Strategies Against Violence: Design for Nonviolent Change

Westview Replica Editions

This book is a Westview Replica Edition. The concept of
Replica Editions is a response to the crisis in academic and
informational publishing. Library budgets for books have been
severely curtailed; economic pressures on the university presses
and the few private publishing companies primarily interested in
scholarly manuscripts have severely limited the capacity of the
industry to properly serve the academic and research communities.
Many manuscripts dealing with important subjects, often representing the highest level of scholarship, are today not econom-
ically viable publishing projects. Or, if they are accepted for
publication, they are often subject to lead times ranging from
one to three years. Scholars are understandably frustrated when
they realize that their first-class research cannot be published
within a reasonable time frame, if at all.

Westview Replica Editions seem to us one feasible and practical solution to the crisis. The concept is simple. We accept
a manuscript in camera-ready form and move it immediately into
the production process. The responsibility for textual and copy
editing lies with the author or sponsoring organization. If
necessary we will advise the author on proper preparation of
footnotes and bibliography. The manuscript is acceptable as
typed for a thesis or dissertation or prepared in any other
clearly organized and readable way, though we prefer it typed
according to our specifications. The end result is a book produced by lithography and bound in hard covers. Edition sizes
range from 200 to 600 copies. We will include among Westview
Replica Editions only works of outstanding scholarly quality or
of great informational value and we will exercise our usual
editorial standards and quality control.

Strategies Against Violence:
Design for Nonviolent Change

edited by Israel W. Charny

"What would you do to advance the cause of peace in this mad world?" An outstanding group of professionals in psychology, psychiatry, sociology, political science, law, education, journalism, philosophy, and the arts answer this question, working with the concepts and tools of their fields to build a plan or model for behaviors that are likely to advance man toward peace and nonviolent change. They provide a rich sampling of the new ideas for human life that are needed if we are, in fact, ever to evolve into a more peaceful species.

The book grew out of a series of sessions organized and chaired by Israel Charny at the annual meetings of the American Orthopsychiatric Association and the American Association for the Advancement of Science. The contributions are organized around three themes: the person, the community and the culture, and the world. Topics include a model for nonviolent strength to counter aggression by others; an examination of the psychology of Adolph Eichmann, with some startling conclusions about how men should cultivate their normal aggressive emotions and enjoy fantasies of violence; how the American democratic process can be turned unknowingly toward disastrous collective violence; and the problem of reducing the contagion of violence spread by daily newscasts of violent events.

Israel W. Charny is senior researcher at the Henrietta Szold National Institute for Research in the Behavioral Sciences in Jerusalem and associate professor of psychology at Tel Aviv University's Center of Criminology and School of Social Work.

Strategies Against Violence:
Design for Nonviolent Change

edited by
Israel W. Charny

Westview Press
Boulder, Colorado

A Westview Replica Edition

Copyright © 1978 by Westview Press, Inc.

Published in 1978 in the United States of America by

Westview Press, Inc.
5500 Central Avenue
Boulder, Colorado 80301
Frederick A. Praeger, Publisher and Editorial Director

Library of Congress Catalog Card Number: 78-3135
ISBN: 0-89158-151-0

Printed and bound in the United States of America

Contents

Section One

THE PERSON: DESIGN FOR NONVIOLENT INTERPERSONAL RELATIONSHIPS

Peace researcher, ALAN NEWCOMBE, deftly and even playfully integrates previous scientific studies of the escalation of violence to construct a remarkable model; from this model, he is able to advise us at one and the same time how to best pursue peace both in our individual relationships and in our international relationships.

Israel psychiatrist, SHLOMO KULCSAR, who together with his psychologist wife examined Adolph Eichmann before his execution, presents a stunning comparison of Eichmann and the infamous Marquis de Sade. He argues that Eichmann, the known administrator of terrible mass killings, feared and defended against normal aggression within him; and that De Sade in real life actually was an exponent of nonviolence who offers all of us who would understand a creative model for nonviolent release of aggression.

Philosopher, LIONEL RUBINOFF, author of *THE PORNOGRAPHY OF POWER*, has written a profound and poetic study of the nature of evil, and how man may triumph over true evil by owning and enjoying the "evil" within him. (It is impressive how independently of one another, Rubinoff and Kulcsar are both developing the same critical concept of integrating the good and bad within us, the latter based on psychiatric thought, and Rubinoff through a process of philosophical inquiry.)

Sociologist, ELISE BOULDING, builds an artful picture of the scientific informations we now have how to best guide children to develop into nonviolent, altruistic social activists who seek to shape their society's future towards peace.

BETTY REARDON, Director of the School Program of the Institute for World Order, writes eloquently of the place of the individual in massive war systems, and proposes an impressive array of educational programs for evoking commitment to the dignity of individuals and to peace.

Folksinger, JOAN BAEZ, in an interview for
PLAYBOY speaks of her concepts of man and
how she translates her social convictions
into everyday life choices and militant nonviolent actions.

Section Two

*THE COMMUNITY AND CULTURE: DESIGN FOR
NONVIOLENT COMMUNITIES AND CULTURES*

Psychologist, ISRAEL CHARNY, identifies several key social science principles whose infusion into man's cultural mainstreams might
help advance our evolution towards peace as
an accepted goal of mankind.

Psychologist and newspaper columnist, WIL-
LIAM BLANCHARD, analyzes the insidious do-
gooder sources of America's violences (in
contrast to the announced genocidal policies
of totalitarian nations), and argues that
democratic nations must carefully monitor
against the unwitting emergence of their violences in the name of peace.

Attorney, SAMUEL RABINOVE, examines the realities and challenges of working within our

democratic system, and considers a variety
of mechanisms of nonviolent social action
that offer promise of securing real results.

Psychologist, ISRAEL CHARNY, works from an
understanding of our natural feelings towards violence to propose surprisingly simple devices for countering the characteristic tonal theme of most American newscasts
of violent events which seem to say, "Well,
folks, it's happened again, it will always
happen again, and there's nothing we can do
about it."

Sociologist, PAUL WEHR and educator, ROBERT
DEHAAN look to the growth potential of conflict in the college student's actual life
experience, also as a framework for meaningful college study of positive and negative conflict; their setting is an inner
city work-study program that is socially
meaningful in its own right.

Psychologist, DORIS TWITCHELL ALLEN, a pioneer in the translation of behavioral science theory into real life applications for
nonviolent change, describes the marvelous
history of the *Children's International Summer Villages (CISV)* which she conceived in

1946, and then her new 1972-initiated *International School-to-School Experience (ISSE)*.

Section Three

THE WORLD: DESIGN FOR NONVIOLENT INTERNATIONAL RELATIONS

Sociologist, A. PAUL HARE, a courageous participant-observer behavioral scientist, reports from the two widely separated real-life laboratories of Kent State and India how groups of people can take effective action against threats of imminent violence.

Psychiatrist, BRYANT WEDGE, describes remarkably simple applications of basic psychotherapeutic concepts to a model of behavioral scientist intervention in violent intergroup conflict; and offers a fascinating report of doing just that in a South American intrigue.

Peace researchers, ALAN NEWCOMBE and HANNA NEWCOMBE, tell of cities across our world twinning with each other, and of many heartwarming experiential opportunities that are then opened to large numbers of people.

Political scientist, J. DAVID SINGER, looks
at feedback forces in society that unexpect-
edly support a government's escalation of
conflict, including the unwitting role of a
government's opposition; alternatively, he
considers examples of "self-correcting feedback" such as building resistance to mobilization appeals, international early warning systems, and alternatives to traditional
styles of international negotiation.

IAN BALDWIN tells the intriguing story of
world-wide teams of scholars creating new
models for a one world system.

Psychologist, JAMES CRAIG, and former public relations consultant, MARGUERITE CRAIG,
innovate a profoundly new approach to international negotiations, where the tradition
of maneuvering for the greatest advantage
is replaced by a commitment to "no-lose"
solutions in which both parties are to be
winners, and neither second best or worse--
as is generally the goal of traditional negotiations.

Acknowledgements

This book grew out of a series of symposiums and workshops organized and chaired by the author at the annual meetings of the American Orthopsychiatric Association and the American Association for the Advancement of Science which were entitled "Design for Nonviolent Change." The participants were a group of respected behavioral scientists who were asked to present some plan for fighting the epidemic of violence that is everywhere in human affairs. Since it was entirely clear that no one proposal could possibly address the total range of human destructiveness, the speakers were specifically advised that any single idea or plan in even a small area of human experience or societal organization would be welcomed so long as it was believed this approach might contribute to reducing the toll of violence. The meetings drew huge audiences and national press and television coverage.

Warm appreciations are due the American Orthopsychiatric Association; its Council on Social Issues; its Study Group on Mental Health Aspects of Aggression, Violence and War; and Herman Schuchman, M.S.W., University of Illinois at Chicago, who was first chairman of the Study Group and then of the larger Council on Social Issues. Although the book necessarily includes only a few of the original participants in the meetings, the conception of the book and many of the ideas developed owe a good deal to those who participated, including George Bach, Ph.D., Beverly Hills, California; William H. Blanchard, Ph.D., Woodland Hills, California; Harry Kaufman, Ph.D., Hunter College, New York: Elise Boulding, Ph.D., University of Colorado; Jerome Frank, M.D., Johns Hopkins University Hospital; A. Paul Hare, Ph.D., Haverford College, Penna.; Senator Vance Hartke of Indiana; Shlomo Kulcsar, M.D., Tel-Hashomer Hospital, Israel; Robert J. Lifton, M.D., Yale University; David Rosenhan, Ph.D., Stanford

University; Marvin Wolfgang, Ph.D., University of Pennsylvania; Lawrence Kohlberg, Ph.D., Harvard University; Peter Scharf, Ed.D., Harvard University; Albert Pepitone, Ph.D., University of Pennsylvania; Herbert C. Kelman, Ph.D., Harvard University; Lee Hamilton Lawrence, Ph.D., Harvard University; J. David Singer, Ph.D., University of Michigan; Joseph D. Ben-Dak, Ph.D., Bureau of Social Research, Washington, D.C., and Robert T. Porter, M.D., New York, N.Y.

In Israel, the book found a home for its completion at the Henrietta Szold National Institute for Research in the Behavioral Sciences in Jerusalem. The Institute is under the able and warm leadership of Chanan Rapaport, Ph.D., whose own professional interests are particularly in social indicator researches and innovative social planning.

For the editor, there has been considerable pleasure in working with the contributors to this volume and watching the book come to life. It can be said honestly that the cooperative experience of developing STRATEGIES AGAINST VIOLENCE went smoothly and happily--with little of the "violences" that have been known to mark collaborative professional projects.

Special appreciations are extended to Mrs. Frances Johnston, SICOM (Secretary in Charge of Manuscripts) in Paoli, Pennsylvania for so many years, and then to Mrs. Doris Sherman, fellow American in Herzliya, Israel for her able handling of the manuscript and publication correspondence.

Appreciations are also due for several kind permissions to reprint or adapt earlier publications. In addition, permission was given by the editor of this book for prior publication of several chapters which were created for STRATEGIES AGAINST VIOLENCE, and these bibliographic citations are also noted:

An earlier draft of "Lovemate: A Personal and International Foreign Policy for Peace" appeared with the editor's permission in *Gandhi Marg*, October, 1972, *16*(4), 254-265. An earlier draft of "De Sade and Eichmann" by Shlomo I. Kulcsar appeared in *Mental Health & Society*, 1976, *3*, 102-113, published by S. Karger AG, Basel, Switzerland. An earlier draft of "The Child and Nonviolent Social Change" appeared with the editor's permission in Christoph Wulf (Ed.), *Handbook on Peace Education*. Oslo, Norway: International Peace Research Assoc., 1974, 101-132. "The Human Person and the War System: A

Problem for Education" by Betty Reardon was developed from two earlier articles, "The Human Person and the War System" in *Intercom*, 1972, *13*(1), 21-26, and "Transformation into Peace and Survival: Programs for the 1970's" in the *Association for Supervision & Curriculum Development Yearbook*, 1973. "Personal Commitment to Nonviolent Social Change (A *Playboy* Interview of Joan Baez)" is excerpted from "Playboy Interviews Joan Baez," *Playboy*, July, 1970; copyright 1970 by *Playboy*.

An earlier draft of "A Cultural Press for Peace" by Israel W. Charny appeared with the author's permission in *Voices: The Art & Science of Psychotherapy*, 1973, *9*(3), 70-78 under the title, "How Can Psychotherapy Contribute to a Cultural Press for Peace?" "Aggression--American Style" by William Blanchard has been expanded into a book, *Aggression--American Style*. Los Angeles: Goodyear, 1978. "Between 'Order' and Violence: The Middle Ground" by Samuel Rabinove appeared in abbreviated form as an article in *America*, October 23, 1971. An earlier draft of "A Human Language for Newscasts of Violence" by Israel W. Charny appeared with the author's permission in *International Journal Group Tensions*, 1972, *2*(3), 52-62 under the title "We Need A Human Language for Reporting the Tragedies of Current Violent Events."

"Dealing with Collective Violence: With Examples from India and Kent State" by Paul Hare was presented at the American Association for the Advancement of Science in Philadelphia in December, 1971. The research was conducted under National Institute of Mental Health Grant No. 5 R01 MH1 7421-03 SP. "Intercession in Violent Intergroup Conflict" by Bryant Wedge appeared as "A Psychiatric Model for Intercession in Violent Intergroup Conflict" in "The *Australian & New Zealand Journal Psychiatry*, 1971, *5*, 84-100. "Transition from Violence in the International System" by J. David Singer is adapted from an earlier article, "Escalation and Control in International Conflict: A Sample Feedback Model" which appeared in *General Systems*, 1970, *15*, 163-73. An earlier draft of the World Order Models Project: Toward a Planetary Social Change Movement" by Ian Baldwin, Jr. appeared with the editor's permission in *IDOC International, North American Edition*, April, 1973.

Preface

This book is for every social science reader who has ever dreamt that man might someday live in peace with his fellow man.

Obviously the time has not yet come that any of us know exactly how this can be achieved. But we have begun to develop ways of designing our human experiences to help men to be less violent, and to bring about constructive changes in our communities and societies. In this volume, the challenge to each contributor has *not* been to attempt a master plan for nonviolent change or peace in any one or another area of human affairs. In fact, the contributors have been specifically cautioned not to attempt to draw the *Big Picture*, but rather to propose any demonstration, however small, of how social science understanding of the nature of man can provide a basis for redesign of the social environment to reduce violences.

Each contributor to this book has been invited specifically to demonstrate the possibility of moving from social science theory or philosophy to designs or applications of the theory in the real world that are likely to help people make choices for nonviolent change. So that over and above what there is of value in the various intriguing and innovative suggestions offered by the writers, our intent is to demonstrate how to build new transitions from social science theory or understanding to action on behalf of peace, and to stimulate other social science thinkers to innovate further designs and strategies against violence.

In *STRATEGIES AGAINST VIOLENCE*, we seek innovative designs for nonviolent change wherever man is, in his everyday interpersonal relationships, in the workings of larger communities and cultures, and in international relations. Contributions to the book are organized along these three axes of the person, the community and culture, and the world:

xvi

Section One - THE PERSON: DESIGN FOR
NONVIOLENT INTERPERSONAL RELATIONSHIPS

While our attentions are normally riveted to
the larger explosions of man's violences, the
facts are that, ultimately, we must also come
to grips with how it is that an individual human being is pulling the trigger or pushing
people into all-too-real "Hansel and Gretel"
furnaces. Furthermore, the sad truth is that
our everyday "small" interpersonal relationships on this planet, although a far cry from
the overt murders of wars and genocides, are in
their own right little hells of injustice and
rage and metaphoric murders. These "little
murders" are the rule even in our family lives
where we would have imagined ourselves to be
especially safe and beloved.
So that we have a great deal to learn how to
educate individual human beings to the dignity
of life.

Section Two - THE   COMMUNITY   AND   CULTURE:
DESIGN FOR NONVIOLENT COMMUNITIES AND CULTURES

In the extended family of man, we humans characteristically divide ourselves against one another along a never-ending variety of contrived
oppositions, north versus south, black versus
white, believers in the true god versus the
heathen, and so on. (Predictably, some day
earthmen will also divide against non-earthmen.)
If we were only able to see from a distance
just how often we all divide against one another, we would know without hesitation that all
these divisions--even the ones we ourselves
succumb to against our particular Others--are
fundamentally a nonsense born of man's primitivity. Yet, time and time again, virtually
all of us are drawn by the grip of these fic-
tions, to the point of sacrificing our lives
and other peoples' lives in their name. Time
and time again, men march all too willingly to
the martial drums of their motherland, or in
the name of their god or political philosophy.
So often, other peoples are relegated to the
role of *not-human* and *lesser-than-us,* therefore,
even deserving of extinction.
We desperately need new ways to help men from
being frozen into the divisions and antagonisms
that spur and legitimate violences.

Section Three - *THE WORLD: DESIGN FOR*
NONVIOLENT INTERNATIONAL RELATIONS

We are an awesome international system of nations, coalitions of nations, regional groups,
and hemispheric organizations. Daily, trans-
atlantic planes fly back and forth connecting
once remote areas of our globe. International
exchanges hum with trades that provide the un-
derstructure for gigantic international economic developments. Yet, behind it all there also
stand tell-tale stockpiles of atom bombs and
missiles and all manner of science-fiction wea-
pons--here, there, and everywhere portending
the very destruction of mankind. It then seems
almost a favor to us that rather than destroy
all of mankind, men engage in chess-games of
little wars and the small violences of "local"
wars such as in Vietnam or the Middle East.
Yet, obviously, these little wars too are enormous killers that are nothing less than tragic.
Might there be newer ways for peoples to communicate with one another on our Planet of Babel?
Is it possible for us to share more of a part-
nership in our planet?
We need imaginative designs for greater communication between peoples, nations and their negotiators so that the *real* issue of international negotiations becomes the well-being of
human beings. We especially need dramatically
new forms of communication between peoples when
they are most needed, at times of bitter conflict.

Throughout, it is fascinating to see the different ways that the various authors in this volume
build towards real-life programs for action from
their particular bases in social science theories
and philosophies. We have all come a long way from
our once simplistic, messianic hopes, when we were
first drawn to the social sciences, that somewhere
in the world of our scholarship we would find a
single critical key to man's betterment.
For some of us, the hope was that a fairer distribution of the goods of this world would somehow
remedy the many evils that befell mankind. Some of
us thought about this issue in economic terms, others more in political terms, and still others saw

the issue in psychological terms that if only we could eliminate *all* human frustration, men would no longer be violent. All of us, it turned out, were pitifully naive.

For others, there was another naive image that if only all of us, especially our national and international leaders, could undergo psychoanalysis, the world would be a better place. (So many of us, in fact, pinned our own hopes for better personal lives on such psychoanalyses, and while some of us did in fact gain much that we hoped for, many others of us did not). Those of us who were, in fact, professionally engaged in the fledgling art and science of psychotherapy sensed, correctly, that the same powerful streams of anxiety and irrationality that lay behind the anguish of the mentally ill ultimately were at work as powerful undercurrents in the minds of *all* people, and had something to do with fomenting all manner of destructiveness and war, even when these were seemingly the work of quite rational human beings. But we had no idea how to apply psychotherapeutic understanding to the critical real-life issues of destructiveness by seemingly normal, rational people. Periodically, seasoned older therapists cried out in horror at the absurdity of normal man's destructiveness and cautioned us of the demonic, primitive unconscious that pressed towards death in us all, but even these greats did not know how to contend with these seemingly limitless forces of destruction in our nature.

But now we have entered a new era where, slowly but surely, we have more and more practical ideas about how to counter man's tendencies to violences, and how human beings might make contact with one another across the chasms of their ever-divided groups and nations. Perhaps it is the passage of time and the relief of distance from the last terrible war. Perhaps it is that we can finally bear to look at the tell-tale mushroom cloud that announced the dawn of the atomic era. Perhaps it is the special soul-shattering awareness that grows of that special event of the Holocaust. In part, it is probably the further perspective that grows from brilliant space-ship probes of worlds beyond. Certainly our various social sciences daily grow more mature and effective in many different areas of human experience.

Whatever the sources, it is now clear to most of us that we are all a single people--no matter our differences in color or language, and that we need the social sciences to help us to design many new

ways for experiencing and honoring the fantastic opportunity that is life.

   *STRATEGIES AGAINST VIOLENCE is dedicated to the
brilliant human potential for finding new undreamt-
of-ways not to succumb to our likely destiny of violence. This book is an invitation to evolution
through demonstrations of man's ingenuity to free-
associate, brainstorm and invent new plans and designs for a safer human environment. No doubt many
readers will also want to join with their own innovations and inventions for peace and nonviolent social change.*

Strategies Against Violence: Design for Nonviolent Change

Section One

The Person: Design for Nonviolent Interpersonal Relationships

1. "Lovemate": A Personal and International Foreign Policy for Peace

Alan G. Newcombe, Ph.D.

Peace Research has found an approach to foreign policy which, if followed, should produce friendship between nations if there is any possible basis for friendship. Such a policy may turn hostility into friendship; the policy would fail only if an Adolf Hitler personality was on the other side; the policy would be self-adjusting to clearly reveal the presence of such a personality so that the pit-falls of appeasement and Munich would be avoided.

Before describing how this policy operates against a hostile power it is advisable to first consider the situation of two friendly, or two indifferent powers, and also to consider other policies that have been advocated for use against hostile powers.

It is often *assumed* that two nations can learn to live in peace together only after they have had a friendly relationship for many years. Such an assumption automatically produces a corollary that the world can only achieve peace when all possible pairs of nations have achieved a friendly relationship. Since the odds against this situation developing are rather high, it is often argued that the world can never achieve peace. Only rarely is the assumption made that nations can learn to live together even if they do not love one another.

If one proceeds on the basis of the first assumption, namely, that peace between nations can only be produced as a product of friendship between nations, then it is logical to ask, "Is there a foreign policy which tends to produce friendship between nations?" If friendship already exists, as for example, the friendship between Norway, Denmark

and Sweden, then the question of how to produce
friendly responses is simply answered by the continuation of present policy. These three nations are
so friendly that not only do they share ownership in
the S.A.S. airline, but also adjust the symbol of
the airline according to the country where the airline literature is distributed. One finds in Denmark that the symbol of the 3 crowns in a triangle
has the Danish crown on top, whereas in Norway it is
the Norwegian crown which is at the apex of the triangle.

      If a state of indifference exists between two
nations, then one nation, Sylvania, to use a mythical example, may decide to end this situation by
making a friendly initiative to the other, Metaguay
(to continue with our mythical example). If Metaguay makes a friendly response, we have the beginning of a friendly interchange and no problem exists.
If Metaguay has an indifferent response (i.e., no
response at all), then Sylvania can make an even
more friendly initiative; if Metaguay still remains
indifferent, Sylvania can either decide to become
even more friendly or may decide that the situation
resembles the title of the Shakespearean play,
"Love's Labour Lost" and can decide to return to a
state of indifference. This situation does not often arise in international affairs and does not constitute a problem when it does arise.

KNIGHT's STRATEGY

      The problem that appears very often in interna-
tional affairs and one which divides hawks from
doves is the question of what one should do when
Sylvania and Metaguay are hostile to the other. The
hawk (or, alternatively, the Knight) argument is
that the only response Sylvania can make to Meta-
guayan hostility is to arm in order to defend Sylvania against a possible attack by Metaguay. Such advice is, of course, correct if Metaguay is governed
by a power hungry, aggressive individual such as
Adolf Hitler, or if it is governed by a cabinet or
committee which believes that military solutions to
political arguments (or national disputes) are the
only way to conduct affairs. The difficulty with
this approach is to be able to know if one faces an
Adolf Hitler or a committee dominated by Militarist
minds.* If one is faced with this situation, any

_____

*When I use Militaristic with a capital "M", I mean

attempt to be friendly with Metaguay will be interpreted by the Militaristic committee in Metaguay as
a sign of weakness in the same way that Chamberlain's appeasement policy was viewed by Hitler. But
what happens if the committee in Metaguay, while
hostile to Sylvania, is *not* dominated by Militaristic minds? Will they not perceive the Sylvanian
military build-up as a threat? Will they not then
feel compelled to increase their own military expenditures in order to defend themselves? This in turn
will increase the percentage of militarist minds on
the committee, for only such minds believe in such a
policy. The Sylvanian Militarist approach is thus a
self-fulfilling prophecy. The logic above is the
logic of any arms race; this has been explored by
Richardson (21,22) and more recently by Newcombe (7-
16, Tensiometer Series); these arms races very frequently end in war. When there is sufficient provocation, the "seed of war" (Sarejevo, for example),
presents itself. Thus the advice given by the Militaristic minds, the Knights, is right when one faces
an Adolf Hitler and wrong if this is not the case.

BISHOP'S STRATEGY

Religious men, such as Bishops, often advise
diplomats to meet hostility by turning the other
cheek and returning love for hate or friendship for
hostility. Such advice is certainly right if the
cabinet of Metaguay is basically friendly and has
mistakenly been perceived as hostile (perhaps because the military of Metaguay has been making foreign policy through military action). But what happens if the cabinet of Metaguay is not quite that
friendly? May they not perceive that Sylvania returns friendship for friendship and friendship for
hostility as well and decide to take advantage of
Sylvania? Thus the Bishop's Strategy may actually
induce aggression on the part of the cabinet of
Metaguay and provoke a war. This is the objection
that the Knights customarily raise to the Bishop's
Strategy.

---

a person who scores high on the Militarism Attitude
Scale devised by William Eckhardt (3). Such people
are found both in civilian life and in the armed
forces.

KING'S STRATEGY

Followers of Martin Luther King and Gandhi will advocate nonviolent action as the appropriate response to hostility. These advocates do not concentrate their advice in terms of the shaping of foreign policy, but rather deal with a method of meeting violent hostility from the opponent. Nor is it often realized by them that their nonviolent resistance is perceived as hostile by the other side. Thus, the British would much rather have seen the Indians buying tickets and using the railroads the way the British wanted them to do than sitting on the tracks in a nonviolent demonstration; the British, very correctly, perceived such an action as hostile and at the same time very correctly perceived it as clearly lacking in violence or the potential of violence. Gandhi's actions lacked the potential of violence because Gandhi insisted on discipline within the ranks of his demonstrators and ordered anyone who did not believe that they could maintain a nonviolent response to stay home. The words *hostile* and *violent* are often used incorrectly as synonyms, although the first refers to an emotional attitude and the second to a form of action. Another source of semantic confusion is that many people believe that the only antonym to *violence* is *nonviolence* and do not realize that a third possibility, *minimization of violence,* exists despite the fact that in the cities of the world we curb the potential violent behaviour of our neighbours (and ourselves) by creating a social order based on laws which strive to minimize violence rather than use nonviolent techniques to confront the violence or hostility of others. Learning to live with our neighbours even though we do not love them is a more realistic alternative to the Knight's approach than "Make Love, Not War."

Nonviolent action is not a choice in terms of developing a foreign policy to produce friendship. Both the Bishop's and the King's Strategy are in agreement in their opposition to the Knight's reliance on defence and weapons production. To the extent that Richardson and Newcombe have shown that military expenditures create political tension which in turn causes an increase in military expenditure and this arms race produces war, the Bishop and the King are right. To the extent that the only reaction to Adolf Hitler that would have been realistic was to prepare for war, the Knight is right. *The difficulty in finding a foreign policy that will*

*turn hostility into friendship (a state that may be
related to peace) is to find a policy which is self-
adjusting to the situation. What is required is a
policy which will allow an Adolf Hitler to reveal
himself in his true colors and which, on the other
hand, will not compound a minor hostility into an
arms race, with its subsequent increase in hostility, and produce a war which might have been avoided.
Such a policy has now been found.*

QUEEN'S STRATEGY

Tit-for-tat. Experiments using the Prisoners'
Dilemma Situation (see Rapoport (10) or Newcombe
(6), in which a confederate of the experimenter was
instructed always to play a given strategy against
the subject, have shown that when the confederate
played the strategy associated with the person high
on the Militarism Attitude Scale (the Knight), the
subject cooperated only 6% of the time. When the
confederate was instructed to play the equivalent of
the Bishop's Strategy, half the subjects cooperated
all the time and half the subjects exploited the
Bishop on every play; thus the level of cooperation
from all subjects was 50%. When the confederate was
instructed to play a tit-for-tat strategy, i.e., to
return good for good and evil for evil, the level of
cooperation from the subjects rose to 85%. The major objection to this strategy is that it gives all
of the initiative to the other player who has the
basic decision in his hands as to whether he will
play good or evil. The Tit-for-Tat Strategist only
responds to the initiatives of the other player. He
can, however, gain the initiative by using the GRIT
Strategy devised by Charles Osgood.

G R I T. Charles Osgood, in a series of publications (17,18,19), has described a strategy for
Graduated Reciprocation in International Tension-re-
duction which suggests that tension can be reduced
between two actors if one of them, unilaterally,
communicates, either by word or by deed, an initiative (which is not directly involved with the sali-
ent issue increasing tension at the moment) which
the actor believes the other side will perceive as
being conciliatory. Osgood believes that the other
side would accurately perceive this initiative and
would reciprocate. A number of political scientists
then attacked Osgood's idea because it is contrary
to the Siegel and Fouraker (23) hypothesis which

suggests that such a conciliatory move would be perceived by the opponent as a sign of surrender and would cause the opponent to increase his demands.

Otomar Bartos (1) conducted a series of experiments to discover the conditions under which Osgood's hypothesis was correct and under what conditions the Siegel and Fouraker hypothesis was correct. Bartos' results, when interpreted (6) through the study of attitudes conducted by Eckhardt (3), shows that the Osgood hypothesis is correct for most people and fails only with those people who score exceptionally high on the Militarism and Nationalism scales (the Knights). It is for these people only that the Siegel and Fouraker hypothesis applies. Thus it is likely that those political scientists who suggested that the Russians would not understand a GRIT initiative and would not reciprocate it did so not because of any inherent characteristic of the Russians, but rather *because of their own Militarist and Nationalist feelings.*

Not only did the Russians understand it (see articles by Waterkamp (24) and also by Dmitriev (2), they liked it so much that they renamed it the "Policy of Mutual Example."

In 1967, Etzioni (4) published his paper, "The Kennedy Experiment," in which he showed that in 1963 President Kennedy used the GRIT initiative on 16 separate occasions and each time the Russians made an equivalent response *within 24 hours.*

The Queen's Strategy. In my Review of 1969 (5), I combined the Tit-for-Tat Strategy and the GRIT hypothesis and called the product the Queen's Strategy because the Queen is the most powerful piece on the chessboard, and this strategy would be, in my mind, the most powerful strategy for achieving friendship between two nations. The Queen's Strategy suggests that when the other nation is perceived as sending a hostile signal (either by word or deed), then one should respond with an equally hostile signal; and if one finds that one is locked into an exchange of hostile signals one should, at some frequency, determined in advance by oneself (say, with every third communication), use the GRIT hypothesis to make a friendly initiative. If, after several attempts (or perhaps 7 times 70 as the Bible suggests), the other side has not reciprocated, then one could conclude that you were faced with an Adolf Hitler and should proceed at once to arm in order to defend oneself. If, on the other hand, the GRIT iniative was reciprocated, one should continue with

such initiatives until a friendly state was reached.
This aspect of the policy would fit in with the testament that one should love one's enemies, and the
over-all policy approach would not leave one vulnerable to those people who would take advantage of the
Bishop's Strategy. The Queen's Strategy is better
than the plain Tit-for-Tat Strategy because it gives
an occasional initiative.

*If you utilize the Queen's Strategy in your
normal contact with people, you will be surprised to
discover how well it works. If you meet hostility
with only hostility, as the Knight does, you will
find that you live in a world populated with many
hostile people. If you are always turning the other
cheek as the Bishop does, you will find that the
world is populated with many people prepared to take
advantage of you and your faith will be strained.*
Human beings are very flexible and very willing to
create themselves in the image that you project onto
them. This is very similar to Leary's "Principle of
Self-Determination" which states (5, p. 117), "Your
own interpersonal behaviour has, more than any other
factor, determined the reception you get from others.
Your slowly developing pattern of reflexes has
trained others and yourself to accept you as this
sort of person--to be treated in this sort of way.
You are the manager of your own destiny."

*If you use the Queen's Strategy in your inter-
personal behaviour, you are projecting the image of
a person willing to meet hostility with hostility
but also willing to be friendly if the other person
will respond to your initiative. If, furthermore,
you make the assumption that other people are
friendly, your initiatives towards them will be
friendly and they will respond in the same way.*

It is not surprising that a policy advocated
for the conduct of les affaires étrangère should also apply to your affairs with strangers. For either
at the foreign policy level or the two person interaction, we are dealing with communications between
human beings. Leary states that your own behaviour
determines the reception that you receive from others and raises the question of how one communicates
to others the way that you wish them to treat you;
he states that these communications "are partly in
the content or verbal meaning of the communication,
but primarily in the tone of voice, gesture, car-
riage and external appearance" (5, pp. 96-97).
These last four items could be summarized in the
phrase "non-verbal communication." A nation which
has large military expenditures, glorifies its army

and holds its secret police in great respect, while
subjecting some of its citizens to second class citizenship, cannot be regarded as peace-loving by other nations. The amazing phenomenon during the Thirties was that Mr. Chamberlain and M. Daladier were
able to be as blind as they were to the menace of
Hitler's Germany. The other side of this argument
is that a nation with a low military expenditure
(with respect to its GNP[1] and a high degree of tolerance towards minority groups, is not regarded as
hostile by a neighbouring nation.

A MODEL FOR MAPPING STRATEGIES

We can construct a theoretical model to encompass these strategies. Assume that the number of
attitudes which individuals (or nations) can perceive is relatively few in number and can be summarized as friendly, hostile, indifferent, and nonviolent. (If you can suggest a fifth attitude which is
qualitatively different to these four, it does not
destroy the model but merely changes the arithmetic.)
I am aware that there are differences in degree between giving a girl flowers and proposing marriage
to her, but these two events are of the same kind
and differ only in degree of friendship, and this degree can be represented by a multiplier which would
affect the symbol we use for a friendly perception;
thus, we could represent a marriage proposal as 900+
and a gift of flowers as 5+ where the "+" sign represents the friendly perception and the multipliers
represent the different utilities or values that the
other person would place on these initiatives. The
same type of multiplier could be used to rank hostile acts so that 15- and 50- could be used to represent how a national leader would view the breaking
of diplomatic relations and the imposition of an oil
embargo. The last example reveals why I have talked
about the perception by the other of my action; the
utility of the act is a subjective decision which is
made by the recipient of the communication and not
by the sender. For example, if the U.N. imposed an
oil embargo on the importation of oil into Iran or
Venezuela, both of these countries would merely
laugh because they are oil exporters, but the imposition of an embargo on the importation of oil into
Japan or the U.S.A. would be regarded as a hostile
act by both of these nations, and in each case to a
different degree, because Japan is totally dependent
on oil imports and the U.S.A. does have some oil re-

serves of its own.

At the same time, we have another type of communication which lies between friendship and hostility and could be called the region of Indifference.
Nations which do not recognize each other, or nations which do not answer communications from a nation they do recognize, are not behaving in either a
friendly or hostile way, but rather are behaving in
an Indifferent way. In terms of voting at the
United Nations, this area would correspond to an ab-
stention. If you smile at someone on the bus and
they merely turn and look in another direction, they
are behaving in an Indifferent way. The attitude of
Indifference could be represented by a 0. We could
also represent Nonviolent behaviour by the letters
NV and presumably such actions might also have multipliers (for example a Nonviolent demonstration by
500 people might be viewed as 5 times as impressive
as a demonstration by 100 people).

In our own personal lives, we are aware that
the events which occur between our spouses and ourselves exist as a chain of events in which one event
leads to the next event. In terms of representing
this chain of events, we need a model in which this
link between events is an inherent part of the model.
If we merely list these events we do not have such a
linkage. We have the same situation as the photog-
rapher who has taken the picture of 20 people standing side by side by taking 10 pictures of them two
at a time; when he obtains his prints he knows the
relationship between pairs but not between each pair;
the way he can avoid this problem is by taking a
picture of a & b, c & d, etc. and also of b & c, d &
e, etc., and when he makes his final composite picture, half of his photographs are eliminated and
drop out but have been quite useful to relate Smith
and Jones to Green and Brown. Thus, we can create a
useful model by coding each perception twice and
grouping the perceptions in sets of four. For example, we can record *the perceptions* of two people in
the following way:

He +, She +, He 3+, She 2+, He 6+, She 3+
which means that his perception of the first communication between the two (she smiled at him) was perceived by him as friendly, and that her perception
of his response (he smiled back) was perceived by her
as friendly. It also tells you that his perception
of her attitude when she spoke to him was a 3+, and
that her perception of him when he replied in a
friendly way was only 2+. By recording perceptions
in this way, we do *not* have a model in which the

linkage between his 6+ perception is clearly dependent in part on her 2+ perception and to a lesser
extent on his previous 3+ perception. But if we
code each perception twice and break them into sets
of four, then the example above would be written in
the following way:

   (He +, She +, He 3+, She 2+),
   (He 3+, She 2+, He 6+, She 3+)

Now the last two symbols in the first set of four
are identical with the first two symbols in the second set of four, because they describe the same perceptions, and we can say that the first set produced
the second set because of the overlap.

   If we are interested in how to achieve friendship between people, or friendship between nations
(on the *assumption* that friendship is a prerequisite
for peace), we are concerned with achieving the set
(+,+,+,+) and this set can be achieved only from a
set ending with +,+. Because we have four symbols
and four positions in each set, there are, we know,a
total of 256 sets; of these there are only 16 types
ending in +,+, and they group themselves into 5 general types which can be represented by *(-,+,+,+);*
(-,NV,+,+); (-,-,+,+); (-,0,+,+); and *(+,+,+,+).*

   The first of these general types represents the
successful use of the Bishop's Strategy in which the
hostile person has been redeemed, and also represents the successful use of the GRIT Strategy and of
the Queen's Strategy. The second type represents
the successful use of the King's Strategy. The
third type represents the successful use of the Tit-
for-Tat Strategy and also of the successful use of
the Queen's Strategy (which is a combination of Tit-
for Tat with GRIT). The fourth type represents the
successful use of the Castle's Strategy in which one
actor has ignored the hostility of the other and the
other has rectified his error. The last type represents an existing friendly situation which may be a
very special case of Tit-for-Tat Strategy. If someone can identify another qualitatively different human response in addition to the four mentioned here,
we would have a total of 625 different response sets
but would gain only one more strategy for turning
hostility into friendship, which we would represent
as (-,*,+,+) where the * represents the, at present,
unknown, additional human response. These response
sets are dealt with more extensively in my *Peace Research Review* (6). The interesting thing about this
model is that it tells us that there are *only four*
strategies for turning hostility into friendship,
namely, Queen's, King's, Bishop's and Castle's, and

it also tells us that the Knight's Strategy of meeting hostility with hostility with increasing hostility cannot produce friendship but only surrender.

Earlier I said that we were assuming that peace can only come about through friendship. If we do not make this assumption, we are left with the idea that two individuals, or two nations, can live together in peace while being very hostile to each other. This idea is quite real, for we have numerous examples of neighbours who are quite hostile to each other who live together in peace because each has essentially renounced the violent expression of hostility and each has decided to resolve conflicts with the other by recourse to law. On the international scene, this idea is reflected in the World Federalist organization which seeks to strengthen the body of international law by strengthening the United Nations, especially through reform of the U.N. Charter, and also to strengthen the International Court of Justice through repeal of the Connally Amendment in the U.S.A. and similar reservations in other countries. Because of differences on the assumption of whether countries must be friendly before peace can break out, we essentially have two peace movements, the emotional and the rational. The emotional (this word is not used pejoratively) peace movement concentrates on people-to-people exchanges--on the assumption that the better you know the stranger the more you will be friendly with him (which may not be true!), increased trade, and disarmament. The rational peace movement concentrates on increased trade, strengthening the U.N., more use of the International Court, and disarmament. These two peace movements are not mutually exclusive and may both be right in their approaches. Perhaps the reality of the situation is that unless we have a certain minimum level of hostility (or friendship), we cannot achieve the structural and legal changes which the rational peace movement seeks. In other words, if hostility is high, one cannot even agree on the rules of the game (structural and legal rules) or on what kind of table to sit at. Perhaps one needs to have a certain minimum level of friendliness to achieve such agreements. Alternatively, the rational peace movement suggests one does not even need any friendliness, but only a certain minimum level of hostility. The slogan of the emotional peace movement is "Make Love, Not War"; the slogan (if one existed) of the rational peace movement should be what I call the Bachelor's Slogan, namely, "We don't want to love our enemies, all we want to do is to live with them."

The two peace movements described above should
not be confused with the so-called "peace movement"
in the U.S.A. which has been not so much a peace
movement as an anti-war movement, and which is also
an anti-establishment movement. The anti-war movement in the U.S.A. consists of people who are in favour of peace and opposed to violence, and also of
others who are not in favour of peace and not opposed to violence. With the end of the war in Indochina, this anti-war movement no longer had reason
to exist, but both an emotional and a rational peace
movement have every reason to develop.
Peace is more than the absence of war; if we have a
year in which there is no war but the U.S. and the
Soviet Union continue to spend billions upon arma-
ments, we will not have a year in peace but merely a
year in armistice. Peace then has to be defined as
a state in which war does not occur and in which war
cannot occur because the nations of the world disarm.

*The Knight's reaction of meeting hostility with
hostility and violence with violence is the reaction
of primitive men. The Queen's Strategy of meeting
hostility with hostility, and (at a frequency determined in advance of using the GRIT initiative) of
meeting hostility with a friendly response is the
response of civilized and disciplined men. Using
this strategy, one finds that one can love one's enemies to death, not in the physical sense to their
physical death, but rather to the point at which
they cease to be enemies and become friends, (that
is, to the death of enmity).*

NOTES

1. We all realize that the Military Expenditure
(M.E.) of a nation must be a fraction of its Gross
National Product; for example, Canada can never have
a M.E. as large as that of the U.S.A. because the
American M.E. is larger than the GNP of Canada. (In
1966, the Canadian GNP was 58,950 millions of dollars and the U.S. M.E. was 63,283 millions of dollars.) In a series of research papers on my Inter-
Nation Tensiometer, I have, with my co-workers, found
a relationship between GNP/Capita and Military Ex-
penditure/Capita such that any nation with an M.E./
Capita larger than the value due to the GNP/Capita
is termed "supra-critical." Supra-critical nations
are 30.6 times more likely to be involved in a war
with another nation in the five years following the

year under study than are the sub-critical nations.
Supra-critical nations fight wars with other supra-
critical nations; for 96.5% of the nations at war in
the period 1950-1970 had been supra-critical before
the war began.

Few people realize how big the Military Expenditures of the various nations really are. To help
people visualize these sums, I tell audiences that
a million dollars in thousand dollar bills makes a
stack 7.5 inches high, and the 1975 world military
expenditure of 371.26 billion makes a stack of thousand dollar bills some 43.95 *miles* high! NATO contributes 17.2 miles and the Warsaw Pact 16.2 miles
of thousand dollar bills to the world stack.

REFERENCES

1. Bartos, Otomar. Concession making in experimen-
    tal negotiations. Paper at the Annual Meeting
    of the American Sociological Association, Chi-
    cago, August, 1965. (PRA Ref. No. 21332)*
2. Dmitriev, Boris. Policy of mutual example.
    Izvestiia, Dec. 15, 1964, p. 1. *Current Digest
    of the Soviet Press*, Jan. 6, 1965, *16*, 16.
    (PRA Ref. No. 34270)
3. Eckhardt, William. *Ideology and Personality in
    Social Attitudes*. *Peace Research Reviews*, April
    1969, *3*(2). (whole no.)
4. Etzioni, Amitai. The Kennedy Experiment. *West-
    ern Political Quarterly*, 1967, *20*(2), part 1,
    361-380. Also in Etzioni, Amitai, & Wenglinsky,
    Martin (Eds.), *War and its Prevention*. New
    York: Harper & Row, 1970, 215-296.
5. Leary, Timothy. *Interpersonal Diagnosis of Per-
    sonality*. New York: Ronald, 1957.
6. Newcombe, Alan. *Initiatives & Responses in For-
    eign Policy*. *Peace Research Reviews*, June,
    1969, *3*(3). (whole no.)
7. Newcombe, Alan. *Towards the Development of an
    Inter-Nation Tensiometer*. *Peace Research Soci-
    ety, Papers XIII*. The Copenhagen Conference,
    1969, pp. 11-27. (Tensiometer Series No. 1)
8. Newcombe, Alan G., & Andrighetti, Robert. *Na-
    tions at Risk: A Prediction of Nations Likely
    To Be in War in the Years 1974-1978. Interna-*

---

*PRA numbers refer to *Peace Research Abstracts*.

tional Interactions, 1977, *3*(2), 133-158.
(Tensiometer Series No. 9)

9. Newcombe, Alan G., Barber, John D., Wert, James, Haven, Mark, & Hiebert, Cathy. *An Improved Inter-Nation Tensiometer for the Prediction of War.* *Peace Research Reviews*, February, 1974, *5* (4), 1-52. (Tensiometer Series No. 5)

10. Newcombe, Alan G., & Klaassen, Frank F. The Tensiometer Prediction of Nations Likely to be Involved in International War in the Years 1977-1980. A research report prepared especially for the United Nations Preparatory Committee for the Special Session of the General Assembly on Disarmament. Presented to the International Peace Research Association Conference in Mexico City in December, 1977. (Tensiometer Series No. 10)

11. Newcombe, Alan G., Köhler, Garnot, & Wert, James. *The Prediction of War Using an Inter-Nation Tensiometer.* IPRA Studies in Peace Research No. 6 (IPRA Secretariat, P.O. Box 5052 Majorstua, Oslo 3, Norway). (Tensiometer Series No. 6)

12. Newcombe, Alan G., Köhler, Gernot, & Dugan, Maire. *The Inter-Nation Tensiometer for the Prediction of War.* In press. (This book will be No. 7 in Tensiometer Series)

13. Newcombe, Alan G., Köhler, Gernot, & Dugan, Maire. *The Inter-Nation Tensiometer for the Prediction of War.* In *Peace and Violence: Quantitative Studies of International, Civil, and Structural Conflict.* New Haven: Human Relations Area Files Press, 1977. (Tensiometer Series No. 8)

14. Newcombe, Alan G., Newcombe, Nora S., & Landrus, Gary. *The Development of the Inter-Nation Tensiometer.* *International Interactions*, 1974, *1*, 3-18. (Tensiometer Series No. 2)

15. Newcombe, Alan, & Wert, James. *An Inter-Nation Tensiometer for the Prediction of War.* Canadian Peace Research Institute, 1972. (Tensiometer Series No. 3)

16. Newcombe, Alan G., Wert, James. *The Use of an Inter-Nation Tensiometer for the Prediction of War.* Peace Research Society Papers, 1973, *21*, 73-83. (Tensiometer Series No. 4)

17. Osgood, Charles E. Suggestion for winning the real war with Communism. *Journal Conflict Resolution*, 1959, *3*, 295-325. (PRA Ref. No. 21330)

18. Osgood, Charles E. *A Plea for Perspective and Patience in the Conduct of Foreign Policy.* Urbana, Illinois: Institute of Communication

Research, University of Illinois, 1965. (mimeo.)
(PRA Ref. No. 21331)

19. Osgood, Charles E. *Perspective in Foreign Policy*. Palo Alto, California: Pacific Books, 1966.
(This is expanded version of previous item (12).

20. Rapoport, Anatol. *Games Which Simulate Deterrence and Disarmament. Peace Research Reviews*,
1967, *1*(4). (whole no.)

21. Richardson, Lewis F. *Statistics of Deadly Quarrels*. Chicago: Quadrangle, 1960.

22. Richardson, Lewis F. *Arms and Insecurity: A Mathematical Study of the Causes and Origins of War*. Chicago: Quadrangle, 1960.

23. Siegel, Sidney, & Fouraker, Lawrence. E. *Bargaining Behaviour*. New York: McGraw-Hill, 1963.

24. Waterkamp, Rainer. The policy of mutual example in the approach to disarmament. *Frankfurter Hefte*, 1965, *20*(3), 186-194. (PRA Ref. No. 37788)

ALAN NEWCOMBE was born in Hamilton, Ontario in 1923. He received a B.A. degree in Chemistry from McMaster University in 1945, and M.A. and Ph.D. degrees from the University of Toronto in Organic Chemistry in 1947 and 1950. He worked as a Post-Doctorate Fellow in the Banting Institute from September 1949 to April 1951 when he joined the staff of the Ontario Research Foundation; he worked there on wood chemistry until November 1953 when he became Research Director of Porritts & Spencer (Canada), a firm making industrial fabrics. In the autumn of 1961, he initiated the campaign for voluntary donations in the Hamilton area to help establish the Canadian Peace Research Institute and in February 1963, he joined its staff. His long interest in world affairs has shown itself over the years in memberships in the World Federalists of Canada (since 1947), the United Nations Association (since 1958), and the Canadian Institute of International Affairs.

Together with his wife, Hanna, he organized the Hamilton Branch of WFC (1961), and founded the Canadian Peace Research & Education Association (1966), a membership organization for academics. They began PEACE RESEARCH ABSTRACTS JOURNAL in 1964 and PEACE RESEARCH REVIEWS JOURNAL in 1967. As an outgrowth of the first Review, they developed the Canadian form of mundialization (see Chapter 15), and participated in the mundialization of Dundas, Hamilton, Kitchener, Toronto, Ottawa, Oakville, Victoria, and

Waterloo. Alan was the first National Chairman of the Mundialization Committee of WFC. From September 1971 to June 1972, he served as the part-time Executive Officer of the World Federalists of Canada. In this position, his function was to lobby with Canadian Members of Parliament and with diplomats in the Department of External Affairs on behalf of the World Federalists, with particular attention to the subject of United Nations Charter Revision. From June 1972 to June 1974, he served as National President of the World Federalists of Canada.

He joined the Religious Society of Friends (Quakers) in 1961 and has served on the Executive Committee and the Peace Committee of the Canadian Friends Service Committee. From 1964 to 1969, he was Chairman of the Planning Committee of the Quaker-UNESCO Seminars which subsequently became the Canadian School of Peace Research in which he now serves as a Co-Director.

Alan and Hanna were awarded the Lentz International Peace Research Award in 1974. They have 3 children: Nora (26), George (24) and Ian(21).

Alan taught from 1972 to 1974 in the Department of Political Science at York University in Toronto, and a course in peace research in Conrad Grebel College of the University of Waterloo from 1972 to 1977.

On July 1, 1976, Alan & Hanna founded the Peace Research Institute-Dundas which continues the work that they did as part of the Canadian Peace Research Institute, namely, the publication of PEACE RESEARCH ABSTRACTS JOURNAL, PEACE RESEARCH REVIEWS JOURNAL and the operation of the Canadian School of Peace Research. Alan's research includes the development of the Tensiometer for the prediction of war.

SOME OTHER PUBLICATIONS BY ALAN AND HANNA NEWCOMBE

- Newcombe, Hanna & Newcombe, Alan. A new start in Vietnam. *Pugwash Newsletter*, July, 1965, *3*(1), 19-23. Reprinted in *Gandhi Marg*, April, 1966, 1-6.
- Newcombe, Hanna, Newcombe, Alan, & Ross, Michael. United Nations voting patterns. *International Organization*, 1970, 24(1), 100-121. (Longer version of same in *Proceedings of IPRA Conference*. Assen, The Netherlands: Van Gorcum, 1969, 51-89).
- Alcock, N.Z., & Newcombe, Alan. The perception of national power. *Journal Conflict Resolution*, 1970, 14(3), 335-343.
- Newcombe, Hanna. The case for an arms embargo in the Middle East. *War/Peace Report*, March, 1971, 17.

2. De Sade and Eichmann

I. Shlomo Kulcsar, M.D.

EICHMANN

The memory of the tragedy revived by the Jerusalem trial has already faded in the mind of the nations. Violence, terror and wars are devastating
the world, and behind the actual storms, there lurks
in dumb silence the menace of a mechanical, imper-
sonal--perhaps final--destruction of humanity. Politicians, sociologists, psychologists, hippies and
terrorists, freedom fighters and peace apostles are
seeking to understand and prevent the imminent catastrophe by analyzing, traveling, proselytizing--
or, by using violence to try to expel the evil spirit by Beelzebub (an accepted expression for black
homeopathy).
Eichmann, the protagonist of the tragedy,
turned within a short period of history into a symbol similar to Nero, Genghis Khan, or Richard III.
I feel some hesitation and repulsion in remembering
him again. However, since I am the sole psychiatrist ever to have examined him (11,12) I shall try
to overcome my resistance in the hope that perhaps
in my way, I may contribute something to the clari-
fication of humanity's fatal problem, and join the
venerable camp of good-minded social scientists,
freedom fighters and hippies.
In the history of humanity man was never in
need of images for personification or representation
of human evil. In order to determine the peculiar
traits of the destructive principle, I shall try to
examine the protagonist whom I knew personally--com-
paring him with a figure who lived two centuries ago,

and gave his name to the representation of human
cruelty as he is known to posterity, the Marquis de
Sade.

Eichmann's examination, its details and conditions have previously been published in a separate
paper (13). Here I shall group and stress only
those details relevant to the comparison with de
Sade.

The life history of Eichmann does not reveal
any peculiar pathogenic traits. Eichmann was born
in 1906 in South Germany, the eldest of six children
in a typical middle class German family. The father
was a strict, somewhat obsessive man, controlling
his children's behavior and learning. The mother
was a sickly woman who died after a long illness
when Eichmann was 13, after which the father remar-
ried a fanatically religious woman. The family had
moved to Austria in 1913. The young Adolf was a
poor pupil, often playing truant, interrupted his
general humanistic studies, and registered at a
technical high school. After graduating from there,
he was employed as a salesman in the Vacuum Oil Company and entered politics. At first he joined an
Austrian monarchistic organization; later he went
over to the Nazi Party, returned to Germany and made
a career with the N.S.D.P.

The details of his life history were obtained
from personal interviews and his prison memoirs.

In our examination of Eichmann in prison, we
based the findings more on the psychodiagnostic ex-
aminations than on his own reports. His drive
structure was revealed by the Szondi (13) test, analyzed by Szondi himself as a blind test. He chose,
in the Szondi test, on the average, 5 out of 6 murderers, and showed 10 times the characteristic Cain
syndrome out of 19 profiles. After the publication
of these results, there arose some doubts as to
whether Szondi at that time had not guessed that the
material sent by me was none other than that of
Eichmann. For those familiar with the test, it cannot make any difference. The results have a statistical relevance, and according to Szondi, among the
6,000 tests made and revised by him, there was not
a single one which gave the test signs of murderous
impulses in such a quantity as that of Eichmann (19,
p. 47).

Szondi's essential conclusion reads: "This man
is a criminal with an insatiable killing intention."
Later on, "We are confronted here with an almost
unique case. Besides the traits I mentioned previously, 88% of the vector reactions were of a social-

negative character (19, p. 46).

On the basis of the personal interviews and the other projective and intelligence test results (Wechsler, Bender, Draw a Person, Rorschach, T.A.T.) I shall sttempt to reconstruct the way in which Eichmann succeeded to live and function, with these murderous drives, what were his defenses and where did they fail.

In his everyday life, he was a bureaucrat, and he did not participate personally in the executions he commanded. His emotional life was constricted, and only rarely crude emotions broke through the barriers of the defenses. In some instances, he felt the vertigo of existential anxiety. This was the case when he met his own irresistible aggressive impulses which threatened to flood his ego-functioning and sweep him away, like "the perils of the soul." He was cynical towards the world, and towards himself as well. He had no empathy, understanding only the actions of others and not their experiences.

On the Picture Completion Test, twice he arranged the pictures in the correct order without grasping the story (11). People were not subjects for him, they were only objects. They were not co-actors, but merely "extras" in the infernal comedy of his life. He was unable to create, or feel, any direct interpersonal relations.

On the subject of sex, he proved to be very shy in the interview situation. It was the only time where he showed resistance in cooperating. The psycho-diagnostic test hinted at a repressed sado-masochistic sexual constitution (11,20).

His intelligence was a good average. He actually succeeded in formal perception and obtained good results as long as he was not required to grasp the deeper, inner meaning of what was going on. His style was extremely dry and pedantic. It was anything but natural. Words, and not concepts, sufficed for the expression and communication of feelings (11).

His education was very poor--he read almost nothing except party literature, did not visit the theater, and although he played the violin, never attended either concerts or opera performances.

He had his philosophy of life. The subjective world in which he lived was inhuman, biological at best, and fundamentally mechanical. "There is no death," he said to me, "only life. When I shall end my form of existence as a man, I shall go on to live in various organic and inorganic forms. The soul is a system of relays connected to a magnetic field. Its center is somewhere in the brain." This mechanical state of things was ruled by an impersonal mechanical God. Eichmann developed a peculiar kind of trivial fatalism which released him from every responsibility.

Eichmann's philosophy of life was a reflection of his dehumanized life experience.

The same aspect appeared in his style, his test responses, his definitions and other expressions.

The highest form of his ideal was expressed through his concept of the Reich: "The Reich, not only in the pragmatic, but in the ideal sense...the steady, the conforming, the not-disrupted."

* * * * * * *

De SADE

There were few figures discussed so vehemently and contradictorily during the last two centuries as the "divine Marquis." Restif de la Bretonne--as quoted by Gorey called him the "Monster Author" (7, p. 15). Krafft-Ebing (10) took his name for the classic example of perverted cruelty. Appolinaire called him "l'esprit le plus libre qui ait encore existe" (7, p. 16) and Baudelaire "l'homme naturel" (1, motto). His early life history is scant and not particularly noteworthy. Born in 1740 to an aristocratic French family, he was very little cared for by his parents, was raised by a series of tutors, and already, at the age of 14, served in the French Cavalry during the Seven Years War. In 1763 he married the daughter of M. de Montreuil, a mésalliance, with a strong, ambitious woman and a powerful mother. In the same year, he was already imprisoned for excesses in a "petite maison." In 1764, the inspector of the police in Paris "without going into details" advised the madame of the petite maison not to supply girls to de Sade. Nevertheless, he continued his libertine ways in a provocative manner, spent more and more time in prison, and was eventually banished from Paris. He ran away with his sister-in-law and had love affairs with several women. In 1768, his name became known through the notorious Rose Kailair affair, where he was accused of having flagellated and tortured a woman. In 1772, another "infamous" deed took place. He gave annise and cantharide (popularly known as Spanish Fly) to two prostitutes who filed a complaint of poisoning. He was sentenced to death but managed to escape.

During the time spent in prison, the dormant

writer in him awoke. Many of his works were destroyed by the authorities and the agents of his
mother-in-law. In 1789, he was interned in the lun-
atic asylum of Charenton. Between one imprisonment
and another, he published his works. During the
Revolution, he got different positions, wrote revolutionary pamphlets--but by 1792 he was already dis-
illusioned with the Revolution. As the reign of
terror grew, he became more and more nauseated by
its butcheries. In December, 1793, he was arrested
by the police on suspicion of moderantism. Years of
imprisonment started again. During his periods of
freedom he lived in misery. He attacked in anony-
mous pamphlets Bonaparte and Josephine.

In 1803, he was once more transferred to Charenton where he was described an "an incorrigible man
in a perpetual state of sexual dementia." In the
asylum, he organized theatrical performances, and it
became "chic" in the high society to visit de Sade's
theater. In 1808, the head surgeon of the asylum,
Roger Collard, recommended the suppression of de
Sade's dramatic organizations as "harmful to the patients," and in 1830, all his theatrical shows were
forbidden by ministerial order. In 1814, de Sade's
misery ended in Charenton. In 1830, his body was
exhumed, and his cranium examined by phrenologists
(7).

What were the *factual* crimes in de Sade's life?
In his day, flagellation of prostitutes belonged to
the "cream" of the aristocracy and there were more
famous flagellants than de Sade. The case of Rose
Kailair was based on the evidence of two hysterical
women--one of whom had no personal experience of the
incriminating facts. The "affair of the poinsoned
sweets" was a tasteless joke with aphrodisiacs.
That is the entire list of real facts.

*De Sade was actually persecuted because of his
fantasies,* his philosophy of life, and the obstinate
demonstration of them through his writings, in his
public and private performances, and in his intimate
plays. It was his obstinate nonconformism which
made him enemies among his contemporaries, and
turned his name into a symbol of evil among German
professors and sexologists.

Sadism in its present meaning is only one of
de Sade's imaginative preoccupations. In his pro-
saic writings, one can find the entire list of the
known sexual perversions: incest, lust murder, torture, sodomy, bestiality, arson leading to sexual
frenzy, simultaneous combination of several sexual
and parasexual acts. Parallel to the "deviations,"

he had a lot of love affairs, lived during his last
years in a faithful human intimacy with Madame Ques-
net, whom he called "this angel sent to me by heav-
en." In a letter sent from the prison of Vincennes,
he described his vision of Laura the love of
Petrarch, the eternal image of pure love, who appeared to console him in his misery.

One of de Sade's erotic trends, which appears
as much in his life history as in the content of his
writings, was his perpetual seeking of a public.
The lust felt in his characters' indulgences was no
true lust if not participated in by a public of on-
lookers. Minsky, the mysterious monster in
"Juliette" (17) who represents de Sade's ego-ideal
ad absurdum, invites Juliette's society into his
fear-inspiring secret castle, not in order to kill
and eat them, as was his way with other travelers,
but so as to serve him as companions in his sadistic
indulgences.

*De Sade's fantasies, writings and deeds are a
continuous experimentation with the emotions derived
from sex.* The effects are always dramatic, exaggerated, heightening the tension of the "nerve fluid,"
the action is pointed out *ad absurdum*, ending in
climax and catharsis--in the concrete and figurative
sense, in sexual climax. De Sade's works are sexual
and sexualized not only in their content, but also
in their function--in the expansion of the theme to
an explosive finish. The form of the narrative is
mostly dialogue, never descriptive characterizations.
Their essence is drama, written for a public of on-
lookers.

It is interesting to follow the obsessed preoccupation with play in de Sade's life. He acted as
playwright, director, producer, and during the periods of material misery, as a simple scene shifter in
the theater. Having already been successful with
his novels, he never desisted from presenting his
plays on the stage. When he finally succeeded, he
was tragically booed off as a man of the "ancient
regime." In his castle, he gave theatrical performances for the neighboring gentry, and when in Charenton, he at last found his long longed-for satisfaction, he was denounced by the wise doctor of the
asylum.

The erotic scenes performed in the brothels and
in his castle are nothing other than drama! Gorer
(7) who sees the principle of Sadism in coercing
one's will on other people, sees a connection between
sadism and theater within this frame. According to

him, the dramatist tries to influence his public.
In my opinion, sadism and drama both are playful ex-
perimentations with emotions. They demonstrate in
an absurd and surrealistic way some principles of
life, and the techniques of both are similar. In
de Sade's view, to listen to a story is more exciting than to participate in the action, and in "Les
120 Journees de Sodome," the four women who relate
to the public their sexual experiences he names "ac-
tresses" (2, p. 114).

De Sade's "plays"--from the scenes performed in
the brothels of Paris, to the theatrical organization in Charenton--seem to be a continuous psychodrama of his life. With the improvisations of his
perpetual comedia, he seems to have neutralized and
channelized powerful destructive impulses. It is
worthwhile to note how contrary were his political
and philosophical writings and actions to his erotic
imaginings. *He was always opposed to the death penalty and to legal oppression.* In August, 1793, he
wrote, "Yesterday...after having been forced to
withdraw twice, I was forced to abandon my seat to
the vice-president. They wanted me to put to the
vote a horrible and inhuman project. I desperately
refused" (1, p. 26). During his presidency, he had
the occasion to take revenge on his greatest enemy,
his mother-in-law and her family. "If I had said a
word, they were lost. I kept my peace. I have had
my revenge" (1, p. 26).

"Murderers! Imprisoners! Fools of every country, and of every government," he exclaims, "When
will you prefer the science of knowing man to that
of shutting him up and killing him!" (1, p. 62). As
mentioned above, he was imprisoned and sentenced to
death because of moderantism, and only due to a bureaucratic error, escaped the guillotine.

In the period when State and Society were held
in the highest order, de Sade remained a fanatical
believer in Nature, which justified his erotic and
individual extravangancies.

COMPARING EICHMANN AND De SADE

In summing up the personal traits of our two
characters, we may classify them into eight groups:

Eichmann	*De Sade*

1) An incomparable mur-
    derous tendency.
	1) De Sade's aggression
	    was always eroticized.

Szondi did not find among his 6,000 tests a single case who gave in such quantity the Cain syndrome. His aggression was de-eroticized, death instinct and libido were unmingled.

2) Eichman's was an alienated personality. The definition of alienation taken according to that of F.H. Heinemann: "The facts to which the term 'alienation' refers, are objectively, different kinds of dissociation, break or rupture between human beings and their objects, whether the latter be other persons, or the natural world, or their own creations in art, science and society; and subjectively the corresponding states of disequilibrium, disturbance, strangeness and anxiety" (8, p. 13)

3) Eichmann was a bureaucrat par excellence--taking as a definition that of Marx: "The bureaucrat relates himself to the world as a mere object of his activity" (15, p. 61). When Eichmann characterized himself as a "cogwheel in a machine,"

He despised the death sentence, oppression and impersonal violence.

2) Was in constant touch with 'the other'--when not in reality, at least in imagination. He had no pleasure in his factual and imaginative acts without on-lookers.

3) He hated all manisfestations of bureaucracy--state, religion, legal.

it was not simply
a juridical defense,
but an expression of
his self-image.

4) Eichmann had no em-   4) His sadistic pleasure
pathy.   was inconceivable
                             without feeling his
                             partner's experience.

5) Eichmann was in-   5) De Sade's sins were,
human--more correct-   according to Baude-
ly, *a-human* in the   laire, *human*.
strict sense of the
word.

6) Eichmann's highest   6) De Sade was an anar-
ideal was the Reich.   chist to the bottom of
                             his heart.

7) Eichmann hid him-   7) De Sade was a fighting
self behind conform-   nonconformist.
ism.

8) Eichmannism is a   8) Sadism is a dialogue.
monologue.

THE SADISTIC DRAMA AS THERAPEUTIC AND PREVENTIVE

From these comparisons arise some philosophical
problems: Is violence deeply rooted in human nature, or is it only a reaction to frustrations, or a
social product, like some late protagonists of the
"noble savage" claim? If it is rooted in human nature, how is it correctable? *Might replacing Eichmannism with Sadism be one way of correction, and
could it be justified?*

I would like to try to follow a path to its
final consequences, in the wame way as Freud entered
into the discussion of the death instinct. "It is
...an attempt to follow out an idea consistently out
of curiosity to see where it will lead" (4, p. 23).
Besides, if I have already invoked Freud, let me
cite him again in another statement (*ibid*): "It
might indeed be said that sadism which has been
forced out of the ego, has pointed the way for the
libidual components of the sexual instinct and these
follow after it, to the object" (4, p. 58).

After having known de Sade's philosophy about
impersonal violence on the one hand and eroticized
cruelty on the other, we shall not be surprised to
find in his writings some practical suggestions for
a way of translating violence into eroticism.

One of the most competent scholars of de Sade,
Gorer, points out that de Sade held self-love and

despotism "especially when deprived of direct satisfaction...the most dangerous of all antisocial
forces: and therefore suggested to channel them into
playful and erotic activities. De Sade thought of
women as being more cruel than men, and therefore
suggested for them active flagellation. "Society,"
he writes, "would profit by means of this outlet for
female cruelty, for if they cannot hurt in this way,
they will in another, spreading their poison in society and driving their husbands and families to de-
struct" (7, p. 166).

He also suggested adaptation of sports like
bullfights, gladiators, boxing and wrestling. "Who
knows," he askes, "if by thus giving issue to human
cruelty, we wouldn't dry up at the source of their
mysterious crimes?" (7, p. 167).

These suggestions even if they weren't called
sublimation, might be defined as "socialization" of
instinctual trends--to use the concept of Szondi
(19).

In his work "La philosophie dans le boudoire,"
de Sade gives a practical solution for the problem.
He suggests the organization of special brothels
where, in a protected setting, everyone could act
out his cruel wishes in a psychodrama with prostitutes as auxiliary egos. For women who according to
his view "have far more violent desires for the
pleasure of lust," he plans special brothels (7,
p. 166).

Anyone who had interest and time for such a research could find countless examples in de Sade's
works for role-playing as a means of protected acting out and prevention of antisocial forces. Not
only in his writings, but even in his life history,
in his private life, in the "petites maisons" and in
his castle, and, returning once more to a subject
discussed briefly above, he endeavored to get rid of
antisocial instincts and was obsessed by a preoccupation with theater. From a distance of two centuries and with the possession of psychological knowledge and historical perspectives, let us try to follow de Sade's paths and to find some way of preventing destruction through drama.

According to modern theory, drama originated in
cult, it was a personification of the myth. The con-
tents of the original Greek Drama were: incest, murder and guilt, punishment, immolation. It is not
difficult to recognize in its script the antique
tragedy of the totem sacrifice. Human emotion and
passion were still identical with Destiny. Originally the public participated--literally--in the play,

and later on by identification. The theater goer
felt the violence, the suffering, the guilt and the
punishment and found the solution in the final cath-
arsis. In Medieval drama, from the 13th century on-
wards, the *Passion Play* replaced pagan tragedy. The
Catholic Church made a wide use of this correcting
experience, and later it spread also among the lai-
ty, and in some places it is performed up to the
present time. The word "passion" meant, originally,
the sufferings of Jewus Christ, and later the word
was used as a translation of the Greek philosophical
term "Pathos." In modern usage, it means "strong
and uncontrolled emotions." When a man who was not
brought up in the Christian faith and traditions enters a Catholic Church, he is struck by the multi-
fold and impressive depictions of cruelty and suffering, those of the Pagans and Christians respec-
tively. These expressions seem to have flowed from
a deep pyschological need for the artists, but let
us remember that the artists, in those days, were
not yet individualists and worked according to the
order of the Church. As the Catholic Church was one
of the greatest and most successful educators of all
ages, the Fathers who gave the orders, knew exactly
for what they gave them. It was very likely intended to pacify the aggressive instincts of medieval
man by educating him to feel the "passion" by identification. The stories of the Saints abound in descriptions of martyrdom and suffering, but, even before Christendom, we find the same motifs in the
mysteries of the Near East, e.g., in the Cult of
Adonis, Osiris.
     Through the ages, we find the dramatization of
passion, passion in both senses, as a means of education of human aggressive instincts. *The psychodrama directed by Hamlet in the presence of his parents should have been played before the murder--in
which case it would not have happened!*
     "Imperious, choleric, irascible, extreme in
everything, with a dissolute imagination, the like
of which was never seen..."(1, p. 11)--with these
words de Sade characterizes himself. It is a char-
acterization of the passionate man. The plays of
his life served to depassionate him.
     Now "to follow out an idea consistently," we may
arrive at very strange results. *The consequence may
be that in order to mitigate human aggression we
must develop some kind of "neo-sadism"* following the
way Freud (5) hints at as early as in 1905 and develops into a basic idea in "Das Ich und das Es" (6).
     To increase a sense for passion is not a new

idea. In Western civilization, especially in the
United States, its lack is felt more and more. Very
often, exaggerated experiments in its development
such as sensitivity training, encounter groups, T-
groups strike more conservative European tastes as
testimony to the feelings of emotional deprivation
of the American people. The counter-culture movements such as the pop-culture, perhaps serve the
same purpose. The faces of the participants in the
encounter groups as depicted in the journals, and
the distorted mimics of pop-singers, sometimes remind one of the facial expressions of ecstatic believers of all religions.

Again "to follow out consistently," one had to
find some means of expression that are more scienti-
fically based, applicable to the education of masses, fitting human nature, and somewhat more taste-
ful.

As mentioned above, the *sine qua non* of sadism
is *empathy*, and this in dramatic opposition to
Eichmannism. The problem is how to develop something of which, until this time, we do not have a
satisfactory definition. The term "empathy" formulated by F.T. Vicher in 1846 (20) refers originally
to an esthetic experience, and the word was transferred into psychology in a different meaning. The
only substrate of this semantic game which we are
able to grasp through our psychological concepts is
one of its intrinsic components: identification.
Thus, the more circumscribed task of neo-sadism
might be defined as "how to train for identification." Though I don't like to use the verb "training" in the meaning of forming human character, I
would like to formulate it in this way, in order to
stress that I do not mean a Salvation Army approach,
but a method like training in basketball or mathematical skill.

The Bible gives an eternal example of this approach: "Love thy neighbor as thyself." From the
logical and rationalistic context wherein it appears, it is clear that this command is not a mawk-
ish appeal, but an adequate expression for a social
law. The same sense is expressed in the law demanding tolerance toward the stranger: "For thou hast
also been a foreigner in the land of Egypt." *This
kind of identification with fellow men is the faculty which Eichmann, and potential Eichmanns do not
possess.*

IDENTIFICATION WITH HUMANITY

In wishing to develop identification, we have
to clarify:
    (1) Identification--with whom?
    (2) How to develop it?
The first question arises because of the poor
identification in Western Culture on one hand, and
the development of hyper-identification in minority
groups on the other--religious, political, social,
racial, ethnic, or whatever they may be. In Communist countries, as Bronfenbrenner (3) gave an account, the object of the identification extends from
the narrower group to the wider group to the abstract Society. Still, it seems to me, that this
ideal does not fit the Western way of life, and especially not the American ideal of education initiated by Dewey. Western people were, at least until
the last century, raised on the Bible and its spirit
of individual responsibility. The Western ideal
stressed individuality often in an exaggerated way,
and forgot, meanwhile, the code of "Love thy neighbor as thyself." Still, it does not mean that we
must throw out the baby with the bathwater.
The Western type of identification might only
be with a fellow man but through that fellow man it
should continue to other fellows until it attains
its object, which is abstract Humanity.
How can one attain identification? This is a
question for educators, psychologists, social scientists. One of the methods may be a new kind of Passion play, new school dramas. Moreno (16) caught
the idea as early as during the devastating World
War I, developing the method on wayward children of
Vienna, and he was heroic enough to suggest that international conflicts could be solved by psychodrama.
Modern theater also tries to take its performances
out to the streets, and to invite the public to join
in the action. Many experiments were initiated outside the frame of professional science. Has the
science of today alienated itself?
*The "divine Marquis" may be one of the answers
to the question put before humanity by the infernal
Obersturmbannfuhrer. Perhaps it is not yet too late
to respond.*

REFERENCES

1. Beauvoir, Simone de. *The Marquis de Sade*. Lon-
    don: Calder, 1962.

2. Beauvoir, Simone de. Selections from the Writ-
    ings of the Marquis de Sade. *Ibid.*
3. Bronfenbrenner, Urie. *Two Worlds of Childhood.*
    New York: Basic Books, 1970.
4. Freud, S. Jenseits des lustprinzips. *Ges.*
    Werke, XIII. London: Imago, 1952
5. Freud, S. Drei abhandlungen zur sexualtheories
    Ges. Werke, V. London: Imago, 1952.
6. Freud, S. Das Ich und das Es. *Ges. Werke,*
    XIII. London: Imago, 1952.
7. Gorer, G. *The Life and Ideas of the Marquis de*
    Sade. London: Panther, 1963.
8. Heinemann, F.H. *Existentialism and the Modern*
    Predicament. New York: Harper, 1958. (as
    cited by Josephson (9))
9. Josephson, Eric, & Josephson, Mary. *Man Alone.*
    New York: Dell, 1962.
10. Kraft-Ebing, R.V. *Psychopathia Sexualis,* 1886.
11. Kulcsar, Shoshanna: The Psychodiagnostic Exam-
    ination of Adolf Eichmann, 1961. (Unpublished)
12. Kulcsar, I.S. The psychopathology of Adolf
    Eichmann. *Proceedings of the IV World Congress*
    of Psychiatry. Madrid, 1966.
13. Kulcsar, I.S., Kulcsar, Shoshanna, & Szondi,
    Lipot. Adolf Eichmann and the Third Reich. In
    Ralph Slovenko, (Ed.), *Crime, Law and Correc-*
    tions. Springfield, Illinois: Charles C.
    Thomas, 1966, 16-52.
14. Kulcsar, I.S. The education of the psychother-
    apist through the medium of psychodrama. *Brit-*
    ish Journal Social Psychiatry & Community Health,
    1972, *6*(1), 20-25.
15. Marx, Karl. *Das Kapital,* 1967. (as cited by
    Josephson (9))
16. Moreno, J.L. *The Cradle of Psychodrama.* New
    York: Beacon, 1964.
17. Sade, de. *Juliette.* New York: Langer, 1965.
18. Sade, de. *Quartet.* London: Panther, 1963.
19. Szondi, L. *Kain, Gestalten des Böses.* Bern:
    Huber, 1969.
20. Vischer, F.T. *Aesthetik oder Wissenschaft des*
    Schönen, 1846.

ISTVAN SHLOMO KULCSAR was born in 1901 in Buda-
pest, a city of revolutionaries, poets and psychia-
trists. He received his education--from grammar
school till postgraduate training--at the same
place. For some time, he hesitated between a liter-
ary and a medical career, and in the end chose as a

compromise, psychiatry. Though practicing and teaching psychotherapy, in his publications he has tried to stress the clinical and pharmocological side in order to overcompensate for his literary inclination.

He met organized violence first during the "White Terror" of Horthy's military junta and was later imprisoned as a participant of a half-literary conspiracy against the Horthy regime.

The second time he was struck by violence was during the Nazi invasion of Hungary, when it became his turn to see murdered children and women. He became active in a group of Resistance rescuing Jewish children. After the liberation of Hungary, he worked for some years with the psychiatric consequences of concentration camps and the orphans of the Holocaust, and in the year 1950 emigrated to Israel. There he immediately was assigned the task of building up a modern psychiatric hospital within the walls of the medieval castle of Akko. At the age of 56, he visited for the first time European psychiatric institutions, towns and museums. Until this day, he has not achieved the B.I.A. degree (Been In America). In 1958, he organized a psychiatric ward within the framework of a general teaching hospital (Chaim Sheba Medical Center) where he worked until his retirement in 1971. Since that time he has been active in the Youth Clinic of the same hospital, and continues teaching psychiatry at the University of Tel Aviv.

His third meeting with the problem of violence occurred when in 1961 he was appointed to perform a psychiatric examination of Adolf Eichmann. Since that time the problem does not give him rest any more.

He is living in a garden suburb near Tel Aviv. His late wife was a clinical psychologist working with him for two decades. One of his sons is a journalist and writer, the other a fisherman, thus realizing their father's hidden wishes.

Besides his professional activity, his chief interests are drama and water sports--including fishing, though the latter is a violence against our cold-blooded fellow creatures.

SOME OTHER PUBLICATIONS BY I.S. KULCSAR

- The education of the psychotherapist through the medium of psychodrama. *British Journal Social Psychiatry & Community Health,* 1972, 6(1), 20-25.
- The Duo-drama. *Mental Health & Society,* 1976, 3, 286-299.

3. In Nomine Diaboli: The Voices of Evil

Lionel Rubinoff, Ph.D.

INTRODUCTION: THE INSTITUTIONALIZATION OF EVIL

The most significant and astonishing phenomenon of recent history is the sophistication with which the performance of acts of evil and the violence through which such evils are perpetuated have been institutionalized and integrated into the normal routines of everyday living and working.[1] The chief symptom of this state of affairs is the fact that we seem to have lost our certainty about what evil is, as well as our capacity to identify with it. The result is that we find ourselves engaging in evil acts without experiencing them as such. Take, for example, the tendency in our society to subsidize a pornography of violence masquerading as art and literature. As George Steiner puts it:

> We live in a world in which art not only flirts with but pays homage to the genius of cruelty and brutality. This kind of art prepares the imagination to believe that certain things could be tried or might be fun to look at, so that very subtly it undermines its own overt moral values. The concentration camp is the symbol for these ideas. But there are other symbols....man's murder of animal species and his destruction of the ecology...Something in man has made him murder thousands of species-- not for food, but in gratuitous waste. Something in man makes him ravage landscapes and demolish the last places of beauty. Some suicidal demon in our civilization sees the evil that it does, yet continues to do it.[2]

The character of our age is thus formed by the dedicated pursuit of incongruous goals. As the poet W.B. Yeats once put it:

> The best lack all conviction, while the worst
> Are full of passionate intensity.

The very same reasoning and the very same language that produces science, philosophy, technology and art, on the one hand, produces at the same time the excuses and the ideologies by means of which our energies are employed towards the corruption of rationality and the support of evil, often through the most violent means. We believe that the rationale of our society serves the interests of justice. As one reflects on the matter, however, the suspicion is aroused that our society has been rationalized *in nomine diaboli,* in the name of the devil.

ACCEPTANCE OF EVIL

How is this possible? How has the institutionalization of evil come about? By what magic has it become possible for men to serve the devil without being aware of it? Sometimes we find ourselves doing things without any awareness of the fact that the consequences are evil. At other times, we find ourselves doing things which we openly recognize to be inconsistent with our avowed moral beliefs, but which we are nevertheless unable to resist. We may admit that what we are doing is regrettable or even wrong but not that it is evil. Thus, we believe that it is wrong to kill, or to deprive one of his civil liberties, but when this is done in the name of law and order and the national interest, then we regard these very same acts as heroic. How is it possible to reconcile such gross inconsistencies?

In answer to this question, social scientists have drawn attention to the fact that all human societies have evolved procedures, in the form of rituals, which have the effect of hiding such inconsistencies from their members. Erich Fromm, for example, in his book, *The Sane Society,* refers to the process whereby evil is so normalized as the mechanism of the "socially patterned defect."[3] This is a process whereby a defect is raised to a virtue by a culture through the uncritical acceptance of the majority of members of that culture. In this way, those who exemplify such a defect in their conduct are able to enjoy a feeling of achievement rather than guilt. Notice, for example, the way in which many members of the North American public responded to the atrocities committed at Kent State and My Lai. In the eyes of many, the National Guardsmen and Lt. Calley were heroes.[4] There was also the incident, some years ago--in the late fifties and early sixties--in which a certain Major Claude Eatherly' attempted to raise questions about the morality of the bombing of Hiroshima in which he had himself participated. But rather than accept his self-confessed guilt for having committed a crime against humanity--which would mean coming to terms with their own complicity in the crime--his critics chose instead to brand him insane, thus neutralizing the effects of his criticisms. As Eatherly himself put it, "The truth is that society cannot accept the fact of *my* guilt without at the same time recognizing its own far deeper guilt."[5] The American public was prepared to honour him for his part in the massacre, but when he repented, it turned against him rather than face its own condemnation. And the reaction of the same public to the Kent State and My Lai massacres was no different years later.

Further examples of such behaviour are the uncritical acceptance by large numbers of Canadians of the Federal government's decision to suspend the civil liberties of all Japanese Canadians on the West Coast during the second world war, or the decision to suspend the civil liberties of all Canadians during the FLQ crisis which occurred inthe Fall and Winter of 1970.[6]   Finally, I would like to cite the typical policy of Western support for the former military dictatorship in Greece. A typical example is the following editorial from the *Wall Street Journal*:

> We do not deny that the junta is, on the record, repressive. It has squashed freedom and other liberties associated with a free society. It relentlessly punished political dissent. On these scores it is presumably repugnant to most Americans, including U.S. policy-makers.
> *Yet to make such repugnamce the criterion of policy would be to indulge in diplomacy by emotionalism--never a wise exercise. Diplomatic recognition, or its recision, should not depend on emotional reactions but on considerations of the national interest.* (my italics)
> If Washington can use whatever influence it has

to induce more democratic conditions in Greece,
that is worth doing. But the administration
has evidently decided, so far, that for strategic and international political reasons, the
present basic policy is in this nation's interest. For that evaluation, it seems to us, it
does not deserve chastisement.[7]

The above cited incidents are particularly significant because they suggest the possibility that
large numbers of persons can be socialized to perceive certain acts as evil when committed by foreigners, but not when committed by members of their
own nation. Such persons flatter themselves with
the belief that evil is something committed by unac-
countable foreigners, or by those among us under the
influence of foreigners, or else by alienated and
deranged persons who have failed to be properly socialized. And anyone who thinks differently and
tries to place guilt where it does not belong must
also be deranged.
The chief rituals through which the circumstances I have described have been brought about are
those which tend to indoctrinate one into the virtue
and piety of obeying orders, and doing one's job, or
doing whatever is in the national interest.
But just as there are rituals of indoctrination
which hide discrepancies, thus producing uncritical
acceptance of defects and acts of injustice, so
there are other kinds of ritual whose purpose is to
produce just the opposite effect. As opposed to the
rituals of "indoctrination," there are what I propose to call, rituals of "attention" whose effect is
primarily therapeutic. Through rituals of attention, men come to experience themselves as creatures
of temptation and ambivalence. *The therapeutic effect of this self-knowledge is that by identifying
the sources of evil within the drama of their own
inner consciousness, men come to acquire a kind of
immunity from the temptation to indulge in uncrit-
ically accepted behaviour.*
In the next section of this paper, I will be
concerned primarily with the rituals of indoctrination whereby men lose their capacity to recognize
evil, which in turn acts either as an incentive to
violence or else tends to inhibit our capacity to
resist it. In the following part, I will be concerned with the therapeutic rituals of attention
through which consciousness is able to transcend its
capacity for rationalizing evil.

THE PSYCHOLOGY AND SOCIOLOGY OF EVIL

The questions to which I shall address myself in this section may be stated as follows. What are the psychodynamics whereby an individual can freely engage in evil without visible signs of guilt? And what are the social mechanisms which facilitate and encourage this behaviour?

Some help may be obtained by exploring the structure of evil as represented in myth and literature. Of particular importance in this regard, is the image of Satan. In a very interesting and important paper on the devil, David Bakan suggests that the image of Satan can be analyzed into two components.[8] The first may be designated as "ultra-realistic," the second as "ultra-mythic." The "ultra-realism" of Satan lies in the fact that for those who believe in him, he is experienced as a foreign intruder and as an embodiment of external reality. At the same time, Satan is typically represented as the "Tempter," and as "calling forth the beast in man." It is he who manipulates our inner drives. The pleasures and pains which the individual experiences with respect to the committing of evil acts are experienced as having been evoked from without, from some point in external reality called "hell." In this way, the individual projects the inner-felt reality associated with evil on to an external source which must now bear full responsibility for the impulses, drives and experiences of pleasure which constitute the content of that inner reality.

Now there is a close parallel between the image of Satan as an external source of temptation and compulsion, and contemporary man's view of his behaviour as compelled by forces over which he has no control. *Just as Satan represents a mythological solution to the need for finding some way of relieving us of full responsibility for our actions, so contemporary man has invented "bureaucracy," with its emphasis on uncritical acceptance of authority.* Bureaucratic authoritarianism makes it possible for the individual to experience his behaviour not as an expression of something internal to himself, but simply as a response to an external command, and as something over which he has no control. "I am simply doing my job, merely following orders." The bureaucrat is "compelled by his job description" in much the same way that in both ancient and contemporary times certain individuals believed themselves to have been "possessed" by the Devil.[9] And just as

the Devil relieves individuals from the burden of
responsibility for their own behaviour--for doing
what they secretly crave to do--so bureaucracy relieves individuals of a similar sense of responsibility.

This tendency to identify with one's job description, irrespective of the moral consequences,
can be further elucidated by interpreting the symbolism of the Devil's fall from heaven, and man's
subsequent expulsion from paradise. In the case of
the Devil, to have been cast out of heaven is to
have been separated from being and cast into hell,
the realm of nothing. The Devil is thus the messen-
ger of "nothing." He is activity without purpose.
It is important also to remember that although the
Devil has fallen from being, in which case he has
lost all sense of vision and purpose, he has not
lost any of his techniques, his knowledge, or his
skills. He is like a lover who no longer believes
in love, but still retains his power of seduction.
He is a tireless worker, who dedicates himself to
bringing about whatever happens to be *desired* without regard to whether or not it is also *desirable*.
And whatever is done skillfully but without regard
to the moral consequences of pursuing such ends
bears the imprimatur of the Devil.[10]

The problem to which I am drawing attention may
be further illustrated by appealing to the following
images from classical mythology. When the name
Prometheus comes to mind, one tends to think of the
compassionate hero who was so inspired by his concerns for the miseries of man that he risked the
wrath of God by stealing fire from heaven so that
men might become their own masters and thus allevi-
ate the adversity under whih they lived and suffered. But there is another association that derives from the etymology of the word itself. The
word "Prometheus" comes from the Greek words "pro"
and "mathein" which together means forethought or
thoughtfulness. Putting these various meanings together, then, *Promethean* may be understood to mean
*the compassionate but thoughtful concern for leading
mankind towards greater and greater degrees of self-
mastery through understanding and knowledge.* Viewed
this way, Promethean aptly describes the professions
of science and technology in their ideal form.

A much different image derives from the mythological figure of Faust. Faust too has an interest
in knowledge. But unlike Promethean knowledge,
Faustian knowledge serves the appetite for personal
self-interest and power. So defined, Faustian ra-

tionality is clearly the opposite of the rationality upon which science and technology are ideally founded. Yet Faustians have a peculiar talent for disguising their real interests under the guise of Promethean rationality and creativity. For this reason, we are often deceived by Faustians pretending to be promethean; by politicians, scientists and technologists who claim to be dedicated to the classical humanistic ideals of western culture, but for whom in fact the entire resources of science and technology present themselves primarily as instruments for the satisfaction of an irrational craving to exercise power.

As I have used these terms, the Promethean and the Faustian suggest two distinct interpretations of rationality which can easily be confused. Promethean rationality is "thoughtful." It seeks th application of means to the realization of ends that are worthy of being realized because they are understood to contribute to justice and the general happiness of mankind. For such rational thinking which aims at the evaluation of ends has priority over thinking which preoccupies itself exclusively with the determination of means. Faustian tradition is "thoughtless." It is concerned exclusively with the organization of means irrespective of the ends; indeed, the extent to which it is concerned with ends at all, is only insofar as they serve the irrational need to gain recognition through the manipulation of the means. Faustian rationality is the rationality through which the ego seeks selfhood through mastery over others. It arises in the course of the dialectic of self-consciousness, as outlined by Hegel in the *Phenomenology of Mind,* which leads eventually to the relationship of Lordship and Bondage. Consider, for example, Hegel's claim that desire is the first form of self-consciousness and the first category for understanding the growth of both individual and collective consciousness. Desire arises as a consequence of the fact that self-consciousness, as opposed to mere consciousness, depends for its sense of self-certainty on the negation of the other, whether in the form of nature or other selves. Self-consciousness regards itself as the truth of the other, and in the eyes of self-consciousness, the other is nothing until it derives its truth from its being appropriated by self-consciousness. This is the ontological source of the desire to negate the other.

DESIRE TO NEGATE OTHERS

Self-consciousness thus arises in the context of a desire to appropriate or negate the independence or otherness of the other. What makes the other an object of desire is the mere fact that it exists as other.

How does this doctrine affect our understanding of interpersonal relations and international relations? To begin with, we should become immediately suspicious of the excuses and rationalizations that we are accustomed to employ in order to justify our aggressive attitudes towards each other. Such rationalizations may be nothing more than masks which hide the true meaning of our behaviour. For alas, we are in real life less prone to philosophical self-understanding than is Hegel's philosophical consciousness. Let us suppose that the selfhood of the nation, like the selfhood of the single individual, depends for its selfhood on the annihilation of the selfhood or sovereignty of the other. The nation in search of selfhood thus conceives itself as the truth of all other nations; the other is nothing until it has been consumed by the desire of the aggressor nation. But for reasons having to do with the nature of the collective super-ego, no nation can explicitly adopt this point of view. Instead it will manufacture excuses in order to justify its conduct.

This is a phenomenon to which Freud has perhaps contributed more understanding than Hegel. Thus, Pericles conceived Greek imperialism as a form of education. Woodrow Wilson justified the messianic nationalism of America by appealing to the "manifest destiny." President Nixon attempted to justify his policy of annihilation in South Vietnam and Cambodia on the grounds that he was fighting for liberty against communist aggression, while his colleagues, the Watergate conspirators, pleaded that they acted always in the "national interest." If Watergate and its related events signify anything it is that for the demonically inspired consciousness, it is not enough merely to defeat one's political enemies in an election, it is necessary to annihilate them. In the White House horrors, as John Mitchell has so aptly described them, we witness once again the pornographic exercise of power through which human consciousness has sought to escape from its finitude ever since mankind stepped out of the timeless innocence of paradise into the sensuous domain of history.

The urge to escape from the conditions of finitude by gaining mastery and power over persons as well as things is thus one source of the Faustian urge to implement goals whose simple *possibility* presents itself as *desirability*. The mere fact that it is possible to do something with the technological means at hand, which at the same time increases one's power, is sufficient to render it desirable. This is the attitude of a corruption of consciousness which expresses itself in the form of "technological nihilism." *Technological nihilism is the assertion of function over substance and the elevation of technique to the rank of a deity.*

As represented by the myths and religious traditions of Western man, the most potent symbol of technological nihilism is the Devil or Satan. He is represented as a passionate, preternatural intelligence whose sole mission is to tempt man to follow the same path by means of which he himself fell from divine Grace. But demonic temptation always presents itself in the form of Promethean creativity. Thus, for example, Satan tempts Eve to eat the forbidden fruit by promising her that if she does so then her eyes shall be opened and she shall be as gods, knowing good and evil (Genesis 3: 3-4). It is for this reason that the Satanic impulse is present even in such normally commendable desires as the desire to succeed at something. At its very best, the urge to achieve embodies the Promethean desire to reach transcendental standards of excellence. In itself the desire for excellence is not necessarily productive of evil. Indeed such a desire should be a factor in all motivation. But when this desire is converted into a Faustian compulsion to achieve for the mere sake of acquiring the power that achievement makes possible, and when the idea of achievement conceived as the pursuit of the possible is elevated or deified into an absolute goal, then such desires are inherently Satanic. *Whenever a person submits to the temptation of technological nihilism under the cover of such language as "I was only following orders," "I was only doing my job," "I was serving the national interest," that person is in reality speaking* in nomine diaboli, *in the name of the devil.*

THE DEVIL'S DECEPTION: EVIL AS A PROMISE OF GOOD

According to the symbolism of the myth, demonic temptation never appears as the prospect of evil per se, but appears rather as the prospect of achieving

some good. *The Devil's chief weapon is deception.*
It is always through the mediation of some vision of
the good that a person surrenders to the Faustian
impulse. The Promethean and the Faustian derive
from the same common origin--the human urge for
self-transcendence. This is the source of what I
had earlier called, following David Bakan's analysis, the "ultra-mythic." "Ultra-mythicism" is a
preoccupation with an eschatology or ideology, the
belief that the events of one's life are the playing
out of some grand cosmic drama inspired by a vision
of the Good, in which man rises from his humble origins to a position of divine infallibility. According to the mythic representation, the Devil is a
skillful nihilist, hence the plots of these dramas
and the goals pursued can be invented at will without regard to their truth or falsity. It is thus
that as we were once called upon to act in the name
of God so we now find ourselves called upon to act
in the name of a cause, destiny or national purpose.
As Kurt H. Wolff puts it, in a paper dealing with
the sociology of evil:

> Evil is no longer committed in the name of God,
> is less than ever "legitimated" by religious or
> even moral motives, and is covered over by po-
> litical, economic and technological reasons,
> and on a larger scale than ever.[11]

Wolff suggests that the reason why we are so
captured by these new forces of order is because we
find ourselves living in the midst of a paralysing
suspension between two impossible worlds: a world
ordered by religious directives in which we can no
longer believe, and a world without such directives
which we cannot bear. The result of this alienation
is that we are driven to fill in the vacuum by finding new gods to worship: and these are made readily
available to us in the form of political, economic
and technological incentives. Since the latter are
experienced in the context of the logic of a "functional rationality," which, as I hope to point out,
tends to be confused with the very essence of reason
itself, it does not occur to us that anything committed in the name of such goals could be evil. It
is perhaps, as Wolff points out, for this reason
that "we have not succeeded in articulating a conception of evil that would be adequate to the secu-
larized world in which we in fact live, but which

has left evil itself, in contrast to space, cancer, the Greenland Icecap, and innumerable other phenomena and problems, comparatively unexplored, ominously sacred and threatening."[12]

Other ways of filling in the vacuum which arises from contemporary man's growing sense of alienation are the pursuit of an absolute religious and moral authority that will relieve the discomfort of making decisions, and the restless pursuit of novel and exotic experiences, gratuitously called "alternate states of consciousness," which one seeks to experience for the mere sake of experiencing, and which one believes will bring one into touch with "the absolute." But the irony is that in his effort to overcome alienation, and to protest his captivity to the materialism of contemporary society, his newly acquired "gluttony" for experiences (as Harvey Cox aptly describes it) turns out to be nothing more than a continuation of his former greed for the consumption of things.[13] The "consumer" is replaced by the "searcher," and as such remains the prisoner of the logic of consumerism, which as Cox points out transforms experience as such into a commodity and thus transforms the entire range of human ideals and emotions into a well-stocked pantry. The searcher is now possessed by a demonic passion to transcend the limits of ordinary experience, even if it means participating in a "Black Mass." In keeping with the logic of demonic possession, one's Faustian temptations and appetites are satisfied under the guise of Promethean creativity. One readily accepts the deception that all psychobiological experiences, no matter how bizarre, are revelations of Spiritual reality. What might previously have been regarded as a life of simple debauchery is now mystified into a new and exotic celebration of "the deliciousness of beauty bestialized and of the beast beautified." For the demonically possessed "searcher," the very thought that there remains an experience that has not yet been savoured is enough to inspire an anguish and a craving similar to that of the Christian for God's Grace. And as the anguish and the appetite grow, so will the coterie of entrepreneurs and merchants of experience who are only too willing and able to stimulate and feed the new gluttony to its insatiable limits.

The structure of technological nihilism which tends to characterize the secular world can be further explicated in terms of a distinction, drawn by the sociologist, Karl Mannheim, between "substantial" and "functional" rationality.[14] Substantial

rationality is an act of thought which reveals intelligent insight into the interrelations of events
in a given situation. It is akin to what is sometimes called "common sense." By functional rationality, on the other hand, is meant the way some-
thing--a given industry or administration, for ex-
ample--has been "rationalized." In such cases, the
term "rational" refers not to the fact that the person carries out acts of thinking and knowing for the
purpose of realizing what is for the best, that is
to say, morally desirable, but rather to the fact
that a series of actions is "organized" in such a
way that it leads to a previously defined goal.
Consciousness is no longer subject to the *cognito
ergo sum*. It is rather a *facto ergo sum*. Every
element in this series (or repertoire) of actions
receives a functional position and role. Such a
functional organization of a series of actions will,
moreover, be at its best when the most efficient
techniques are employed in order to attain the given
goal. The latter, according to Mannheim, is a disguised form of irrationality.

ORDER--THE PRETENCE OF RATIONALITY

        The irrationality of so-called "functional ra-
tionality" derives not only from the kinds of goals
pursued, but also from the fact that the agent becomes obsessed with means and techniques and is virtually anaesthetized into adopting an attitude of
passive indifference to (or acceptance of) the
goals. What gives the enterprise the pretence of
rationality is the fact that it is *organized* in such
a way that the realization of the goal is rendered
possible. Thus, Eichmann, in his pursuit of the
"final solution: regarded his actions as rational.
He had organized a repertoire of technologically
functional means toward the solution of a specific
goal; and any action which is experienced as having
a functional role to play in achieving the ultimate
goal, by virtue of this fact alone is regarded as
rational. The nature and content of the goal is
secondary to the satisfaction of achieving it.[15]
Not only is the nature and content of the goal secondary to the satisfaction of achieving it, but the
agent's perception of the rationality of the goal
itself is determined primarily by the success and
efficiency with which it is achieved. If it is
possible to achieve a given goal, then the goal itself must be rational.
        It is thus that one acquires a completely false

sense of rationality. Just as Hume pointed out, in
his well known analysis of causation, that we tend
to confuse the psychological experience of "ful-
filled expectancy" with the perception of "necessary
connection" or "force," so the bureaucrats and tech-
nocrats tend to confuse the psychological experience
of the means bringing about the end with the reason
or rationality for the sake of which the end exists.
So also do searchers after the "Absolute" and seek-
ers of "Truth" confuse every possible psychobiological experience with the true modes of spiritual reality.

Human action thus becomes the agent of what
Hannah Arendt has called "the banality of evil," *the
capacity of engaging in evil without experiencing it
as evil, to perform evil acts as part of one's job
description*. Such behaviour, as Hannah Arendt and
others have pointed out, is not so much the expression of innate aggressiveness or sadism, as it is
the result of the agent's inability to challenge
whatever discrepancies and irrationalities he might
perceive between what he does and his moral beliefs.
This is especially true of the way in which certain
acts of violence become assimilated to the agent's
perception of what is rationally appropriate.

One of the best and most dramatic examples of
the extent to which this inability to challenge authority has come to characterise the average person
is provided by a set of experiments conducted by the
social psychologist, Stanley Milgram, during the
1960s.[16] The aim of these experiments was to determine the amount of pain (in the form of an electric
shock) that a subject is willing to inflict on another, when ordered by an experimenter to do so.
This study shows that it is possible for quite normal individuals to engage in violent and morally in-
decent behaviour (including inflicting pain and suffering on others, even when they are explicitly
aware that it is in conflict with their moral beliefs) at the instruction of some authority, provided that they perceive that authority as legitimate.

> Despite his numerous, agitated objections,
> which were constant accompaniements to his ac-
> tions, the subject unfailingly obeyed the ex-
> perimenter, proceeding to the highest shock
> level on the generator. He displayed a curious
> dissociation between word and action. Although
> at the verbal level he had resolved not to go
> on, his actions were fully in accord with the

experimenter's commands.[17]

Milgram's general findings, as stated in his most important article, deserve to be reported in full:

> With numbing regularity good people were seen
> to knuckle under the demands of authority and
> perform actions that were callous and severe.
> Men who are in everyday life responsible and
> decent were seduced by the trappings of author-
> ity, by the control of their perceptions, and
> by the uncritical acceptance of the experimen-
> ter's definition of the situation, into per-
> forming harsh acts.
> The results, as seen and felt in the laboratory,
> are to this author disturbing. They raise the
> possibility that human nature...cannot be
> counted on to insulate its citizens from bru-
> tality and inhumane treatment at the direction
> of malevolent authority. A substantial propor-
> tion of people do what they are told to do, ir-
> respective of the content of the act and with-
> out limitations of conscience, so long as they
> perceive that the command comes from a legiti-
> mate authority. If in this study an anonymous
> experimenter could successfully command adults
> to subdue a fifty-year-old man, and force on
> him painful electric shocks against his pro-
> tests, one can only wonder what government,
> with its vastly greater authority and prestige,
> can command of its subjects.[18]

In Milgram's experiments, the mechanism of the projection of internal necessity, as embodied in the image of Satan, is exemplified in the situation in which average, normal, individuals are induced to inflict pain on another person under the compulsion of a structured social situation. In that situation, the Satanic temptation is represented by the social structure of authority. But I would maintain that the social structure itself is legitimized by means of what we have earlier called the projection of in- ternal necessity. As against the interpretation that individuals were in fact compelled to their be- haviour by the necessary laws of the authoritarian situation, I would thus argue that they *chose* to perceive and to react to such a "compelling" situation *in order* to express internal necessities, in particular the necessity to express violence without bearing responsibility for it.

I would also draw attention to a similar mechanism which operates in a variety of familiar cases in which people resort to what the sociologist, Lewis Coser, calls the device of "denial of common humanity."[19] Thus, the representation of Jews as sub-human was an important device for facilitating the evil that was done to them. It is by creating a distinction between "good decent people" and "inferior sub-human creatures" that one is able to engage in or witness evil without guilt and without moral indignation. And, as Coser puts it, when the conscience of so-called "good people" rather than being protected by the devices identified above, which tend either to hide evil entirely or else project responsibility for it onto some external necessity, atrophies instead for good, then God help us all.[20]

But just as the "dehumanization" of the victim facilitates the exercise of authority, so authority itself can similarly be delegitimized by being dehumanized. It is thus not surprising that those who currently engage in acts of violent disobedience refer to the authorities they are defying with such language as "pig," "swine," and so on. The very language itself plays an important role in the process. It is one way of breaking down the super-ego defences which might otherwise exercise a restraining influence on the behaviour.

There is one further association of the image of Satan which throws light on the implications of Milgram's experiments as well as on the phenomenon of Eichmann's "final solution." One of the characteristics of Satan, as we already pointed out, is that he is always represented as a master of ingenious and artful physical and chemical devices. Indeed, we cannot help but notice that one of the first products of technology was the weapon, the instrument of warfare and torture. David Bakan observes that historical images of hell are filled with all sorts of clever torture devices, and the "screw" has no doubt been used as a torture device more often than as part of a machine for the production of goods.[21] The fact that Milgram's naive subjects were taking part in a scientific experiment, using electronic and technological devices as instruments of punishment (or "teaching") may have had some effect on the success with which authority prevailed. Likewise, the gas chambers and the ovens and the scientific experiments of Eichmann may also be understood as a mani-

festation of the Devil's ingenuity. Indeed, it
might well be the case, that in a world such as
ours, driven as it is by pragmatic considerations,
and functional rationality, and by the compulsion to
"solve" everything, the application of technology to
the "final solution" of the Jewish problem comes as
no great surprise.

The phenomenon of the Third Reich expresses yet
another of the archetypical structures of evil,
which I have earlier identified as the "ultra-mythic"
preoccupation with an eschatological ideology, the
belief that the events of one's life are the playing
out of some grand cosmic drama. Just as in the
myth, the devil is represented as playing out a cosmic role, so the Nazis presented the final solution
as the fulfillment of a cosmic destiny. Thus, Gert
Kalow declares in *The Shadow of Hitler:*

> Would Hitler have been able to rouse the masses
> ...to such delirious enthusiasm, if there had
> not existed in Germany an idea or expectation
> that something in the nature of collective re-
> demption was possible? A "messianic expecta-
> tion among the common people"...combined with a
> superstitious belief in a world history which,
> by evolution and impelled by a higher automatic
> power, was moving forward to fulfillment?[22]

Here too, language plays an important role.
Just as the language of "I was only obeying orders"
facilitates the mechanisms of ultra-realism, so the
language of ideology: "it is our destiny," "it is
our mission," "it is our purpose," introduces an
equally compelling external force which is made to
bear full responsibility for one's acts.

In the end, then, the one overriding characteristic of the human tendency to engage in evil without compunction is that in all such cases, one acts
in accordance with what is experienced as "an external demand," whether that demand be interpreted as
the demand of authority or the demands of a cosmic
plan. In both cases, the burden of responsibility
is shifted away from the self to the "other."

The diagnosis of evil suggested by an analysis
of the myth of Satan raises the question: If evil is
such a natural part of the human condition, being a
result of man's inherent need to project his inner-
felt reality onto an external source, how can we begin to exercise and transcend it? The problem of

exorcism becomes particularly acute in view of the
fact that society provides as a part of its institutional structure a variety of rituals which easily
facilitate the mechanisms of projection.

The answer lies in the introduction of a series
of counter rituals which direct attention to the inherent fallibility of man *qua* man which constitutes
the source of the will-to-evil. It is a question of
learning to experience the source of evil as an element in the drama of consciousness *per se,* to recognize that evil is not simply the outcome of pathological consciousness, but is a possibility inherent
in even the most natural and normal patterns of behaviour. It is only when evil and the violence to
which it often gives rise is experienced as originating
within the will that the study of evil can
have a therapeutic and healing effect. Otherwise
the study of evil itself runs the risk of degener-
ating into just another process of rationalization.
We must do more than point out that evil results
from the influence of an imperfect environment on
the formation of human character.

*It is not simply that I find myself committing
violent and evil acts* because *of the way in which I
have been brought up. It is rather that I have allowed myself to be so brought up* in order *to so behave. It is not that I am violent and evil because
I was compelled by a command to do so. It is rather
that I choose to be so compelled* in order *that I may
do what I do. It is not that I go to war* because *my
freedom is threatened. It is rather that I perceive
my freedom as threatened* in order *to go to war.* The
substitution of *in order to* for *because,* and the experience of the implications of that substitution,
marks the beginning of the therapy of evil.

THE EXCORCISM OF EVIL

It has been a long-standing conviction among
philosophers, poets, and psychologists that one of
the major sources of violence and evil lies in the
failure of mankind to cope with the demonic dimensions of the human condition.

The problem, of course, is not simply to recognize that one is a creature of passion and a bearer
of the demonic, but to learn how to assume responsibility for it as well. If we are to learn anything
at all from the examples of history and literature,
it is that anger, rage, resentment, sexual passion,
lust for power, violence and pleasure, if simply ig-

nored or repressed, will only return to "infect,"
"sicken," and ultimately to destroy. Western man
has become so anaesthetized by the bad-faith of pretending that he is an angel, that he is in danger of
being totally consumed by the demons and the furies.
    One of the deepest drives in man is to cele-
brate his existence at the centre of eternity; at
the still point of the turning world, as T.S. Eliot
put it. There is a sense of this yearning for eternity, for returning to the ground of being, in many
of the lyrics of our contemporary folk songs. As
Joni Mitchell says, in her song "Woodstock":

> We are star dust, we are golden and we've got
> to get ourselves back to the garden.

    But eternity can be reached only by first tra-
velling the corridors of hell. It was, after all,
only after Adam and Eve had been cast out from Paradise that the drama of redemption and creativity
could begin. As the myth makes plain, the drama of
redemption is a drama of temptation, a drama in
which consciousness grows, and man makes himself, at
the centre of strife, tension, and suffering--the
suffering of both craving to be and being unable to
be as gods. Or, as Nietzsche puts it:

> There is a personal necessity for misfortune;
> terror, want, impoverishment, midnight watches,
> adventures, hazards, and mistakes are as neces-
> sary to me and to you as are their opposites,
> yes, that to speak mystically, the path to
> one's own heaven always leads through the lusts
> of one's own hell.[23]

In a world which denies access to the corridors of
hell, which has repressed man's access to the irrational, it sometimes becomes necessary, in order to
reach into the centre of eternity, to go mad. For
this is what the desire to be God finally amounts to.
As God creates, so he destroys. God does not hide
the destructive from the creative, does not hide the
fact that in order to restore creativity to the cos-
mos He not only allowed but encouraged the Devil to
šeduce Eve, does not hide the fact that man's ascent to eternity begins with the loss of innocence.
Whereas God does not hide all of this from Himself,

it is man's peculiar weakness to err in precisely this direction, by pretending that he has not yet lost his innocence, that he is an unfallen angel who reaches eternity through the exercise of reason alone.

The result, as writers like Dostoevsky, Jean Genet, and Normal Mailer have suggested, is that *men are sometimes driven to destruction in order to be men.* Because we have been unable to create, we are left with no alternative but to destroy, as in the case of Dostoevsky's "underground man" who "vomits up reason" in order to affirm his refusal to be de-humanized. Thus also speaks Stofsky, the hipster hero of John Clellon Homes, well known beat novel of the fifties, *"Go":* "The way to salvation is to die, give up, go mad....To suffer everything. To be. To love...well, ruthlessly." The key to salvation for the hipster is to live in the "enormous present" by engaging in every manner of drunkenness, dope addiction, lewdness, and perversion, imaginable and unimaginable.

For some the life of polymorphous perversity is exclusively an exercise of imagination. As Simone de Beauvoir puts it on behalf of her generation of "immortalists":

> All around me people deplored falsehood, but were careful to avoid the truth; if I found so much difficulty in speaking freely now, it was because I felt it was repugnant to make use of the counterfeit money that was current in my environment. I lost no time in embracing the principles of immoralism. Of course I did not approve of people stealing out of self-interest or going to bed with someone for the pure pleasure of it; but if these became quite gratuitous acts, acts of desperation and revolt--and, of course, quite imaginary--I was prepared to stomach all the vices, the rapes, and the murders one might care to mention. Doing wrong was the most uncompromising way of repudiating all connections with respectable people...The important thing was to use whatever means one could to find release from the world, and then one would come within reach of eternity.[24]

A similar approach to an imagination of violence has been taken by Norman Mailer. Contemporary man, according to Mailer, has been cast into a society

that threatens to extinguish all expressions of
Dionysian vitality. The soul of contemporary man
has been marooned in constipation, emptiness, bore-
dom, and a flat dull terror of death, violence, can-
nibalism, loneliness, insanity, libidinousness, perversion, and mess. At the same time, we are caught
in a vicious irony which stems from the fact that
the fear of violence is itself a major source of violence. The lunacy of our world lies precisely in
the fact that we are cannibals and perverts who pretend to be angels. The world is not lacking in violence, terror, and death, albeit a great deal of
this has been institutionalized beyond recognition.
What is lacking in our world is creativity and life.
But, Mailer argues, if we are to make our way back
to life and restore creativity to the world, the violence and irrationality from which we now flee must
somehow be passed through, confronted and digested,
instead of being counterfeited. In short, says
Mailer, the way to transcend violence is to commit
it; get it out of your system once and for all. The
decision is "to encourage the psychopath in oneself."

> To explore that domain of experience where se-
> curity is boredom and therefore sickness, and
> one exists in the present, in that enormous
> present which is without past or future, memory
> of planned intention, the life where a man must
> go until he is beat, where he must gamble with
> his energies through all those small or large
> crises of courage and unforeseen situations
> which beset his day, where he must be with it
> or doomed not to swing.[25]

IMAGINATION OF EVIL

But how does one commit violence? Not *in fact!*
For to commit it in fact is to surrender to it. To
enter it through the imagination, however, is to
transcend it. The existential moment is therapeutic
precisely because it is imaginative. Because it is
imaginative, it permits the necessary psychic distance without which there can be no transcendence.
Through the imagination, one can endure all manner
of sin and corruption without becoming corrupt.
Even the act of murder can lead the imagination to
the altar of holiness. In the course of an interview, Mailer himself is reported to have made the

following statement concerning the idea of a brutal, gratuitous murder:

> Let's use our imaginations. It means that one human being has determined to extinguish the life of another human being. It means that two people are engaging in a dialogue with eternity. Now if the brute does it and at the last moment likes the man he is extinguishing, then perhaps the victim did not die in vain. If there is an eternity with souls in that eternity, if one is able to be born again, the victim may bet his reward. At least it seems possible that the quality of one being passes into the other, and this altogether hate filled human, gridning his boot into the face of someone...in the act of killing, in this terribly private moment, the brute feels a moment of tenderness, for the first time perhaps in all of his experience. What has happened is that the killer is becoming a little more possible, a little bit more ready to love someone.[27]

But sometimes the madness ceases to be merely imaginative and becomes terrifyingly literal, as in the case of Richard Wishnetsky who on the morning of February 12, 1966 murdered Rabbi Morris Adler in full view of the congregation of Shaarey Zedek synagogue in Detroit as a protest against the forces of modernity which he claimed had dehumanized his life beyond recovery. In a note written the day before the fatal event occurred, this pathetic young man left us a lucid account of his motives and of the significance of what he was about to do:

> My distorted, disoriented voice, either barely uttered or tremendously violent, gives you a slight horrifying glimpse into the dehumanized future that awaits you and your unfortunate children, who will be healthy, comfortable, and secure beyond your fondest dreams and just as diseased. *Since I feel that I am no longer able to make any significant creative contributions, I shall make a destructive one.* What happened in Shaarey Zedek happens only once in a lifetime...Suffer in your forzen hells of apathy, boil in the self-hate of outraged impotence. Listen to my voice, you deaf one. Lis-

ten to how sick, sad, lonely, and forlorn it is.[27]

    Thus does the drama of redemption through an imagination of violence devolve through confusion into a tragedy of self-destruction. It is one thing, as Kenneth Rexroth once declared, to live by the faith that the creative act is the only defence against the ruin of the world. It is quite another matter to substitute the violence of self-destruction for creativity and still call it art. Cast amidst a catastrophic world, human consciousness finds refuge in a Dionysian affirmation of existence through art, love, and faith. The consciousness of modern man has had to find endurance in a world of gas ovens and burning cities. But as the world itself began to take on the guise of an immense gas oven, such expressions of imagination become suddenly meaningless--with the result that consciousness punishes itself by indulging in a orgy of self-destruction. The net results--as Rexroth himself put it--can only be "the desperation of shipwreck--the despair, the orgies, ultimately the cannibalism of a lost life-boat. And in a remark which is as prophetic as it is disquieting, Rexroth exclaims: "I believe that most of an entire generation will go to ruin--the ruin of Celine, Artaud, Rimbaud, voluntarily, enthusiastically."[28]
    But how is the corruption of imagination to be accounted for? What are the chief factors accounting for the distinction between the imaginative encounter with violence, as expressed in art, religion, and self-analysis, and the pathological, pornographic acting out of one's fantasies resulting in a literal orgy of destruction? For it is clear that the pathological acting out of violence is often, if not always, accompanied or preceded by fantasies of violence, so that the imagination rather than displacing the need to act out one's impulses, may in some cases actually stimulate the need to act.
    The analysis thus points towards factors which precede the employment of imagination and which account, therefore, for the distinction between the constructive and the corrupt forms of imagination. These factors may be identified, at least in part, through a comprehensive and systematic study of the symbolism of evil as presented in myth and literature, in particular as associated with the image of the Devil already referred to. The purpose of such a study, which is beyond the scope of this present

essay, would be to uncover the charactertistics associated with the creative celebration of the demonic as distinct from neurotic captivity to the demonic characteristic of the corrupt imagination. It was, after all, to the demonic impulses inherent in the nature of man *qua* man that the Devil appealed in his seduction of Eve. And it was in the manner in which Eve yielded to temptation that the demonic impulse, the Faustian urge, was converted into the neurotic compulsion for power which, whether in the service of "good" or evil," turns towards destruction.

The chief symptom of this neurosis, as our discussion of the myth has already suggested, is the compulsive manner in which one acts and the tendency to experience this compulsion as external. The role of the Devil, according to the interpretation summarized earlier, is to facilitate this mechanism of projection in such a way that the agent no longer experiences his acts as originating from within. By thus experiencing them as compelled from without, the agent disclaims any sense of responsibility for what happens. It is with respect to understanding the precise workings of this mechanism that the psychology and sociology of evil set their goals. The hypothesis to be sounded out through the combined resources of the social sciences is to the effect that whenever the environment is designed so as to facilitate projection and externalization, the imagination develops in a neurotic manner, whereas an environment designed so as to encourage the internalization of responsibility stimulates a more constructive imagination.

VICTIMIZATION

The intentionality of the agent or victimizer is not the only factor of concern in the study of evil. Of equal importance is the process of victimization itself. As Philip Hallie argues in his important book, *The Paradox of Cruelty*, "Intentions are not always as important as ruination."[29] The most outstanding factor, according to Hallie, in the process of victimization, is the powerlessness of the victim. Hence the incredible, ingeneous, and imaginative efforts of victimizers to render their victims powerless before executing their violence upon them. In this regard the study of institutionalized cruelty deserves special attention. The outstanding feature of institutionalized cruelty is its capacity to conceal the fact that it is destroying its victims. This concealment or mystification is accomplished by means of a public logic, or public rationale, which not only protects the spectator from feeling disgust with the destruction of human life but manages also to secure the consent of large numbers of "ordinary," "decent" people--including the victims themselves. Here indeed is the imagination at work in its most corrupt form.

Hallie's study suggests that the very perception of the powerlessness and innocence of the victim acts as an incentive to violence and triggers an appetite for the most bizarre acts of violation. To understand why the perception of innocence incites such passions leading to the violation of innocence constitutes another of the primary tasks of the social sciences. Here again the myth provides a clue. It is perhaps, as Freud suggests in his study of myth and ritual, *Totem and Taboo,* that because of the guilt associated with the original Fall, the crime is excorcised through repetition. *Thus arises one of the most profound paradoxes in the history of consciousness: the assassination of innocence becomes a factor in restoring the psychic balance threatened by memory of the original event responsible for the loss of innocence.*

What is required if we are to be rescued from self-destruction, then, is not a repression but an integration of the demonic into the psyche of Western man. The demonic powers must be taken up into consciousness in such a way that they become co-workers with consciousness rather than its master. But, as I have already suggested, the most effective barrier to the integration of the demonic is man's infinite capacity to misrepresent the nature of his reality. The *hubris* of contemporary man, like the *hubris* of Pentheus and Oedipus, is his deep-seated fear of self-knowledge. The institutions of our society have mutilated most opportunities for confronting and celebrating the mystery of being. Contemporary social existence is no longer an invitation to partake in the Bacchanalian revel through which truth and reality are born. The absurd, the inspiring, the uncanny, the awesome, the terrifying, the ecstatic--none of these fit into a production and efficienty oriented society. As the theologian Harvey Cox once put it: "Having systematically stunted the Dionysian side of the whole human, we assume that man is naturally just a reliable, plane-catching, Appolonian."[30]

Another distressing symptom of our malaise is the way in which we are held captive by history:

that is to say, by routine, by conventions, and by
traditions, thus ignoring the need in man to rebel
and to confront tradition,violently, imaginatively
and with passion. For while it may be true that
revolution without tradition is blind, tradition
without revolution is empty.

Robert Lindner has argued that when men are denied the opportunity for creative rebellion, they
turn inevitably to pathological and mutinous forms
of rebellion.[31] The latter can be avoided only by
innovating more imaginative opportunities for revolt
and rebellion. Bergson once argued that in order
for mind to penetrate the essence of reality, it becomes necessary, under the systematic guidance of
metaphysics, to do violence to itself, to reverse
the direction of the operation by which it ordinarily thinks.[32] Much the same approach can be taken
to the processes of society. Just as metaphysics,
for Bergson, reaches reality through symbol and met-
aphor, so society reaches towards its inner reality
through ritual and festivity.

The rituals through which the structure of social reality is uncovered may be designated as rituals of attention--as distinguished from the rituals
of indoctrination which I discussed earlier. The
chief forms of the rituals of attention are mockery
and parody. Through mockery and parody, consciousness provokes a confrontation with routine and convention. Consciousness does symbolic and ritual violence to its traditions and conventions in order to
live more openly with them. Through festivity, man
reaches into his orphic depths and recreates himself
as man.

But before we can restore festivity to the
world, we must first learn to resist the temptation
to deodorize it. Freud suggested that the origin of
civilization lies in man's willingness to renounce
instinct. But perhaps we have gone too far in that
direction. It is perhaps this renunciation of instinct which has produced the odourless world depicted by T.S. Eliot in *The Wasteland:* a world where
the wholesome tides of passion which alone fertilize
the imagination and action, have dried up; a world
in which the passions which once came to the aid of
innocence are shrunk to nothing; a world in which
men are imprisoned in themselves, becalmed in a wind-
less selfishness. It is a world without *eros* and
without compassion. The only emotion left is fear:
fear of feeling itself; fear of living. It is a
world in which, as Yeats wrote:

the centre cannot hold;
mere anarchy is loosed upon the world,
the blood-dimmed tide is loosed, and everywhere
the ceremony of innocence is drowned;
the best lack all conviction, while the worst
are full of passionate intensity.[33]

I am not suggesting that we give in to our instincts, but only that we find ways of ritualizing
them in order to avoid the need for pathological
fantasizing. Now we may ritualize instincts in such
a way that we are able to indulge them without being
conscious of them, without thinking about them, and
without bearing responsibility for the consequences
of indulging them. Such rituals, as I argued earlier, lead to the institutionalization and normali-
zation of evil, or, if you like, to the banality of
evil. I am not, of course, recommending such rituals. I am recommending rather the kind of rituals
that draw attention to the inherent discrepancies
of our conduct. to the duality and ambivalence of
our experiences, to the violence of our natures and
the degree to which we are seized with passion. I
am recommending rituals which draw attention to the
fact that the irrational and demonic are implicit in
even the most normal patterns of behaviour, in behaviour which exemplifies the highest moral standards. I am recommending rituals which force us to
the disquieting but nevertheless honest recognition
that the very same gesture with which I reach out in
love is implicitly a gesture of destruction, that my
feelings of deep love for the other cannot be di-
vorced from feelings of resentment and hostility,
and that behind the masks of sanity and respectabil-
ity is to be found the lecherous leer of the por-
nographer.

THE TASK OF IMAGINATION: TO EXPRESS EVIL

To so ritualize instinct has important therapeutic effects. Through the ritualization of instinct man rediscovers and identifies the temptations which threaten the stability of culture. At
the same time it is only through the imaginative reliving of temptation that we develop the strength of
character to resist it when it appears like the devil disguised as reason--for the Devil, if you remember, is the master of disguises. Just as Eve was
tempted by the prospect of achieving good, so man is
constantly tempted towards evil in the name of good.

It is the task of the critical imagination to expose this deception.

The imaginative encounter with evil and temptation takes many forms. I have so far identified the forms of ritual, celebration and festivity. One could just as effectively point in the direction of the arts, of history and the social sciences, as well as to religion and even to games. Through the study of history, for example, we encounter not only the evils which have already appeared but the perennial possibilities of evil which derive from the very nature of man's being as man. Through the imaginative reliving of history the individual discovers, perhaps for the first time, the potentialities implicit in his own consciousness. It may be, for example, that as I come to understand the ruthlessness of Renaissance politics, I come to understand that I, too, am capable of such behaviour. The historical process is thus a process in which man creates for himself this or that kind of human nature, by recreating in his own thought the past to which he is heir. And as the human mind comes to understand itself better, it thereby comes to operate in new and different ways. Indeed, I would go so far as to argue that, just as in medicine we acquire immunity from disease by injecting ourselves with small doses of the infecting agent, so the whole point of social theory, whether it be derived from the study of history, philosophy, the social sciences, or the arts, is to develop forms of immunity to evil and bad-reasoning by immersing ourselves in these very phenomena themselves. Or, as Machiavelli once put it: "I believe that the shortest way of getting to heaven is to learn the way to hell in order to avoid it."[34]

What applies to history applies equally to other imaginative encounters, such as the aesthetic and religious encounters in which again the perennial possibilities and dispositions of human nature are lived through and transcended. Just as the historian who has imaginatively lived through the past can better cope with whatever contingencies may arise in the future, so a man who has imaginatively lived through the demonic and barbaric dimensions of his own nature is less likely to surrender himself to evil when circumstances arise which might tempt him in that direction. And that such circumstances will continue to arise is one of the chief lessons to be learned from the study of man. Edward Dahlberg sums it up well in his somewhat unusual meditation, *The Carnal Myth:*

One will honour neither a man who abstains from a lust of which he has no knowledge nor a teacher who feigns that pleasure does not exist ...The men that are most interesting are those who have valiantly resisted the delights for which they ache....Who can brag of the goodness of a dead phallus? And what bravery is there in the abstemiousness of a man who has a worthless prepuce? Moreover, it is redundant to be temperate when one is already impotent...It is wrong to cocker vice, but we grow narrow and pithless if we are furtive about it, for this is at best a pretense, and the sage knows good and evil are kindred....Man is always tempted, and it is what he avoids rather than what he does that enobles his character.[35]

In short, since the conditions which give rise to evil cannot be eliminated, because they are co-terminous with the conditions of reality itself, man's future depends on acquiring a character with which to resist it. Which means that we might be better advised to follow Socrates and Freud down the path to self-knowledge before following Plato and Marx down the path to social reform.

NOTES

1. The foregoing essay, which was prepared especially for this volume, brings together a number of themes and materials which have appeared separately and in different forms and contexts in the following publications: *The Pornography of Power,* Chicago: Quadrangle Books, 1968; Violence and retreat from reason. In Sherman M. Stanage, (Ed.), *Reason and Violence.* Totowa: Littlefield Adams, 1974, 73-118; The conflict between Faust and Prometheus, *Philosophy in Context,* 1974, *3*, 7-22; and Technology and the crisis of rationality: reflections on the death and rebirth of dialogue, *Philosophy Forum,* 1977, *15* (3 & 4), 261-287.

2. *Psychology Today,* February 1973, p. 23.

3. New York: Holt, Rinehart & Winston, 1962, p. 15. Cf. also, Malachi Martin, *Hostage to the Devil,* New York: Reader's Digest Press, 1976. "No one," writes Father Malachi, "wants to believe in evil, really, above all, not in evil and evil being, and

evil spirit. Everyone wants to abolish the idea.
To admit the existence of evil means a responsibility. That is the opening through which [Satan]
crawls, stilling all suspicions, making everything
seem normal and natural. This is the 'thought,' the
unwariness of the ordinary human being which amounts
to a disinclination to believe in evil. And if you
do not believe in evil, how can you believe in or
ever know what good is" (p. 389).

4. *Burning Conscience: The Case of the Hiroshima
Pilot Claude Eatherly Told in his Letters to Gunther
Anders*. New York: Monthly Review Press, 1962.

5. *Wall Street Journal*. Editorial. 12 January,
1970, p. 12.

6. On this occasion a handful of terrorists belonging to an organization called the "Quebec Liberation
Front" kidnapped the Quebec cabinet minister, Pierre
Laporte and the British Trade Commissioner, James
Cross. Laporte was subsequently murdered while
Cross was released after several weeks of imprisonment. Shortly after the kidnappings, the Prime Minister, Pierre Eliot Trudeau, invoked the "War Measures Act" which resulted in the suspension of civil
liberties throughout the country. The War Measures
Act made it possible for police to arrest and inter-
rogate without warrant. In order to justify his actions, the Prime Minister claimed that a state of
affairs existed amounting to an "apprehended insur-
rection." This means that evidence was available
which proved that there was a plot, involving large
numbers of persons, to overthrow the Quebec Government by violence and involving a series of scheduled
political assassinations. In fact, no such evidence
was ever produced. The most that could be established was that a small band of fanatics, without
evidence of wide-spread support, had resorted to
gangster-like tactics on behalf of what they claimed
to be the cause of separation in Quebec. The situation thus appeared no different from any other situation in which violence is employed by individuals
or small groups of individuals for whatever criminal
purposes. There would appear to have been no justification for invoking such extreme measures as the
War Measures Act. To do so was, in my opinion, and
in the opinion of many others, an irresponsible exercise of power which itself helped to generate the
very crisis atmosphere it was supposed to reduce.

7. For further discussion of this event, see
Haggart, Ron, & Golden, Aubrey E. *Rumours of War*.
Toronto: New Press, 1971; Rotstein, Abraham. *Power
Corrupted*. Toronto: New Press, 1971; Smith, Denis.
Bleeding Hearts, Bleeding Country. Edmondton: M.G.
Hurtig, 1971.

8. Bakan, David. Psychological characteristics of
man. projected in the image of Satan. *Catholic
Psychological Record*, Spring 1967, *5*(1), 8-15. Cf.
also Bakan, David. *The Quality of Human Existence*.
Chicago: Rand McNally, 1966, 38-101.

9. For a highly significant discussion of this phenomenon of possession see Freud, Sigmund. A neurosis of demonical possession. In *Collected Papers*,
Vol. IV. New York: Basic Books, 1959, 436-472.
For a somewhat different perspective on possession
see Malachi, Martin, *Hostage to the Devil, op. cit.*

10. As an example of what I am talking about, I cite
the following distinction drawn by Herbert C. Kelman
in his article: Social consequences of social research. *Journal Social Issues*, 1965, *21*(3), 21-40:
"On the one hand," says Kelman, "there is the involvement of those social scientists who...are concerned
with social issues. Their primary orientation is
toward social change or toward the resolution of social problems in accordance with human values...on
the other hand, there is the involvement of those
social scientists who possess special skills relevant to the execution of certain policies and who
have, therefore, been drawn into the process by officials in charge of it. Unlike the social scientists oriented toward social issues, they are not
trying to change the system but rather are responding to the demands of the system in making their
technical skills available to it" (pp. 22-23).

11. Wolff, Kurt H. For a sociology of evil. *Journal Social Issues*, 1969, *25*(1), 111-125 (p. 115).

12. Wolff, Kurt H. *Ibid*.

13. "Why young Americans are buying Oriental religions," *Psychology Today*, July, 1977, p. 40. Cf.
also, Hanley Cox, *Turning East*, New York: Simon &
Schuster, 1977.

14. Mannheim, Karl. *Man and Society in an Age of
Reconstruction*. London: Routledge & Kegan Paul,

1966, p. 52.

15. As an example of how this works in practice, I cite the following passage from a book which presented an on-the-spot story of the Vietnam war: "Dixie Station had a reason. It was simple. A pilot going into combat for the first time is a bit like a swimmer about to dive into an icy lake. He likes to get his big toe wet and then wade around a little before leaping off the high board into the numbing depths. So it was fortunate that young pilots could get their first taste of combat under the direction of a forward air controller over a flat country in bright sunshine where nobody was shooting back with high-powered ack-ack. He learns how it feels to drop bombs on human beings and watch huts go up in a boil of orange flame when his aluminum napalm tanks tumble into them. He gets hardened to pressing the firing button and cutting people down like cloth dummies, as they sprint frantically under him. He gets his sword bloodied for the rougher things to come." (Harvey, Frank. *Air War Vietnam*. New York: Bantam, 1967, p. 2).

16. Milgram, Stanley. Some conditions of obedience and disobedience to authority. *Human Relations,* 1965, *18*(1), 57-76.

17. *Ibid,* p. 67.

18. *Ibid,* pp. 74-75.

19. Coser, Lewis. The visibility of evil. *Journal Social Issues,* 1969, *25*(1), 101-109.

20. *Ibid,* p. 108.

21. *Op.cit.,* p. 124.

22. Kalow, Gert. *The Shadow of Hitler.* Chicago: Quadrangle, 1967, p. 31.

23. Nietzsche, Friedrich. *Joyful Wisdom.* New York: Frederich Ungar, 1960, p. 266.

24. De Beavoir, Simone. *Memoirs of the Dutiful Daughter.* Cleveland: World, 1959, pp. 206-7.

25. Mailer, Norman. The White Negro. In *Advertisements for Myself.* New York: Putnam's, 1959, 363.

26. Cited by Trilling, Diana. The radical moralism
of Norman Mailer. In N. Balakian & C. Simons (Eds.)
The Creative Present. New York: Doubleday, 1963,
168. Cf. also Mailer, Norman. The White Negro.
Advertisements for myself. Ibid, 369.

27. Cited by T.V. LoCicero. The murder of Rabbi
Adler. *Commentary,* June 1966, *52,* 49-53.

28. Rexroth, Kenneth. Disengagement: the art of
the beat generation. In Gene Feldman, & Max Garten-
burg. *The Beat Generation and the Angry Young Men*.
New York: Dell, 1959, 367.

29. Wesleyan University Press, 1969, 14.

30. Cox, Harvey. Religion in the age of Aquarius:
a conversation with Henry Cox and George T. Harris.
Psychology Today , April 1967, p. 47.

31. Linder, Robert. *Must You Conform?* New York:
Grove, 1956, 23, 26.

32. Bergson, Henri. *An Introduction to Metaphysics*.
New York: Philosophical Library, 1946, p. 190. See
also, *Creative Evolution*. New York: Random House,
1944, p. 214.

33. Yeats, W.B., *Collected Poems*. London: Macmillan , 1952, 211.

34. Machiavelli, Niccolo, in a letter to Francesco
Guicciardini dated 17 May 1521.

35. Dahlbert, Edward. *The Carnal Myth: A Search
into Classical Sensuality*. New York: Weybright &
Talley, 1968 , p. 73.

*LIONEL RUBINOFF writes: I was born, raised and
received my early education in Toronto. My interest
in violence derives partly from the fact that as a
young Jewish boy growing up in a predominantly non-
Jewish part of the city, I was the victim of violence
both in the streets and in the classroom. I grew up
during the days when teachers and ministers thought
nothing of reminding their audiences every year that
the Jews killed Christ. The phrase "Christ-killer"
became a daily abuse which I eventually came to ex-*

pect with the rising of the sun.   Later on, as an
adolescent, I became aware of the quiet more institutionalized forms of anti-semitism which operated
under the surface of our society, through "gentle-
men's agreements," and private unofficial policies
concerning such things as "quotas" for gaining admission to medical and dental schools, restrictions
on club memberships, and residential restrictions.
I was constantly astonished by the ease and efficiency with which anti-semites violated the normal
codes of decency while still remaining respectable
and guilt-free.

     In 1951, as a young man of 20, I travelled to
Europe for a year where I encountered the aftermath
of one of the most violent periods in the history of
Western man.   I had originally travelled there to
pursue my interest (and by now well-established career) in the theatre.   I had begun acting professionally as a child on CBC radio and during the late
Forties began acting with professional theatre
groups in Toronto.   During my career as an actor, I
often played the role of a violent and disturbed
child or teenager, as a result of which I became interested in the psychology of violence.   Insofar as
I was called upon to achieve emotional identification with the role I was performing, I came to recognize the sources of violence in my own psychic
make-up.   My experiences in Europe, combined I suppose with my early experiences as a child, drove me
to pursue a more academic and scholarly approach to
phenomena like violence, war, cruelty, and so on.   I
returned to Canada and to Queen's University where I
pursued a course of studies that eventually led me
to a degree in philosophy and history in 1956.

     From 1956 to 1959, I was a graduate student and
instructor in philosophy at the University of Toronto, and in 1960 I joined the newly created faculty
of York University where I remained until 1971 when
I moved to the Philosophy Department of Trent University in Peterborough where I am currently teaching.   My first serious attempt to come to grips with
the origins of violence came in 1966 when I delivered a series of lectures on the CBC national radio network entitled, "Human Nature and the Pornography of Power."   These lectures were expanded into
a book during the Fall of 1967 while at Harvard University, on sabbatical leave from York.   This book
was published in 1968 under the title THE PORNOGRA-
PHY OF POWER.   The present essay represents an attempt to further develop ideas expressed in THE
PORNOGRAPHY OF POWER.

SOME OTHER PUBLICATIONS BY LIONEL RUBINOFF

- Historicism and the *a priori* of history. *Dialogue: Canadian Philosophical Review*, 1964, *3*(1), 81-88.
- Editor, *Faith and Reason: Essays in the Philosophy of Religion by R. G. Collingwood*. Chicago: Quadrangle, 1968.
- *The Reform of Metaphysics: Collingwood's Philosophy of Mind*. Toronto: University of Toronto Press, 1970.
- Editor, *Tradition and Revolution*. Toronto: Macmillan of Canada, 1971.
- Herman Kahn on thermonuclear war. *Philosophical Forum*, 1971, *10*(2), 109-114.
- The dialectic of work and labour in the ontology of man, *Humanitas*, 1971, *7*(2), 147-176.
- Auschwitz and the theology of Holocaust. In Paul Opsahl, & Mark Tannenbaum (Eds.), *Speaking of God Today*. New York: Fortress Press, 1974, 121-143.
- Auschwitz and the pathology of Jew-Hatred. In Eva Fleischner (Ed.), *Auschwitz: Beginning of a New Era*. New York: Ktav, 1976, 347-371.
- The state and the individual. *Queen's Quarterly*, 1977, *84*(2), 267-272.
- The logic and metaphysics of evaluation in political theory. In Harold J. Johnson, J. Leach, & R. Muehlmann (Eds.), *Revolutions, Systems and Theories*. Dordrecht, Holland, & Boston, Mass.: D. Reidel Publishing Co., in press.

4. The Child and Nonviolent Social Change

Elise Boulding, Ph.D.

Any design for a nonviolent world must take special account of what happens to children, and what they are prepared for. Since in any case they are the shapers of the future, we cannot avoid an examination of the nature of the child and the impact of various socialization experiences on the child's capacity to act nonviolently on a changing social order.

The socialization model developed here draws on several different disciplinary frameworks and research areas that have not been brought together before in just this way. Included are (1) animal and human ethology, with emphasis on both genetic and developmental aspects of animal-man potentials; (2) a variety of social learning theories; (3) a delineation of the social spaces within which the individual receives social shaping and acts out roles; and finally (4) a review of studies on altruism and nonviolent activists in recent protest movements.

THE SITUATION OF THE CHILD IN TODAY'S WORLD

The bind that children are in--and they recognize that they are in it, to an extent that would astound most adults--is that they know they are being trained for role performance to maintain the society in which they are growing up and they realize that adults somehow expect them to make a system work that the adults themselves have had great difficulty with. They are to pull off this miracle after having lived a childhood segregated from the system. To further compound the difficulty they are in, all the training they receive in society's nur-

68

series is for performance on yesterday's patterns--
all socialization is for the past--while the social
rhetoric to which they are exposed is couched in
terms of "far-reaching social change." How do children deal with these dilemmas?

The rhetoric of rapid change which is such an
all-pervasive part of the child's environment has,
like all social rhetoric, a sharply uncomfortable
empirical referent the words cannot obscure--though
they try. Children really do need socialization for
the role of change agents. It is to society's interest to prepare its new members for non-destruc-
tive change behaviors, since this enables necessary
and inevitable change to take place with a minimum
of hurt to the society and its individual members.
When no provision for the development of innovative
role-taking is made, then the stage is set for a
necessary resort to violence to disrupt and destroy
inflexible structures. Are there, in our sharply
age-graded socialization process, any experiences
available to children which can trigger perceptions
of the possibility of creative change instead of de-
fensiveness or aggression in situations where old
behaviors are inadequate?

An even more basic question is, can a healthy
normal human being respond non-aggressively to situations of tension and rapid change, or are aggressive tendencies so powerful in human beings that
there is no socialization process that can effectively rechannel them without doing harm to the human temperament? Can drastic social change only be
brought about by violence? For a few decades the
doctrine of the infinite malleability of the human
infant has held sway, and social theories of learning have blossomed in this period. Now we are back,
however to historically recurring ideas about the
killer instinct in man, the "Cain-tendency" as in
Szondi (82) and Ardrey (2). In the eighteenth century, Rousseau championed the doctrine of the natural
good in human nature against the Hobbesian view of
man as beast. At the turn of the twentieth century,
it was Kropotkin who championed the good (1903)
against Thomas Huxley (1888). Once again today the
capacity for human goodness has a champion, Eibl-
Eibesfeldt (19), to face the supporter of the man-
as-beast view, Ardrey (2).

Eibl-Eibesfeldt suggests that there are innate
bonding drives which counterbalance innate aggressive tendencies, and that careful attention to both
sets of drives will enable humans to use their genetic resources to the maximum on behalf of social

order. As a human ethologist he utilizes human societies for his research, rather than generalizing
from animals as is usually done.

Marshaling photographic evidence from a wide
variety of geographic and cultural settings from
tribal pre-literate to urban western, he makes a
serious case for preprogrammed behavior that is set
in motion by innate releasing mechanisms in specific
stimulus situations, independent of social learning.
While these can be culturally modified or repressed,
the transcultural similarity of greeting, nurturant
and protective gestures of adults toward children
and towards one another in situations that call for
this behavior, and of threat gestures in hostile
situations, points to a behavioral repertoire of inherited coordinations. The presence of such inherited coordinations is clearly significant for the
learning of social behaviors. It means that in giv-
en situations some behaviors will be more easily
learned than others.

Since the term "behavioral programming" lends
itself to an excessively mechanistic interpretation,
I will use the term "predisposition to learn" as the
operational equivalent of behavioral programming.
An understanding of the stimuli which will release
bonding behavior in a threat situation could be of
great importance in trying to understand the potentials for training for nonviolent behavior. The innate discharge controls releasing aggressive or
bonding behavior have through phylogenetic adaptation in humans been reduced to secondary status, but
the drives themselves remain intact, Eibl-Eibesfeldt
suggests (19, p. 32). The enormous gain in adapta-
bility in this replacement of innate controls by
cultural ones is clear. The Eskimo needs different
arrangements for diversion of aggressive or sex impulses than a Masai or urbanite, and rigid innate
patterns would be of little use to her. The fact
that any kind of response structure at all exists,
however indeterminate, is significant both for
learning theory and for socialization, however.

INGREDIENTS FOR A SOCIALIZATION MODEL

In our search for a descriptive model of socialization that will throw light on how some children
come to perceive themselves as creators of alternative futures, and can remain unthreatened and nonviolent in the face of changes and tensions that
bring out aggression or withdrawal in others, we

will look at a variety of inputs to the socialization process. The genetic resources for behavioral response will be given substantial attention, because our knowledge of developmental and learning processes is only useful to the extent that we are aware of the genetic substrate of these processes. The social spaces and the socializing agents in a child's life will also be given particular attention.

Figure 1 shows schematically eight sets of inputs to the socialization process chosen for their relevance to our problem, grouped according to whether they are internal or external to the child.

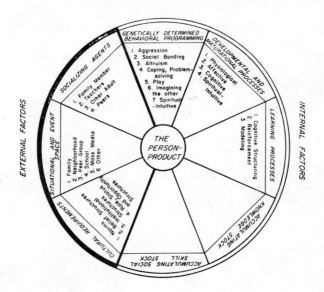

Figure 1.   Inputs to the Socialization Process

The internal factors are (1) the genetic substrate, (2) developmental and maturational processes, (3) learning processes, (4) accumulating knowledge stock, and (5) accumulating social skill stock. The external factors are (6) cultural requirements, (7) socializing agents, and (8) situational and event spaces. We will explore the nature of the interplay between these factors.

I suggest that the life experience of persons committed to a belief in and action on behalf of nonviolent social change includes the following features:

1) optimal opportunities as a child for development of emotional, cognitive and intuitive capacities in home, school and community, in settings that
allow for maximum expression of a wide range of innate behavioral repertoires;
2) substantial exposure to events in the
larger society, and the knowledge stock of that society;
3) substantial exposure to a variety of adult
and peer role models in different kinds of social
settings;
4) opportunities to play out a number of different social roles in childhood and adolescence,
and to deal actively with problem-solving situations;
and
5) experiences of rewarding social feedback in
the playing out of roles and solving problems.
We will now examine each of the factors proposed for the socialization model, beginning with
the genetic component.

THE PHYLOGENETIC SUBSTRATE OF BEHAVIOR

One unifying theme in a great diversity of literature on personality characteristics of leaders,
activists and change agents, is that of the presence
in these individuals of basic feelings of optimism,
competence and self-esteem. Change-agent roles are
selected by persons who feel they can effectively
act on society to change it for the better. Nonviolent activists, while often alienated from the society they are in, display a capacity for social trust
which is sometimes very marked (21). These feelings
may be established in the neonate, in part determined by the genetically given neural thresholds of
the infant. The high neural threshold infant can
take a lot of brusk handling and bumps without any
discomfort, while the low neural threshold infant
may feel pain from even gentle handling. This presence or absence of physical discomfort at being
touched is independent of the handling parent's felt
and expressed tenderness.
Beyond this generalized responsivity to the environment, there are according to Eibl-Eibesfeldt a
variety of phylogenetic adaptations which take the
form of preprogrammed response capacity for a variety of situations. While this theory is bound to be
controversial, it seems too promising to be ignored
in the light of the present controversy about the
degree to which children can be socialized to nonviolence. Using his work as a point of departure, I

am suggesting seven areas in which there may be behavioral programs, or predispositions to learn, for
the human being that provide the basis for response
repertoires in situations of tension and change.[1]
These areas are (1) aggression, (2) social bonding,
(3) altrusim, (4) coping, problem-solving, (5) play,
(6) creation of the other, and (7) spiritual bonding.

I will provide a definition of each behavioral
area, and indicate research that relates to the possibility of some type of behavioral predispositions.
The material which follows is intended mainly to be
suggestive and to provide a basis for some new ways
of thinking about socialization.

Aggression. Human aggression, the stumbling
block on which so many theories of human betterment
fall, has been defined by Feshbach (23, p. 161) as
"any behavioral sequence or subset thereof, which
results in injury to or destruction of an animal,
human, or inanimate object." Aggression has been
difficult to use as an analytic concept because it
has been treated as a catch-all phenomenon covering
a very wide range of behaviors. Corning (15) draws
attention to Moyer's work of separating out eight
functionally different types of behavior, each differentiated by the stimulus configurations that
trigger them (63). Although hard evidence for the
existence of specific neural and endocrinal substrates for each class of aggression is still rudi-
mentary, there is relevant research on humans as
well as animals (62). The most important thing is
the classification scheme itself, which provides an
entirely new way to think about aggression. The
thinking of Moyer and Corning also converges in a
remarkable way with that of Eibl-Eibesfeldt. Each
sees the neural and biochemical mechanisms as a
product of phylogenetic adaptations in the evolutionary process, and each emphasizes that the actual
behaviors are "partially programmed by the individual's interaction with his social and ecological environment." (15, p. 7) The proposed types of aggression, classified by the triggering stimulus-con-
figurations, are predatory, inter-male,* fear induced, irritable, territorial, maternal, instrumen-

---

*Having recently been the horrified witness of (and
intervener in) an attempt by one woman to kill another in a hotel corridor, I would add inter-female
here.

tal and sex-related. These are not all mutually exclusive; territorial and inter-male aggression, for
example, may overlap.

The material on aggression brought together by
Wilson in *Sociobiology: The New Synthesis* (93) while
questionable in its application to human beings,
contains valuable insights into the behavioral dynamics of animal aggression. I have recently explored the implications of the need for the mother
to expel male offspring from the "nest" for later
aggressive behavior of human males (11).

The Corning review of aggression studies makes
it clear that aggression is not spontaneous or plea-
sure-seeking, as it is often described to be. Eibl-
Eibesfeldt points out that there is no evidence of
any vertebrate forming a bond with a conspecific
primarily and exclusively via aggression. The innate inhibition against the pursuit of aggression to
the point of killing, widely noted in the animal
world, exists in the human in the impulse to pity.
This impulse is of course subject to social programming, and in fact became progressively more useless as an inhibitory device with the invention of
weapons that killed at a distance (19, pp. 98-102).
The history of the failure of this inhibition to
serve humankind in conflict dates back to the invention of the first prehistoric flint hand-ax.

While the failure of inhibitory responses in
group conflict is a serious matter, the understanding of aggression as a series of highly differentiated, situation-specific responses allows much more
scope for social reprogramming, or socialization.
Furthermore, aggressive response patterns must be
considered in the broader context of the whole repertoire of response patterns, including *bonding
responses,* which will be discussed next.

Social bonding. Using Eibl-Eibesfelt's work as
a point of departure, I will define social bonding
as the development of reciprocal expectations of
sympathy and supportive, nurturant and aiding behavior between two or more individuals through ritual
and nonritual acts of recognition, affection and
nurturance. Eibl-Eibesfeldt suggests that the
mother-infant's behavior is clearly genetically programmed as is the mother's nurturant response. The
infant sucking at its mother's breast has its fists
tightly closed, a reminder that among our primate
ancestors babies had to hold on to mother's coat for
survival.

Man is by nature a parent-clinger, "Elternhock-
er" as Wolfgang Wickler (92) calls it. We are
not only programmed to these conditions by numerous behavior patterns, we are also equipped
with appetitive behavior for restoring con-
tact--to begin with by crying out and later
through active seeking. Our drive activities
of clinging and snuggling are adapted to the
mother as object. It is this appetitive behavior for contact that is the true root of the
bond between mother and child. (19, pp. 212-12)

All spontaneous adult gestures of greeting,
reaching out with the hands to help another, or com-
forting another, and of fleeing to another for protection, as well as sexual caresses, all derive from
the infant's clutching and the adult's nurturant response. In spite of the heavy cultural overlay of
bonding behavior among adults, the spontaneous gestures of nurturing and seeking nurture are starting-
ly similar in all societies, as Eibl-Eibesfeldt's
photographic research demonstrates.
    Research on the determinants of reciprocating
beneficent behavior on the part of another (27,12,
76) indicates that activities such as food-sharing
are much more likely to take place in a context
where the food donor has previously been the recipient of a clearly voluntary act of beneficence from
his partner. As soon as compulsion or constraint
enters the picture, reciprocated sharing is reduced.
While this is hardly evidence for a genetic basis
for nurturance, it is suggestive. Eibl-Eibesfeldt
suggests that the adequate development of these
bonding capacities depends very much on the character of the environmental influences in the earliest
stages of ontogenetic development.

In man's development there are sensitive periods in which certain basic ethical and aesthetic attitudes become fixated as in imprinting,
as for example "primitive trust" (Urvertrauen).
If such a period is allowed to pass unfulfilled,
then this can lead to lasting damage. (19,
p. 27)

Socialization theory has worked hard to free us
from excessively deterministic views about the role
of early experience in later development. This

notion of fixation of attitudes at a critical period
should not be taken too seriously, but may be taken
as one of the ingredients in the early socialization
process that may have to be dealt with again in
later stages of adult life. In any case, the bonding experiences of infancy, and the parenting experience in adulthood, may be considered as very valuable resources in meeting unfamiliar and stressful
situations.

One of the least likely candidates for preprogrammed behavior is *altruism*, yet precisely because
of its unlikelihood and its relationship to social
bonding, it is challenging to examine this type of
behavior for possible preprogrammed dispositions.

Altruism. A distillation of work by E. Midlarsky (57) and Justin Aronfreed (3) on aiding responses and altruism suggests the following definition of altruism: A subset of bonding behavior oriented towards desired outcomes for another with minimal or no expectations of reciprocity; the behavior
is undertaken at some cost to the initiator, with
little or no gain relative to the magnitude of the
investment. The prototype of aiding behavior undertaken at some cost to the self is parenting, in both
the human and the animal world. The presence of
this kind of aiding response in all cultures points
to a stimulus-specific predisposition. Lois Murphy
(64) established some decades ago that children under four react sympathetically to the stress of others, and Chester Pierce (69) has observed how nursery school teachers thwart spontaneously helpful
behavior among children by stepping in to replace
child helping behavior by adult helping behavior.
Empathy is a necessary but not sufficient condition
of altruism, since it may or may not lead to dis-
tress-alleviating behavior (3).

Another important resource, to be discussed
next is the predisposition to explore and cope with
the unusual.

Coping and problem-solving. Exploratory problem-solving responses to unfamiliar situations, and
coping behavior in the face of difficulty or stress,
as opposed to freezing up in the face of the unfamiliar and threatening, are contrasting responses
that have long interested social psychologists. For
M. Brewster Smith, the competent self is one which

...is perceived as causally important, as effective in the world--which is to a major extent a world of other people--as likely to be
able to bring about desired effects, and as accepting responsibility when effects do not correspond to desire. (79, p. 281)

Competence is accompanied by feelings of self-esteem
and optimism, and an "array of knowledge, habits,
skills and abilities that are required to translate
hopeful expectations and active orientations into
effective behavior "(79, p. 282).
    Can one conceive of a genetically-based predis-
position to engage in coping behavior? Piaget,
watching the young infant "construct" his world
through his early sensory-motor explorations, evolving behavioral schemas which

    ...are presymbolic action-patterns, the
    achievement of which involves mastery of the
    instrumental resources of the body and stabil-
    ization of a world of objects as two sides of
    the same coin (79, p. 293).

would say yes. Kavanau's mice, who consistently
prefer altering their environment to leaving it in
the experimentally arranged state, whenever the
choice exists, and who choose the harder tasks in
their little mouse world rather than the easier
ones, also seem to say yes (79, p. 292).[2]
    In fact the drive to engage in exploratory be-
havior for its own sake and to do things competently
is a human trait frequently commented on by sociologists, psychologists and economists alike. This is
one of Thomas' four wishes (85, pp. 741-4),and it is
also Veblen's instinct of workmanship (1918). It
would be extremely difficult to determine stimulus-
specific neuro-chemical substrates for varieties of
coping behavior, and yet perhaps no more difficult
than for bonding behavior or aggression.
    Studies of aiding behavior will be discussed
later under socialization, but one curious characteristic of a certain kind of aiding behavior will
be mentioned here. In the Fellner and Marshall
study of kidney donors (22, pp. 269-281), the decision to become a donor was instantaneous and preceded the long educational process medical teams insist on with potential donors. Once the decision

was made, it was never subsequently questioned, and the "official decision time" from the point of view of the medical team came long after the actual decision time. It appears as if there had been some kind of internal triggering mechanism that set off the original instantaneous response. Along the same lines, one characteristic feature of all aiding behaviors studied was that the recipients of aid were clearly perceived by aidors to be dependent on them. The capacity for this kind of response is clearly relevant to dealing with stress and change.

Another predisposition which no one will challenge as genetically programmed, and which may have special relevance for nonviolence is *play*.

Play. Drawing on a synthesis of Huizinga (34) and Simmel (95, pp. 42-43); I will define play as behavior which involves the removal of social forms and physical materials from the instrumental contexts of ordinary use and engaging in more or less patterned recombinations of these forms and materials as a free exercise of mind and body for the mutual delight of the participants. Homo sapiens freely empathizes with animals at play, so it is one of the few activities in which we take delight as a member of the animal world. No matter what the cultural overlay, we have no difficulty in recognizing play activity. Its significance in terms of behavioral repertoires is the resource it provides of free energy and spontaneous variability, which may be drawn on in unsuspected ways in times of environmentally imposed stress.

Imagining the other as a possible predisposition overlaps somewhat with both play and coping behavior, but the act of projection into another time gives this behavior unique properties.

Imagining the other. I define the imagining of the other as the construction of alternative models of some or all aspects of the social order in a deliberate effort to reorganize reality in terms of a conceivable other state placed either in the past or the future. This definition covers a range of activities from social planning through science fiction fantasy to conceptions of heaven and hell. It covers both utopianism a la H.G. Wells and counter-utopianism a la Orwell. All societies imagine an other condition, though some imagine chiefly a past, which is why this category is not labeled futurism. It is by no means clear that the imagining of the other is in any way stimulus-specific, but a well-

developed capacity to imagine alternative futures
would clearly be an asset in dealing with stress and
social change. Kavenau's mouse rearranging his
mouse world (79) hints at imagining the other, as do
the nest-building activities of birds, though there
is no reason to believe that they imagine what they
are preparing for. Fred Polak has analyzed the human capacity to envision the other in *The Image of
the Future* (71) on the basis of historical materials
from all the major civilizations. A quantity of related literature on achievement motivation (54,55)
and aspiration levels (42) bears on this theme of
imagining the other, but is couched entirely in
terms of socialization practices. The neurochemical
substrate for this activity, if any, has yet to be
identified.

   Spiritual bonding as a preprogrammed response
may seem like an odd concept to introduce into a
study of socialization for nonviolent social change.
Yet, increasingly research on mystical experience in
the religious traditions of both East and West is
being considered in relation to behavioral science
research. Evolutionary emergence of new potentials
for Homo sapiens is an important new theme, as evi-
denced in John Platt (70), Lecomte duNouy (67)
Teilhard de Chardin (84), and in the Stanford Research Institute's *Changing Images of Man* (51) and
in Jantsch and Waddington, *The Evolution of Human
Consciousness* (39). It therefore seems useful to
try to incorporate a spiritual-intuitive response
capacity into the socialization model being developed
here. While the spiritual refers to the transcendent,
its relevance to the social order is the theme of
all the great religions.

   Spiritual bonding. I will define spiritual
bonding as the development by the human of a relationship with the divine involving both reciprocity
and surrender: reciprocity of love and responsibility as reflected in the teachings concerning a
divine-human covenant, and surrender of will as required by the recognition of the omnipotence and
beneficence of divine wisdom as contrasted with the
fallibility and ambiguity of human understanding.
The divine-human bonding involves a reordering and
reconstruction of all human identities and relationships as the human comes in contact with a cosmic
order that works back on and transmutes the social
self and all social relationships while incorporating
them in a trans-specific (in the sense of trans-spe-
cies) evolutionary process. This definition draws

on Evelyn Underhill's *Mysticism* (89), Sri
Aurobindo's *The Divine Life* (4), Teilhard de
Chardin's *Phenomenon of Man* (84), Walter Nigg's *The
Great Saints* (66), and William James' *Varieties of
Religious Experience* (37).

This type of bonding is not ordinarily engaged
in by the average Homo sapiens. Nevertheless, it is
a recurring event in all cultures, and William Sargeant in *Battle for the Mind* (75) presents evidence
for a patterned sequence of buildup of stress that
leads to conversion experiences (both political and
religious). Conversion experiences are by no means
synonymous with mystical experiences, but they are
usually the precondition for them. William James
and Evelyn Underhill present similar evidence relating more directly to the mystical experience. One
could at least hypothesize a neural-chemical substrate for mystical experience, triggered only by a
very specialized set of circumstances. As a kind of
super-bonding capacity, it may well have long-term
relevance for the survival of Homo sapiens.

The material we have introduced on genetic predispositions to learning suggests a major resource
for creative and peacemaking responses to be taken
account of in the socialization process. We will
now go on to examine developmental and maturational
processes in the socialization context, and link
these with the genetic substrate when we are ready
to put the model itself together. One of the most
interesting uses that has been made of developmental
theories has been in the area of political socialization drawing on the work of Piaget. Researchers
in this field have tried to answer the question,
"What shapes the child as an actor on the political
and civic scene?"

DEVELOPMENTAL AND CHRONOLOGICAL SEQUENCES

Piaget's work (68) has enabled other researchers, notably David Easton (18), Lawrence Kohlberg
(44) and Judity Torney (86) to focus on certain maturational factors as having particular significance
for the child's ability to take on creative political and social action roles. These include the
ability of the child to view situations from more
than one perspective, to make abstract conceptuali-
zations independently of concrete situations, and to
use abstract moral principles in arriving at decisions or judgments. Clearly these maturational phenomena have something to do with the fact that the
tendency to confuse God and the President of the

United States, and to confuse the Lord's prayer with
the pledge of allegiance to the flag, disappear in
the early elementary school years. They also have
something to do with the increased capacity of children by eighth grade to engage in more analytic discussions of the political system than they could in
kindergarten.

Cognitive maturation has probably been given
more explanatory loading than it can carry, however,
and the question of how emotional maturation is
linked to the cognitive has been largely ignored.
Adequate maturational studies on the development of
empathy and altruism are still to be undertaken.
The work of Hartshorn and May (31) and Lois Murphy
(64) laid a foundation which was for a long time
ignored. E. Midlarsky (57) in a recent review identifies two studies done in the 1950's relating age
and altruism (88,30), and she herself has used age
as a variable in studying altruism (58). All the
indications are that the capacity for empathy and
social warmth mature along with the cognitive capacities, but how they interact in the maturing
child's perceptions of self and society we do not
know. The subject has apparently not been of interest to educators. When we discover findings such as
that of Lambert and Klineberg (47) that American
children's interest in foreigners and persons very
dissimilar to themselves peaks at age 10 and then
declines,[3] we would like to know what mixture of
cognition and affect produces that result.

A third type of maturation, related to the capacity for spiritual bonding, can be labeled spiritual-intuitive. In cultures that give the same
careful training to the spiritual-intuitive faculty
as to the socio-emotional and cognitive in the
child, social behavior is given another dimension
because it is conceived in what might be called a
nonspheric context (84). Gandhi's satyagraha (9)
and some traditions of training within religious orders are good examples of a complex of thought,
feeling and behavior that draws on this third capacity. In our model, a balanced continuing development and training in all three of these capacities
is seen as contributing to the growth of the creative peacemaker.

The development of social role-taking skills
goes hand in hand with the development of cognitive-
emotional-intuitive capacities. This is not maturational in the sense that these other capacities are,
but rather represents the building up of a kind of
repertoire with which the maturing child can work

more and more effectively. These social skills are
partly a result of complex Meadian "taking the role
of the other," (56), which depends on the role models present in the individual's life space, partly
the product of extended social play in the peer
group as children "try out" different social roles
as they perceive them, on each other--and at times
on adults.

If we do not understand the interrelationship
of cognitive and emotional maturation, we understand
much less the complex four-way interrelationship between physiological maturation and the other processes. Eibl-Eibesfeldt's (19) suggestion mentioned
earlier that certain ethical and aesthetic attitudes
become fixated at early stages of development and
are highly resistant to later change needs to be
systematically explored in longitudinal research.
Cross-sectional research cannot possibly deal with
this problem. If the development of a healthy capacity for social trust is critically affected by the
four-way interaction of these factors at an early
age, it would be helpful to know about this.

In addition to developmental sequences there is
another chronological sequence which is of great
importance to the life of the growing child: the
succession of historical events in the child's time
stream. As the child "survives" event after event
in the world "out there"--wars, elections, assassinations, technological breakthroughs--an "event
stock" is built up which can be drawn on in constructing an image of the world and the child's role
in it. The event stock is part of the objective environmental reality. Growing with it is the child's
own "knowledge stock," compounded of perceptions of
events and of information acquired via teachers,
books, TV and all other sources of information to
which children are exposed.

The child's personal-social maturation inter-
acts with the event stream in a way that is crucial
for determining the style of that maturation. Children who have had first-hand experience of war have
different images of the world, and different responses to it, than children who have not (29).
Critical public events in the time-stream during
childhood help set a world view that persists
through life. The Munich trauma determined the attitudes of a whole generation of citizens and policy makers. The war in Indo-China certainly had an
equally potent, but very different, effect on today's children. The view of the earth from the moon
which is now a basic ingredient in the feeling about

the planet for the children of the 60s, provides a
context for all the information we impart to them
about the world with effects we cannot begin to
imagine.

Figure 2 provides a diagrammatic representation
of the relationship between the developmental sequences **we** have been discussing and the social or
event spaces in which learning takes place.

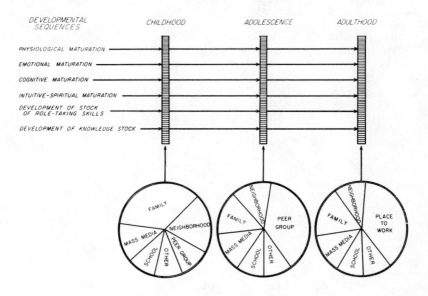

Figure 2

Up to this point we have viewed the biologically maturing child with genetically given predispositions to learn as acquiring on the one hand a set of
perceptual and analytic skills based on developing
emotional-cognitive-intuitive equipment, with a set
of behavioral, role-taking skills to match, and acquiring on the other hand a stock of "survived historical events" and an accompanying knowledge stock.

The interaction between developmental processes
and learning is a complex one. Inhelder and Sinclair point out that

...although learning may accelerate development
(within certain limits), such acceleration
obeys limitative conditions of assimilation
which, in turn, are subject to temporal regula-

tions reminiscent of the "chronological succession of competences" in embryology, as Waddington calls them. (36, p. 19)

LEARNING PROCESSES

The types of learning we will be concerned with
in analyzing the socialization process are cognitive
construction, social learning through reinforcement,
and social modeling. In the analysis of the event
spaces in which socialization takes place which follows, it will be well to keep in mind these three
types of learning, which will be briefly reviewed
here. Cognitive construction is the interior work
of assembling data from the perceived world, relating them to data already stored in the mind, and
organizing them into ordered images and concepts.
The degree of sophistication of the constructs depends on the developmental stage of the child, but
in no case does understanding

...consist in simply incorporating ready-made
and readily available data, but rather in re-
discovering them or reinventing them by one's
own activity. (36, p. 21)

Social learning through selective reinforcement
of responses has been the major focus of socialization research since the thirties when Dollard, Doob,
Miller and Sears (17) began their social learning
studies. Bandura, Walters and Aronfreed, cited
elsewhere in this chapter, work from this theoretical base. Behavioral modification through operant
conditioning is a more recent variant of this, and
has found many uses in therapy settings. A pathological behavior sequence in a child or adult can be
redirected by focusing on one segment of that behavior and withdrawing previous positive reinforcements
for that behavior. Similarly, new behaviors can be
created by positive reinforcements for new sequences
(16,90,53,43).
While older social learning theory would emphasize reinforcement as the basic learning process
that goes on in the family, and in the other event
spaces to be discussed, modeling has come to be increasingly recognized as a special form of social
learning not directly dependent on reinforcement to
the modeler (5). Modeling is not a new concept, but

Gabriel Tarde's work in *Les Lois D'Imitation (Laws of Imitation)* somehow never entered the mainstream of social learning theory.[4] It is of special interest to us because modeling represents a unique "instant" type of learning of a very complex set of interrelated behaviors which the learner is able to emulate without having added each component in piece-by-piece learning (5). It is learning through observation, and can take place at a distance; for example, through watching a person on TV, reading about a fictional or real-life heroine, or knowing about a community leader with whom one never has personal contact. It is much more economical than reinforcement learning, which involves simpler units of behavior, learned sequentially. Also, modeling represents the possibility of unintended socialization in contexts where no teaching is planned (40).

After an examination of the event spaces in which social learning takes place, we will present the socialization model which incorporates all of the elements discussed so far in the paper.

THE CHILD'S SET OF SOCIAL SPACES

Six important categories of social space within which the child receives significant socialization are the family, the neighborhood, the peer group, the school, other institutional settings (church, scouts, the Y's) and the world as imaged in the mass media. While each of these spaces continues to be part of a child's life into adulthood, they change in relative importance, from early childhood to youth, as reflected in the social space "pies" in the diagram (Figure 2). Family and neighborhood are most important in early years; peer group, school and other formal institutional settings are most important later. The TV set is the one social space that remains significant and unchanged in its relative importance from pre-school through the high school years, according to a study of sources of attitudes on war and peace in Canadian and American children by Haavelsrud (29).

The family. As a socializing agent, the family provides the child with role models for the management of tension and conflict (20,46,33), with training for problem-solving (73), with a self-image reflecting perceived adequacy and competence (17), with opportunities for aggressive or creative play (72), and with an image of the world as set or changeable, friendly or hostile (78). So much has been written

on the family's role in determining the personal and
social adequacy of the child that there is no need
to expand on these points here.

The neighborhood. While the pre-schooler is
socialized primarily through the family, the primary
social environment outside the home, i.e., the
neighborhood, gradually increases in importance as a
socializing agent for the pre-adolescent. Neighbors,
policemen, the family doctor, and other local figures interact with the growing child in neighborhood
events and (1) provide alternative role models and
(2) reinforce or contradict the training given in
the family setting.

School. The socializing influence of the school
is felt (a) through the teacher as a personal role
model, (b) through the teacher's ordering of data
concerning the structure, organization and values of
society, and (c) through textbook presentation of the
world. The last two, (b) and (c), contribute explicitly to the child's cognitive mapping of the world,
though there is an implicit contribution to the cognitive mapping from all the sources listed earlier.
There is some evidence that there may be a direct
relationship between the complexity of the cognitive
structure of the elementary school teachers and the
degree of acceptance of groups and cultures different from one's own on the part of elementary school
students, independently of the type of textbook used
(52).
Not only does the teacher's own cognitive structure mediate the learnings of the students, but
styles of teaching foster either an active intellectual search on the part of the students which enables
them to sustain cognitive dissonance and engage in
creative problem-solving, or a passive "receptacle"
stance which induces compartmentalized stereotyped
thinking and an inability to confront new situations.

Other institutional settings. The child has an
opportunity to play out a variety of alternative
roles in play groups, church association settings
and formal groups such as Cub Scouts and Brownies.
The degree of rigidity and level of aggression with
which these roles are played, and openness to alternative solutions to problems, is largely determined
by socialization experiences in the other settings
mentioned. However, the opportunities for anticipa-
tory socialization into possible change-agent roles
in this play behavior are significant in themselves;

Huizinga (34) has pointed out the importance of play in generating social innovation.

THE SOCIALIZATION MODEL AND THE REAL-LIFE ACTIVIST

We have now built up a picture of the child with a set of genetic predispositions to learn both aggressive and bonding and problem solving behaviors, maturing in cognitive, emotional and intuitive capacities, acquiring role-taking skills and a knowledge stock, and engaging in social learning in a variety of event spaces. Figure 3 links these factors together.

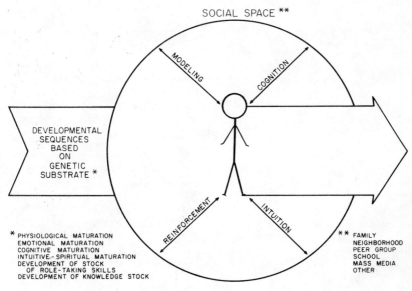

Figure 3

It will be remembered that when the ingredients for the socialization model were first presented, it was suggested that the life experience of a nonviolent activist would include the following features: (1) optimal opportunities for emotional, cognitive and intuitive development; (2) exposure to events and knowledge stock; (3) exposure to a variety of adult and peer role models; (4) role-playing and problem-solving opportunities; and (5) rewarding feedback for problem-solving.

These statements are all qualifying statements about the way in which different parts of the socialization process included in the socialization model

move forward in the life experience of the growing
child to produce peacemaking behavior. Now we will
look at some of the research on development of peaceful attitudes and peaceful dissenting behavior in
recent protest movements for confirmation or discon-
firmation of these postulates.

*DEVELOPMENTAL OPPORTUNITIES IN HOME AND SCHOOL
AND EXPOSURE TO EVENTS STOCK*

Research in support of points (1) and (2) were
presented in the discussion of social space. We
need add here only a mention of the convergence of
research findings on student activists and their
families. Two issues of the *Journal of Social
Issues* devoted to this topic, October, 1964 and July,
1967, especially the articles by Flacks (25),
Gelineau and Kantor (26), Christian Bay (6), Fishman
and Solomon (24), and the Rosenhan study of the civil rights movement activists (74), plus the Block,
Haan and Smith study of activism and apathy in adolescents (8) all point to the fact that liberal parents who have close, warm relationships with their
children and also provide intellectual stimulation
in the home often produce children who become committed activists, acting out their parents' views in
ways their parents have not done. While children
and parents may now disagree, the fact remains that
in these families there has been more open communication between parents and children than in the average family. These activist students are better
informed than their nonactivist counterparts.
Heckman's study (32) of theological students
who turned in their draft cards as a protest against
the war and risked prison sentences rather than take
the draft deferrment permitted them by their choice
of the ministerial vocation shows similar family
closeness, together with encouragement by parents of
independent thinking on the part of the sons.
Maccoby's discussion (50) of the development of moral behavior in childhood also makes very clear the
crucial role of parental child-rearing styles which
combine emotional warmth with encouragement of autonomy in producing children with both a sense of competence and of social responsibility. Since warmth
without autonomy can mean overprotective childrear-
ing and produce timidity in children, the willingness of parents to stand back and let their children
experiment on their own and think for themselves appears to be equally important with warmth in the development of the creative peacemaker.

EXPOSURE TO ADULT AND PEER ROLE MODELS

The importance of the peer group as a source of role models is often ignored in favor of a focus on significant adults. The importance of the peer group is particularly pronounced in the development of attitudes toward peace and peacemaking. Haavelsrud's (29) study shows that friends are considered a more important source of information about peace than any other agent by tenth-graders. In fact, these teenagers report that teachers, textbooks and the media all teach them much more effectively about war than about peace. The significance of informal and formal peer-group associations in structuring and strengthening commitment of young people to new behaviors can hardly be overestimated in the light of their reported judgments that they learn about peacemaking from each other, not from any sector of the adult society or the mass media.

We have other evidence, however, that the effect of special adult role models at this age may be very great. Studies of critical influences in the lives of young adults who were conscientious objectors in World War II (28) and of women who became active in the Women's Strike for Peace in 1962 (10) reveals the importance of an encounter, often in the early teens, with a minister, teacher or other community figure who represented a dynamic role model for social change in contrast with earlier role model exposure for these individuals. Encounters with great social innovators through reading were also reported as significant experiences. Heckman's (32) seminary draft resisters also reported the great importance of male adults other than their fathers in their intellectual and moral development.

COMPETENCE-GENERATING SOCIAL EXPERIENCE

Combining points (4) and (5) listed above, we find the researches on socialization for competence and on development of altruistic behavior emphasize the importance of the following:

a. Successful past experience with problem-solving and ability to cope with stress (57,60,75, 8,3).

b. Feelings of optimism about society, confidence in self (59,57,61,6,48,79).

c. Feelings of responsibility for the well-being of others (32,24).

d. Experience of emotional warmth and reward for helping behavior (41, p. 104, 3).

A variety of research on altruism from different points of view all make clear the relationship between competence and altruism. People do not engage in aiding behavior, particularly at cost to themselves, unless they feel competent and this feeling of competence is based on past successes. E. Midlarsky (57) makes clear that what looks like very costly altruistic behavior to an outsider may be a trifle to the aider who has the competence to do what others would find difficult. Aiders can also endure more stress than the average person (94, 38). It is *not*, however, an exclusively middle class phenomenon, although much of the research on competence emphasizes the training for competence of middle class parents. E. Midlarsky (57, p. 237) reports different patterns of aiding behavior in the lower and middle class, but aiding itself is not class-linked. The word autonomy is frequently used in describing the personality of the altruist.

An enormous optimism about the future and confidence in self as actor characterizes the activist-altruist. London (48) describes the characteristics of the rescuers of Jews in Nazi Germany as including a pronounced spirit of adventurousness. This was all the more notable because their aiding responses were taken at very great risk and they were a very tiny social minority with no reinforcement possible for their behavior except a sense of acting on behalf of a future, better society (and of course the gratitude of the rescued). Sorokin's good neighbors in his neighbor study were notably optimistic people (81). Christian Bay in his study of college students (6) considers optimism about the future one of the key characteristics of activists.

Feelings of responsibility for others extending beyond particular claims made personally by the activist are marked. Heckman's seminary students (32) who risked jail needlessly to resist the draft expressed deep concern about how society was going. "What kind of people are we becoming?" "I want to be able to face my children." These feelings begin to develop early. Fishman and Solomon state:

> In studies of peace and civil rights demonstrators we have tentatively noted that "first memories" of social concern and sympathy seem to cluster around the ages of 5-7 and 12-15. This coincides with period of great personality and role transition in the individual. Perhaps the awareness of and discomfort with change in the

> self increases the tendency to displacement and
> projection and thus enhances sensitivity to and
> sympathy with suffering in others. (24, p. 6)

The notion that spurts in personal growth and in
sensitivity to others may go hand in hand is an interesting one for parents and educators to explore.

One of the most delightful of all researches
into altruism was undertaken recently by Elizabeth
Midlarsky and James Bryan (59), in which they demonstrated that joyous hugging of children when they
engaged in an altruistic response in an experimental
situation (sharing candy or other goodies) greatly
increased the frequency of altruistic responses in
future runs of the experiment. The rewards of altruism can be felt through positive responses of rewarding others, or through the simple perception
that the person helped is in fact now better off.
Aronfreed (3) argues that the altruist is automatically reinforced by the fact of desired outcomes being produced for the person helped. This simple observation removes a lot of unnecessary mystique from
altruistic behavior.

Children who become altruists, activists, and
nonviolent shapers of the future are then persons
who feel autonomous, competent, confident about
their own future and the future of society, able to
cope with stress, relate warmly to others and feel
responsibility for them even when they are not directly dependent on the aider-activists. They have
had many opportunities to solve problems and play
out different social roles in the past and their
successes have been recognized and rewarded; they
have been exposed to a wide variety of events, ac-
cumulated a fair amount of knowledge, and have a
cognitively complex view of the world. They have
been inspired by adult role models, but also nur-
tured and helped by their own peers. In terms of
our model, they have had optimal opportunities to
develop each of their capacities, cognitive, emotional and intuitive, during their maturing years;
their predispositions for bonding, for altruism,
play, creating alternatives have more than counter-
balanced their predispositions for aggression.
Their social spaces have been filled with challenges
they could meet, role models which provided rich
sources of complex learnings about possible social
behavior, and positive reinforcements for their attempts to make constructive changes around them.

These shapers of the future are something of a

miracle, since as Christian Bay points out:

> Every new human being is potentially a liberal
> animal and a rebel; yet every social organiza-
> tion he will be up against, from the family to
> the state, is likely to seek to "socialize" him
> into a conveniently pliant conformity. (6,
> p. 90)

If we look at the daily lives of children and teenagers, we get a very powerful impression that they
are extracting something from their various environments and from the time-stream that most adults are
missing. Vietnam, President Kennedy's assassination, the space-walk, tightly-packed urban misery,
loneliness in the midst of affluence--all these have
filtered through the formal socialization agencies
and contributed to a set of images of the world inside children's heads quite different from the ones
held by the older generation. The autonomous role
of cognition and intuition in social learning must
not be forgotten. In acting on their own images
young people are engaging in a kind of social creativity that defies encapsulation in any theory of
socialization.

NOTES

1. There is no attempt here to suggest what the
full range of behavioral programs might be. We are
discussing only those relevant to our topic.

2. These enthusiastic little explorers seem to give
lie to Berger's poetic presentation of Homo sapien
as the only creature who comes into an unfinished
world and must, by his very nature, actively engage
in continuous creation (7).

3. "By the age of 14 these same young people appeared less open to positive views of foreign nations" (87).

4. Tarde's name does not even appear in the standard
work on socialization, Clausen's *Socialization and
Society* (13).

REFERENCES

1. American Association for the Advancement of Science Annual Meeting, Session on "Biological Basis of Destructive Behavior," General Science Symposia, Value and Knowledge Requirements for Peace, December 28, 1971.
2. Ardrey, Robert. *African Genesis*. New York: Atheneum, 1962.
3. Aronfreed, Justin. The socialization of altruistic and sympathetic behavior: some theoretical and experimental analyses. In J. Macaulay & L. Berkowitz (Eds.), *Altruism and Helping Behavior*. New York: Academic Press, 1970.
4. Aurobindo, Sri. *Future Evolution of Man*. New York: Dutton, 1963.
5. Bandura, A., & Walters, R.H. *Social Learning and Personality Development*. New York: Holt, Rinehart & Winston, 1963.
6. Bay, Christian. Political and apolitical students: facts in search of theory. *Journal Social Issues*, 1967, *23*, 76-91.
7. Berger, Peter L. *A Rumor of Angels*. New York: Doubleday, 1969.
8. Block, Jeanne H., Haan, Norma, & Smith, M. Brewster. Activism and apathy in contemporary adolescents. In James F. Adams (Ed.), *Understanding Adolescence*. Boston: Allyn & Bacon, 1968.
9. Bondurant, Joan V. *Conquest of Violence: the Gandhian Philosophy of Conflict*. Berkeley: University California Press, 1955.
10. Boulding, Elise. Who are these women? A progress report on a study of the Women Strike for Peace. In Milton Schwebel (Ed.), *Behavioral Science and Human Survival*. Palo Alto: Science & Behavior Books, 1965.
11. Boulding, Elise. *The Underside of History: A View of Women through Time*. Boulder, Colorado: Westview, 1976.
12. Brehm, J.W., & Cole, A.H. Effect of a favor which reduces freedom. *Journal Personality & Social Psychology*, 1966, *3*, 420-426.
13. Clausen, John A. (Ed.), *Socialization and Society*. Boston: Little, Brown, 1968.
14. Corning, Peter, & Corning, Constance Hellyer. An evolutionary-adaptive theory of aggression. Paper presented Annual Meeting, American Political Science Association, Chicago, 1971. (mimeographed)
15. Corning, Peter, & Corning, Constance, Hellyer.

Toward a general theory of violent aggression. Boulder: University of Colorado, 1972. (mimeographed)

16. Creer, Thomas L., & Yoches, Carol. The modification of an inappropriate behavioral pattern in asthmatic children. *Journal Chronic Disorders,* 1971.

17. Dollard, J., Doob, L., Miller, N.E., Mowrer, O.H., & Sears, R.R. *Frustration and Aggression.* New Haven: Yale University Press, 1939.

18. Easton, David, & Dennis, Jack. *Children in the Political System:* New York: McGraw Hill, 1969.

18. Eibl-Eibesfeldt, Irenäus. *Love and Hate.* New York: Holt, Rinehart & Winston, 1972.

20. Elmer, Elizabeth. *Children in Jeopardy.* Pittsburgh: University of Pittsburgh Press, 1967.

21. Escalona, Sibylle K. *Roots of Individuality.* Chicago: Aldine, 1968.

22. Fellner, Carl H., & Marshall, John R. Kidney donors. In J. Macaulay & L. Berkowitz (Eds.), *Altruism and Helping Behavior.* New York: Academic Press, 1970.

23. Feshbach, Seymour. Aggression. In Paul H. Mussen (Ed.), *Manual of Child Psychology, Volume II.* New York: Wiley, 1970.

24. Fishman, Jacob R., & Solomon, Fredric. Youth and social action: an introduction. *Journal Social Issues,* 1964, *20,* 1-21.

25. Flacks, Richard. The liberated generation. *Journal Social Issues,* 1967, *23,* 52-75.

26. Gelineau, Victor A., & Kantor, David. Prosocial commitment among college students. *Journal Social Issues,* 1964, *20,* 112-130.

27. Goranson, R.E., & Berkowitz, L. Reciprocity and responsibility reactions to prior help. *Journal Personality & Social Psychology,* 1966, *3,* 227-232.

28. Guetzkow, Harold. Unpublished data from a study of drafted conscientious objectors resident in camps for conscientious objectors operated jointly by the Federal government and the peace churches during World War II, 1945.

29. Haavelsrud, Magnus. Development concepts related to peace and war: an international perspective. Paper presented at annual convention, American Psychological Association, Washington, D.C., September 7, 1971.

30. Handlon, R.V., & Gross, P. The development of sharing behavior. *Journal Abnormal Social Psychology,* 1959, *59,* 425-428.

31. Hartshorne, H., & May, M.A. *Studies in Service*

and Self-Control. New York: Macmillan, 1929.

32. Heckman, Dale M. World views of students who take risk for ethical conviction. Stockton, University of the Pacific, unpublished Ph.D. dissertation, 1972.

33. Hefler, Ray, & Kemp, Henry C. *The Battered Child*. Chicago: University Chicago Press, 1968.

34. Huizinga, Johan. *Homo Ludens: A Study of the Play Element in Culture*. Boston: Beacon, 1955.

35. Huxley, Thomas. *The Struggle for Existence and its Bearing upon Man*. London, 1888.

36. Inhelder, Barbel, & Sinclair, Hermina. Learning cognitive structures. In Paul Mussen, Jonas Langer, & Martin Covington (Eds.), *Trends and Issues in Developmental Psychology*. New York: Hold, Rinehart & Winston, 1969.

37. James, William. *Varieties of Religious Experience*. New York: Modern Library, 1902.

38. Janis, I.L. Psychological effects of warnings. In G.W. Baker & D.W. Chapman (Eds.), *Man and Society in Disaster*. New York: Basic Books, 1962.

39. Jantsch, Erich, & Waddington, Conrad H. (Eds.). *Evolution and Consciousness*. Reading, Mass.: Addison-Wesley, 1976.

40. Jessor, Richard, & Jessor, Shirley. Some issues related to nonparental socialization. Paper prepared for working conference on Social Aspects of Socialization, organized by the National Institute of Child Health and Human Development, Washington, D.C., December 7-9, 1967.

41. Kaufmann, Harry. *Aggression and Altruism*. New York: Holt, Rinehart & Winston, 1970.

42. Kausler, D.N. Aspiration level as a determinant of performance. *Journal Personality*, 1959, *27*, 346-351.

43. Kimble, G.A. *Hilgard and Marquis' Conditioning and Learning*. New York: Appleton-Century-Crofts, 1961.

44. Kohlberg, Lawrence. Moral education in the schools: a developmental view. *The School Review*, 1966, *74*, 1-29.

45. Kropotkin, Peter. *Mutual Aid*. London, 1903.

46. Laing, R.D. *The Politics of Experience*. New York: Ballantine, 1967.

47. Lambert, W.E., & Klineberg, O. *Children's Views of Foreign People*. New York: Appleton-Century-Crofts, 1967.

48. London, Perry. The rescuers: motivational hypotheses about Christians who saved Jews from the Nazis. In J. Macaulay & L. Berkowitz,

(Eds.), *Altruism and Helping Behavior*. New
York: Academic Press, 1970.

49. Macaulay, J., & Berkowitz, L. (Eds.). *Altruism
and Helping Behavior*. New York: Academic
Press, 1970.

50. Maccoby, Eleanor E. The development of moral
values and behavior in childhood. In John A.
Clausen (Ed.), *Socialization and Society*.
Boston: Little, Brown, 1968.

51. Markley, O.W. (Ed.), Changing Images of Man.
Report CSSP-RR-4. Menlo Park, Calif.: Stanford
Research Institute, 1974.

52. Maruyama, Linda. The effect of teachers' belief
systems on children's ethnocentric behavior.
Unpublished paper for Professor Elise Boulding,
Problems and Prospects for Peace class, University Colorado, Boulder, May 1969.

53. Mattos, R.L., Mattson, R.H., & Walker, H.M.,
et al. Reinforcement and aversive control in
the modification of behavior. *Academy of Therapy*, 1969, *5*, Report No. 147.

54. McClelland, David C. *The Achieving Society*.
Princeton, N.J.: Van Nostrand, 1961.

55. McClelland, David C., & Winter, David G. *Motivating Economic Achievement*. New York: Free
Press, 1969.

56. Mead, George. *Mind, Self and Society*. Charles
W. Morris (Ed.). Chicago: University Illinois
Press, 1934.

57. Midlarsky, Elizabeth. Aiding responses: an
analysis and review. *Merril-Palmer Quarterly*,
1968, *14*, 229-260.

58. Midlarsky, Elizabeth, & Bryan, James H. Training charity in children. *Journal Personality &
Social Psychology*, 1967, *5*, 408-415.

59. Midlarsky, Elizabeth, & Bryan, James H. Affect
expressions and children's initiative altruism.
University of Denver, 1972. (mimeographed)

60. Midlarsky, Elizabeth, & Midlarsky, Manus. Some
determinants of aiding under experimentally-in-
duced stress. University of Denver and University of Colorado, 1971. (mimeographed)

61. Midlarsky, Manus, & Midlarsky, Elizabeth. Status inconsistency: aggression attitudes and
helping behavior. University of Colorado and
University of Denver, 1972. (mimeographed)

62. Moyer, K.E. Internal impulses to aggression.
Transactions of the New York Academy Sciences,
1969, *31*, 104-114.

63. Moyer, K.E. *The Physiology of Hostility*. Chicago: Markham, 1971.

64. Murphy, Lois. *Social Behavior and Child Person-
    ality: An Exploratory Study of Some Roots of
    Sympathy*. New York: Columbia University Press,
    1937.
65. Mussen, Paul H., Langer, Jonas, & Covington,
    Martin (Eds.). *Trends and Issues in Developmen-
    tal Psychology*. New York: Holt, Rinehart &
    Winston, 1969.
66. Nigg, Walter. *The Great Saints*. London:
    Francis Aldor, 1948.
67. duNouy, Lecomte. *Human Destiny*. New York: New
    American Library, 1949.
68. Piaget, Jean, & Weil, Anna Marie. The develop-
    ment in children of the idea of homeland and of
    relations with other countries. *International
    Social Science Bulletin*, 1951, *3*, 561-578.
69. Pierce, Chester. The preschooler and the fu-
    ture. *The Futurist*, 1972, *5*, 13-15.
70. Platt, John. *The Step to Man*. New York:
    Wiley, 1966.
71. Polak, Fred. *Image of the Future*. Translated
    and abridged by Elise Boulding from the Dutch,
    1955. (Original two volume translation pub-
    lishedin 1961 by Oceana Press). San Francisco:
    Jossey Bass/Elsevier, 1972.
72. *Psychology Today*. Society, morality and the
    Gun. *Psychology Today*, 1968, *1*, entire issue.
73. Rosen, B.D., & D'Andrade, R. The psychosocial
    origins of achievement motivation. *Sociometry*,
    1959, *22*, 185-218.
74. Rosenhan, David. The natural socialization of
    altruistic autonomy. In J. Macaulay & L. Berko-
    witz (Eds.), *Altruism and Helping Behavior*. New
    York: Academic Press, 1970.
75. Sampson, Edward. Student activism and the dec-
    ade of protest. *Journal Social Issues*, 1967,
    23, 1-33.
76. Sargeant, William. *Battle for the Mind*. Garden
    City: Doubleday, 1957.
77. Schopler, John. An attributing analysis of some
    determinants of reciprocating a benefit. In
    J. Macaulay & L. Berkowitz (Eds.), *Altruism and
    Helping Behavior*. New York: Academic Press,
    1970.
78. Sigel, Roberta (Ed.). *Political Socialization.
    The Annals of American Academy Political & So-
    cial Science*, 1965, *362*. (whole issue)
79. Smith, M. Brewster. Competence and socializa-
    tion. In John A. Clausen (Ed.), *Socialization
    and Society*. Boston: Little, Brown, 1968.
80. Solomon, Fredric, & Fishman, Jacob R. Youth and

peace: a psychosocial study of student peace demonstrators in Washington, D.C. *Journal Social Issues*, 1964, *20*, 54-73.

81. Sorokin, P.A. *Altruistic Love*. Boston: Beacon Press, 1950.

82. Szondi, Lipot. *Gestalten des Böses*. Bern, 1969.

83. Tarde, Gabriel. *Les Lois D'Imitation (Laws of Imitation)*. New York: Peter Smith.

84. Teilhard de Chardin, Pierre. *The Phenomenon of Man*. New York: Harper & Row, 1959.

85. Thomas, W.I.   The four wishes and the definition of the situation. In Talcott Parsons, Edward Shils, Kaspar D. Naegele, & Jesse R. Pitts (Eds.), *Theories of Society*. New York: Free Press, 1961.

86. Torney, Judith. Contemporary political socialization in elementary schools and beyond. *The High School Journal*, 1970, 153-163.

87. Torney, Judith V., & Morris, Donald N. Teaching in the international perspective in the elementary school. *Intercom* (in press).

88. Ugurel-Semin, R. Moral behavior and moral judgment of children. *Journal Abnormal Social Psychology*, 1952, *47*, 463-474.

89. Underhill, Evelyn. *Mysticism*. New York: World, 1955.

90. Veblen, Thorstein. *The Instinct of Workmanship*. New York: Kelley, 1918.

91. Walker, H.M., & Buckley, N.K. The use of positive reinforcement in conditioning attending behavior. *Journal Applied Behavior Annual, 1*, 245-250.

92. Wickler, Wolfgang. *Sunder? naturgesetze der Ehe*. Munich, 1969.

93. Wilson, Edward O. *Sociobiology: The New Synthesis*. Cambridge, Mass.: Belknap Press of Harvard Univer. Press, 1975.

94. Withey, S.B. Reaction to uncertain threats. In G.W. Baker & D.W. Chapman (Eds.), *Man and Society in Disaster*. New York: Basic Books, 1962.

95. Wolff, Kurt H. (Ed.), *Sociology of George Simmel*. New York: Free Press, 1950.

ELISE BOULDING is Professor of Sociology at the University of Colorado and Project Director at the Institute of Behavioral Science. She was the first editor of the INTERNATIONAL PEACE RESEARCH NEWSLETTER, and was Chairperson of the Consortium on Peace Research, Education and Development. As a peace re-

searcher, she has tried to link research on the family and socialization processes with the international order.

Professor Boulding was born in Oslo, Norway. She received her B.A. degree in English from Douglass College, her M.S. in Sociology, and her Ph.D. from the University of Michigan.

A sociologist with a global view, she has undertaken numerous transnational and comparative cross-national studies on conflict resolution, war and peace, family life, and women in society. Her work in the area of future studies dates from 1961 when she translated, from the Dutch, Fred Polak's classic work, IMAGE OF THE FUTURE (San Francisco: Jossey Bass/Elsevier, 1972). She has worked internationally on problems of peace and world order both as a scholar and as an activist.

Her major historical study of women's changing social, economic and political roles over four millenia entitled, THE UNDERSIDE OF HISTORY: A VIEW OF WOMEN THROUGH TIME, has just been published (Boulder, Colorado: Westview Press, 1976). In addition, three other books have recently been published: HANDBOOK OF INTERNATIONAL DATA ON WOMEN (New York: Halsted Press, 1976); WOMEN IN THE TWENTIETH CENTURY WORLD (New York: Halsted Press, 1977); and FROM A MONASTERY KITCHEN (New York: Harper & Row, 1976).

In addition to current work on global-local linkage and examining the human life span as a social system, Professor Boulding is exploring religious dimensions of human growth.

SOME OTHER PUBLICATIONS BY ELISE BOULDING

- Child as shapter of the future. *Peace and Change: A Journal of Peace Research*, 1972, *1*, 11-17.
- *Children and Solitude*, Pendle Hill Pamphlet Number 125. Wallingford, Pennsylvania, 1962.
- Adolescent culture: reflections of divergence. In Nobuo Kenneth Shimahara & Adam Scrupski (Eds.), *Social Forces and Schooling*. New York: McKay, 1975, 187-220.
- Children's Rights and World Order: A Global Survey of the Role and Status of Children and Youth in the 1970s. University of Colorado, Institute of Behavioral Science, 1977. (mimeographed)
- Global altruism and everyday behavior. In Theo F. Lentz (Ed.), *Humatriotism: Human Interest in Peace and Survival*. St. Louis, Missouri: Futures, 1976, 39-65.

5. The Human Person and the War System: A Problem for Education

Betty Reardon, M.A.

"War is cruelty and there is no refining it!" This often misquoted statement by General Sherman goes to the heart of one of the major dilemmas facing policy makers, educators, and citizens. Since World War II, policy makers have been caught between the purposes of avoiding war and "reaffirming a belief in fundamental human rights" as stated in the U.N. Charter, and pursuing the interests of their individual nation states viewed as so competitive with and exclusive of the interests of other states that force and violence must be used. Since then we have seen the Korean War, the killing of hundreds of thousands of alleged Communists in Indonesia, the mass starvation of children in Nigeria, civilians of many nations held hostage or hijacked from their intended air destinations, the murder of political kidnap victims, and, of course, a war in Vietnam resulting in civilian deaths estimated at over 300,000, with total civilian casualties of perhaps 1,000,000, and which necessitated a series of criminal proceedings against American military personnel. We have also witnessed the escalation of violence in Ireland, and the pouring out of Pakistan of a million refugees into India, until that nation saw fit to take up arms to end the causes of the refugees' flight. A bitter civil war in Lebanon with over 10,000 dead, and many other tragedies have shadowed the history of the mid-20th century. Humanizing the conduct of war, when most wars by their very nature involve large numbers of civilians and the use of highly sophisticated weaponry, much of it deliberately designed as anti-personnel, has become about as difficult as abolishing war, while the need to abolish war becomes even more urgent.

It has become clear to many that to survive as a species on this planet, human beings must overcome the major threats to their existence. First and foremost of these is war. Beyond survival, war must be abolished so that we may preserve our humanity. War, more than any other dehumanizing force of contemporary life, prevents humankind from establishing a human community in which all may live in dignity.

The process of education is intended, in part, to enable persons to achieve their human potential and to realize their human dignity. If we are to fulfill this intention, then educators must raise questions about the war system as an instrument of dehumanization, and citizens must make it clear to policy makers that the waste of resources on such an instrument in the face of the overwhelming need of vast numbers of the human race to be freed from the oppression of poverty, poor health and ignorance will no longer be tolerated.

Neither of the foregoing aims can be achieved until human beings begin to perceive each other as fellow humans wtih the same needs and fears, caught in the same critical crisis of survival. Although some may be threatened by starvation, others by violence and still others by the lethal quality of the environment, all humans face the survival danger. It is this fact which underlies the suggestions which came forth from the study made by the Foreign Policy Association for the U.S. Office of Education on *Recommendations, Needs and Priorities in International Education,*[1] particularly as reflected in two of the major conceptual bases it recommends for international education.

The first is *the species concept of mankind.* For some years now, those educators who sought to be more effective in their attempts to teach "international understanding" as a means to peace have searched for an appropriate mode of teaching about the common characteristics of all peoples in all nations. Clearly the most simple and probably the most functional approach is through their membership in a single animal species. As the FPA study points out, now that the planet earth can be viewed as a single ecosystem, with most behavior of individuals, groups, and nations ultimately affecting everyone on earth, a working understanding of the single species concept may be essential to human survival. Certainly without such a conceptual base there can be only a dim hope of forming a single human community on this planet. Every member of our species is a

human person, and all attempts to improve the quality of life and extend human rights must apply to
everyone equally. The exhortations of *Pacem in
Terris* and the rights enumerated in the Universal
Declaration of Human Rights refer to every human
person, whether memebers of our own groups, or of
all groups opposed to our own, and even to the "enemy." Indeed, the Papal encyclical is quite clear
on this point. It warns that:

> ...one must never confuse error and the person
> who errs, not even when there is question of
> error, or inadequate knowledge of truth....The
> person who errs is always and above all a human
> being, and in every case he retains his dignity
> as a human person. He must always be regarded
> and treated in accordance with that lofty dig-
> nity.[2]

The second recommendation of the FPA study
which reflects the survival concern is that *the present international system be studied as one of the
operating levels of human social organization.* It
is, in fact, this particular conceptual base which
was the subject of the research and curriculum development program of the Institute for World Order;
the Institute's special concern being the war system, that aspect of the international system reflected in the unrestricted use of violence for resolving conflict and pursuing the particular goals
and interests of individual nation states. *The international system is the only unit of human social
organization which does not enforce prohibitions
against the use of violence.* All other units have
done so or attempted to do so, recognizing that the
absence of such prohibitions erodes the viability
and cohesiveness of the unit and is likely to lead
to its destruction.
    *World order is a field of study devoted to
seeking nonviolent modes of international conflict
resolution and social change.* It seeks to achieve
on a global scale certain goals sought internally by
the nation state, namely peace and order, economic
welfare, and social justice for every member of the
human species.
    The major focus of the world order inquiry is
on violence as a political device, exploring its use
by nation states, groups within nation states, and
individuals. It is also concerned with the ways in

which these categories of actors within the international system attempt to devise alternatives to, or
prevent violence. The study of world order, therefore, provides a responsible base from which to examine the specific problems of humanizing the conduct of international relations, of war and war
crimes, and the general issues related to the rights
and responsibilities of the individual in the international system.

HISTORY AS A CHRONICLE OF CRIMINAL WARFARE

Another responsible base from which education
might approach these issues is the historical perspective. Human history is a chronicle of warfare,
and the history of warfare is a chronicle of crime.
In spite of the chivalric traditions from previous
centuries and the rules of warfare established in
1863, war crimes before the present century were not
considered anti-normative, much less anti-legal. It
is significant to note that the Dutch government
would not surrender the Kaiser to the Allies after
World War I to be tried for violation of "moral" not
legal principles. The Allies afterwards recognized
all war to be a crime against humanity, and that
principle was supposedly written into law by the
Kellogg-Briand Pact in 1928. It took another war to
get most nations to recognize the principle, now
stated in the United Nations Charter, and to engen-
der a statement defining the minimal rights of all
human beings. The Universal Declaration of Human
Rights of 1948 was promulgated about the time of the
United Nations endorsement of the Nuremberg Principles. If either of these documents were retroac-
tive, there is good reason to believe that not a
single nation state could avoid charges of having
violated these principles.

An interesting question for teachers of history
to pose to their students would be: How might the
history of civilization have differed had law, as it
evolved, included the concept of war crimes? Would
those gifted lawmakers, the Romans, have sacked
Jerusalem and destroyed Carthage? Would the Norman
Christians have desisted from rape, pillage, and
murder of their fellow Christians of slightly different persuasions as they marched to the Holy Land?
Would the Christian colonizers of the Americas have
enslaved and tortured the native inhabitants of
these continents in the name of Christian conversion? Would hundreds of thousands of Armenians have

died in the process of being expelled from their
homelands? Could Belgian soldiers have brought to
the colonial officers in the Congo baskets filled
with human hands as proof of the severity of punishment imposed upon those who did not work for their
imperial masters? If the Nuremberg Principles had
come after the First World War, would the second
have produced a history of wanton death and destruction, including such horrors as the Nazi death
camps, the Katyn Forest massacres, Lidice, and the
saturation bombing of Dresden in the European theater? Or would the Asian theater have seen the
Bataan Death March, the annihilation of a Philippine
village for which a Japanese general was later executed as a war criminal, or the unleashing against
civilian populations of the greatest weapon of mass
destruction that had yet been devised and used?

How might the history of this nation have been
changed? Would the majority of the Continental Army
prisoners taken by the British in our Revolutionary
War have died during imprisonment? Would the in-
famies of Andersonville in the Civil War, or the
massacre at Samar in the Philippines which brought
about the court-martial of American officers at the
turn of this centruy, or in fact the shame of Mylai,
be on our nation's conscience?

Although it is obvious that we have not yet
fully established the Nuremberg Principles as invi-
olable legal norms for the conduct of international
relations, it is also true that they do represent a
significant landmark in Western history, one which
should be given far greater attention not only in
classes dealing with the history of World War II but
also in those courses concerned with the development
of Western traditions and moral values.

There is no doubt that many thoughtful young
people today look cynically upon the Western moral
tradition, and their feeling was reinforced, if not
magnified, by the Mylai disclosure, the official
"cover up" of the events and subsequent acquittal of
all but one of the accused. The historic perspective may offer a reasonable framework through which
the teacher can present the issues, and the world
order perspective may provide lines of inquiry about
how to prevent such events in the future. However,
for high school students who approach the age of
military service, there is an urgent emotional and
intellectual need to confront the problem directly.
They certainly deserve the opportunity to study the
events, the precedents, and the possibilities for
prevention of, and restitution for war crimes. Even

more important, they must understand what their own individual rights would be should they ever find themselves faced with the moral dilemma of being called upon to commit inhuman acts in warfare.

HOW CAN HUMAN BEINGS DO SUCH THINGS?

No matter how high a level of analysis we achieve in exploring these issues in discussion groups and classrooms, there is still the basic emotional-moral question which always emerges when we confront inhuman practices. *How can human beings do such things to their fellow humans?* How does an average citizen become an inhumane killer? The average citizen does not become a killer per se, but a soldier, an honorable defender of his own nation or group against the threat of an enemy. The "enemy" is always dehumanized, and the soldier believes that his opponents are those against whom "it is allowed to exercise all means necessary....The first consideration is to crush the...enemy."[3] The true trauma of Mylai was that it has revealed the "defenders" of humanity in the inhumane role formerly reserved exclusively for the enemy. Those who condemn such acts generally tend to view the victims as fellow human beings; those who condone them, view the dead as the "enemy." Unless the people of the world come to acknowledge the common humanity of all people, there can be no practical, nor legitimate acknowledgement of the concept of "war crimes."

In situations such as those in Bangladesh and Northern Ireland, one sees clearly how limited are the rights and humanity of the individual in a violent political struggle. The present system of international relations seems unable to provide protection for individuals consistent with the spirit of the Universal Declaration of Human Rights or *Pacem in Terris,* or for that matter, with the Geneva Conventions. This problem is sharply illustrated by the Shimoda Case, in which the suit of victims of the atomic bombings of Japan was dismissed on the grounds that individual persons had no standing in international law. Significantly, though, the ruling also condemned the bombings on the basis of their producing unnecessary human suffering, the reason for which gas warfare was made "illegal." Like the Nuremberg Principles, this concept was then totally ignored in the massive bombings by American Air Force in Vietnam. In addition, the use of certain weapons and practices in Vietnam showed the close relationship between types of weapons employed and the unavoidable violations of the rights of human persons in war. It also fixed on the major problem of war crimes: *Is it, in fact, possible to conduct warfare without committing gross violations of the human rights of large numbers of persons, civilian as well as military?*

There are those who assert that it is war itself which constitutes the crime. Some contend that there are no circumstances and no causes which can possibly make war an acceptable strategy for the achievement of political or human goals, and will argue this position on pragmatic as well as moral grounds. Martin Luther King was such a man, and for his espousal and use of nonviolence he was awarded the Nobel Peace Prize. There are others, some also clergymen like the Reverend Michael Scott, who took stands in South Africa. Long before social and political scientists had defined the phenomenon of institutional violence, Michael Scott had not only recognized it, but had begun to struggle against it when he joined the black miners where he was jailed for struggling for their rights. *While institutional violence exists both inside and outside the war system, wherever it continues without relief it almost inevitably leads to open warfare.* This problem, therefore, is also central to any inquiry into the dilemma of the human person in the war system. When modes and methods by which some rule others negate humanity, then those political, social, and economic processes constitute violence. Michael Scott is one individual who has acted within the international system, using the institutions available, as he does in his annual appearances before the U.N. on behalf of Southwest Africa, to try to gain dignity and justice for victims of political violence. His work indicates that, although limited, there are still nonviolent recourses open to those who will not, or cannot, use the war system. Certainly the principles and practices of such persons should be a significant subject of study in all our schools.

There are many other problems affecting the human person in the war system. The fate of prisoners of war is a source of anxiety to their families and fellow countrymen. The needs of the poor are given low priority. Parents may face the return of sons in coffins, or be forced to visit them in military stockades, or sit as spectators as they are tried for war crimes. Homes are razed, crops destroyed, and death, injury, and anguish reach far beyond the

field of combat. The acute problems of limitations
on civil rights and the risks involved in dissent
from foreign policy in wartime affect in one way or
another every citizen, and the press and other media
must grapple with delicate questions of censorship.

These are all problems to be raised in any disciplined examination of the human condition and
principles guiding human institutions, and they must
become a central focus of education. Hopefully,
such reflection upon these issues will contribute to
a better understanding of the war system and consequently to its abolition. Without significant
changes in education, we will be unable to respond
to the challenges of the war system.

A REVOLUTION IN EDUCATION

There are many project and program possibilities for such changes within the growing survival-
curriculum movement and also in projects dealing
with social issues and human development. Many of
these projects have an admitted crisis orientation,
rather than problem-centered, because there is a
general recognition that our present structrues and
processes for problem solution are inadequate to
meet the current situation. Michael Scriven was the
first to put forth a suggestive outline for a survival curriculum which must be developed to replace
the "war curriculum."[4] Other notable contributions
on the relationship between education and survival,
together with suggestions for curricular and pedagogical approaches, have been made by William H.
Boyer, of the University of Hawaii,[5] and Fannie R.
Shaftel, of Stanford University.[6] Although these
researchers carry out their work in the tradition of
social reconstruction, their writings call for an
activist commitment and, indeed, tend to be more
revolutionary than reformist, in that they document
the need for immediate and drastic changes in educational organization and practice.

It is our opinion that while there is a general
recognition of the need for educational change of
revolutionary proportions, there has been no systematic general diagnosis from which we may project a
comprehensive vision of change and design strategies
for bringing the vision into reality. Criticism and
problems are dealt with separately, if at all, and
consequently little or no headway is made toward
meeting the real needs of the schools.

Programs such as those advocated by Gordon[7] and

world-order educators should have top priorities,
not only because of their concern for peace, but
also because of the related goals espoused as essential to peace, social justice and economic welfare.
Such programs would make operational Earl S. Johnson's definition of the "politicization of social
knowledge," which is "the purposeful turning of
thought and action, collectively and individually,
toward the realities of our time--war, the rape of
nature, racism, hunger."[8]

World order seeks not only nonviolent solutions
to conflicts but *just* solutions to conflicts. It is
a normative, value-centered discipline which aspires
to more than the elimination of war, aiming also at
relieving human suffering resulting from drastically
disparate distribution of the world's wealth; from
the prejudices, discrimination, and oppression which
deprive far too many human beings of their rights
and dignity; and from the wanton exploitation of the
earth's resources by that powerful minority which
controls and uses them without regard to the interests of the people of this and succeeding generations. The search for just solutions is expressed
by world order as an attempt to achieve five goals:

1. *The minimization of violence or war preven-*
    tion
2. *The maximizing of economic welfare, or the*
    providing of better standards of living for
    more people
3. *The increasing of social justice by reliev-*
    ing discrimination and oppression
4. *The broadening of the democratic base of*
    public policymaking by increasing the par-
    ticipation of minorities and individuals in
    decision-making processes
5. *The improving of the quality of life*
    through restoration of ecological balance

World order examines these goals by asking some
significant questions: What is the present state of
the world with regard to peace, economic welfare,
social justice, political participation, and ecological balance? If we make no significant changes in
the international system, what is the state likely
to be in the next generation? If that state is, as
most trend analyses indicate, not one likely to
achieve peace and the other related world-order
goals, what changes in the system would be most

likely to do so? How can we bring about those changes?

The methodology of world order encompasses many techniques of inquiry and active learning which offer some hope for improving education on values and public issues. There are five basic steps to this methodology. The first is the *diagnosis;* a summary and analysis of world problems, their causes and their relationship to the values. The second step is a *prognosis* or a projection of the evolution of these problems and the potential for the emergence of other problems over a twenty-to-thirty-year period. These two are preliminary to a third step which actually attempts to deal with the future in the *positing of several alternative international systems* designed to resolve the problems defined in the first step. This projection is followed by the *evaluation of the alternatives* and the *selection of a preferred system*--the alternative which emerges from the evaluation as the one most likely to achieve peace, economic welfare and social justice in the world community. The final step, *transition,* plots the strategies and policies needed to transform the present world system into the "preferred world."[9]

It is these processes and questions which should be addressed to all students in every school in terms appropriate to their age and environment. It is the goals implicit in these questions which should form the central purposes of education not only *at all levels* but also *in all subjects*. They are raised in only a few of our schools now; if they are not raised in most schools long before the end of this decade, the schools will have made no contribution to survival or to peace. These issues and problems should provide the main content of curriculums in the 1970s.

PERSONAL IDENTITY AND WORLD CIVILIZATION

The personal realm is a major focus of the rapidly developing human-potential movement, another important area of survival programs and one which could well serve to complement world-order studies. In its efforts to help people regain or develop a sense of self, to cultivate, manage, and enjoy emotional responses and aesthetic experiences, the human-potential movement offers much promise of turning us away from some of the dehumanizing aspects of a complex technological society.

I would recommend the inclusion of such techniques as complements to world order rather than as primary program components, because they have less to offer in terms of immediate crisis management and institution building. While learning from these fields may help assure that new institutions may avoid the antihuman elements of the old and encourage the institutions' designers to include the possibility of human fulfillment as criteria for the desirability of proposed institutions, it does not contribute directly to the design of the structures. That is clearly a system problem, and systems change is our most immediate survival problem, the crucial component in establishing peace, and the main focus of world-order studies.

Another resource for program development in the personal and social realms lies in the field of world cultures and the emerging world civilization. Thus, there has been advocacy for the establishment of a center for inquiry and study aimed at bringing forth a world civilization (a network of common values and human institutions mixed with a plurality of cultures and life styles), the purpose being to aid in the deliberate synergizing of such elements to formulate a community of mankind. Programs such as this would offer us opportunities to study the various philosophies, interpretations of life, and definitions of what it is to be human which have been devised in diverse cultures and at different periods of human history.

With such a rich variety of resources to call upon, human beings may be better able to develop identities giving each one full personhood while enabling him to relate fully to his species. A person so identified may be better able to survive crises in the other realms and to adapt and expand his or her identity as his or her community grows. Schools therefore should teach world cultures with this purpose in mind, *not simply as they relate to American culture or compare to each other but as the infinite variety of human qualities, values, and life styles which form the total pool of human resources, the heritage of all humanity.*

LANGUAGE FACILITY FOR A MULTICULTURAL COMMUNITY

One of the prime requisites for peace is full
and accurate communication among peoples. The study
of other cultures, therefore, should include emer-
sion in another language, one in which the logic,
structure, and harmonies connote thought patterns,
sensitivities, and values vastly different from the
native culture of the learner. For generations,
educated Asians and Africans have learned about the
cultures of their conquerers by gaining fluency in
French, Dutch, Portuguese, or English. Westerners
should become equally fluent in languages, not to
command another tool for exploitation but to gain a
key to a wider portion of their own human heritage,
to come to understand more deeply other members of
their species, and thereby gain a wider sphere of
identification as part of humankind.

Mutual respect and human dignity for all can
only exist in a polyglot global society. Enforcement of one language for instruction and for the
economic and political life of a society is a phenomenon of the age of nationalism. If peace and human community building are major goals of education,
then the development of multiple language facility
should be one of the chief strategies in achieving
that goal. If human fulfillment is also one of the
goals, there is further need for teaching and learning in various languages, including the nonverbal
ones.

World institution builders should be able to
shift from one language to another with the same
ease and full appreciation of the medium being used,
as an accomplished musician displays in shifting
from one musical mode of composition to another.
Multilingual persons are more fully able to enjoy
and contribute to varieties of human experience and
to expand their identities to include still more
groups. Certainly such proficiency should be a major aim of educational programs for human development.

There are also important aspects of individual
survival to be benefited by polyglotism. The human
rights of minorities have often been violated by
states and societies in which power is applied and
justice rendered in the language of the governing
elites. There should be no room in a human community for such scenes as are now witnessed--persons
being tried in court procedures of which they do not
understand a word, in which they are charged with
violations of laws imposed on them by an alien cul-

ture in a language which to them is utterly "foreign." If the individual is to play an effective role in the world community, he or she must not be limited by the lack of language facility.

SYSTEMS APPROACH AND SURVIVAL SKILLS

Since groups who find a system intolerable may turn to violence to alter or overthrow the system, this should indeed be a core question in the curricula of the 1980s, as should these parallel questions: How can one change systems? How can one establish justice without violence? When legal recourses are inhumanly slow or stacked against the oppressed, what other alternatives can be projected to ameliorate their lot?

Scriven raises his question about systems in his list of recommendations for "survival skills." He also lists as a skill (because he asserts that in part it can be learned) that quality called "creativity," a skill I would refer to as "constructive imagination" or utopianism at its most pragmatic. Unless we can learn to create practical alternatives to violence, there can be no peace and little chance of long-range survival. The schools of the 1980s should be preparing students to conceive and put into effect alternative systems which are human, moral, and practical. They should be encouraging disciplined speculation on alternative life styles, forms of government, and social orders. They should as well be developing skills of evaluation to aid the young to select from various alternatives their preferences for modes of survival. Further, they should be helping the young to formulate strategies for change, and should be making it possible for them to test their strategies in practical action programs, such as the Omega program, which was born in a Jesuit high school in New York in the late 1960s, and is now spreading to schools in other areas. Omega students plan and carry out community-development projects, some in their own city, some going as far as Appalachia. They determine their own success by what they accomplish, and they are given academic credit for their work. The Omega program takes its philosophy from the ecumenism of Pope John, with special reference to his encyclical, *Pacem in Terris*, a document which has a mankind focus, and much of its strategy from Paulo Freire's concept of "conscientization," the process of becoming aware of the social and political structure, or "system," of which each individual is a part, and of striving to motivate and equip individuals not to "adapt" to the structures but to "use" them and where necessary to change them to meet their own needs. There is a frank and well-conceived moral element to the program, one which might well be emulated by "secular" schools, for, as Scriven asserts, "The survival curriculum is largely about morality in practice."[10]

There must be in our survival inquiry a careful investigation of the relationship between means and ends. Scriven recommends that "curricula at the *moment* should be organized around studying and *creating* the great revolutions of the past, present and future."[11] Yet most of us, educators and/or liberals, are caught in the *most acute moral dilemma of our time, the tension between the unacceptability of deliberate violence and the intolerability of gross injustice*. Discussion of this dilemma should be an integral part of the survival curriculum. Its resolution cannot be left either to those who will act without reflection or to those who reflect without action. To avoid this moral issue would be the greatest cop out of education, and indeed failure to confront it may make survival impossible.

NOTES

1. A summary of the Office of Education study is available from The Center for Global Perspectives, 218 E. 18 St., N.Y.C. 10013.

2. Pacem in Terris, Part V.

3. Richard A. Falk, & Saul H. Mendlovitz (Eds.), *The Strategy of World Order*. Vol. 1. New York: Institute World Order.

4. Scriven, Michael. Education for survival. In G. Kinley (Ed.), *The Ideal School*. Wilmette, Ill.: Kagg Press, 1969.

5. Boyer, William H. Education for survival. *Phi Delta Kappan*, January, 1971. (reprints available from the Institute for World Order)

6. Schaftel, Fannie R. A Survival Curriculum in the Social Studies. Address to the Southern California Social Studies Council, October, 1970.

7. Gordon, Edmund W. Building a Socially Support-

ive Environment. ERIC-IRCD Urban Disadvantages Series, No. 16, June, 1970.

8. Johnson, Earl S. Commentary on social studies
curriculum guidelines. *Social Education*, 1972, *36*,
(3), 260.

9. Reardon, Betty. Prologue. *Media and Methods*,
October, 1969. (Reprints available from the Institute for World Order)

10. *Ibid*, 52.

11. *Ibid*. Italics added--and please note that the
"moment" was dated 1969.

*BETTY REARDON has been Director of the School
Program of the World Law Fund and then Institute for
World Order in New York since 1963. This post coor-
dinates programs of teacher services, teacher education, and secondary curriculum development in the
various areas of world order.*
*She received her B.A. from Wheaton College,
Norton, Massachusetts, and her M.A. in history from
New York University.*
*Her professional experience includes nine years
of teaching the social studies at the secondary level. During these years as a classroom teacher, she
also served from 1958 until 1963 as a member of the
Executive Committee of Leadership and World Society,
a grant-giving organization which awarded funds to
high schools for experimental and innovative programs in world affairs teaching. Responsibilities
consisted of reviewing and evaluating applications,
and visits to schools to observe experimental programs in action.*
*From 1963 until 1967, she served as Associate
Director of Leadership and World Society, a post
which involved administration of the program, the
pre-evaluation of applications, presentation to the
Committee, and nationwide visits to schools involved
in such experimental programs.*
*Among other professional affiliations, Betty
Reardon is Chairman of the Advisory Committee on International Activities of the National Council for
the Social Studies. She is on the National Task
Force on International Education (founder and organizer). Between 1963 and 1969, she was a member of
the Social Studies Committee of the National Association of Independent Schools (organizer of Wing-*

*spread Conference on the New Social Studies). In
1968, she served as a member of the International
Relations Committee of the National Council for the
Social Studies, and as a member of the Social Science Education Consortium. More recently, she has
served as Chairperson of the Consortium on Peace Research, Education, and Development.*

SOME OTHER PUBLICATIONS BY BETTY A. REARDON

- With Margaret Carter. Procedures for analyzing
  and clarifying values related to human rights.
  Pennsylvania Council Social Studies Journal, Winter, 1972.
- Beyond Nationalism: Education and Survival. In
  Dwight Allen, & Jeffrey Hecht (Eds.), *Controversy
  in Education,* volume of the Massachusetts University Series in Education. Philadelphia: W.B.
  Saunders, 1973.
- With Jack Fraenkel, & Margaret Carter. *Peacekeep-
  ing,* part of the Perspectives in World Order Ser-
  ies. New York: Random House, 1973.
- With Jack Fraenkel, & Margaret Carter. *The Strug-
  gle for Human Rights: A Question of Values,* part
  of the Perspectives in World Order series. New
  York: Random House, 1974.
- Women's movements and human futures. *Convergence,*
  1975, *8*(3).
- With Curtis Colby. *War Criminals, War Victims:
  Andersonville, Nuremburg, Hiroshima, My Lai,* part
  of the Crises in World Order Series. New York:
  Random House, 1974.
- With Margaret Carter, Estela Matriano, & Barbara
  Stanford. *Discrimination: The Cycle of Injustice.*
  Sidney: Holt-Saunders, 1977.

*Reprints of articles and booklets by Betty A. Rear-
don are available from The World Without War Book-
store, 67 East Madison St., Chicago, Ill. 60603.*

6. Personal Commitment to Nonviolent Social Change (A Playboy Interview of Joan Baez)

A Candid Conversation with the Dedicated Anti-War Activist and Folk Singer [1970]

It's been 11 years since a slim, long-haired 18-year-old girl appeared at the Newport Folk Festival and transfixed the audience with what one writer called her "achingly pure soprano." After dominating all accounts of that event, she returned to Newport the next year, 1960, and her first album (on Vanguard) was released that fall. Its sales were unprecedented for a folk singer self-accompanied on guitar, and her subsequent concert appearances were unfailingly triumphant.

This gifted young woman was Joan Baez. Born on Staten Island in 1941--her mother Scotch-English in background, her father of Mexican parentage--she grew up peripatetic, because her physicist father moved his family often in the course of his work as a researcher and UNESCO consultant. Much of that growing up took place in small towns in New York and California, where she sang in school choirs and eventually taught herself to play the guitar. When the Baezes moved to Boston, Joan studied drama briefly at Boston University, but her increasing involvement in the Cambridge-Boston nexus of folk clubs then flourishing pulled her out of school and into a singing vocation that led to her ascent into the national consciousness in the early Sixties.

Although the music scene has changed radically since then--having become rock-driven, electrified and ecumenical--Joan Baez still draws huge audiences and remains a singular presence. Her attraction now, however, is based on much more than the undiminished power of her voice. She has become a leading activist for nonviolence as a way of life, as a way to create what she calls "the revolution"--a society in which the sanctity of life transcends all other values, including nationalism.

The emergence of Joan Baez as a battling and embattled force for her extramusical convictions began in 1963, when she refused to appear on ABC-TV's "Hootenanny" because that network was black-listing fellow folk singer Pete Seeger. The next year, she began to engage in tax resistance to the Vietnam war and to defense spending and, ever since, has refused to pay that part of her income taxes which she estimates will be used for death. The Government doggedly collects it, anyway--usually by attaching her income--along with a penalty for nonpayment.

During the Sixties, she also became a highly visible and vulnerable civil rights activist, marching and singing in the South as well as in the North. Among other causes, she has assisted Cesar Chavez in his organizing efforts and boycotts on behalf of Mexican-American migrant farm workers. But her primary focus in recent years has been against the war and the draft. In October 1967, she was arrested with 118 others for blocking the Armed Forces Induction Center in Oakland; after serving a ten-day sentence at Santa Rita Prison Farm, she was arrested again in December for sitting in front of the Oakland Induction Center. The result was another prison term--this one for 31 days.

PLAYBOY's interview with her--the longest and most comprehensive she has ever given--was conducted by Nat Hentoff in New York, where she had come to appear at a concert in Madison Square Garden. As is now the rule--at her insistence--none of the seats at her concerts costs more than two dollars. Twenty thousand came and several thousand more were turned away. Her program ranged from the old labor-union organizing song, "Joe Hill," to the Rolling Stones' "As Tears Go By." Between songs, she spoke of her implacable opposition to violence, nationalism, hate and exploitation.

As critic Marlene Nadle wrote of the event in *The Village Voice,* "Baez, by her presence, reaffirmed the positive, now dimming side of the movement, its humanity, its love, its moral choices. In her continuing faith in the power of nonviolence, she was the symbol of (what) many in the audience would have liked to have been if disillusion or temperament or fashion or reason hadn't taken them on to different things." They listened to her and cheered her; for, as a member of the audience said, "Baez may not be fashionable or hip. But she's discovered the secret. She always knows who she's coming as."

Hentoff talked with Miss Baez throughout the
day following the concert. "I've known Joan for ten
years," he writes. "She's always had immovable integrity; but at the beginning, it occasionally manifested itself in a rather aloof manner, and those
whom she resisted on matters of principle sometimes
mistook her shyness for arrogance. Through the
years, I've watched Joan become noticeably more re-
laxed as a performer--and evolve into a growing figure of controversy. Simultaneously, her dedication
to nonviolence has become deeper and much more
knowledgeable. What most impressed me in this interview with Joan was how thoughtfully and honestly
she has faced the ambiguities and the practical difficulties inherent in a total commitment to active
pacifism.

"We talked in her nondescript room at a large,
equally nondescript motel on the West Side of Man-
hattan. In the elevators and the corridors, Muzak
was inescapable and the place itself was equally ar-
tificial--everything, from walls to carpets, having
been made of a material intended to imitate some
other material. I asked her why she had chosen such
plastic surroundings. She laughed. 'Traveling with
the boys who accompany me, we all get to looking a
little weird, and it's just not worth the sweat of
going into a fancy hotel. And I'm more comfortable
not being waited on with the silver trays and all
that stuff. So I just wanted somewhere that was as
totally mediocre as you could get, and this is it.
They've put the Jefferson Airplane in this wing with
us--you know, keeping all the freaks in one quarter.
But that's fine. We can go get ice barefoot and do
just what we want.'

"In the room, Joan sat down and stretched back
in her chair. Her black hair, which used to fall
past her shoulders, was now cut short. With some
women, short hair evokes hardness and toughness, but
Joan had never seemed more feminine. In a blue-
flower-print dress, her feet bare, her figure still
lithe, there was a glow in her that I'd never seen
before. Perhaps it was the pregnancy, which ended
on December second, with the birth of a boy, Gabriel.
Perhaps it was the assurance she has gained as a
practicing pacifist who knows how much she can sacrifice and yet do much more than survive. I wondered how much room was left for music, now that she
was so wholly involved as an activist; the interview
began on that note."

PLAYBOY: You've said several times in the past
year, "Music isn't my thing anymore." Why not?
BAEZ: What I meant was that music *alone* isn't
enough for me. If I'm not on the side of life in
action as well as in music, then all those sounds,
however beautiful, are irrelevant to the only real
question of this century: How do we stop men from
murdering each other, and what am I doing with my
life to help stop the murdering? Whatever I do in
music now has to be part of that larger context. I
used to be called the folk-singer pacifist; now I'm
considered a pacifist folk singer. It's just a new
set of priorities.
PLAYBOY: When did you begin to change those priorities?
BAEZ: I can't answer that with a definite date.
But there are certain assumptions, certain basic
convictions I've had since I was a little girl--be-
ing against violence, knowing that I didn't have the
right to do injury to anyone. The problem all along
for me has been trying to define what I see happening and what I see coming and then knowing what to
do about it. Gradually, the means and ends of ac-
tion--and means and ends have to be the same--became
clearer. In 1964, I began refusing to pay the
amount of my income taxes that would go for defense
spending. The next year, I got deeper into civil
rights activities, and I also started the Institute
for the Study of Nonviolence. Then there were the
anti-war demonstrations I was part of; and by the
summer of 1967, I was helping organize a national
draft-card turn-in day. Then I served jail terms
for refusing to move from in front of induction centers; and in 1968, I went on a college tour with my
husband, David, to talk about resistance, about
finding ways to really change things--ways that
don't use violence as a means of change.
PLAYBOY: After one of your appearances on the *Dick
Cavett Show*, ABC commentator Howard K. Smith delivered an angry editorial in which he called you self-
righteous and negative and said that, in trying for
utopian perfection, you were copping out on realistic, pragmatic approaches to change. Others have
gone on to say that you provoke the very violence
you're against by demonstrating and encouraging
draft resistance.
BAEZ: I know the arguments. First of all, people
like to talk about being "pragmatic" because it's
easier that way to avoid the extraordinarily hard
work necessary to really change things. And the violence they say I provoke is already there; we

haven't caused it. That argument is like people in
the South a few years ago saying, "Things were all
calm around here until those troublemaking civil
rights people came barging in." But things weren't
calm. All kinds of tensions and hostilities had
been festering below the surface. Things are at the
bursting point all over the world. Every once in a
while, they explode--in the Middle East, in Vietnam,
somewhere else. It's as if the entire world were
infected with a disease and the people in power were
running around with this great big hypodermic nee-
dle, jamming it into one place after another. The
only catch is that they're injecting the wrong
fluids. When there's an eruption, they jam in the
same fluid that's part of the disease, which is violence.

    I know how difficult it is to even think about
giving up this pet solution to problems. If you
hang onto violence, you have something that kind of
carried people through all these centuries. And if
you go along with it--even in a nuclear age--you
figure it might carry you through this, too. But if
all recourse to violence is taken away, you're
forced to really use your mind to search for alternatives. And you're forced to acknowledge--and this
is what *I* mean by revolution--that no man has the
right to do injury to another person or to be an accomplice in the doing of injury. This means you
have to recognize that everybody is equal and
there's no such thing as an enemy.

PLAYBOY: Wouldn't you have considered Adolf Hitler
an enemy?

BAEZ: He was a human being, too. But recognizing
his humanity didn't mean you had to like him and it
certainly didn't mean you had to carry out his orders. In a civilized society, people wouldn't have
followed him. They would have seen that he was a
wreck, a very sick man; and, seeing that, they would
have gotten him some help. The term enemy just gets
in the way of understanding that we are all human
beings. Admittedly, it takes an awful lot of un-
brainwashing to come to that point. To be this kind
of revolutionary requires the right-winger to throw
away his flag and the left-winger to forget all
those posters about power coming out of the barrel
of a gun.

PLAYBOY: Then you are against any violence for any
cause, however just that cause might be?

BAEZ: Yes, I see only one way. I don't think anybody said it better than Tolstoy: The difference be
tween establishment violence and revolutionary vio-

lence is the difference between dog shit and cat
shit. But insisting on nonviolence doesn't mean remaining passive or giving up. It means always
searching for that third alternative. Sure, it's a
hard search. We've had thousands of years of training in violence, so it's very difficult to bring
people around to even bother looking for that alternative.

PLAYBOY: You say you're absolutely against violence; but what would you do if you yourself were
being attacked violently, if David were being attacked or if you saw a child being physically attacked? Would you just stand there and do nothing
to counter the violence?

BAEZ: That remains to be seen. But after all, I'm
limited in what violence I could do. I don't carry
a gun. I don't know how to use a knife. So I'd be
reduced to having to use my feeble mind to get us
all out of a situation like that. Look, all I can
say is that I know people who have trained themselves to think of the third alternative rather than
faint from fright or club somebody on the head. And
those people have done well in situations like the
kind you describe, not only with regard to their own
self-defense but also in the defense of people near
them. I remember one night, a group of protesters
was sitting in at the San Francisco Federal Building. A guy was out there with a knife, swinging it
around, threatening them. And Ira Sandperl, who's
been with me in the Institute for the Study of Nonviolence from the beginning, walked up to that man
and said, "Give me the knife." Ira took it out of
his hand. You have to overcome the fear in yourself
when you walk into a situation like that. You don't
know whether he's going to get you in the gut or
not, but you know what you have to do.

PLAYBOY: Have you ever been in a situation where
you were able to stop violence through nonviolence?

BAEZ: One of the times I was in prison, there was
a girl who had done six months of dead time. She
didn't know what her sentence was. She had no money
and there was no lawyer working for her. She just
sat there, waiting to appear in court. And when she
finally did get sentenced, the time she'd been waiting wouldn't count; it wouldn't come off her sentence. Periodically, she used to get just furious
and pick a fight with somebody. She was a black
girl, and one time she picked a fight with a white
girl from the kitchen. I knew the white girl was a
nonfighter, so I went over to try to talk to the
black girl. "Get out of my way!" she said. But I

stayed where I was standing, so that she couldn't
move unless she kicked me aside. She didn't want to
kick me. She had hold of the white girl's hair and
was trying to kick her in the stomach, and there I
was--in the way. Finally, her kicks got milder and
then she exploded in tears. And I hugged her.
PLAYBOY: Do you call that an example of nonviolence
that isn't passive?
BAEZ: Yes, I *did* something. I got in the way. But
I wish that word nonviolence could be junked. I
mean, nonviolence doesn't really *say* it. We haven't
thought of a word yet in English that does say it.
But the Indians have. They use the term *Satyagraha*,
which means "truth force." The word force begins to
give you some idea of what the third alternative involves. To be part of this kind of fighting, you
have to be forceful; you have to be aggressive.
Passivity is, in a sense, a worse enemy than violence.
PLAYBOY: Gandhi once said that as deeply as he was
committed to *Satyagraha*, he would rather a person
took violent action than none at all.
BAEZ: Yes, he said that; and in a way, it's fortunate he did, because passivity is so huge an obstacle
to change. But in another way, it was an unfortun-
ate remark, because that's the one thing everybody
seems to pick out of everything Gandhi ever wrote.
And they try to use it to justify some violent act
of their own, ignoring the fact that Gandhi spent
practically his entire life trying to teach people
the other way.
PLAYBOY: How would you describe this other way?
BAEZ: Putting the sanctity of life above everything
else.
PLAYBOY: In all circumstances? Would you have
placed the sanctity of Nazi lives above the fact
that they were murdering millions of Jews and other
people?
BAEZ: Killing is killing, whether it's killing a
Nazi or anyone else. And killing leads to more
killing. If the Jews in Germany under the Nazis had
known anything about organized nonviolent resistance, I think fewer of them would have been killed.
Most, however, were passive; God knows that's understandable, because they were so afraid. But if they
had refused to cooperate, consider how much manpower
it would have taken to simply move them. Why, at
one point, it took only two storm troopers to round
up more than 600 people. But if millions of Jews
had refused to move, they could have slowed down the
Nazi machinery enormously and, in the process, there

would have been no way the other Germans could have
avoided knowing what was going on. The resistance
of the Jews would have been too visible. And there
would have been no way to keep the information about
what was going on from people in other countries.
The whole world would have been watching; and with
the Jews resisting inside and the pressure building
outside, I think there would have been far less
killing and perhaps it might have stopped entirely.
PLAYBOY: Your critics would say you're unrealistic
to allege that violence can't cure violence, since--
to cite a contemporary example--you don't take into
account what might happen to America if violence
were done against it and it offered no armed resistance. Would you leave the country defenseless?
BAEZ: Yes, because as long as you go on defending
the *country*, you go on killing--others and yourself.
You see, the defense of country has absolutely nothing to do with the defense of people. Once we get
rid of the obsession with defending one's country,
we will begin defending *life*. We will begin to have
a real sense of what it's like to take care of
people instead of trying to watch over a piece of
land. That's why I hate flags. I despise any flag,
not just the American flag. It's a symbol of a
piece of land that's considered more important than
the human lives on it. Look at what happened over
the attempt to create a People's Park in Berkeley.
PLAYBOY: Isn't defending a country very different
from fighting over a piece of real estate in Berkeley?
BAEZ: Is it? I don't think so. We have to rear-
range in our minds what defense actually means, and
that includes defense of country. Does it mean
you're going to try to protect the boundaries of a
piece of land, or does it mean you're going to try
to help the people on that piece of land--and all
other pieces of land--live a better life? What I'm
saying is that we have to begin to dispose of the
very concept of nation. I don't think we can survive if nations stay.
PLAYBOY: How would you deal with an invasion by another nation that didn't share your zeal for the
abolition of all nations?
BAEZ: To begin with, you have to examine the American people's paranoia about invasion. It simply
isn't rational to seriously consider that possibility. But, all right, let's say all of a sudden,
here they come--those little yellow bastards--just
as you always expected. Well, if we're in the state
we're in now, there will probably be a nuclear war.

But if we've gotten our heads together to the point of recognizing that a nuclear reaction would be insane, we will already have made some assumptions about how to deal with invaders. We will have begun to understand the concept of a general strike by the people, and that means understanding the logic of invasion. When an invader comes into a country, he doesn't run the country. He gets *you* to run it. If enough people in a country are really involved in truth force, they can't be pushed by its invaders into running it.

PLAYBOY: Then you would advocate that Americans resist invasion nonviolently.

BAEZ: More than that. If the invader were rushing into your home town, about to take over all your hamburger stands and used-car lots, you would say, "If you're hungry, I'll feed you. If you're thirsty, I'll give you something to drink. But if you intend to run my life, forget it."

PLAYBOY: Suppose, after listening to all that, the invader decides to shoot you down or ship you off to a concentration camp. Then what?

BAEZ: Obviously, you can never be certain of the response to any action you take   All you can do, therefore, is be consistent with your own beliefs; and if that leads to death or imprisonment, at least you won't have broken faith with yourself.

PLAYBOY: For your approach to work as a deterrent to violence, wouldn't the invader have to be reachable on a human level, and wouldn't the vast majority of the invaded people have to feel and act as you do? Otherwise, isn't it likely that large-scale sniping would take place and that the invader would take revenge on everyone in sight?

BAEZ: That's right. That's why, if there were an invasion now--at the stage most Americans are now in--I think we'd be doomed. One can only hope our circle will grow until, eventually, most Americans would act in a different manner. But if you feel strongly enough about working for this kind of revolution, you have to act anyway, hope or not. You see, people say about the Germans under Hitler: "Why didn't somebody do something *back then?* Why did they all follow him like that?" Well, that's exactly where we're at right now. That's exactly what draft resistance is about. This country is the biggest bunch of "good Germans" on the face of the earth right now. And the resistance is saying: "We're not going to take part in it. We're pulling out now and we're going to do what we can to convince others to join us to stop the killing." I

grant it doesn't look too hopeful. We're fighting
not just a wave; it's more like a tidal wave. But
we do exist. People are saying: "I refuse to take
part in violence--any violence. I refuse to take
part in the nation-state, in the United States military, in the institutions supporting it." That
means they're also saying: "I am one molecule in a
tidal wave, but I'm going to go the other way." Of
course, it's not an easy thing to do, but it gets
easier as you find your brothers. That's why the
draft-resistance movement is a very exciting thing.
It started with only three people about four years
ago, and now there are at least 10,000 and maybe as
many as 50,000 of us.

PLAYBOY: About 1000 of that number--all of them
draft resisters, including your husband--are serving
prison terms. Why have so few opponents of the war
been willing to put themselves on the line?

BAEZ: Don't underestimate the number of resisters.
In addition to the thousands in Canada and abroad,
many more than 1000 have stayed in America and are
subject to prison terms. They just haven't been
arrested or imprisoned yet. No one knows exactly
how many there are. A woman I know who worked for
the San Jose draft board was told that 2000 people
had sent their draft cards back to that particular
board. "What do you do with them?" she asked. They
said, "We stick them in a drawer and we shut it, because we don't *know* what to do with them." Now, if
there are at least 2000 cards filed in a drawer in
San Jose, think of what must be going on in other
draft centers. There may well be at least 50,000
draft resisters in that situation.

PLAYBOY: On what basis does the Government move
against some and not against others?

BAEZ: The loudest ones are prosecuted first. David
was indicted within 13 days after he refused induction. Or someone may turn in his card and wait a
year to engage in some political action, some kind
of demonstration. If they hear about him--bingo--
he's indicted. But there simply isn't enough court
time to handle everybody who's resisting. Many
haven't heard a thing yet. Their cards are blowin'
in the wind.

PLAYBOY: Do young men still turn in cards to you at
concerts?

BAEZ: Lots of times. I remember particularly at
Ann Arbor a while ago, as I walked off after the
last encore, a deliriously happy guy handed me his
card. I took it and asked him into our little room
backstage, where I kind of grilled him. "How long

have you been thinking about it?" He smiled and said
said, "It's been months." "OK," I said, "what do
your want me to do with it?" "I don't care," he
said, "anything." "Let's burn half of it." I suggested, "and send the other half--with your name on
it--to the Government. If you burn it all, it might
take a long time before they'd know you'd done it.
This way, you're telling them what you've done and
they have to go looking for you. It adds a bit more
nuisance for them." He said, "Fine." So we burned
it in an ashtray and sprinkled the ashes all over
the room. I also get mail from people who have
turned in their cards or are about to. That kind of
mail has been increasing. More and more guys are
finally coming to the edge, and there are others who
have begun thinking of resistance as a reality for
the first time.
PLAYBOY: There are also increasing numbers of college students who pledge--as many did at graduation
ceremonies last year--to resist the draft if called.
BAEZ: I don't hold those pledges to be worth much.
Sure, then sympathies are in the right direction;
but when the penalty is as heavy as it is for draft
resistance, I'll believe they really mean it when I
see it. Some do, others may not. Sometimes it's
just a fad and, therefore, meaningless. Last year,
a boy in a school we visited told us, "I'm going to
run for office on a resistance ticket. Everybody
who votes for me has to turn his card in." "Have
you turned your card in?" I asked. "Well, I will,"
he said, "after I've won."
PLAYBOY: Is Resistance, the group to which David
belongs, any more important or effective than the
other alternatives to the draft?
BAEZ: Well, let's look at the alternatives. Everybody has four alternatives if he doesn't want to accept the draft. First, you can try to be classified
a conscientious objector. I understand the C.O.
position, but I don't think it's politically effective. It acknowledges the right of the Government
to make that decision, but it should be *your* decision.
    A second alternative is to leave the country
and go somewhere like Canada. Now, I've been in
Canada a couple of times and from what I've seen of
the people who have gone there to avoid the draft,
I'd say that those who haven't made up their minds
yet ought not to kid themselves about what going to
Canada means. If you're going there because you
don't want to go to jail, that's fine. But if
you're going to Canada because you think you can be-

come more effective in working for peace, you're
pulling a phony on yourself. The people I've met in
Canada who went there under that impression are dis-
illusioned and sad. I don't condemn anybody for going there, but I do feel you have to be really clear
in your head as to why you're going. To save yourself is one thing, but if you're concerned with more
than that, the battle is here.

   The third alternative is going underground.
There's a lot of that and it seems damn unhealthy to
me--people hiding and changing their names. That's
the official underground--people who know they're
being chased and have to keep running. But there's
also another kind of underground: You don't register and you don't let yourself be known. You hope
your name never turns up. But when you do that,
you're not clear with yourself. You don't know what
would happen if you even had to really face up to
the confrontation. You're never really sure where
you stand. I don't think that's a healthy way to
live, either.

   The fourth alternative is to resist. You are
open in public about what you're doing and why. You
refuse to carry a card. You refuse to be given a
number. You refuse to say to the Government, "OK,
here are the next years of my life." And you do
more than refuse: you organize resistance. And
thousands are making that decision. They're making
that eminently sane decision in the midst of all the
insanity around us.
PLAYBOY: Why do you call that decision sane?
BAEZ: My definition of sanity in this context would
be *seeing* again, seeing each man as your brother,
getting back your vision, so that you couldn't do
harm to another.
PLAYBOY: What makes you so certain that you won't
eventually be driven by desperation to take part in
some form of violent revolution?
BAEZ: As long as I see one kid's face a day, that
will be enough to remind me that I can't take part
in killing. You remember that movie, *The Battle of
Algiers*, about the Algerians' fight for independence? There were people in this country who saw it
as a handbook for violent revolution. But what I
saw in it was an insistence that, in their terms,
the most revolutionary act anybody can perform is to
be able to blow up a room full of people after having seen children in it. They made it clear in the
movie that to be really brave and really with it,
you could look at a little kid with ice cream all
over his mouth--and then blow him up. All for the

revolution! Well, I don't think that's revolutionary. I think it's insane.
PLAYBOY: What leads you to believe--speaking of the
world now, not just about America--that there will
ever be enough people who feel as you do?
BAEZ: I don't in the least underestimate how difficult it's going to be to end this insanity of dependence on violence. In fact, Tanzania is the only
place I've ever heard of that had a rational discussion about nonviolence and the nation-state. Its
leader, Julius Nyerere, called in Quaker types from
all over to discuss the question of how he could defend Tanzania nonviolently. I don't know how many
days it lasted, but the discussion ended with the
conclusion that there was *no way*.

   This goes back to what I was saying before.
There is a fundamental difference between nonviolently defending the *people* of Tanzania and the *country*
of Tanzania. You can't do the second; but it's possible to do the first. It took even Gandhi a long
time to recognize that difference. In his early
years, when somebody asked how his family was, he'd
say, "All of India is my family." But by the end,
he knew better. If he were alive today, his answer
would be, "All the *world* is my family." He saw that
when India gained her independence, not only India
but two competitive nation-states had been born.
There was also Pakistan. And then he started to
fast again, because he realized that, in a sense, he
had blown it. The nation-state, any nation-state,
has nothing to do with brotherhood. But that took
him a lifetime to learn.
PLAYBOY: Dr. Martin Luther King, Jr., often referred to Gandhi as a major influence on him. Do
you see any major differences in their philosophies?
BAEZ: The main difference was that King represented
what historian Staughton Lynd calls "petitionary
nonviolence." That means you get a lot of people to
agree to put pressure on Congress to change a few
things, so that the society will be a little less
corrupt. It amounts to your always being in a position of *asking*. That's what King was involved in--
having his people patiently ask for some degree of
power. Gandhi, on the other hand, assumed that the
power was the people's and that they must act on
that assumption. He'd say, "Today we're going to
take salt from the ocean, no matter what the government says about its right to tax and control it."
And by the time he got to the ocean, thousands of
people were walking with him and they had done it!
They weren't asking anybody for anything and they

weren't waving guns around, either.
PLAYBOY: Didn't you agree with Dr. King's celebration of love as a force for change?
BAEZ: I loved Dr. King and wanted to work with that
revolution, but he and I agreed on very few things.
I kept asking him, "What is it you're trying to do?
What are you really trying to change?" At that
point, for instance, banks run by blacks were growing out of some of his organizations; and this development was considered revolution! He'd say,
"Well, the black keys and the white keys on the
piano are out of tune. We have to get them into
tune, and this is one way." My answer was: "But
the whole fucking orchestra is shot, so what good
are black banks going to do?"
PLAYBOY: There are black people who would consider
that statement exceedingly smug. From their point
of view, banks run by blacks are essential in an
economy so weighted against black people. If black
banks will help black neighborhoods, how can you--
white and nonpoor--justify that kind of criticism?
BAEZ: I'm not preaching to anybody. Obviously, until there are alternatives that make better sense to
black people, they'll go on doing what seems to fit
this society's definition of progress. And that includes building black banks. It boils down to what
you're going to do with your energy, and I'm not going to put any of mine into advocating or supporting
blue, yellow, pink or black banks. I think the
whole economic system is bad, and having black banks
isn't going to make it any better. But I understand
those who think that since there are white banks,
there ought to be black banks, too. To me, however,
it's shortsighted. And I thought King was shortsighted. His context wasn't any broader than America as it is. I think King was an American first, a
good citizen and a preacher second, a black man
third and an exponent of nonviolence fourth. If you
remember, King delayed in coming out against the
Vietnam war. He had terrific pressures from some of
his own black brothers, who kept saying, "That's not
our revolution. It will get in the way of what we
have to do here." But we'd say, "For Christ's sake,
spit it out. You can't sit on something like that
when the world's blowing up." Then, little by little, he got to the point at which he finally felt
strong enough to speak out.
PLAYBOY: More and more black people are doing
things now--organizing for power in their own communities, trying to gain control over their schools,
trying to improve their housing. Many blacks would

tell you that you have an enormous amount of gall to preach the doctrine of nonviolence while they're still living in poverty and their kids are still locked into ghettos.

BAEZ: First of all, I don't go around preaching to them. That's a sin--going to somebody you've been oppressing all your life and telling him how to act. But, on the other hand, if someone were seriously looking for an alternative, if someone were to ask me about ways to become really unoppressed, I couldn't in good conscience say, "The Black Panthers have some hints for you," because I don't think what they propose is a real solution. I think violence leads to more violence and finally to disaster. But if I were asked, I'd say that some other people might have some hints. Like Gandhi. He was an oppressed person. He began his career in *Satyagraha* when he was thrown off a train in South Africa for being the wrong color. And I would say that probably the best example now is Danilo Dolci. He was a student of architecture who went to Sicily to look at ruins and ended up seeing ruined people. He then forgot all about being an architect and started organizing in villages against the Mafia, against the Church and against the Sicilian government.

Dolci has done some very revolutionary things there, but because they're not spectacular in size, hardly anyone here has heard about them. The reverse strike, for instance. I don't think anybody has tried that in this country, but he has in Sicily. The roads from village to village were dilapidated and worthless; they needed rebuilding, and the people needed jobs. He asked the government to pay the people to rebuild the roads. Petitionary nonviolence again. But then, after working with Dolci, they said: "The hell with it! We'll rebuild our own roads." So they had a reverse strike and went out and rebuilt roads for themselves.

PLAYBOY: How would you apply that technique in America?

BAEZ: Well, let's look at what alternative there might have been to all that violence at San Francisco State last year. Suppose the people who were fighting over that piece of land and screaming "Get the pigs off our campus" had, instead, gone to one apartment building in San Francisco and organized a strike--a strike involving renters in a deteriorating building refusing to pay the rent and using that money to fix up the place. That would have been a more intelligent thing to do than scream about who controls the campus. Sure, a rent strike

wouldn't have gotten the press coverage the fighting
did. But it would have directly benefited the lives
of some of the people who were being claimed as
brothers by those screaming on the campus.
PLAYBOY: That is precisely what the Panthers claim
they're already doing--organizing people in neighborhoods around such basic issues as housing and
schools.
BAEZ: Well, I can't claim to be up on what everybody in the Panthers is doing. But I did read a recent issue of their newspaper and it looked pretty
scary to me. All the cartoons, all the articles in
it were so loaded with hate rhetoric that I can't
identify with it. More than that, I want to fight
it. I want to say, "Don't you see what all that
hate is going to lead to?" One time in San Francisco, David and I attended a conference of people who
had decided not to register for the draft, and there
were, like, 50 high school kids there--boys and
girls. And somebody invited a Panther, because he
felt that group should have its say, even if it had
nothing to do with nonregistration. The Panther
came in with three guards, stationed them at the
doors and then started waving around a book on the
Mafia. "This is a good guide," he was saying.
"They know how to get power." David and I re-
strained ourselves as long as we could and then we
finally said, "Do you see the logical conclusion of
what you're doing? If your equation is A plus A
plus A plus A, you're not going to get B. You're
going to get A. If you use shit plus shit plus
shit, you end up with a pile of shit."
PLAYBOY: There is another thesis, expounded most
notably in Frantz Fanon's *The Wretched of the Earth,*
that regards violence as a key stage of self liberation in which those who have been oppressed purge
themselves of feelings of impotence through acts of
violence.
BAEZ: I don't agree, and I would point out that
Fanon himself shows in his book a number of people
who experienced that kind of purge and weren't in
such good shape afterward. When you do violence to
another, you're also doing violence to yourself;
your're diminishing your own humanity. That's true
even when, in the Panthers' case, it's just the
rhetoric of violence they're indulging in. I do
recognize that they've been doing some good things--
the less flashy stuff, like giving children break-
fast. I'm not about to knock that. But in their
publications and their speeches, the emphasis is on
sticking pigs. I can't see how you're going to nur-

ture or increase anyone's humanity by thinking and
talking like that.
PLAYBOY: The Weatherman faction of SDS insists that
a fully humanistic society can't be achieved unless
actual violence is committed against the symbols of
what they call the present imperialist-capitalist
society. Only that kind of violence, they say, can
awaken people to the repressiveness and brutality of
their national institutions. We would think you
disagree.
BAEZ: Yes, that's a completely stupid approach.
You don't enlighten people by frightening them; you
create more barriers that way, more divisions between people. And all you accomplish for yourselves
is to get your heads busted. It's utterly self-defeating. There's no violent way to get people together in brotherhood. It's like killing for peace.
It makes no sense.
PLAYBOY: Can't electoral politics be a way of
changing society?
BAEZ: I've tried on and off to act on that assumption, but it's the wrong base for action. If you
remember, the peace candidata against Barry Gold-
water in 1964 was Lyndon Johnson. David puts it another way when people start talking about who
they're voting for. "You see a gigantic wave," he
says, "and there's a surfer on top. You don't
shout, 'Wow, look at that surfer pushing that wave
around!' Obviously, if you look at what's happening, there's only a limited amount of distance the
surfer on top of that wave can travel from right to
left." Well, that's what right and left in our
electoral politics is all about. Until you can
change what's underneath--the wave itself--and not
just ride the top, you can only go a certain distance either way. We're not going to be able to
build institutions that really work for everyone until there is first a fundamental change in the way
people live and in the way they relate to one another. When people have their vision back, new institutions will then grow out of that new kind of
society. And they'll be flexible, responsive, open
to change. I know that it's hard for a lot of people to see this. The first thing I hear is: "In
this new society of yours, what are you going to do
about traffic and about collecting the garbage?"
PLAYBOY: How do you answer that?
BAEZ: If the revolution were for real, people would
care for one another, and out of that caring would
come real agreement on how to deal with traffic and
garbage collection. What it comes down to is that

if people can get to really *see* themselves and others, they'll find ways to take care of all the problems of living together. That's essentially what I mean when I say I'm politically ahead. It's not that I have a blueprint detailing exactly how the new society is going to work. But I do see far enough ahead to know that unless people have the vision to care about one another, no blueprint is going to lead to fundamental changes in the way we live.

PLAYBOY: Your detractors would call those ideas ingenuous and naive. Critic Ellen Willis, for example, reviewing your book *Daybreak*, wrote: "I find ...her moral approach to politics offensively escapist."

BAEZ: It really annoys me when people talk about me as being an escapist and impractical. Is it escapist, when we're on the very edge of World War Three, to act againt violence? Is it practical to be so tied up with the nation-state mentality that we couldn't get food through to Biafra? I'll tell you who's impractical and escapist: anybody who thinks we're going to survive this century if we continue as we are--putting our taxes where we put them now, letting our brothers be sent off to war. *That* person is impractical and naive and foolish. You see, what we're doing now isn't just imperfect. It's insane.

PLAYBOY: You're calling millions of people insane or accomplices in acts of insanity. Doesn't that indictment come through as a kind of moral elitism that might well alienate the masses of people you want to reach?

BAEZ: Yes, I'm familiar with that criticism, and part of it is very good and very real. There are times when you get to thinking that you have the one true light and you want to spread it around. Then, when someone reminds you that you don't know all the answers, you come crashing down. It's a good thing to be told your ego's running away with you; and I know I talk too much. But I'm sincere in trying to communicate and I also try to listen, because I'm aware of how far I have to go in terms of learning about people.

PLAYBOY: You didn't seem to be listening when you said publicly a year or so ago, "No woman should go to bed with a man who carries a draft card." Isn't that self-righteous preaching?

BAEZ: I'll tell you how that started. Some women were asking one another, "What can we do to help?" And the first thing that came to my mind--as a joke,

in a sense--was to refuse to go to bed with anyone
carrying a draft card. It's not a new idea. You
remember Aristophanes' *Lysistrata?* The women in
that play said, "No more screwing until you put down
your arms." Well, the more I thought about it, the
more serious the idea seemed to me, and not in a
self-righteous sense. Women *can* help if they change
their own conception of what "hero" means. As long
as a hero is John Wayne coming home from the battlefield with blood dripping from his forehead, having
killed X number people, we'll keep perpetuating
violence. So the base of that idea is more than refusing to sleep with people who don't break away
from the institutions of violence; it's a matter of
women deciding what qualities in a man they can
really respect.
PLAYBOY: William Sloane Coffin, Jr., the Yale chap-
lain, has said that he hopes a new definition of
courage may come out of the resistance to the war in
Vietnam. Are you hopeful that might happen?
BAEZ: I think there *has* been a change in the past
three years. Very few people say "chicken" anymore
when somebody refuses to be drafted. That kind of
thing used to be an almost automatic response:
"Draft dodger!" "Yellow!" "Scared to go into the
Army!" That's changed. Even people who totally
disagree with the resistance have come to see, I
think, that it does take courage to face jail for
your convictions.
PLAYBOY: Your husband, David, has remained active
even in jail. What's the basis of the protest he's
involved in?
BAEZ: Well, part of it was the food. But it's important for us to look at this and the other complaints as being not about this particular jail but
about *all* prisons. America should look at the whole
system that prison represents. She should look at
the idea of punishment and the idea of rehiabilita-
tion, which is just a farce. They say rehabilitation, but what they mean is just more of the same
old punishment. What prison actually does is murder
people's spirits. But to take the prison David was
sent to--one of the people in his cell had been in
for 137 days and had lost about 40 pounds. It
wasn't because the food tasted bad; it was because
there was no real nourishment in it. I mean, it's
intended to make you so quiet and dead that you can
just about move. David also said in a letter he
wrote me from there that the lights are turned out
at nine o'clock, but if you stay up late, you can
hear the guards beating the prisoners in the hole.

The hole is a room about five feet by seven, with
rubber walls, and in the middle of the floor is an
opening through which sewage backs up into the cell.
When the grand jury went through the prison, the officials had to put down a new floor because they
couldn't wash out the bloodstains. At the time
David was in that prison, there was someone in the
hole screaming every night.

He also wrote me about medical attention. A
man in his cell was coughing up blood and they asked
for the guards, who took the man, put him on a concrete floor and gave him sleeping pills. That's all
they'd do for him. The last lines in David's letter
were: "In here, you see the logical conclusion of
American society. What happens here isn't really
different in kind compared with what happens outside; it's just different in quantity." We're all
so used to oppression and exploitation and the many
more subtle kinds of murder we do in our daily lives
that a revelation of what happens in prison
shouldn't come as a shock to us. It does, however,
because this particular area of brutality has been
so hidden away from us. But David's right. It's
not a difference in kind.

PLAYBOY: Isn't that an extraordinary exaggeration?
Surely there's a great difference between being behind bars, subject to that kind of brutality, and
being on the outside.

BAEZ: Of course it's worse to be locked up; but
what I'm talking about is the insensitivity of most
of us to the brutality that *isn't* hidden from us--
the brutality that allows people to go hungry, the
brutality that allows racism. Sure, people who are
hungry and who are discriminated against would suffer even more if they were put into a literal jail,
but my point is that what goes on in jails is a result of people deadening themselves to what is done
to other human beings. And what goes on outside is
a result of the same kind of complicity by silence.
Still, it *is* worse in prison, and what we allow to
happen there is something from the Middle Ages. It
shouldn't exist, any more than nuclear weapons
should exist.

PLAYBOY: How do you deal with those who insist they
have the right to break up meetings and shout down
anyone with whom they disagree?

BAEZ: First of all, you have to make distinctions.
There are times when meetings *have* to be pretty
stormy. If, for instance, there's an internal hassle, you ought not to try to impose your "wisdom"
from the outside until that hassle is cleared up.

You've got to get all that pent-up stuff out. But
on the other hand, when people rigidly insist that
only their side has the right to be heard, that's
something else. I suppose the person who's shouting
you down feels that if you finally leave the room,
he's won. But he hasn't won anything except a deci-
bel contest.
PLAYBOY: What do *you* do in that kind of situation?
BAEZ: Well, once when David and I were talking,
some black radicals were trying to shout us down.
First I joked with them, but finally I said, "Hey,
hold it! I've got just one thing to say. Do you
have any interest in hearing it?" And there was a
shout, "No!" I said, "That's what I thought." And
everybody laughed, including a couple of the heck-
lers. Well, that made the man leading the shouting
feel a little funny. So he said, "Yeah, sure, go
ahead." Sometimes you can get through that way--
showing how silly it is to not even try to listen to
what the other person has to say.
PLAYBOY: What did you say when you finally had the
chance?
BAEZ: The man who'd been doing the shouting had
been talking about Irish this and Jewish that and
what an Italian son of a bitc h someone else was.
What I said was, "Listen, if you're going to end
racism, you're going to have to stop *being* a racist.
You're going to have to stop putting down people in
groups." I mean, how can you be part of real change
unless you see, or try to see, each person in terms
of who he is? When I say you can't end racism if
your're a racist yourself, I'm also trying to show
that you can't make a new kind of society by forgetting that every one of us is valuable and unique,
that the most important thing--before all others--is
the sanctity of each human life.
PLAYBOY: There's one area in your concern about the
sanctity of life that seems somewhat unclear. During the parade in Berkeley for the People's Park in
the spring of 1969, John Lennon called KPFA, a local
radio station, to encourage the march. He also said
that the marchers should keep their cool and realize
that there are no principles worth dying for. You
objected publicly to that last line. Why?
BAEZ: I don't think I was being inconsistent. I
called KPFA and said that I didn't think any principle is worth *killing* for, but obviously there are
things worth *dying* for. Not necessarily the People's Park, but there are times when you may have to
be willing to face death if you're acting for life.
PLAYBOY: What would you find worth dying for?

BAEZ: People. Of course, it's much too easy when
you say it like that. But I can imagine putting myself in the way of violence to prevent violence being done to another.
PLAYBOY: You said earlier that you've already done
that--in jail, when you stopped a black girl from
beating up a white girl.
BAEZ: I suppose so, but that's not real danger.
When I speak and act for draft resistance, though,
I'm making myself really vulnerable. Just about
everywhere I go, I know there's a possibility that
somebody's going to want to pop me off. But if I
started worrying about getting killed for saying the
things I say, I'd quit doing most of everything I
do. There are a million places and times when it
could happen, but I just have to forget about them.
Let me make it clear, though, that I'm by no means
looking for martyrdom.
PLAYBOY: But there are still so few of you, and
it's the majority view that keeps being buttressed
by all the claims that man is inherently and unal-
terably aggressive. What argument do you have
against those who point to history as proof that human nature is violent and cannot be fundamentally
changed?
BAEZ: All the examples in history are not on that
side. Anthropologists can tell you of societies in
which nonviolence is the norm. I can think of one
tribe in Africa to whom it never occurred *not* to be
civil to anyone who wandered in off the desert.
There were about 2000 in that tribe, and once, after
a flood, they were overwhelmed by about 40,000 outsiders. This tribe fed and clothed them all for as
long as was necessary and didn't grumble aobut it or
worry about whether they'd replenish their supplies.
This was just their way of thinking, their human nature.
PLAYBOY: But that kind of behavior is very much an
exception in human history.
BAEZ: Oh, I'll grant that the statistics, if you
want to argue that way, are certainly in favor of
the other side. But I'm not interested in that kind
of argument. I tell you that I keep seeing people
making changes in themselves that I didn't think
they could make. I've seen it in myself--changes I
didn't think were possible.
PLAYBOY: How do you feel about the argument that
women in particular have had their "vision" taken
away from them, that their options are much more
limited than those of men because this remains basically a male-supremacist society? Are you in-

volved in women's liberation groups?
BAEZ: I'm not, but I feel I should take a closer
look. I've been turned off so far because I live
near Berkeley and most of the stuff I've seen came
out of there and I didn't like it at all. It seemed
to be saying, "I'm a woman. I demand my rights. I
can be as good a soldier or a competitor as any man."
You're not going to have a new kind of society, a
real sense of brotherhood, that way. On the other
hand, I've heard of some good, less flashy things
coming out of women's liberation activities--like cooperative nurseries, so that women who've been
stuck in a house for ten years can get out. I expect there are other things going on that I should
know about. But it's going to take a big effort for
me, partly because I've spent the last year and a
half trying to be less aggressive, trying to play
less of a man's role. All those years before, I was
by myself as an entertainer on a stage, and that's a
very odd position. It's doing what a man usually
does--learning how to project to a lot of people.
But being married to David, I wanted to get away
from that kind of aggressiveness--and in the process,
by the way, I've learned how to cook and I love it.
No women's liberation front is going to take that
away from me.
PLAYBOY: Whatever your personal feelings about some
of its more militant exponents, do you feel there is
a necessity for the liberation of women as people?
BAEZ: I see very, very clearly the need for women
to free themselves of many things--having to wear
brassieres and make-up and take those pains to fit
into a stereotypical pattern of how you're supposed
to act. And beyond that, the still-prevalent concept in this country that the woman's place is in
the home. Well, it isn't or shouldn't be for many
women. And even for those who refuse to accept that
role, the jobs open to them are equally sterotyped
and limited and they earn about half what a man does
for the same work. But as to how to go about changing all that, it boils down again to means and ends.
And when the means are as crazy as some of them are
now, the end result isn't going to be real.
PLAYBOY: As you pointed out earlier, the identity
of means and ends is central to your thinking. But
are you an absolutist on the question? Can't a particularly desirable end ever justify bending the
means to reach it?
BAEZ: Absolutist is a pretty rigid term. I prefer
to say that I don't think there's any difference between ends and means, because what you do always de-

termines what you get. We have all of human history
to prove that. Men have always said, "We want
peace; we want brotherhood; we want tranquility.
Just one more war and we'll have it." But after
just one more war, you've laid the whole groundwork
for the next war. To be more specific, take the
Cuban revolution. There are some beautiful things
about that revolution that I refuse to knock--like
ending the system of economic privilege. But at the
same time, a certain mentality grew out of the way
that revolution was fought. I know that children in
Cuba now start the day saluting the Cuban flag,
singing nationalist songs, and that by the age of
ten, they're carrying rifles. That doesn't seem to
me like a very sturdy groundwork for anything but
another nation-state and the dependence on violence
that goes with protecting the nation-state.
PLAYBOY: Young people in Cuba say there is no alternative to keeping the country militarily alert
with the American colossus only 90 miles away.
Without cultivating nationalism and without a citizenry that knows how to handle guns, they insist
"the revolution" couldn't be preserved.
BAEZ: My answer is what it always is: How do you
think you're going to preserve any revolution in
that way, particularly when there's a colossus right
over your heads? Being a bristling, armed nation-
state is going to make it that much more tempting
for the colossus to want to crush you. The one alternative is to do something very different from
what any nation-state has done in the past. I mean,
the development of a nonviolent society. But you
can't do that if your primary concern is preserving
the nation-state rather than the people in it. So I
would say that the Cuban revolution hasn't been revolutionary *enough*.
PLAYBOY: Given the odds against you--and the lessons of history--how do you sustain a belief that
your way will work, in Cuba or anywhere else?
BAEZ: It's not easy, because one can never tell how
much he's fooling himself. Sometimes I get very encouraged through the people I work with and the context in which I work. But then I get brought down.
I meet someone like a woman who interviewed me recently. She's very much into Black Pantherism and
she told me, "You're all by yourself. How do you go
on thinking that way when nobody else does?" I kept
saying, "But there *are* others. If you're interested,
get out of New York City and look around outside the
context you're operating in. We do exist. There
are people who believe that blowing other people's

heads off is a dumb idea. I'm not the only one on
earth who thinks as I do." But then, when she'd
left, I thought of the reality of her own experience
to her. She really hasn't known anyone else who
thinks as I do. Maybe I *do* overestimate the numbers
and the force on our side, because I surround myself
with people who more or less believe as I do. We do
exist, but it may be that there won't ever be enough
of us.

PLAYBOY: When you get discouraged, what lifts you
out of it and gets you going again?

BAEZ: The thing that keeps me doing the things I do
and makes me think they may work, in spite of everybody's arguments about human nature and in spite of
the wars and the exploitation, is that I've never in
my travels met a person who didn't want to live and
be loved by other people. I think that need can be
as powerful a force as any of the forces we've been
talking about. That's the force I try to work with.
It's *there.* The makings for the revolution I'm
talking about are there. Oh, you often talk to the
guy down the street and he's sure *he* can do it, but
he adds that first you've got to get that *other* guy
out of the way, because he might start after us with
a machine gun. Everybody feels *he's* capable of being part of that real change I call revolution; but
so far, only a few have gotten over that frenzy
about the other person. That's what we have to work
on, but we do have a base: that need everybody has
to love and be loved.

PLAYBOY: Are there times when you feel there is no
real hope at all, even with that base?

BAEZ: I'm acquainted with that feeling. It usually
goes away fairly fast, but I have it once in a
while. I can't pretend not to have had it. It's
then I think: What if the revolution never happens?
Well, I want to have lived my life in such a way
that I won't regret any of the things I've done. So
even if we never reach the goal, I'll at least have
attempted to live a decent life all the way through.
I'll have kept on trying to reach people, trying to
keep myself open, so that *I* can be reached, trying
to be kind, trying to learn about love. In my most
down moments, I think maybe that will be the most
we'll be able to do--to live a life of *trying* to do
those things. And if it comes to that, it will,
after all, have been quite a lot to have done.

JOAN BAEZ is a well-known, beloved folk singer. She was the founder of the Institute of Nonviolence in Palo Alto, California, and for many years served as its vice-president.

Her life history is a running diary of involvement and courageous innovation on behalf of peace. Thus, in the 1960s:

April 1962: Embarked on first of three concert tours to southern campuses and recital halls under an unequivocal no-discrimination policy. To Nashville and Atlanta, then to Miles College and the 16th Street Baptist Church at the time students on strike were met with water hoses. On to Mobile and Tuscaloosa, Alabama, and Toogaloo, Mississippi, among many other locations.

March 1963: Refused to appear on ABC's "Hootenanny" because of that network's blacklisting of Pete Seeger.

April 1964. In a letter addressed "Dear Friends," Joan informed the "Eternal Revenue Service" she would not pay the 60% of her taxes on 1963 earnings that would be used for defense spending.

November 1964. IRS filed a $50,182 lien against her for nonpayment of 1963 taxes.

April 1965. Announced her refusal to pay 65% of tax due on her 1964 earnings. Informed Mormon church officials she would refuse to return to the Mormon Tabernacle in Salt Lake City unless they changed their policy toward Negroes. Took part in anti-war demonstration in front of the White House.

July 1965. Revealed plans to convert a former schoolhouse in Carmel Valley, California into the Institute for the Study of Nonviolence. Nearly 450 local residents signed a petition to protest expected invasion of "hippies and free-love subversives."

November 1965. After a bitter 4-hour debate, Monterey County Board of Supervisors OK'd a school use permit for the Institute but attached numerous restrictions.

December 1965. IRS filed a $37,000 lien against her for nonpayment of 1964 taxes. Informed local officials she intended to defy school restrictions, claiming use permits are not required for institutes.

April 1966. Led (Easter Day) anti-war march in West Germany. Gave a studio performance for an East German television audience.

September 1966. Joined silent march in Grenada, Mississippi to protest beatings of black elementary school children by parents of white students. March blocked by police at school grounds.

December 1966. Performed in Santa Monica, California at a benefit for striking Delano farm workers. Announced an increase to 75% of income tax portion she would refuse to pay due to war escalation. Participated in Christmas vigil at San Quentin Penitentiary to urge commutation of death sentences for 64 Death Row prisoners.

January 1967. Demanded a retraction from Li'l Abner cartoonist, Al Capp, for his Joanie Phoanie comic strip parody of her peace activities, claiming the strip was damaging to the movement. As representative of America at a Tokyo anti-war rally, signed a Japan-U.S. Civil Pact condemning war.

February 1967. Japanese press reported that during her concert tour of Japan, CIA pressured Miss Baez' interpreter to mistranslate her political remarks under threat of refusing his future entry into the U.S.

August 1967. Received permission to give free concert at base of the Washington Momument after Daughters of the American Revolution refused to let her use DAR-owned Constitution Hall because of her "unpatriotic activities." Appearing before 30,000 at the Washington Momument, she thanked the DAR for denying her use of the 3800-seat hall.

September 1967. Helped organize a national draft card turn-in day for the Resistance; 500 cards were turned in.

October 1967. Arrested along with her mother, sister, Mimi Farina, and 700 others at Armed Forces Examining Center in Oakland, California. Charged with refusing to disperse, creating a public nuisance and blocking a public street. All three received ten-day jail sentences at Santa Rita Prison Farm.

December 1967. Arrested along with 190 others at the Oakland Induction Center for similar violations. Sentenced to 90 days at Santa Rita, 45 days of which were suspended.

January 1968. Released prior to completed sentence before press could be notified because prison officials felt "rehabilitation has been accomplished."

March 1968. Began college tour with Resistance leader David Harris, urging girls to say yes to boys who say no.

Summer 1969. Embarked on a summer tour with the usual stipulation that all her solo concerts should have a maximum admission charge of $2. This applied to Madison Square Garden as well as other large facilities.

Summer 1970. Embarked on another European tour covering Milan, Rome, Montreaux, France, Sweden, Denmark, Poland, and the Isle of Wight Festival, England.

In recent years, Joan continues her concerts and recordings, and she carries on her involvement in nonviolence through the Resource Center for Nonviolence in Santa Cruz, California, a new group that grew out of the old institute.

The excerpts that were taken from a sensitive PLAYBOY interview in 1970 admittedly refer to much that is now "ancient history" for America, and for Joan personally. Nonetheless, even at this much later date, the story of Joan's commitment to nonviolence in the 60s is not only a fascinating document of the era, but a model for people to have the courage of their convictions on behalf of peace, at any time and in any country.

Section Two

The Community and Culture: Design for Nonviolent Communities and Cultures

7. A Cultural Press for Peace

Israel W. Charny, Ph.D.

Psychotherapists as a group care very, very much about the destinies of people everywhere on this troubled planet. Many of us originally were drawn to our field in search of understanding how mankind might shape its future. In recent years, more psychotherapists have involved themselves openly with the larger issues concerning the evolution of man. Perhaps our awakening stems from the fact that we now have come through the first stunned, paralyzed post-holocaust and post-atomic decades and the first shocked inability to bear seeing our species moving relentlessly, diabolically towards extinction (20). Perhaps our emerging new perspective of our own being grows from our new sight of ourselves and our planet from the far-off position of a space ship in the heavens. Perhaps it is the dawn of awareness of a new possibility of ecological suicide that propels us to a new spirit of activity. Also, we therapists have now evolved professionally enough to know that we are accepted members of the scientific community, permitting us to serve as delegates of our worried species to seek new tools that might give us a measure of direction over our destiny.

The particular dimension of man's future that is our concern is man's moth-to-flame history of warring and genocidal destruction.

There *is* a beginning social science of real proposals for peace. Recent years have seen fairly sophisticated treatments of proposed approaches to arms reduction and control (33,34). There is very significant press at the frontiers of new conceptions of international and global peace (24). There is a solid beginning of a peace research literature drawing on the convergence of a variety of social

147

and behavioral sciences: *The Bulletin of Peace Proposals* and the *Journal of Peace Research,* both published by the International Peace Research Institute at the University of Oslo, Norway; the *Journal of Conflict Resolution* in the United States; a responsible key to the peace research literature is available through *Peace Research Abstracts* published by the Peace Research Institute, Dundas, Ontario, Canada; these to mention but a few of the variety of publications emerging around the globe--and without our touching on the fact that there are such publications now in a variety of languages.

However, if we ask how much these beginnings represent development of psychological understanding of how man, to begin with, is *humanly* capable of his terrible destructiveness, we find that we have not much to show.

In an earlier article (10,11), I struggled with the recognition that the most terrifying genocidal destructiveness is essentially the work of *normal* human beings, like ourselves; and that we need a psychology of man that honestly sees us as the loving, creative creatures we are, as well as simultaneously open to the worst beastiality (see, for example the study of SS killers by Dicks [18]). I suggested that in our professional failure to confront this destructiveness in our basic image of man, we psychologists too have been victims of a species-wide pathologic defense in denial. This same failure to incorporate destructiveness in our basic image of man has in turn severely limited us from developing a more relevant psychology for peace-seeking efforts.

I would like now to consider some such ways in which our psychotherapeutic science might contribute to a cultural press for peace even at the stage of knowledge and theory presently available to us. I propose to develop ideas towards this goal on two levels: first, on the level of *basic psychological principles* that could be infused into the very lifestream of our cultures, and hence into the machinery for everyday human experiencing of our species; and second, on the level of several *illustrative psychoeducational projects* which embody the previous principles in efforts with target groups in the community of man.

PSYCHOLOGICAL PRINCIPLES TOWARDS DESIGN OF A
CULTURAL PRESS FOR PEACE

1.*Psychology can contribute to evoking awareness of
   man's war-making.*
        In teaching man to be conscious of his repeated
war-making, we will be reinterating a basic principle which has proven of real value to people in other aspects of life. We experience increasing capacity for choice and mastery of our destiny the more
we free ourselves to be open to the honest awareness
of the many, often paradoxical, often distressing
sides of the real feelings within us.
        The natural function of *denial* of awareness is
to spare us pain beyond the level of our ability to
endure. The hazard of this defense mechanism is
that it removes the greatest gift of our evolutionary development, the capacity to be conscious, aware
and self-observing, and therefore capable of planning future actions knowledgeably in our best interests. Psychology directs us to teach man to be
aware of the historical repetition compulsion towards war and towards genocide; also, the truth of
how it is both homicide and suicide that man pursues
through his compulsion of war-making and genocide
(3,15,22,28). Sharing the pain of our collective
past, present and future, we may stimulate the significant strength of man's profound instinct for
seeking life. We would hope in this way to stimulate the best of our minds to efforts towards new
ways for society. We also may provide some measure
of relief for our quite terrified species if only
through the courage to acknowledge the reality we
live in, rather than leave ourselves open to the
more terrifying unconscious dread (of war and death
with which we all live and which we know also adds
to destructiveness (36).

2.*Psychology can teach us how the roots of our destructive aggressions are based in natural processes designed to assist us in the struggle for
   survival and mastery; how we must learn to employ
   angry feelings without acting on them in overt
   acts of destruction.*
        Here again our psychological field will be re-
iterating a basic principle by which we have already
been credited wtih real helpfulness to our species,
beginning with the much more tantalizing if also-
troublesome area of sexuality. There we have taught
man to recognize and accept the naturalness of his
impulses in affairs (sic) of sex. We have taught

man that psychologically healthy or moral choices regarding one or another sexual experience are the more possible when built on a foundation of acceptance of the naturalness of just about any wish, and yet, where we know not to equate wish with action. Thus, the old-fashioned injunction against adultery means don't even think of it. But in twentieth century psychology, this commandment is revised to include an invitation to all normally attractive people to think of it quite a lot, for we are understandably attracted to many potential partners; yet to think carefully before we act on all our wishes. Wishing for another partner is one thing, but acting on this wish had best be considered carefully in relation to all manner of considerations before taking the plunge (sic).

The same goes for hostile impulses. We all *think* or *feel* like killing others; far be it from our *doing* so. Such consciousness of man's destructive inclinations affords a powerful new base of truth for programs of education towards nonviolence, intergroup relations, and international friendship. Specifically, it is the possibility of psychology teaching people that *all* human beings get very angry when frustrated, limited, or in any way driven to a sense of resourcelessness; that under conditions of heightened intimacy, all people feel parts of themselves wishing to hurt their loved ones; that hurting in the unconscious mind is equivalent to, or at least draws on historic images of doing away with or killing the other person; and that it is one of the developmental tasks of each human being, begun in the early preschool years, to learn to separate feeling from act. To feel angry is a universal and necessary experience, but to act on the wish actually to hurt another's person is humanly wrong (8,9, 31,37).

Were the mental health fields effective in teaching just such consciousness of man's capacity for separating actual destructive acts from angry feelings, we would be making a great contribution to man's historic search for means for peace. There will be many other doors to be opened for contributions to peace once we are consciously committed to extending our search for how man might naturalistically tap his aggression on his own behalf.

3. *Psychotherapy can teach men how natural it is to*
   fight in self-defense against would-be threats to
   our life; yet, we must learn to control the often
   unwitting cycle of overanxiety and overdefensive-
   ness that builds to a holocaust in the name of
   self-defense.

Obviously it is useful that man-animal is en-
dowed with the capacity to perceive and to anticipate threats to his being. Day by day, we seek to
extend the range of our safety-monitoring equipment
in the tumultuous natural world, such as increasing
sophistication in prediction of weather systems that
once hurricaned unsuspecting victims to their
deaths. Yet, in our interpersonal relationships, we
are all too ready to be *overvigilant* in perceiving
threat from others, and then launching, unwittingly,
a kind of self-fulfilling cycle of prophecy and destructive fulfillment.

There are those of us who care so much about
man's destructive madness that we say the only way
to break out of such cycles is to commit oneself
never to attack another human being, and certainly
never to take a life. To my mind such a well-inten-
tioned pacifist principle has within it the seeds of
further destruction of man, beginning with the very
ones who in their sincerity would offer us such a
guide to stopping the hell. The peaceloving pioneer's life, too, is the very human life we must
seek to protect; a pacifist's martyrdom is no less
tragic than the loss of life of another he is seeking to prevent. It is a fundamental rule of nature
to wish to live; under those circumstances where it
is *entirely* clear that someone comes to attack us,
it is only right to trigger a vigorous self-defense,
including living out the risk of *actually* proceeding
to hurt another. When someone seeks to murder us,
it is natural that we surge with wishes to hurt this
other, yes to kill him--to see him hurt even far beyond what is actually necessary for self-defense.
That is what happens naturally when one feels his
very life threatened by the attacker.

The trouble is, we are so often wrong, self-
fulfilling prophets in our judgments. It is frequently the cyclical flow of our legitimate wishes
for self-defense that build warlike retaliatory actions which in turn trigger all that is fearful and
terrifying in the attacker; he too, all too often,
is caught up unwittingly in cycles of response to
unknown terrors (23). Clearly, man must learn to
cut these vicious circles. Let us take somber, humble note of the fact that virtually every aggressor

in this world has seen himself as fighting in self-
defense, the genociders included. It is much like
the smaller-scale play of marital battles where
there is never a spouse who does not sincerely see
himself as the attacked one who is the victim to the
other. When a spouse yields to awareness of the
pain and threat also being experienced by his mate--
notwithstanding his own emotional conviction of being the victim--the hazards of escalation into a
holy war are much reduced. In time, we would look
to the social sciences to develop new systems approaches to help men and nations to monitor and correct their overvigilant perceptions of threats.

4. *Psychotherapy can explore ways to teach human beings all over the world that there is no such
   group of people that is "non-human"; that the
   time-honored rationalization of all killers, that
   the enemies--Jew, Black, Indian, Gypsy,--are of
   another species and less than "us," is a lie.*
     It is precisely this ploy that someone or an-
other is *not-human* which underlies genocidal mani-
festoes through the ages. This definition in effect
permits man to pretend that his destruction of fellow humans is what Lorenz (30) has described as entirely prevalent in other species--attacks against
another species, but not against one's own. Effective psychosocial education towards acknowledgement
of the unity of man would clearly represent a major
evolutionary step.
     Such education would begin with teaching aware-
ness of the primitive, universal defense of *projection*; pressing others into some mold of *not-us, dif-
ferent-from-us, lesser-than-us*; and into symbolic
carriers of evil, whose elimination (ostensibly)
would free us from all manner of dangers that, in
reality, are not more than experiences within us
that we share with our would-be victims; such as
awareness of the ultimate mortality of us all.
     In this century, especially since World War II,
much beautiful work has been done on the positive
side of eliminating barriers to *contacts* between
peoples. One historic contribution is that of psychologist, Doris Allen, who created the program of
Children's International Summer Villages (see her
chapter in this book). Many other programs exist
for increasing contact between peoples from around
our globe, so that people learn how we are brothers
to one another and that the richness of our differences are no more than variations elaborating the
basic evolving 'stuff' of our species (44). Framed

from the side of positive feelings for one's fellow man, there seem to be many experiential techniques for teaching respect and affection for other people, and what has been described as the oceanic feeling reached at the height of the psychotherapeutic process or in other penetrating existential experiences such as religious inspiration, hippie communality, drug release of the inner self, or the tragic clarity of impending death. Here one knows that each of us is part of the one stunning universal reality, and that beauteous life-meaning obtains to each and everyone of us "God's creatures."

It is initially less appealing and far more difficult to imagine how to teach people to anticipate that their so-convincing inner magic of casting one or another group of humans into a junkheap of *not-us* and *not-human* is nonsense, no matter how beguiling the inner rationalization. None of us humans represents a higher species who might "legitimately" end the lives of others as if they are lower species. We must teach men that the cursed devil of such projection wears many forms (17). It is thus that we find psychiatrists and pediatricians, who otherwise cared about their patients, arranging the genocide of those patients who were so retarded or disturbed as to constitute, in their minds, the *not-human* (46,47). It is thus throughout history that we see people who care about a revolution for liberty and equality losing themselves in guillotine-lust to remove those whom they consider the enemies of their liberty and equality (Shoham [41] studies the basic mechanism of attributing evil to others).

Characteristically, a kind of romantic feeling develops around programs for teaching that all men are brothers; but we still suffer a fearful taboo-inability to bear looking at how much we make of one another not-brothers and not humans. We must now learn to vaccinate ourselves against the scourge of this projection process which is originally intended for our defense, but which became a basis for the worst offenses against nature when carried beyond its original self-preserving and terror-reducing intent (for an excellent series of studies of dehumanization, see Sanford and Comstock [38]).

5. *Psychotherapeutic science can seek to teach us to bear experiencing our ultimate mortality; to see our fear of death as a challenge to meaningful living before the time comes when our opportunity for experiencing comes to its end.*

Ultimately, the greatest secret man keeps from

himself is what he knows from the earliest bone-
awareness of life: that life is a developing opportunity that will be marked by an end from which
there is no escape. Yet, man fears his death so
bitterly that he has contrived many ways of es-
caping awareness of its inevitability and therefore
its meaning for his life (2,6,7,21,29,39). Some men
seek to seize life itself, as if to say that they
are masters of the life and death of another and in
turn are not to be vulnerable to their own deaths.
Others race through their own lives grateful for the
Russian-roulette opportunities of war and genocide,
ostensibly to bring death to others, but subtly
courting suicide. We need to learn how to teach men
that despite, and the more so *because* of the inevitability of life's end, we need to respect the opportunity that is life and to seek courage to rise
to the challenge and anxiety of being alive.

How precious will be the psychology that
teaches men such arts for living. In retrospect,
the exciting beginning we made in inviting men to
the natural joy of their sexuality will be a small
matter in comparison to teaching men a larger naturalness and joy in their living.

ILLUSTRATIVE PROJECTS FOR MENTAL HEALTH EDUCATION
TOWARDS NONVIOLENCE

Where Would We Make Our Contribution?
Much of what we know certainly can be taught in
individual, family and group psychotherapies--the
bread-and-butter activities of mental health clini-
cians. Clearly, however, the larger goal of psychological science is to contribute to the evolution of
a culture-wide consciousness of man's capacity to
choose and affirm life over death. Is this a vague
hope like so many other Messianic notions in our
mental health tradition, where in some pious way it
is hinted that we might contribute to saving our
civilization, but where there is no real practical
application of our ideas? Sometimes we have heard
the desperate magical hope that all political leaders should submit themselves to psychoanalysis.
Other times we live off the vague, fear-dulling hope
that somehow a day will come when all people will
love their babies so well that problems of destructiveness will be eliminated. We all know well
enough that these are tranquilizing hogwash, and
that *only as we become skilled enough to translate
our concepts into educational projects that can*

*reach masses of population is there a possibility of
psychology effecting an impact on man's long-range
problems in the real world.*

Following are a number of illustrations of how
mental health professionals might seek to educate
others to become change agents so that we might develop a community of change agents striking out into
society with new humanistic tools for peace.

1. *To the newscasters and newspaper writers of the
world*

So often those who are responsible for inform-
ing us of our everyday, violent human actions present the news of such tragic events routinely, glib-
ly, and even with a covert excitement that would
seem to participate in the frenzy and pleasure of
still another piece of sadism by man, or even a secret masochistic joy in his defeat. Would it not be
possible for newscasters to articulate for us the
sadness and challenge of such events?

Needless to say, it is the newscaster's role to
operate within the framework of the tradition of
"objective reporting" and not as a commentator or
analyst. However, still operating entirely within
this tradition, could not newscasters use simple,
factual adjectives such as, "a sad accident today
claimed the lives of..."? And might not the newscaster construct a subtle tone of quiet depth that
speaks to his sadness, mixed deftly with a note of
anger at the wastefulness of it all? Certainly it
would be reasonably easy for news professionals to
learn to avoid juxtaposing the news of a car accident or deaths in war with banal or undignified com-
mercials. It would be appropriate for a newscaster
to mirror honestly something of the natural excitement that all of us feel in response to the drama of
violence about us; and yet, following the appropriate dramatic quality of reportage of such events,
the newscaster, with all his dramatic talent, then
could move slowly into a quietness and sadness and
angry regret that in itself could convey the evolutionary potential of man to move from unchecked violence to caring which transcends his primitivity
(see other chapter by author in this book).

2. *To the teachers of history*

So often teachers of history speak to pupils
routinely and all too matter-of-factly of so many
human beings who were killed in the war of such-and-
such. Here too, we might stimulate teachers to experience and convey the intrinsic meaning of these

historic events: to focus on what it is for a human
being to die; the meaning to him, the meaning to his
spouse, the meaning to his children. And what it
means when a man goes off to war in our day and age;
to the children who say good-bye, to the spouse who
is left behind, to the man himself as he goes off to
the battlefield. If he survives, how he returns
with memories of blowing men to bits with his gun,
even as others sought to do the same to him.

The learning of history can become a truly
human experience of consciousness rather than a remote depersonalizing consideration of economic or
political forces, relevant as they are. We have
much evidence that even children, in all cultures,
experience an intrinsic sense of right and wrong regarding the dignity of man's life (25,26), and it is
against such a naturalistic frame of reference that
such teaching can be developed--surprisingly enough,
at all ages, even with the youngest. Needless to
say, the same and more is true in teaching the current events of the day (4,5,32,45).

3.To parents and counselors of children
Have we really taught caretakers of children
how to deal with aggressions that spring up in the
natural life of children and in their groups? As we
came to understand that children themselves fear going too far to delinquent extremes, we learned that
limiting a child from acting-out is a statement of
our caring and love of him. But have we gone very
far in teaching parents and child care workers and
counselors how to help children release their angry
feelings, and how to respect their angry feelings?
Have we taught adults to say, "We do feel angry at
one another very often, don't we, but it's wrong to
hit another child so hard that it really hurts him"?

We might teach teachers to encourage children
to talk of their angry dreams of the night before,
just as they are helped to bring in other kinds of
material to "Show and Tell" (35). When cruelty
shows in a child, it can be recognized as a part of
him that springs from what is natural in us all;
yet, a part of him which should not reign so much
over his person that it blocks him from fulfilling
the precious parts of his being that would love and
care and feel with other people. We can teach
adults how to accept that thrust of cruelty without
losing heart for the larger challenge: to learn how
to limit the place of cruelty in the human experience (14,16,19,22,40).

4.To spouses and parents and family counselors
We all know the incredible statistics of family
despair and breakdown. Might we teach people the
truth that family life is a never-ending process of
conflict and struggle, and that the few who manage a
measure of achievement and fulfillment are those who
stay with the painful process? Might we not teach
people that the family is a proving ground for life,
that the whole point is for people who love each
other the most, and who want to love each other,
train each other; so that each person in the family
group, young and old, is in turn trainer and trainee
to the other!
As long as people remain committed to their
caring for one another, go on searching for ways to
convey their caring, and develop their ability to
stop the excesses of their hurting the others, the
whole swirling, buzzing confusion of guerrilla tactics, revolutionary uprisings and open warfare that
is family life might yield a measure of fulfilling
peace. Not the quietness of taking off one's shoes
after work and not being bothered. Not a romanti-
cized effort at total mothering or fathering that in
most cases never existed in one's own childhood.
Nor a doll house of make-believe that children are
to grow up hale and hearty without emotional blemish
because parents now know how to do all the right
things according to the latest psychology books.
Rather, a creative aliveness out of the good and
bad, the loving and hating, the attracting and re-
pelling that is all of us; and this in preparation
for being effective citizens in a world where good
men will know how to resist being drawn into the
mass hypnotic frenzies of each century's violence
(1,13).

5.To religious leaders
Increasingly, we train our ministers in principles of pastoral counseling for the many individuals
who come to them emotionally troubled, but how far
have we gone in teaching ministers to help men face
the sinful, seemingly irreligious part of them that
springs from within the natural self of us all? Religion and all ethical forces for good can help to
bring man to consciousness of his natural drives,
such as aggression, as a more *real* basis for man
reaching and freeing the goodness in him that we all
seek. It is true that we wish men to feel their
brotherhood to all, but how far do we succeed in
teaching brotherhood when we do not also allow how,
in part, men hate their brothers? Indeed, too often

in man's history, religions themselves have been the fomenters of virulent hatred and genocide, spawned in the very piety and pseudopurity of the "righteous" seeking to prevail over the "evil." We can help religious leaders to help man encounter the godliness or naturalness of his aggression and the seductive ease with which it may be turned to rage and destructiveness in the name of one false god or another (43,48).

6.To government leaders and diplomats
    Might we not contribute to the training and education of diplomats and leaders who carry the burden of negotiation in those often tragic-comic international negotiations where war and peace are developed? Teach these men how to perceive the other party to international negotiations as representing a group of human beings like himself and his family. Perhaps to learn how to review these convictions in daily inner emotional exercises paralleling in meaning what traditional religion intends in prayer. And teach these men something of the hazard of the cycle of the self-fulfilling prophecy in which the momentum of fighting back against injustice in turn triggers the others' feelings of danger and imminent persecution. Can we learn how to teach government leaders to appreciate the deep fearfulness that abounds in all human beings and how to seek to speak to their fear rather than to bully, outsmart, or even rely on rightness of logic? Can we teach diplomats new concepts of negotiations which do not aim for victory of one side over the other but for *no-lose solutions* that clearly affirm a victory for both sides? (20,42, see the chapters by Singer, Wedge, and the Craigs in this book).

BUT HOW MUCH GOOD WILL IT DO?

You're kidding yourself: You can't change human nature.
    Agreed, partly! It is my belief that our lifetime will *not* see a solution to man's violence, and that it is better mental health to anticipate, realistically, the likelihood of our own destruction by violent forces than it is to pretend exaggerated "therapeutic hopefulness" for our civilization or to return to outright denial of it all.
    In the long evolutionary run, however, it seems to me quite conceivable that man might give up cannibalism, gladiator sports, religious inquisitions,

and cultures of pistols, cannons, and atom bombing.

In our own time, it is right to try and thus to experience meaning for ourselves by participating in the long-range evolutionary flow of man. Where once we psychotherapists felt an empty helplessness about conceptualizing relevant principles of human behavior concerning such matters as life-destroying forces, we see now our psychotherapeutic science of today and tomorrow can contribute to progress.

REFERENCES

1. Bach, George, R., & Wyden, Peter. *The Intimate Enemy*. New York: Wm. Morrow, 1969.
2. Becker, Ernest. *The Denial of Death*. New York: Free Press, 1975. (paperback)
3. Berg, Irwin A. Cultural trends and the task of psychology. *American Psychologist*, 1965, *20*, 203-207.
4. Borton, Terry. *Read, Touch, and Teach*. New York: McGraw-Hill, 1970.
5. Boulding, Elise. The cold war in the classroom. *Fellowship*, January, 1965, 8-10.
6. Brown, Norman O. *Life Against Death*. New York: Random House, 1959.
7. Bugental, J.F.T. *The Search for Authenticity*. New York: Rinehart & Winston, 1965.
8. Charny, Israel W. The psychotherapist as teacher of an ethic of nonviolence. *Voices: The Art & Science of Psychotherapy*, 1967, *3*, 57-66.
9. Charny, Israel W. Teaching the violence of the holocaust: a challenge to educating potential future oppressors and victims for nonviolence. *Jewish Education*, 1968, *38*, 15-24.
10. Charny, Israel W. Normal man as genocider: we need a psychology of *normal* man as genocider, accomplice, or indifferent bystander to mass killing of man. *Voices: The Art & Science of Psychotherapy*, 1971, *7*(2), 68-79.
11. Charny, Israel W. Psichologia shel hashmadat am. *International Problems* (Israel), 1971, *10* (1-2), XXXI-XXXXVII. (Hebrew; with English summary: A psychology of normal man as genocider, pages 9-10).
12. Charny, Israel W. We need a human language for reporting the tragedies of current violent events: towards a model for the content, tone and dramatic mood of the broadcaster reporting the news of human violence. *American Journal Orthopsychiatry*, 1971, *41*, 219-220. (summary)

13. Charny, Israel W. *Marital Love and Hate*. New York: Macmillan, 1972.
14. Charny, Israel W. And Abraham went to slay Isaac: a parable of killer, victim, and by-stander in the family of man. *Journal Ecumenical Studies*, 1973, *10*(2), 304-318.
15. Clark, Robert A. Psychiatrists and psychoanalysts on war. *American Journal Psychotherapy*, 1965, *19*, 540-558.
16. Clark, Robert A. Friends and aggression. Philadelphia: American Friends Service Committee, about 1969. (mimeo)
17. Dadrian, Vahakn N. The common features of the Armenian and Jewish cases of genocide: a comparative victimological persepctive. In Israel Drapkin & Emilio Viano (Eds.), *Victimology: A New Focus*. Vol. IV. *Violence and its Victims*. Lexington, Mass.: D.C. Heath, 1973, 99-120.
18. Dicks, Henry V. *Licensed Mass Murder: A Sociological Study of Some SS Killers*. London: Heinemann, 1972.
19. Feshbach, Seymour. Dynamics and morality of violence and aggression: some psychological considerations. *American Psychologist*, 1971, *26*, 281-292.
20. Frank, Jerome D. *Sanity and Survival*. New York: Random House, 1967.
21. Friedman, Maurice. *To Deny Our Nothingness*. New York: Dell, 1967.
22. Group for the Advancement of Psychiatry. *Psychiatric Aspects of the Prevention of Nuclear War*. 1964, report #57.
23. Hoedemaker, Edward N. Distrust and aggression: an interpersonal-international analogy. *Journal Conflict Resolution*, 1968, *12*, 69-81.
24. Hollins, Elizabeth Jay (Ed.), *Peace is Possible*. New York: Grossman, 1966.
25. Kohlberg, Lawrence. Moral education in the schools: a developmental view. *The School Review*, 1966, *74*, 1-30.
26. Kohlberg, Lawrence. The child as a moral philosopher. *Psychology Today*, September, 1968, *2*, (4), 24-30.
27. Laing, R.D. *The Politics of Experience*. New York: Pantheon, 1967.
28. Lifton, Robert Jay. *Death in Life*. Random House, 1967.
29. Lifton, Robert Jay, & Harris, T. George. The politics of immortality (a conversation with Lifton). *Psychology Today*, November, 1970, *4*(6).

30. Lorenz, Konrad. *On Aggression*. New York: Harcourt, Brace & World, 1966.
31. May, Rollo. *Love and Will*. New York: W.W. Norton, 1969.
32. Nesbitt, William A. (Ed.), *Teaching Global Issues Through Simulation: It Can Be Easy. Intercom*. Summer, 1974, No. 75 (whole issue).
33. Newcombe, Alan. Initiatives and responses in foreign policy. *Peace Research Reviews*, 1969, *3*, No. 3 (whole no.)
34. Osgood, C.E. *An Alternative to War or Surrender*. Urbana, Illinois: University Illinois Press, 1962.
35. Pikas, Anatol. *We Speak and We Listen*. Uppsala, Sweden: Pedagogiska Institutionen, 1975 (mimeo. pre-publ. edition).
36. Pilisuk, Marc, & Ober, Lyn. Torture and genocide: public health problems. *American Journal Orthopsychiatry*, 1976, *46*(3), 388-392.
37. Rubinoff, Lionel. *The Pornography of Power*. New York: Ballantine, 1969 (Quadrangle, 1967).
38. Sanford, Nevitt, & Comstock, Craig. *Sanctions for Evil*. San Francisco: Jossey-Bass, 1971.
39. Searles, Harold F. Schizophrenia and the inevitability of death. *Psychiatric Quarterly*, 1961, *35*, 631-665.
40. Sheleff, Leon Shaskolsky. Beyond the Oedipus Complex: A perspective on the myth and reality of generational conflict. *Theory and Society*, 1976, *3*, 1-44.
41. Shoham, Shlomo. *The Mark of Cain*. Jerusalem: Israel Universities Press (Keter), 1971.
42. Singer, J. David. Negotiation by proxy. *Journal Conflict Resolution*, 1965, *9*, 538-41.
43. Tillich, Paul. *The Courage to Be*. New Haven: Yale University Press, 1952.
44. UNESCO. *Education for International Understanding*, 1959.
45. Weinstein, Gerald, & Fantini, Mario. *A Model for Developing Relevant Curriculum*. New York: Praeger, 1970.
46. Wertham, Frederic. The geranium in the window: the "euthansia" murders. Chapter 9. In *A Sign for Cain: An Exploration of Human Violence*. New York: Macmillan, 1966, 153-191.
47. Wertham, Frederic. New dimensions of human violence. *American Journal Psychotherapy*, 1969, *23*, 374-380.
48. Winter, Gibson. *Love and Conflict: New Patterns in Family Life*. New York: Doubleday, 1961 (Dolphin Edition).

Dr. ISRAEL W. CHARNY, a Diplomate of the American Board of Professional Psychology, is a clinical psychologist now living and practicing in Herzliya Pituach, Israel, on the seacoast north of Tel-Aviv. Dr. Charny is Senior Researcher at the Henrietta Szold National Institute for Research in the Behavioral Sciences in Jerusalem, and Associate Professor of Psychology at Tel-Aviv University. He is also Senior Consultant to the Kibbutz Child & Family Clinic in Ramat-Aviv, and teaches at the Ministry of Welfare's Institute for the Training of Social Workers. He is the author of MARITAL LOVE AND HATE (Macmillan, 1972 and Lancer paperback, 1973), a forthcoming volume, THE COURAGE TO STAY A FAMILY, and still another forthcoming volume, which was commissioned by the Institute of World Order in New York: GENOCIDE: THE CANCER OF HUMAN EXPERIENCING.

For many years, Dr. Charny practiced in Paoli, Pennsylvania, in the United States, where he directed a private group practice, Guidance Consultants. He also coordinated a small interdisciplinary study group, Group for Research in the Psychology of Aggression and Nonviolence whose activities were later included in the framework of the American Orthopsychiatric Association's Study Group on Mental Health Aspects of Aggression, Violence, and War which he chaired for several years. He was also a founding member of the Consortium on Peace Research, Education, and Development, and then served on its Advisory Council.

Dr. Charny believes the greatest challenge to psychology is to understand so-called normal man's availability to destroy his fellow man: so many men, in so many different cultures condone, stand by indifferently, support, and actually execute destruction and mass murder--not only in "legitimate" wars, but against helpless children, women, and men. He is particularly interested in the possible contributions of psychotherapy to a model of a strong but largely nonviolent man. He enjoys conceiving of the psychotherapy of marital couples, and family therapy, as a small-scale laboratory for the study of violent feelings and human betrayal.

A key underlying theme in much of Dr. Charny's work is his deep concern with the Holocaust. He dreams someday of a center devoted to the study of the Holocaust, not in memoriam (important as this is, such as provided by Israel's Yad Vashem or Martyrs' & Heroes" Remembrance Authority), but as a focus for a broad spectrum of analyses of what makes it possible for human beings to destroy wantonly,

and how can such understanding be tapped to help men
towards affirming their no less brilliant potential
for nonviolent creativity.
    The author enjoys speaking Hebrew, writing,
riding a bicycle, swimming, and occasionally being
a good assistant handyman. Generally, he is occu-
pied in a search for meaning, some pleasure, and a
sense of humor about being.

SOME OTHER PUBLICATIONS BY ISRAEL W. CHARNY

- The new psychotherapies and encounters of the
  seventies: progress or fads? *The Humanist,* 1974
  (2-part series, May-June, July-August). Reprinted
  in *Reflections* (Merck, Sharp, & Dohme), 1975, *10*
  (2: 1-13; 3: 1-17). Reprinted in David Welch
  (Ed.), *Humanistic Psychology: A Sourcebook.* New
  York: Prometheus, in press.
- A Center for Study of Genocide, Human Rights and
  Man's Potential for Peace. Jerusalem: Szold
  National Institute for Research in the Behavioral
  Sciences, 1977. (pamphlet)
- With Rapaport, Ch. A Genocide Early Warning Sys-
  tem (A Pilot Project). Jerusalem: Szold National
  Institute for Research in the Behavioral Sciences,
  1977. (pamphlet)

8. Aggression—American Style

William H. Blanchard, Ph.D.

Many leading political theorists have sub-
scribed to the notion that democratic governments
are more peaceful because war is not in the best interest of the common people and the people are, presumably, free to advance their own interest. The
United States has often been used as an example of
the peaceful consequences of a democratic form of
government. Joseph Schumpeter (18), who felt the
United States was less imperialistic than the other
nations of the world, associated this tendency with
capitalism rather than democracy, per se. It was
not, he said, in the interest of the average citizen
to support a warlike policy and the policy of the
United States confirmed this view. Alexis de Toque-
ville (20) had more reservations about the relationship between democracy and peace. While he believed
that "democratic nations are naturally prone to
peace from their interests and their propensities,"
he felt they were drawn into war by their armies.
Earlier public opinion research supported the
notion of the peaceful inclination of the American
people. In a study of the way nations perceive each
other, Buchanan and Cantril (4) found, in part, that
Americans were generally rated as more peace-loving
than Russians. But the Buchanan and Cantril study
was published in 1953, using data obtained in 1948,
long before we were drawn into the conflict in South-
east Asia. In 1948, the United States was already
beginning to suffer the negative effects of a too
hasty post-war demobilization. Our European allies,
fearful of the Russian presence in Europe, had begun
to feel we were a bit too peace-loving. Today, they
are frightened by our involvement in Asia and the
Soviet Union is carrying off, quite successfully, the
role of mediator and peacemaker. It is unlikely that

the ratings, if taken again, would still show such a universal opinion of Americans as lovers of peace. Images tend to change, depending on the times and the needs of the observer. The fraternity boy and football hero of yesterday has become the Jock of today. The men of the heroic United States Air Force, the wild blue yonder boys of World War II who came to the rescue of an embattled civilization with crushed caps and an engaging American smile, have become part of a major nuclear strike force which terrifies the world. The image of Dr. Oppenheimer has been replaced by that of Dr. Strangelove and Jimmy Stewart, the boy next door, has become a General.

It would be convenient, at this point, to hark back to the warning of Tocqueville and contend that we have been betrayed by the ambitions of our military leaders, the thesis being that the people want peace, but the Generals have conspired against them. However, some of our most successful military leaders have been opposed to our growing militarism. General (and later President) Dwight Eisenhower (7) warned of the ominous alliance between the military and industrial organizations. General Smedly Butler (5) of the U.S. Marines, who was twice awarded the Congressional Medal of Honor, said, with obvious disgust, that he had spent his life advancing the interest of large American corporations. "I spent 33 years...most of my time being a high-class muscle man for Big Business, for Wall Street and the bankers. In short, I was a racketeer for capitalism... I helped purify Nicaragua for the international banking house of Brown Brothers in 1909-1912. I helped make Mexico and especially Tampico safe for American oil interests in 1914. I helped in the rape of half a dozen Central American republics for the benefit of Wall Street....In China in 1927 I helped to see to it that Standard Oil went its way unmolested....I had...a swell racket. I was rewarded with honors, medals, promotions....I might have given Al Capone a few hints. The best he could do was to operate a racket in three city districts. The Marines operated on three continents." While General Butler's remark suggests that there is a dangerous alliance between American capitalism and militarism, it is not at all clear that this mutual encouragement is the result of a conscious conspiracy. Conspirators generally do not fink on one another nor do they warn the public that their colleagues are dangerous. The warnings of Eisenhower and Smedley Butler seem to result from a belated

awareness that they have been a part of something
that is not altogether in the best interest of the
nation, that they are a bit uncomfortable about it
(in Butler's case more than a bit uncomfortable) and
that they would like to make some kind of restitu-
tion--if only a verbal restitution--to the people.
In the remarks of the speakers, as in the earlier
statement by Tocqueville, there is an implication
that the best interest of a democratic people will
not be served by a large military organization. If
the people can be made to see their interest clearly, they will reduce the size of their armed forces.

THE HIDDEN FACE OF DEMOCRATIC IMPERIALISM

But why should this be such a problem? If it
is simply a matter of explaining something that
makes sense from a logical point of view, we should
have ended the problem of military domination long
ago. We should be able to provide a reasonable defense against aggression without proposing to build
a military force large enough to save the world.
The people are more numerous than the Generals. If
they are free to oppose the power of a growing military establishment and fail to do so, we are justified in suspecting that they derive some satisfaction from being represented by such an impressive
show of force. It may not be in their best "interest" to escalate the arms race, but perhaps it satisfies some need that they are not willing to admit
openly. At the time of the Boer War, Schumpeter
(18) remarked that there was not a beggar in London
who did not speak of "our" rebellious subjects. It
is not, of course, acceptable for the leadership in
a democracy to give voice to the satisfactions expressed by Schumpeter's beggar. The thirst for
power in a democracy must be experienced as a painful necessity. It must be cleansed of any obvious
libidinal satisfaction. Thus we hear, in the United
States, that we did not seek our position of world
leadership. It was thrust upon us. During the
ceremony of lighting the White House Christmas tree,
President Nixon (14) remarked, "America did not seek
this role of world leadership...we are the first
power to be the major power in the world that did
not ask for it." If a democratic leader takes joy
in the exercise of power, he cannot remain in office.
To secure the pleasures of command he must put on a
long face. The ancient warrior King, on the other
hand, pounded his chest and challenged his enemies.

He took an open delight in warfare as a form of
sport, and when he was victorious he would drag the
conquered chieftain through the streets in chains
behind his chariot. Democratic imperialism must
take a different form. The aggressive intent of an
action must be concealed not only from the other nations of the world but from the people who help to
perpetrate the aggression.

However, the concelament of motives is not
enough. The military state must have force and discipline. If a nation is to become an international
power, the people must move as a unit. To do this
they must be willing to relinquish some of their independence. They must share some of the pleasures
of their leader without admitting to each other that
they have enjoyed themselves. Freud (8) has suggested that there is a dynamic relationship between
the desire to dominate others and the willingness to
be dominated ourselves. Rousseau has made a similar
point in regard to politics, pointing out that people can only be induced to sacrifice their freedom
and independence if they can be instructed in the
pleasures of command. "Individuals only allow themselves to be oppressed," he said, "so far as the are
hurried on by blind ambition, and, looking rather
below than above them, come to love authority more
than independence, and submit to slavery, that they
may in turn enslave others" (16, p. 24).

PSYCHOLOGICAL REPRESSION

If there is any substance to the belief that a
free people are more peaceloving and autocratic societies more warlike, we should expect to see freedom decline within a nation as it becomes a major
military power. But here America presents a peculiar problem. The outward signs of freedom are on
the increase in the United States. Since the end of
World War II civil rights--in the formal and legal-
istic sense--have improved. The American black man,
who was formerly considered an inferior soldier, is
now welcomed by the armed forces. In fact, if he is
not careful he may find himself part of a large mer-
cenary force designed to advance the cause of white
imperialism. As employment opportunities improve
for the black man he finds himself punching the same
time clocks that white men are privileged to punch.
Nevertheless, in this atmosphere of increasing political and economic freedom we find people com-
plaining that they feel more oppressed than before.
Hazel Barnes (1, pp. 284-5), has remarked that we

seem to be moving in the direction of trying to define a way of life for everyone. When civil rights
are denied the injustice is clear, but it is also
clear that there is a principle worth defending. On
the other hand the more subtle and insidious pressures for conformity are more deadly because they
can never be fully grasped. "It is like those ther-
mal blankets in which the threads are so loosely
woven that they seem to hold more empty spaces than
substance, yet the result is an artfully contrived
insulation against the outer environment more complete than any tight-woven textiles can provide.
Against such suffocating pressure, one must fight
one thread at a time, and each in itself seems too
insignificant to justify a violent revolt." This
sense of psychological repression in the midst of
political freedom is by no means a recent occurrence
in the United States. Tocqueville noticed it in the
1830s when he remarked that Monarchs institute material repression but that democratic republics had
rendered repression entirely an affair of the mind.
"Under the absolute sway of one man the body was attacked in order to subdue the soul; but the soul escaped the blows that were directed against it and
rose proudly superior. Such is not the course
adopted by tyranny in democratic republics; there
the body is left free, and the soul is enslaved"
(20, pp. 274-5).
     In the United States, where the psychological
pressures for conformity are greater, there is a
correspondingly greater political freedom. The
American adult can be "trusted" with this freedom
precisely because he has been thoroughly indoctri-
nated--by his education, the news media and by his
neighbors in the same middle class housing tract.
His notion of individualism is contained within the
social limits and the type of aspirations accepted
by his society. He is interested in discovering his
own unique way of becoming successful, but he does
not question the merits of the success ethic itself.
He has learned to equate freedom of choice with the
freedom to choose among those things his society offers him. He does not recognize that he has the
power to create his own alternatives. He is unaware
that he is free,and there is, therefore, less danger
that he will make use of his freedom.
     The problem is not peculiar to the United
States. It is a phenomenon of mass democratic col-
lectivization, a system of control so effective that
it is being imitated by the totalitarian countries
as well. It is becoming increasingly apparent that

the obvious forms of repression--the sudden cancel-
lation of radio and television broadcasts and the
trial of a writer for unorthodox ideas--are less effective than the more subtle methods of social control. Blank columns in the newspaper cry out to the
people that censorship has taken place. But the
playing down of the significance of information by
printing it in the final pages of the paper, "esti-
mating" a crowd at half the actual size, generating
a contrary source of excitement which will make news
and steal the headlines--all of these techniques affect the mind of the reader without announcing their
intent. The capacity of the individual to find
meaning in information is further reduced by increasing the quantity available to him. His search
capacity is limited. If he is constantly intimidated by the implication that he does not have all
the facts, his sense of closure and confidence in
his data is indefinitely suspended. One could argue
that the very emphasis on knowing everything reduces
comprehension. The effort to relay all the facts to
the public can become a means for flooding the
senses with factual information. Public attention
is directed to the sensation of the event itself,
and the next event, and then the next, and so on.
If the desire of the public to be "informed" can be
interpreted in the technological sense, that is, receiving the maximum number of bits of information
within a given unit of time, it becomes possible to
use the volume of information as a means for con-
cealing its significance.
     Repression is more effective if people can be
sold on the idea of their own foolishness and incompetence. If the police can be kept in the background, the people can be taught to restrain themselves because they will look ridiculous or because
their behavior might be bad for business. If a man
feels himself tremble at his own fear of a beating,
he knows that his manhood is being attacked. If he
is afraid of being socially inappropriate, he is unaware of his own surrender. This is why the revolution of awareness in young people has been directed
toward bringing the repressive aspects of our society into the foreground, i.e., in refusing to cancel
a protest march because it blocks traffic in front
of the business establishments, flouting their own
fears of looking ridiculous by wearing the most out-
landish and unconventional garb. All of these acts
represent an attempt to recapture a lost sense of
psychological freedom. The struggle for power is
moving from the outward field of physical force to

the inner realm. In domestic as in international
affairs the final battle will be fought not for possession of land, but for possession of the human
soul. The United States today is one of the primary
forces in this transformation in the locus of power.
It is reflected in the image making that is characteristic of our domestic politics and in the "mood
engineering" with which we approach international
bargaining and negotiating. It is, in part, a product of the advertising culture in which the "hidden
persuader" plays such an important role.

AUTOCRATIC REPRESSION

Autocratic societies have not been unmindful of
the importance of the control of perception, but in
the development of "propaganda," their objective has
been shortsighted. This was particularly true of
Hitler, who believed he could control the perception
of others by deliberate and conscious lies. Modern
methods of thought control are more subtle. It is
possible for the chief executive to maintain a policy of telling the truth if others learn when to lie
for him and when to conceal information from him.
In this way deception can take place without becoming a part of national policy. The intent of the
national leader is concealed not only from the people but from himself as well.
A similar process obtains in all the echelons
of command. Junior military officers, junior State
Department executives and rookie policemen soon
learn that there are certain practices the "old man"
would rather not hear about. Thus it becomes possible for the "old man" to be "honest" and open in
his dealings with the press and the public. If illegal and repressive acts occur, they occur without
his knowledge and, by implication, without his intent. In a society in which there are laws designed
to provide for freedom of information, it is impossible to conceal acts of injustice--and it is not
really necessary. If such acts can be isolated from
the intent of the administrator they become "mis-
takes" or "failures in communication." If one cannot find a repressive intent in the written directives of the police department or in the words of a
briefing officer, the acts themselves become the
product of individual idiosyncracy, nothing more.
In a similar manner, acts of international aggression are explained in terms of a failure in communication or a failure to get all the facts. This is
particularly true for acts of aggression that turn

out badly for one reason or another.

The emphasis on information contains an implicit assumption that the formulation of policy is a problem with a scientific solution. The very act of gathering information implies that policy is getting better day by day. In this concentration on externals the internal and more human influences on policy are ignored. These are the subtle attitudinal variables which make it possible to have a different form of law enforcement for the wealthy and for the poor, although the policy is ostensibly the same. The information approach assumes that if we can only find out, in great detail, what is going on in the ghetto, we can correct the situation. It takes for granted the good intentions of policy makers and the malleability of the police. In a similar manner, American foreign policy is based on the assumption that international disagreement is caused by some misunderstanding. If only all the facts were known, both sides would see the mutuality of their interests and cooperation would be assured.

AWARENESS OF AGGRESSION

Justice is always rational, but man is not. The understanding of international disagreement must take into consideration the urge for national aggrandizement and the will to dominate. This does not mean that a few clever conspirators have made the United States into an imperialist power against the will of the people. It means that the spokesmen for American imperialism have learned to make use of the urge for power which exists in all of us to forward their own ambitions. But even this statement is suggestive of too much deliberation. Those who have been the most active in advancing American interests have been "decent respectable citizens" with all that this phrase implies for the American middle-class. They are not conscious of their greed. They feel that they have earned the right to what is called "success." They regard competition, in both the individual and the international sense, as a healthy form of sportsmanship. They have managed to avoid looking at its deadly and destructive aspect. This attitude is common not only to the "power elite," but to the majority of the American middle class.

It is this lack of awareness of our aggressive intent that is responsible for some of the most significant failures in American foreign policy. It

applies to those situations in which we have been
attacked without fully recognizing our danger (such
as Pearl Harbor) as well as those in which we have
attempted to suppress revolutions "for the good of
the Free World" (such as Vietnam, Cuba, and Santa
Domingo). In the latter instances we have miscalcu-
lated the degree of resistance we would encounter,
because we have assumed that we were acting to support the interest of the majority of people in the
country we have invaded. We have been surprised by
the response because we did not recognize our own
intentions--though others did. In our concentration
upon policy and upon rational representation of society, we have denied the existence of dark forces
within the human psyche which work against man's rational aspirations. We have ignored the reality of
evil in man, and with it, the whole realm of the irrational.

    If it is true that we can be aggressive without
becoming aware of our aggressive intent, then an important element in the problem of war (and perhaps
domestic violence as well) can be seen as essentially psychological. This does not mean we should attempt to become aware of our aggressive intent in
order to eliminate all aggression. Aggression is a
healthy response in some instances. However, if one
is unaware of the aggressive nature of one's acts,
one may be surprised by unexpected violence on the
part of others. If we are unaware of the significance of our acts, we will be puzzled by this violence and regard it as undue provocation. The
chances for escalation in such a situation are obvious. On the other hand, if we recognize our own
aggressive acts for what they are, we are more inclined to understand the response of others. Understanding alone is not enough for peace, but it is
the prerequisite for any rational discussion.

DEVELOPING AWARENESS

    How, then, does one bring about greater total
awareness? Clearly there is a growing recognition
on the part of many people that they are cut off
from their feelings and lacking in sensitivity to
the world around them. There are a number of centers
for human growth already in existence which are designed to foster greater awareness. Some participants in growth center encounter groups report something that they call a "peak experience," a sense of
the oneness of man with his physical body and the
world around him. They also report that a greater

sense of understanding and tolerance for their fellow man follows such experiences. Some humanistic psychologists have even suggested that the answer to some of our social problems, such as race hatred, corruption and international war, is the proliferation of encounter groups throughout the world. However, there are numerous problems in implementing such a program. The first is that the very people who are most in need of the experience of awareness are most resistant to it. Having built their lives on the basis of the ego, they are more fearful of letting go. The second problem is that the people who do achieve a kind of beautific vision of the unity of mankind from a peak experience are generally unconcerned with changing the world. It is the rare individual who, like Gandhi, turns his vision outward. Most participants in growth centers tend to turn inward to the exploration of their physical sensations and sharing their experiences with others like themselves. There is already an air of cultishness about the growth center movement. It would seem, in short, that, while the peak experience may help a man appreciate the value of world peace, it does not stimulate him to work toward its realization. While there are often moments of anger, fear, and frustration in groups which seek awareness, the final experience is expected to be one of bliss. This statement is based on the descriptions of leaders in the field who report the peak experience as being something that is always good and pleasant--at least in mature people. This seems to be the attitude of most group leaders at the increasingly popular growth centers such as Esalen, Aureon, Kairos, etc. If one has a bad trip, one is considered to be either immature or insufficiently prepared for the beauties of Nirvana.

Yet, the bad trip is not as uncommon as we are led to believe. William James (8) in his *Varieties of Religious Experience,* reports a series of both pleasant and frightening experiences that lead to a marked alteration in the life style of the individual. One of the frightening variety was apparently his own. Colin Wilson (21) in *The Outsider* considers the bad trip almost exclusively. Examining some of the great creative minds of history, he points to the terror that often accompanies or precedes the moment of creativity. Jean Jacques-Rousseau (15) in his *Confessions* reports a peak experience that launched him on his career as a political writer. While his initial experience was pleasant, Rousseau found himself pulled ever more deeply into the con-

sequences of his commitment. The result was inter-
mittent episodes of terror that reached psychotic
proportions (3).
     Apparently, then, the experience of awareness
can be either pleasant or unpleasant, ecstatic or
terrifying. If there is a relationship between the
experience of awareness and the search for peace,
how do these moments of terror fit into the notion
of a brotherhood of man. Certainly they are not
very peaceful. Yet one must also raise the question
as to whether the search for peace can really be a
peaceful process in the world as it is today. The
awareness of the urgency of the problem of world
peace arises from the immediacy of the war threat.
One does not stop war by invoking the notion of
brotherhood, but by confronting the warmakers.
Hence the seemingly incongruous notion of a "fight
for peace," and the caricature slogan of the Yippies
"Kill for Peace."
     However, just as the professional organizations
for the promotion of awareness tend to emphasize the
pleasurable, ecstatic and happy aspects of awareness,
so professional convocations for world peace tend to
emphasize the need for brotherhood, the search for
law and harmony and the achievement of human happiness as part of the total phenomenon of world peace.
The entire structure of our society tends to foster
this idea. Webster (22) defines the word "peace" in
several ways, most of which support the idea of order and calm. Peace is "a state of tranquility or
quiet." It is "freedom from civil disturbance." It
is "a state of security or order within a community
provided by law and custom." It is "freedom from
disquieting or oppressive thoughts or emotions." It
is "harmony in personal relations." And finally it
is "a pact or agreement to end hostilities between
those who have been at war." Now it seems to me
that in order to achieve the condition described by
the last of these definitions, we must be willing to
forego the earlier ones. *The peace that comes about
through the termination of the international system
of warfare will be characterized by a lack of tranquility, an increase in civil disturbance and in
disquieting thought, disharmony in personal relationships and, most of all, a breach in the customs
and laws of a community which provide for a state of
order and security.* It is my contention--and this
is certainly not an original idea--that in order to
prosecute a war efficiently one must have domestic
order, relatively strict adherence to the laws, and
particularly the customs of a society, and minimal

civil unrest. Therefore, in a civilization which
has become habituated to warfare as a way of life,
peace (in the sense of a cessation of war) can only
be maintained by an alert citizenry which is in a
constant state of disquiet: restive, suspicious of
every government prouncement, and ready to erupt into protest at the slightest awareness that it is being prepared for mass mobilization. As we become
more aware of our violence as a nation, we may become more disruptive and openly aggressive as individuals.

     While this study was underway, I came across a
book by Richard Sennett on the problems of the city
entitled *The Uses of Disorder* (19). Sennett deals
with the problem of aggression and conflict on a
smaller scale, but there appears to be some clear
parallels between his work and mine. The tendency
of governments, whether they are city governments or
national governments, to equate advance planning and
control with peace and stability seems to increase
as modern technology gives these governments the
ability to exercise control. Sennett describes the
city planner as one who imposes his concept of a
city upon the real, disorderly, messy conglomeration
of buildings and people. If the city does not develop according to the plan or if some parts of the
plan conflict with others, there is said to be a
"failure" of the plans. But in reality, some degree
of conflict is part of the human experience. It is
the effort to make everything orderly and "purified"
that conflicts most of all with the way people work
and live. The insistence that people function according to plans tends to increase the degree of
conflict.

FAITH AND COMMITMENT

     But one of the chief problems of peace convoca-
tions, particularly those in the United States, is a
predisposition to take a positive view of mankind,
to concentrate on the brotherhood of man, to emphasize the constructive and the creative, in the hope
that peace can somehow be "sold" to mankind as a
whole. A peace-oriented society would require the
complete restructuring of our present system of national and international controls. It would require
a change in the idea of what constitutes manhood and
courage. It would mean a breach of customs, an in-
vocation of the absurd in order to heighten our
awareness of the absurdity of our present way of

life. This awareness that changes the shape of a
human life is, in part, an intellectual experience,
a matter of understanding. But it also has elements
of another kind of experience, a knowing in the
sense of faith and conviction. The experience that
instills such conviction may combine both terror and
ecstacy, but it will certainly involve the whole
person. Norman Mailer has described such an experience among the youth who remained all night on the
steps of the Pentagon during a war protest.

> Yes, the passage through the night against ev-
> ery temptation to leave--the cold, the possi-
> bility of new, more brutal, and more overwhelm-
> ing attacks, the boredom, the middle-class ter-
> ror of excess....Yes, the passage through the
> night brought every temptation to leave...ex-
> cept if they left, and no one was at the Penta-
> gon then but the soldiers through the night,
> well what unseen burning torch of which unknown
> but palpably felt spirit might expire?....So it
> became a rite of passage for these tender drug-
> vitiated jargon-mired children, they endured
> through a night, a black dark night which began
> in joy, near foundered in terror, and dragged
> on through empty apathetic hours while glints
> of light came to each alone. Yes the rite of
> passage was invoked, the moral ladder was
> climbed, they were forever different in the
> morning than they had been before the night,
> which is the meaning of a rite of passage, one
> has voyaged through a channel of shipwreck and
> temptation... Some part of the man has been born
> again and is better, just as some hardly so re-
> markable area of the soul may have been in some
> miniscule sweet fashion reborn on the crossing
> of the markers over Arlington Memorial Bridge,
> for the worst of them and the most timid were
> moving nonetheless to a confrontation they
> could only fear, they were going to the land of
> the warmakers. (13, pp. 310-312)

Such an experience, that exposes all the nerve
ends to both pleasure and pain, is a form of knowing
and discovering. It is an intellectual as well as
an emotional experience. But it is the kind of experience that casts the mind into a different realm
of thought, a new frame of reference. It involves
the notion of intention and commitment, an aspect of

the intellectual life that has been given little attention by modern psychology. It is precisely this
aspect of *commitment* that lends terror to the learning experience, for it may involve not only one's
physical being, but one's identity as well.

TERROR AND POSITIVE CHANGE

The terror in such situations springs from a
feeling that one is no longer in complete control of
one's own consciousness. Unlike the experience of
listening to a lecture or watching a film, one cannot avoid knowing. Awareness arrives because one is
in the experience and part of it. It is my personal
conviction that all learning is superficial which
does not involve this element of terror to some degree and in some form. It is the only kind of intellectual experience that changes human lives.

It should be evident by now that the world cannot be sweet-talked or reasoned into peace. This
does not mean we must discard all our intellectual
resources. It does mean, however, that the intellectual explanation that peace makes good sense is
not sufficient to evoke the necessary action to preserve it. Peace, in the context of really putting
an end to a civilization based on warfare, is a revolutionary idea, and it may require a revolution to
achieve it. Whether or not this revolution involves
violence will depend on the extent to which the established authority in each nation is prepared to
use force to maintain the status quo. This, in
turn, will depend on the character of the people,
their psychological resilience, their capacity for
encountering uncertainty and civil unrest without
panic, their ability to experience an expansion of
awareness and a dramatic change in cultural values
without despair and disintegration.

Such a change would involve not only the mass
resistance to warfare, but the resistance to all
systems of violence and oppression. For we cannot
expect an end to warfare unless there is a vigorous
opposition to all systems of organized oppression,
discrimination and injustice. If crime exists under
the name of law, and if it is not opposed, the inevitable result will be an accumulation of anger and
resentment and the organization of a violent coun-
ter-system to oppose it. The result will be a revolution that replaces one type of injustice by another.

CENTERS FOR POLITICAL AWARENESS

How can a nation provide an atmosphere for this kind of change? It is a problem that could enlist the full resources of those who have had some experience in political awareness. However, the kind of political awareness I am talking about is not the kind that is advertised by nonpartisan organizations which encourage the citizen to know his congressman. A center or an institution which provides the kind of awareness I have been describing would have to develop without help from the federal government. Generally if it developed at all, it would rise up in the teeth of resistance from established institutions.

In spite of the difficulties involved, there have been a few institutions of this kind throughout the world. In 1966, Father Blase Bonpane, a priest of the Catholic Foreign Mission Society in America opened what he called a "Center for Awareness" at the National University of Guatemala. He attempted to inform local peasants of their right to organize and teach them certain fundamental human values such as the dignity of man. More important, in this case, is the fact that he attempted to make them aware of the organized and systematic violence of which they were the daily victims. Speaking of the Guatemalan peasant, he said:

> I believe the well read student can say honestly, the status quo is killing my brother: my brother is suffering as a result of the institutionalized violence in which he lives. He is dying because he doesn't eat. He is dying because he doesn't have any land. He is dying because he cannot organize his labor. He is dying intellectually because he has no schools. (2, p. 61)

Father Bonpane was opposed by the wealthy landowners and finally by the government. He was called a communist and several of his students had to flee for their lives. Had he not been an American citizen he might not have survived as long as he did. In 1968 he was recalled to the United States.

Several centers for political awareness are still operating in Mexico and South America today. One of these is CIDOC, the Center for Intercultural Documentation, which has managed to survive because

it has directed its appeal to intellectuals and has
made no attempt to organize the peasants.

Centers for political awareness are springing
up throughout the underdeveloped countries of the
world. There are a number, of a more informal type,
in the ghettos of American cities. If we are to
bring about change through minor stages of civil
disturbance, as opposed to the more drastic step of
international war and internal revolution, a similar
experience in political awakening must be provided
for the American middle-class. The Institute for
the Study of Nonviolence in Palo Alto, California,
made such an opportunity possible. Although most
participants could hardly be described as middle-
class, I also met businessmen there and two navy officers who were in the early stages of resistance to
service in Vietnam.

With our present notion of tranquility and order as the social ideal, we are conditioned to expect a change that takes place through channels according to designated procedures. Such an attitude
leaves us psychologically unprepared for the future.
Unless we can learn to accept the kind of change
that springs from opposition to the status quo, we
will strive too hard to keep the lid on tight and
thus encourage a buildup of tension. As President
Kennedy (11) has remarked, "Those who make peaceful
revolutions impossible will make violent revolutions
inevitable."

CORRECTING AGGRESSION AMERICAN STYLE

In the United States we have had a number of
shocks in recent years. Each in its own way has
produced a rent in some area of our national identity: Watergate, the Vietnam War, the Arab oil boycott, the campus revolts, Civil Rights marches, militant minorities and a new, more critically perceptive, communications media.

It is possible that the current style of American aggression is a transitory stage in our development which has been maintained because of our geographic distance from other world powers in our early history. Our development was so rapid that we
were not obliged to see the world as others saw it.
It was up to them to understand us and to try to
reach our level of achievement. The mere opening of
the doors of travel through the jet airplane would
not be enough to change this narrow American provin-
cialism, for in the early part of the jet era, we

brought our American money with us and purchased our
own standard of living everywhere in the world with
our powerful dollar. People who share a common culture tend to reinforce each other's beliefs and a
few weeks of travel outside this closed system is
not enough to dispel our illusions.

The Arab oil boycott and the decline of the
American dollar have diminished our physical comfort, but they have expanded our perception of the
world. They have made us aware that the resources
of the earth are not limitless and we have been disturbed to discover that there is nothing permanent
about American economic superiority. The wage-
earner in Sweden and Germany have already surpassed
our average wage and the Japanese are gaining rapidly. The world is changing to the point that we will
soon be forced to deal with the problem of an equi-
table distribution of world resources.

We are not yet certain that this shock is sufficient to bring about change. It may be that we
will require a series of electrical blackouts before
the individual American experiences this problem in
a direct way in his own home. But the leadership of
our nation is aware of it. If they can muster the
courage to make the necessary unpopular decisions,
we may still escape some of the more serious consequences of our declining resources.

The war in Vietnam represented an even greater
shock to American dreams of omnipotence and personal
virtue. We owe much that we have learned from this
experience to the courageous resistance of the young
men who refused to fight in the war and refused all
the legal means of avoiding military service. While
the college campuses are quiet once again, some of
the young people who were part of the revolt of the
60s are now taking their place in the adult world.
The campus revolt had its fringe elements who loved
to trash a city block for the fun of trashing, but
the leadership in this movement represented some of
our brightest and most capable people, as Kenniston
(12) and Hampden-Turner (9) demonstrated.

*Perhaps the most encouraging sign of a movement
away from American innocence is the development of a
more critical press and television.* During the
Cuban invasion, there was a surrender of the press
to the administration. President Kennedy exerted
considerable pressure to bring about press compliance and he was angered by the few reporters bold
enough to print some information on the invasion
plans. But after it was over, he remarked that, had
the press insisted on printing everything about the

invasion, the administration might have been saved
from a colossal mistake. He also arranged for more
private discussions with his staff, urging them to
come forth with their unfettered opinions. In regard to the staff, Schlesinger remarked, "For our
part we resolved to be less acquiescent the next
time. The Bay of Pigs gave us a license for the im-
polite inquiry and the rude comment" (17, p. 278).

Television and press reporting of the Vietnam
War was relentless. If a person could hide from it
during the day, it was there facing him with the
morning paper and it greeted him in the evening from
the television set. There was no escape from the
details of burning peasant villages, the body count,
the defoliation and the slaughter of Hamburger Hill
and My Lai. These constant visual and auditory re-
minders that ours was not a "compassionate army," as
well as the coverage given to anti-war demonstrators, were much criticized by the Johnson and Nixon
administrations. Nevertheless, the media played a
central role in influencing our decision to withdraw
from Vietnam. The media did not manufacture this
information; it simply refused to suppress dramatic
and newsworthy stories that contained direct or im-
plied criticism of the administration.

However, the critical aspect in all of this
movement toward social change is that the American
people must learn to recognize when their desires
are incompatible. This requires the kind of self-
scrutiny that Lasswell recommended in his study of
politics. In the end, the deeper study of politics
means a confrontation with one's self. Churchman
arrived at a similar conclusion about the study of
the universe, but he also added that a deep look into one's self is not without a certain danger, that
it has been viewed with suspicion throughout history.

The suspicion is a sound one, as all the wise
men of history have told us. He who seeks to
understand himself seeks the devil in himself
as well as his God. The view that his understanding may open up may be too much for his
contemplation, for it may display to him what
he really is: perhaps the agent of all that is
decadent in nature....
If men begin to understand what they are trying
to do, they may understand the worse as well as
the better about themselves. Can they stand to
understand? (6, pp. 108-116)

REFERENCES

1. Barnes, Hazel. *An Existential Ethics*. New
    York: Knopf, 1967, pp. 284-85.
2. Bonpane, B. Our Latin Vietnam. *Los Angeles
    Times*, February 11, 1968, pp. 21-22.
3. Blanchard, W.H. *Rousseau and the Spirit of Re-
    volt*. Ann Arbor: University of Michigan Press,
    1967.
4. Buchanan, W., & Cantril, H. *How Nations See
    Each Other*. Urbana: University of Illinois
    Press, 1953.
5. Butler, S. In G. Seldes (Ed.), *Great Quota-
    tions*. New York: Lyle Stuart, 1960 (p. 134).
6. Churchman, C.W. *Challenge to Reason*. New York:
    McGraw-Hill, 1968.
7. Eisenhower, D.D. President Eisenhower's Fare-
    well Address to the Nation. *Department of State
    Bulletin*, February 6,. 1961, 179-182.
8. Freud, S. *The Basic Writings of Sigmund Freud*.
    A.A. Brill (Ed.), New York: Modern Library,
    1938.
9. Hampden-Turner, C. *Radical Man*. Cambridge:
    Schenkman, 1970.
10. James, W. *The Varieties of Religious Experience*.
    New York: New American Library (Mentor), 1958.
11. Kennedy, J.F. Address to Latin American Diplo-
    mats. White House. March 12, 1962.
12. Kenniston, K. *Young Radicals*. New York: Har-
    court, Brace & World, 1968.
13. Mailer, N. *The Armies of the Night*. New York:
    New American Library (Signet), 1968
14. Nixon, R.M. The Pageant of Peace Ceremony.
    Weekly Compilation of Presidential Documents,
    1969, *5*, No. 51, 1757-1758.
15. Rousseau, J.J. *Les Oeuvres Completes de Jean-
    Jacques Rousseau*. Paris: Gallimard, 1959-1964.
16. Rousseau, J.J. *The Social Contract and Dis-
    courses*. New York: E.P. Dutton, 1950.
17. Schlesinger, A.M., Jr. *A Thousand Days*. Green-
    wich, Conn.: Fawcett, 1965.
18. Schumpeter, J. *Imperialism and Social Classes*.
    New York: World, 1966.
19. Sennett, R. *The Uses of Disorder*. New York:
    Random House (Vintage), 1970.
20. Tocqueville, A. de. *Democracy in America*. New
    York: Vintage, 2 volumes, 1955 & 1959.
21. Wilson, C. *The Outsider*. New York: Delta,
    1956.
22. Webster, A.M. *Webster's New Collegiate Diction-
    ary*. Springfield: G. & C. Merriam, 1961.

WILLIAM H. BLANCHARD *is a clinical psychologist. Early in his career with the California Youth Authority, he developed (with Crain and Jacobs) the widely used consensus approach to the Rorschach. After a period in private practice, he spent several years with RAND Corporation and System Development Corporation in the fields of systems analysis and training program development. He became increasingly concerned with the spread of what he has called "the systematization of thought" in the formulation of national policy. He believes that the techniques of systems analysis are too often set up to deal only with quantifiable information, and as such tend to discourage consideration of human values--especially those that deal with nuances and ambiguities. Dr. Blanchard believes that a culture dominated by an analytic approach to policy tends to deny and suppress awareness of its aggressive trends. In such an environment the dangers of war are greater and the chances of preventing and ending wars are diminished.*

During 1962-64, Dr. Blanchard worked in Europe gathering information for a psychological study of the political ideas of Jean-Jacques Rousseau. This was his first venture into the study of the psychology of politics. The book was published in 1967 by the University of Michigan Press under the title, ROUSSEAU AND THE SPIRIT OF REVOLT. He has recently completed a book-length treatment of the subject of his chapter in this book, under the same name: AGGRESSION--AMERICAN STYLE (Los Angeles: Goodyear, 1978). Today Dr. Blanchard spends his time as a consultant, writing and initiating experimental university courses. His course in "The Psychology of Revolution" began at California State University, Northridge, and was also taught at UCLA and the California School of Professional Psychology. He was also a program coordinator for an experimental program in urbanology at the University of Southern California. He is currently working on a psychological study of Karl Marx. He is married, has two children, a boy and a girl, and lives in Woodland Hills, California.

SOME OTHER PUBLICATIONS BY WILLIAM H. BLANCHARD

- Intellectual inhibition and the search for scientific truth. *Journal of Social Psychology,* 1958, *47,* 55-70.
- Psychodynamic aspects of the peak experience. *Psychoanalytic Review,* 1969, *56*(1), 87-112.

9. Between "Order" and Violence: The Middle Ground

Samuel Rabinove, LL.B.

Public opinion polls consistently paint a dreary picture of popular attitudes toward civil liberties. In May, 1970, for example, Louis Harris found that his question, "Do you think protests against the war should be declared illegal?" was answered affirmatively by 37% of those surveyed, with 10% "not sure."(1). And in the winter of 1969, when he had asked, "Do you feel that students have the right to make their protests or not?" 52% of his cross-section responded negatively, with 10% "not sure"(2). True, these questions failed to distinguish clearly between violent and peaceful protests, but the findings are disquieting nevertheless. Going back a bit further, a Harris poll statement in 1968: "Mayor Daley was right the way he used police against demonstrators at the Democratic Party convention in Chicago," elicited 66% agreement, 20% disagreement, 14% "not sure"(3). This refers to the very disturbances which were widely witnessed on television and which were characterized as a "police riot" in the Report to the National Commission on the Causes and Prevention of Violence (Walker Report)(4).

There have been other times in American history, of course, when citizens displayed something less than an impassioned commitment to the principles articulated in the Bill of Rights. But many of us would like to believe that a contemporary version of the Sedition Act of 1798 (which, among other things, made it a crime punishable by imprisonment to speak or write against the President or Congress with the intent to bring them "into contempt or disrepute"(5) or of black slavery or Indian genocide, or, more recently, of the mass incarceration of

184

Japanese-Americans during World War II, could not
happen today because the people would not stand for
such doings. Let us not be too sure. While the
spirit of liberty in America runs wide and deep, so
does the strain of repression, and in crisis situations it is hazardous to attempt to predict what the
public temper may be. In fact, a good many of our
political dissidents in recent years themselves have
exhibited repressive tendencies, having shouted down
speakers they abhorred on numerous college campuses
around the country.

The average American is either unaware of or
else is indifferent to the truth that political and
intergroup violence have studded the national scene
ever since the very founding of our Republic. He
has little acquaintance, if any, for example, with
the dozens of major riots in Boston, Philadelphia,
New York, Baltimore and other cities, between 1830
and 1860, stemming from the conflicts between native
Americans and recently arrived immigrants(6). He is
apt to be enraged by the lawlessness of radical activists, white or black, and typically has closed
his mind to dispassionate analyses or historical
parallels or root causes. About these, regrettably,
he couldn't care less. As Sen. Margaret Chase Smith
has indicated, if our people were forced to choose
between anarchy and repression,"...the American people, even if with reluctance and misgiving, will
choose repression"(7).

There is little question that the apparent re-
ceptivity on the part of so many Americans to repressive measures by government authorities derives,
at least in large part, from the fears induced by
the sharp upsurge in political and racial violence
and disruption during the past few years. All violence, of course, is explainable--if we care to
probe deeply enough. Hitler's Brown Shirts also included a goodly number of disadvantaged youths. Yet
it is equally evident that while to explain all is
by no means to excuse all, the explaining of contemporary violence has been accompanied by a great deal
of excusing.

If we were to believe that the end justifies
the means, that people must "do their own thing" no
matter who gets hurt, that the democratic process is
a myth, that there is no hope for society as presently constituted and that nothing could be worse
than what we now have, then *any* revolutionary action
would be excusable--whether from the left or the
right. Such an ideology would open the door to despotism, with naked force as the major determinant of

social policy. Most people, however, are apt to be
highly selective about the brands of political violence that they are prepared to excuse. Not surprisingly, few apologists for the Weathermen or the
Black Panthers, for example, have been disposed to
be correspondingly indulgent toward the antics of
the Minutemen or the Ku Klux Klan or club-wielding
"hardhats" or the Jewish Defense League. Somebody
once said the trouble with the exciting game of
street-fighting is that any number can play. Always
for "noble" causes, naturally, though the causes
may happen to clash.

It is abundantly clear that much more has to be
done in every quarter to rectify the deep-seated
and, by now, very well-known social and economic injustices that continue to disgrace America. Yet the
tragic reality is that these evils are not likely to
be fully abated in the immediate future. How large
the deficit will be and how long it will persist are
impossible to foretell. This depends not merely on
how much will be done but also on how much will be
expected by people who feel deprived. In all likelihood some degree of acute social unrest, erupting
into disorder, will continue to plague us for some
time to come.

If this scenario is correct, the challenge of
the 1970s and 80s for freedom-loving liberals and
conservatives is not only to achieve as much justice
as is humanly possible, but also to stake out and
consolidate a middle-ground, democratic position between those who endorse or condone revolutionary violence on the one side and those who do the same for
authoritarian repression on the other. It *is* possible for public officials to respond to civil disturbances effectively, with no more force than absolutely necessary, and within the framework of the
rule of law. But it is not easy; it requires skill
and determination, and it is not likely to happen
most of the time as long as the public, by and
large, is willing to countenance the scuttling of
hard-won constitutional guarantees in the name of
preserving "law and order." It is noteworthy that
Attorney General John Mitchell stated, rather be-
latedly, to be sure (August, 1971), that he agreed
with the conclusion of the National Commission on
Campus Unrest (Scranton Commission) that the shooting of the students at Kent State by Ohio National
Guardsmen was "unnecessary, unwarranted and inexcus-
able"(8). It is equally noteworthy that none of the
Guardsmen were prosecuted.

THE NEED TO WIN OVER "MIDDLE AMERICA"

Civil libertarians will have to do a far better job of teaching and "selling" the Bill of Rights than has been done heretofore. One good way to begin is to reach out and seek to communicate with groups in the population which, while they love freedom in the abstract, generally have found their ardor cooled when confronted with a civil liberties problem in the concrete, particularly when an unpopular cause or individual is involved. This will be no easy task.

The average member of the American Legion is not really a bloodthirsty Fascist, bent upon destroying the Bill of Rights. But he is very much concerned, and properly so, about maintaining order and security in his community. He is not likely to be worried that the F.B.I. may tap his telephone without a court order. What does trouble him mightily, however, is that he cannot walk the streets of his own city at night without fear of being mugged. If he can be shown that his objectives are obtainable without sacrificing anybody's civil liberties, in all probability he will be satisfied. If, on the other hand, he concludes that his own safety and that of his family demand certain Draconian measures which civil libertarians label "repressive," he will accept "repression" as a necessary price to be paid.

Middle America will not be convinced of the overriding importance of civil liberties by appeals to lofty principle or a higher morality. What could be persuasive, however, is an approach based on enlightened self-interest. A law-abiding "hardhat," for example, may be induced to take a fresh look at the elements of due process of law for accused persons if he realizes that his own son could be jailed because a search of his clothing revealed a marijuana cigarette. Nor is he likely to be moved to vote for a legislator who advocates sweeping penal reform, including civil rights for felons, by appeals to his sense of mercy or compassion for the poor and the afflicted. But he may be won over by a strategy which asks him whether he would prefer to have a convict (who has served his sentence) released into the community more dangerous or less dangerous than when he entered prison. In other words, middle aged, middle class whites can only be brought into the civil liberties camp by a strategy which is sensitive to and which responds persuasively to their own felt needs. A nationwide program, therefore, to schedule forums, debates and stimulating speakers on

timely civil liberties issues with groups such as
the American Legion, Veterans of Foreign Wars,
Knights of Columbus, Rotary, Kiwanis, Elks, Moose,
etc., many of whose members have exhibited constricted or ambivalent attitudes toward civil liberties, would be an invaluable public service.

> Farmer uprisings are part of our national heri-
> tage; as late as the 1930s debt-ridden farmers
> were blocking mortgage foreclosures, burning
> crops, and buying in foreclosed properties for
> pennies at "shotgun sales."....Businessmen
> hired private armies of their own or allied
> themselves with gangsters to defeat the union
> movement....The same groups which began their
> rise to suburban respectability and middle-of-
> the road politics in the 1930s and 1940s were
> the Molly Maguires, Wobblies, gangsters and an-
> archists of an earlier age....Naturally, mem-
> bers of the ultra-respectable labor movement of
> the 1960s do not like to be reminded of the AFL
> dynamiters of 1910-1920, the Kentucky border
> mining wars of the 1920s or the violent CIO
> strikes of the 1930s (9, pp. 13-14).

There is a critical need for a lively, anec-
dotal, highly readable pamphlet, beamed at Middle
America, which effectively shatters the myth that
social progress in this country typically has been
accomplished peacefully. A publication of this nature, liberally sprinkled with cartoons and photos
graphically depicting turbulent events in the American historical experience, should be subvented by a
public-spirited private foundation for free distribution in quantity. For those who are disposed to
read, this could be an eye-opener. For those who
are not, a more arresting approach is needed: a
series of documentaries on television, targeting and
interpreting little known episodes of group violence
in American.

TEACH CIVIL RIGHTS, LIBERTIES AND RESPONSIBILITIES TO ALL HIGH SCHOOL STUDENTS

Despite anybody's best efforts, a certain proportion of our adult citizens probably are so deeply
fixed in their cherished attitudes and values that,
realistically, they cannot be converted to the civil

liberties cause. But this may not be at all true of
their children. This is why it is so important to
try to bring the Bill of Rights, along with the rest
of the message of constitutional government, to as
many high school students as possible. Most of
them, obviously, are the middle Americans of 1980--
or 1984.

The Essex County OEO Legal Services unit, the
Young Lawyers section of the New Jersey Bar Association, Rutgers Law School, Seton Hall Law School and
the New Jersey Chapter of the American Jewish Committee have collaborated on a useful educational
project. Its objective has been to offer high
school students, within the framework of the social
studies curriculum, a basic understanding of those
aspects of the law which concern them most, as well
as hopefully to instill in them a positive attitude
toward the role of law (and the rule of law) in our
society. At the conclusion of a pilot program conducted with nine classes of seniors at Orange High
School, the students filled out evaluation questionnaires. Their responses reflected a nearly
unanimously favorable opinion of the program and expressed keen interest in learning more about the
laws pertaining to marriage and divorce, drugs, the
draft, crime and student protest.

The important thing about an educational program of this nature is that, unlike much of what is
taught in high school today, the students will
quickly perceive that it is "for real"--provided it
is properly presented. Its content, however, must
be tailored to their live needs and concerns. Nor
need it be restricted to high school students. In
Redwood City, Cal. 7th and 8th graders have been
learning about "rules and rights," and Portland,
Ore. junior high children have been reading case
studies on the Bill of Rights, including U.S. Supreme Court decisions on school desegregation,
search and seizure, etc.(10). These children are
being taught the rudiments of civil rights and liberties, along with civil responsibilities, the idea
being to shape constructive attitudes as early as
possible.

Other programs of this kind have been underway
in Boston, sponsored by the Law and Poverty project
of Boston University Law School; in Harrisburg,
where practicing attorneys have visited the city's
three high schools for weekly lectures; and in St.
Louis, where law students have been instructing
teenagers on landlord-tenant problems, their own
rights in court and on other very practical matters.

In Miami, a legal education undertaking on the high
school level, stressing realistic alternatives to
violence and change through orderly process, was organized by the Young Lawyers Section of the Dade
County Bar Association. Commented one lawyer-teach-
er, "You can't be 'stuffed shirt' with these kids--
they're too perceptive"(11). On the whole, the
Miami program has been well received, as have the
other experimental programs. But even something as
simple and unstructured as volunteer lawyers coming
into high school social studies classrooms just to
answer questions may be an improvement over what
there is now in many schools, though a somewhat more
ambitious program is well within the realm of feasi-
bility.

Yet as valuable as it may be, formal instruction in rights, liberties and responsibilities for
young students will be infinitely more so if these
precepts are translated into living reality in their
day-to-day educational experience, if they are accorded a share in the decision-making process on
matters which vitally affect them. This brings to
mind a cartoon which appeared in *Playboy* magazine in
1969, depicting a group of high school students in a
principal's office, with the caption, "I'm glad you
young people have seen fit to protest nonviolently.
It shows you're civilized. Now get out."

HOW TO WORK WITHIN THE SYSTEM AND GET RESULTS

According to a survey in 1970, commissioned by
the American Council on Education and conducted by
Louis Harris, 63% of American college students believe that "the democratic process is capable of
keeping up with the pace of events and with the need
for action." Among the techniques favored by students for bringing about improvement were the following: working to elect better public officials,
contacting such officials to communicate viewpoints
and protesting peacefully to influence government
policies. About two-thirds of the students rejected
the use of violent tactics to achieve basic changes
in society. One-third, however, believed that violent tactics either were "very effective" (11%), or
"somewhat effective" (21%) as a means to achieve
such changes (12).

The apostles of revolutionary violence in America, if they were ever to gain power, in all likelihood would not succeed in bringing forth either a
more humane society or one with greater liberty and

justice for all. The record of history, as well as
their own frequently nihilistic behavior and rhetoric, has weighed in heavily against them. In the
words of Youth International Party leader, Abbie
Hoffman, in 1970, "Burn down Yale Law School!
That's where it's at!"(13). (During this frenetic
period, somebody actually did try to do just that
[14]). Romantic idealists need to be forcefully reminded of the tragic experience of earlier violent
revolutionary movements which betrayed their promise
and devoured their own young, as in the Soviet Union
under Czar Josef the Terrible, or created a state of
anarchy which culminated in Fascism, as in Italy under the famous ex-Socialist, Benito Mussolini. How
easy it is for the oppressed to become the oppres-
sor. Whittier's allusion to the violent moralist,
John Brown, is apposite: "Perish with him the folly
that seeks through evil good"(15). Violence, of
course, always is distinguishable from recourse to
nonviolent civil disobedience for which individuals
are willing to accept a legal penalty as the price
for bearing witness to what they deem to be a moral
imperative dictated by conscience.

POLITICAL ACTION WORKSHOPS

But it is not enough to tell people who feel
deeply aggrieved that violence is wicked or that, in
any case, it is counter-productive. Results are a
"must." Black militants, scorning the moderates,
have defended rioting as, at the very least, an effective attention-getting device (16). There is an
urgent need for political action workshops to teach
people who need help how to work in various ways to
achieve legitimate ends without employing illegiti-
mate means. Provided it is done on a strictly nonpartisan basis, this is a kind of educational activity which is appropriate for non-profit, tax-exempt
institutions such as universities and public interest agencies. Several years ago this writer participated in an informative (though markedly conserva-
tively oriented) "Action Course in Practical Politics," sponsored by the U.S. Chambers of Commerce in
cities throughout the country.

THE BOYCOTT

The *modus operandi* of a Martin Luther King, Jr.
or a Cesar Chavez, while by no means suitable for
every problem situation, is bound to be instructive.
For example, one of the most powerful and potenti-

ally effective weapons of nonviolent political action is the boycott. This was demonstrated rather
convincingly by King during the civil rights strug-
gles of the 1960s. But a successful boycott requires skill, planning and organization, as well as
a profound sense of injustice. Appropriately enough,
a Boycott Center was established in 1972 by the Institute for Nonviolent Social Change, a component of
the Martin Luther King, Jr. Memorial Center, to provide guidance and assistance to groups which contem-
plate using this particular technique to attain
their goals.

VOTER REGISTRATION

Another worthy agenda item for a political action workshop is the promotion of voter registration
campaigns. Within our constitutional system political power, of course, is the "name of the game," and
a difficult "game" it is. Yet it is common knowledge that many millions of eligible voters, particularly among the poor and the downtrodden, regularly
are self-disenfranchised by their failure to register and vote. It is not easy to overcome the
apathy, ignorance, cynicism or sense of hopelessness
among such people and motivate them to get out and
take the first step of casting ballots, but it can
be done. Organizations such as U.S. Youth Council
and Frontlash have furnished success models for
sharply increased voter turnout in those districts
where they have targeted their efforts. Their en-
deavors need to be replicated countrywide.

The noted constitutional scholar and historian,
Prof. Alexander M. Bickel of Yale, said this:

> Our domestic problems can be solved or allevi-
> ated only through the democratic political pro-
> cess, which is slow, and out of which no one
> gets all he wants. The political process is
> not only slow, it is prone to error, and it
> carries a high frustration factor (17, p. 17).

This is the painful reality. But nobody, it would
seem, has yet devised a better way for government to
operate if it is to serve the interest of the greatest good for the greatest number.

MECHANISMS FOR INTERGROUP CONFLICT MANAGEMENT

Perhaps nothing cuts as close to the heart of any design for nonviolent change as does the need to create workable instruments for the accommodation of disputes between various elements in our society and to teach people how to use them. In fact, one of the key findings of the National Advisory Commission on Civil Disorders (Kerner Commission) as to the underlying causes of major riots was the lack of adequate grievance machinery (18). Scanning the contemporary scene one is struck by the relative frequency of such symptoms of conflict as violent racial confrontations, school boycotts, welfare sit-ins, rent strikes, protest demonstrations, clashes between anti-poverty groups, etc. But what about the courts? Unfortunately, the courts have been weighed repeatedly in this area and so often have been found wanting.

Consider, for example, the efficacy of the present judicial system from the perspective of black people who are poor. The image of "the Court" in the eyes of the black poor is apt to resemble something like this: a complicated, impersonal, menacing, costly, confusing apparatus, marked by delay, technicalities and "red tape," where nobody really cares and where black people don't get justice. Black offenders historically have been apt to draw stiffer sentences than whites for identical offenses (19). Courts all too frequently have been neither sensitive nor responsive to the authentic grievances of the black poor, which continue to fester without remedy. Landlords, for instance, are summoned to court but slum housing violations, it is claimed, remain uncorrected. Courts, after all, are arms of government, and government is equated with the power structure which is perceived as oppressive. An excerpt from a Report to the National Commission on the Causes and Prevention of Violence is illuminating:

> Black, student, and anti-war protesters have come to share a common view that legal institutions serve power and are incapable of remedying social and political grievances...the courts are not suited to the task of resolving the political conflicts which occasion civil crisis and mass arrests (20, p. xxxvi).

CONFLICT RESOLUTION

What are the other options? Starting from the
premise that there are no "quickie" solutions to intractable political-economic problems, it is nonetheless possible to fashion alternative devices for
conflict accommodation and resolution which may be
useful. The Center for Dispute Settlement of the
American Arbitration Association, headquartered in
Washington, D.C. and with branches in several cities,
for example, has achieved some notable successes in
conciliating various types of controversies. The
touchstone of the Center's approach is to encourage
the disputants to adjust their differences by selecting fact-finders, mediators or arbitrators, often
from within their own community, who are acceptable
to both sides. This approach deserves to be proli-
ferated and applied to all sorts of disputes between
students and school administrators, landlords and
tenants, merchants and consumers, local residents
and urban renewal or Model Cities officials, welfare
clients and welfare department functionaries, etc.
In the words of a seasoned professional arbi-
trator:

> The threshold problem in developing an effec-
> tive Neighborhood Mediation and Arbitration
> Service is to inform the neighborhood leader-
> ship that there is a viable peaceful alterna-
> tive to direct confrontation and the escalation
> of hostilities (21).

But even when this initial hurdle is surmounted, the
road is by no means a smooth one. Assuming settlement is reached, a common problem is how to insure
compliance with hard-to-accept decisions or recommendations. If settlement is not reached, obviously
things are worse. How does one bridge an enormous
gap between two bitterly adversary groups? In this
connection a device which ought to be utilized extensively is that of the "most reasonable package."
To avoid the pitfall of "splitting the difference"
(often unjustly) between extreme positions, each
side is asked by an arbitration panel to submit its
best total offer. That package which the arbitrators consider as a whole to be the most reasonable
one is then decreed as a settlement without any alteration whatever, thereby affording a powerful
built-in incentive to both sides to be as reasonable

as possible.

The impediments notwithstanding, on balance the case for employing extra-judicial techniques to attempt to resolve intergroup conflict situations, and for creating the mechanisms to accomplish this, is a compelling one. As recently as 30 years ago, mediation and arbitration in the labor management field were primitive tools, regarded with suspicion by both sides. Today, despite their acknowledged flaws and failures, they are virtually an institution.

OMBUDSMAN

Where one of the groups in conflict is "government" and the other is "citizens," there is available a widely heralded instrument which has been employed in Sweden for 160 years but which is just beginning to take root in the United States. Everybody knows about the Ombudsman--the independent top-level official who receives complaints, investigates them, and seeks to obtain redress of legitimate grievances arising out of governmental misfeasance or non-feasance.

Yet the astonishing fact is that this concept has not as yet been extensively implemented in America, due in large part to bureaucratic resistance to "outside interference." Those in government jobs have a tendency to forget that they are supposed to serve their constituents. They need to be reminded. In a complex urbanized society, where people are prone to feel that government is indifferent, remote and unapproachable, whether their complaints relate to garbage collection, street repair or police protection, there is a vital need for an office of Ombudsman, particularly on the municipal level, but in state and federal government as well (22). In 1971 the U.S. Department of Commerce recognized this need by creating an office of Ombudsman for Business to handle complaints, criticisms, inquiries and suggestions for improving the efficiency of the Department. Not that an Ombudsman is a panacea, but one who is competent, dedicated and courageous surely could improve matters to some degree, even in our cities where conditions are so bad that there is no real remedy but a massive infusion of money, coupled with measures to get "more bang for the buck."

DEMONSTRATION MONITORS

Still another device which, while not strictly a mechanism for managing intergroup conflict, cer-

tainly does relate to the larger problem is the protest demonstration monitor system. The Association
of the Bar of the City of New York has created a
Special Committee on Demonstration Observations (23).
It consists of some 150 lawyers who take turns vol-
unteering to observe and report on all aspects of
demonstrations. Depending upon the anticipated size
of the protest, a team of anywhere from two to
twelve lawyers will be present. All of these volunteers have received special training from police officers and lawyers knowledgeable in civil liberties.
They learn how the police operate, what their instructions and regulations are, and what are the
rights of citizens who participate in demonstrations.
After attending a demonstration, each lawyer observer submits an individual report on what he saw;
all of these reports are then combined into a single
narrative, which is made available to the Mayor,
Police Commissioner, and leaders of the demonstration. Each lawyer volunteer is given a photo identification card which entitles him to pass through
police lines. Reaction to this scheme has been
overwhelmingly favorable, both from demonstration
leaders and from the police. It deserves to be emulated in cities throughout the country.

The value of demonstration monitors was sharply
underscored by this writer's personal experience as
a demonstrator several years ago at a protest march
which, regrettably, was not monitored by impartial
observers. The protest was directed at discrimination against blacks and Jews in admission to membership in the New York Athletic Club. Violence erup-
ted between some of the demonstrators and police,
with each group blaming the other for having preci-
pitated it. Had monitors been present, and had people been aware of their presence, greater restraint
might have been exercised on both sides.

CONCLUSION

In October, 1971, a two-day national consultation on responses to political violence through democratic means, cosponsored by Catholic University
Law School and the American Jewish Committee, was
held near Washington, D.C. Some 90 leadership people participated in this meeting, representing a
broad cross-section of American group life, including students, blacks, women, police chiefs, lawyers,
professors, clergymen, government officials, community spokesmen, media and non-profit organization

people. The chief recommendation which emerged from
their deliberations was that local coalitions be organized to promote humane yet effective governmental
responses to political violence, within the rule of
law, as well as alternative methods of political action, utilizing approaches such as those delineated
in this chapter. All of these disparate approaches
clearly are pathways to a common destination, designed to translate the hallowed American dream of a
free, just and peaceful society into the American
reality. To bring about fundamental improvements in
public attitudes toward rights and liberties has
never been easy, nor will it be any easier in the
future. But the possibilities are there, and it is
hard to imagine a more worthy task for concerned
groups and individuals. Indeed, the ultimate fate
of our society may be said to hang upon its accom-
plishment.

REFERENCES

1. The Washington *Post*, June 1, 1970.
2. The Atlanta *Constitution*, March 31, 1969.
3. The New York *Post*, October 3, 1968.
4. Walker, Daniel. *Rights in Conflict*, Report to
    the National Commission on the Causes and Pre-
    vention of Violence. New York: Bantam Books,
    1968.
5. Morison, Samuel Eliot. *The Oxford History of
    the American People*. New York: Oxford Univer-
    sity Press, 1965.
6. Graham, Hugh Davis, & Gurr, Ted Robert. *The
    History of Violence in America*, Report to the
    National Commission on the Causes and Prevention
    of Violence. New York: Bantam Books, 1969.
7. The New York *Times*, June 2, 1970.
8. The New York *Times*, August 14, 1971.
9. Rubenstein, Richard E. *Rebels in Eden*, Boston:
    Little, Brown, 1970.
10. Reed, Watford. Riot in the classroom. *Liberty*,
    September-October 1970, 7-10.
11. Dearing, Daniel S. Alternative to violence.
    Miami Interaction, June 1969, 18-19.
12. The Boston *Globe*, July 20, 1970.
13. The New York *Post*, May 12, 1970.
14. The New York *Times*, May 3, 1970.
15. Whittier, John Greenleaf. "Brown of Ossawatom-
    ie." In *This Land is Mine--An Anthology of
    American Verse*, Philadelphia: J.B. Lippincott
    Co., 1965.

16. Fogelson, Robert M. *Violence as Protest: A Study of Riots and Ghettos.* Garden City, N.Y.: Doubleday & Company, 1971.
17. Bickel, Alexander M. The tolerance of violence on the campus. *New Republic*, June 13, 1970, 15-17.
18. *Report of the National Advisory Commission on Civil Disorders.* New York: Bantam Books, 1968.
19. Wolfgang, Marvin E. *Crime and Race: Conceptions and Misconceptions.* New York: Institute of Human Relations Press, 1964.
20. Skolnick, Jerome H. *The Politics of Protest*, Report to the National Commission on the Causes and Prevention of Violence. New York: Ballantine Books, 1969.
21. Zack, Arnold M. Dispute settlement in the ghetto. Labor Management Institute, American Arbitration Association. New York, 1968. pamphlet, no page nos.)
22. Report of the Thirty-second American Assembly, Columbia University. *The Ombudsman*, October, 1967.
23. The New York *Times*, September 4, 1970.

SAMUEL RABINOVE, director of the Legal Division in the American Jewish Committee's Domestic Affairs Department, is concerned primarily with the legal and quasi-legal aspects of the Committee's civil rights, civil liberties, intergroup relations and social action activities. In these areas, he provides guidance, counsel and training to AJC national and field staff, National Jewish Community Relations Advisory Council and local Jewish community relations councils.

Working with AJC's National Legal Committee, he also administers the agency's participation, both nationally and on the chapter level, in litigation of programmatic concern to AJC. He is responsible for the filing of briefs and other actions in cases that have significant implications for minority groups in general and for Jews in particular, such as those involving questions of religious liberty, discrimination in housing, education and employment, and freedom of expression.

A native of New York City, Mr. Rabinove received his B.S. degree in Social Science from the College of the City of New York and his LL.B. from Columbia Law School. Prior to joining the American Jewish Committee in 1967, he was a member of the legal department of Allstate Insurance Company.

He has been active in numerous organizations,
including the American Bar Association, American Arbitration Association, International League for the
Rights of Man, National Church/State Committee of
the American Civil Liberties Union, National Coalition Against Censorship and National Council on Religion and Public Education.

A resident of White Plains, N.Y., Mr. Rabinove
has worked with the George Washington Carver Community Center, where he initiated and directed two in-
terracial home visit projects, served as counselor
to a youth group at the center, as well as on its
board of directors. He is a member of the New York
State Advisory Committee to the U.S. Civil Rights
Commission.

Mr. Rabinove has written on a variety of sub-
jects in addition to the law. His interests include
Jewish life and heritage, race relations and envi-
ronmental protection. His articles have appeared
in publications such as American Jewish Yearbook,
Midstream, National Jewish Monthly, Jewish Digest,
American Zionist, Young Judean, Sh'ma, America,
Christian Century, Christian Herald, The Humanist,
Civil Rights Digest, National Parks Magazine and the
Journal of Law and Education.

SOME OTHER PUBLICATIONS BY SAMUEL RABINOVE

- Bridge across the gulf: Catholic-Jewish Dialogue.
  Social Digest, September, 1967, 142-146.
- Crisis in integration. Colloquy, April, 1969,
  16-18.
- A Jewish view of church and state. Christian Her-
  ald, April, 1970, MT18-MT23.
- Private club discrimination and the law. Civil
  Rights Digest, Spring, 1970, 28-33.
- Privacy: everybody's business--and nobody's.
  Christian Century, July 8, 1970, 843-846.
- Intergroup relations and tensions in the United
  States. American Jewish Year Book, 1974-1975,
  83-132.

10. A Human Language for Newscasts of Violence

Israel W. Charny, Ph.D.

As reporters of the contemporary events of mankind, newscasters bring to us day after day the news
of man's insane, incessant destruction of himself
and his fellow man: in small- and large-scale stories of violence on the highways, in the home, on
city streets, in government capitals, on the fields
of national battle, in atomic clouds of destruction,
in genocidal purgatories.

Clearly, at this point in evolution, our species is at a barely primitive point of developing
its potential for self-preservation; and it remains
to be seen whether we will be wise enough and brave
enough to succeed in the evolutionary challenge to
learn how to preserve our lives. To this drama,
newscasters are privy as the reporters and histori-
ans of our contemporary world; as such, newscaster
journalists carry a heavy responsibility for the
ways in which they report to us the tragically re-
petitive events of our destructive violence.

The tradition of the newscaster in a democratic
society is that he is an objective reporter of
events. There can be no disputing the fact it is a
cornerstone of any effort at a free society to seek
to provide the people with as true and uncensored
news as possible.

Nonetheless, we have learned in science--in-
cluding the once-idealized world of physical phenomena, where men once believed they would discover the
"reality" out there that in no way was affected by
the observer--that every observer plays a distinct
role in shaping the reality he describes.

This subtle but critical principle of scientific method shows up immediately in the experiences
we have in listening to our newscasters tell us in
rich baritone voices how many of us have killed how

many other of us. It is *as if* we hear over and over
again the subliminal message, *"Well, folks, it's
happened again, it's still happening, it's always
going to happen, and there isn't a damn thing we can
do about it!"*

Over and over again, we have the experience of
newscasts that tell us the latest of human destructiveness in an indifferent or bored-sounding mechanical "sirupy and glib" reportage of the facts of one
or another of many deaths and injuries of human beings; and often enough there is even a covert excitement that conveys (what we shall indeed acknowledge later is an altogether natural) fascination and
passionate interest in still another piece of sadism
and/or suicide.

We conclude that most newscasts of man's violent ways, subtly and penetratingly, contribute to a
kind of demoralization and hopelessness; perhaps,
too, to passivity and resignation in the face of violence; and perhaps, too, to the further violence
that grows precisely out of the hopelessness that is
never quite tolerable to the inner human spirit.

TOWARDS HUMANISTIC, OBJECTIVE NEWSCASTING

Can it be otherwise?
Is it possible for the newscaster to serve as
agent of man's better hopes for himself, even as he
remains a journalist true to his fundamental commitment to seek to convey accurately and without editorial interpretation the facts of what is going on?
Again, it cannot be emphasized too strongly that in
no way would we consider compromising a free society's principle of factual reporting. We know all
too well that the truth may stimulate men to their
best capacities more than any of the best-inten-
tioned efforts at recasting the news into some pre-
determined philosophical or political framework. Yet,
the objective newscast that actually plays accomplice to glibness and/or covert excitement cannot be
thought of as eliciting man's better potential.

There is little doubt that it is on the horns
of this dilemma that many thoughtful people have
sidestepped their concern with the quality of the
emotional experience generated by the newscast in
our society. The fear is that any effort to guide
the newscaster towards a more humanistic presentation might well involve tampering with the objectivity of the journalistic report. However, there is a
sound way of dealing with this kind of dilemma that

comes to us from the very struggle of science to cope with the discovery that all so-called *objective* representations of *anything* at all of reality are shaped by the implicit judgments, values, and the position of the observer. The solution is to objectify these very influences; in other words, insofar as we make ourselves conscious of our implicit values as observers, and the roles these values play in determining our observations, we are freed from the blind grip of the subjectivity of our observations. Stated otherwise, it is both the effort to present the facts as honestly as possible with the best scientific data-gathering processes at hand, and the effort to describe honestly how one assembles one's data and channels the reporting of information that makes the difference between objective presentation and propaganda. For example, it has always been true of those who would seek to ram anything down our throats, be it their concept of God, or truth or justice, or a claim of who hit the most home runs in 19something or other, that they insist that *their* statement is *the* reality, rather than to say that it is their belief that what they propose is the truth, such and such is the source of their belief, and they believe this source of information to be credible to such and such extent.

Objectivity then is a sequence of fair-minded observations about how one is going about making fair-minded observations.

It is now clear in all areas of science that our so-powerful scientific method for arriving at (the more) real truths of nature always grows out of the ways in which the research question is asked and how one goes about answering the question.

For example, does isolation break people down? Yes, indeed. But there are circumstances and ways in which one can design isolation which can free people for enormous personal growth. Many studies have shown that the inner intent of the persons arranging the isolation largely determines the outcome of the experience.

Another example of how we need to make ourselves aware of what it is and how it is we know something : Does a given medicine heal? Suppose the information we have received from preliminary studies is that one particular medicine helped a fair number of people. But it is often shown that much of the healing power ascribed to a medicine is matched by a placebo given by a physician who conveys the impression of caring for the patient, whereas less healing will follow a placebo whose

apothecary mixture is not associated with much involvement and caring by the dispensing doctor.

We would therefore propose to our newscaster
scientists and doctors of truth to keep telling
things as they are, but also to observe themselves
and train themselves in their work of telling the
truth. Ultimately, they must learn how to commit
their skills as dramatic artists *to convey and foster the greater respect for human life we are all
dying (sic) to feel*.

A PROPOSED MODEL

The model shown in Table 1 is intended to formulate a framework for objective but humanistic reporting of the news of violence. Throughout we insist on the newscaster staying within the framework
of objective reporting; yet, looking at the process
of reporting itself as a subtle shaper of the phe-
noma which it reports, we seek to choose those
styles of content selection, tone, and dramatic mood
that might invite man to develop his better self and
to move away from the despondent fatalism that we
see in much present day reporting.

Thus, still operating within the framework of
objective reporting, the newscaster should avoid
juxtaposing the news of the death of a person in a
car accident, or news of a war with the happy excitement of a commercial for a new toothpaste. Within
the limits of the often hectic pace of assembling
the news, the newscaster might plan to juxtapose the
day's lot of man's murdering with stories of human
aggression in the service of life-building and life-
saving and transcending (the story of a medical
breakthrough and the latest steps towards brilliant
exploration of space, and so forth). And the newscaster might seek to convey as much as possible the
human meaning of violent events by projecting for us
local stories of violence through their impact on individuals, families, and the community. This way the
news of a tragedy has further meaning to us through
its impacts on those human beings who are close to
the tragedy--e.g., the statements of the observers
of a fatal car accident, the shaken excitement of
the peers of a youngster cut down in urban violence,
or the agony of the surviving family of victims of
violence. For instance, the news of a flaming wreck-
age at Main and Fifth Streets can be deftly framed
as a story seen through the eyes of human beings:
"Pedestrians at Main and Fifth witnessed today a

Table 1.   OBJECTIVE BUT HUMAN NEWS OF HUMAN VIOLENCE

Ethical and Psychological Guidelines	Editing Content of the News of Violence	The Broadcaster's Art in Tone and Inner Mood
Destruction of human beings is always deeply regrettable--even of our enemy. One should go to great lengths to avoid overt destructive acts against other human beings.	Separate news of loss of life from sports, commercials, civic developments, etc. Use a local story of violence to project the human reality of loss to violence...and to offer a tone for stories of more distant or organized violence. Where possible, take story of large violence down to its impact on people's everyday lives, to illustrate impact on an individual. Use small words that say that there is something wrong with unending violence: "Still another riot"; "casualties are light; nevertheless, 100 are dead..."	Speak of loss of life with qualities of sadness, reverence.

Also speak with muted anger, hope for the future, not with monotonic indifference or uncaring excitement. |
| | Make a point of stories respecting life; use these as counterpoint to news of violence. | Speak of lifesaving, or fulfilling life, or the search for peace with joy. |

Table 1.   (continued)

Ethical and Psychological Guidelines	Editing Content of the News of Violence	The Broadcaster's Art in Tone and Inner Mood
While overt acts of de struction are basically wrong, feelings of anger and protest, and wishes to destroy and hurt others are frequent and natural in intimate family relationships-- husband and wife, parent and child-- and in relationships of groups and nations.	Report news of angry feelings and protest in group and community and interpersonal life with respect, often with humorous affection; but treat news of overt destruction of property or people as wrong, unless in self-defense against overtly destructive forces such as those who would use force to deny the very democratic right to protest.	*Do* allow excitement to show in reporting various news of life-and-death encounters and violence (as a mirror of the excitement and potential for violence in all humans; also as relief for our own feelings about possibly being hurt sometime); but move from the element of excitement to restraint, sadness, reverence (as a symbolic de demonstration of man's capacity to channel his passions into a fighting commitment for life).
Self-defense (or avoiding destruction of ourselves) is equally valid, as a statement of the same principle that destruction of humans is wrong--we, too, are human. However, caution: nations and people generally explain their wars as self-defense.	In reporting how human beings, individually or collectively, protect themselves in self-defense, emphasize known intents at defense instead of describing both sides' violence as if there were no difference.	Speak of the courage to fight in self-defense with respect and excited pleasure, yet introduce a subtly questioning note that conveys the feeling that one must await a later judgment of history as to whether the sincerity of the self-defense was in fact objectively justified.

fiery crash of two cars in which three people lost
their lives...." Or the newscaster who grows really
confident of his ability to put together the facts
of an event as well as something of its impact on
people could use simple *factual* adjectives such as
"A sad accident today claimed the lives of..." Note
that all of these devices are intended to be used
without any additional demand on broadcast time.

We would ask the newscaster to utilize his dramatic skills on our behalf in his tone, inflection,
rate of speed, and ultimately his very mood. Cultivating the fullest dramatic potential of his
craft, the newscaster might convey to us a dramatic
sense that all killing--whether ultimately or historically tragically necessary, or whether obviously
obscene or absurd--is an occasion for sadness about
the human condition, humility, and a renewed search
for ways to improve the quality of human life.

After all, it is clear that not only is *some*
violence inevitable in the simple nature of our
lives on this planet of earthquakes and storms, but
also that man must sometimes choose to be violent if
he is to be free to pursue his evolution towards
greater decency; for, unfortunately, there are occasions when we must indeed fight in self-defense
against the killers. The trouble is that people and
nations have always explained *their* wars as self-defense; even genociders explain their attempted destruction of entire peoples as their defense against
the threats of these people to them. As our objective reporter of current violence, the newscaster
should report the latest events of wars and counter-
wars and ostensible acts of self-defense in a mood
that is not only sad, but conveys a kind of respectful reserving of judgment towards the claim that one
has acted in self-defense. For example, Americans
finally learned in the tragic decade of Vietnam that
even when one's country claims to be fighting in
self-defense, this may not be the truth or the whole
truth. The newscaster can convey a respectful ten-
tativeness in the way he reports government explana-
tions of a military incursion, expedition, or response, thus implying that there are aspects of the
situation that are not immediately observable or
known.

We have therefore distinguished two mood levels: a basic humility about loss of life, and a
kind of let's-wait-and-see feeling about the announced intent of a country's self-defense. Some
might feel this extent of mood dramatization would
be too demanding for pedestrian newscasters, but we

believe that the fair number of dramatic craftsmen
in the news media would find the evocation of such
moods well within their talent.

However, at least one more major issue does remain, and that is whether newscasters should show
any excitement whatsoever about violences. It is
quite important to acknowledge the psychological
truth that violences do carry with them a kind of
natural fire-excitement for *all of us*.

Whatever the psychological reasons--the relief
that "there but for the grace of God go I"; excitement at seeing in real life the kinds of destructive
wishes and fantasies we are forever experiencing
within ourselves (even toward our loved ones); the
echo of archaic passions deep within; or a fascination with the mortality of others as we struggle to
prepare for our own ultimate deaths--the fact is, we
are all drawn powerfully to some kind of passionate
interest in such events.

It is therefore entirely appropriate that the
newscaster as a reporter articulate for us *some* of
this excitement through all of the news of men hurting each other and themselves.

Some newscasters are able to convey this excitement through a subtle tension in the rhythm of
the story, even as they hold basically to a fact-
objectifying tone. Others will prefer more open
suggestions of emotion.

The important point is, first of all, that such
emotion is appropriate, and then, that the newscaster might seek to move from his representation of
this natural excitement toward a *further* side of our
nature; namely, to our capacity to experience reverence for life, caring for others, and sadness at
wasteful death. *In this way, the newscaster might
well exemplify mankind's evolutionary potential to
move from destructive passions toward a larger, more
enduring commitment to life.* The newscaster's very
sequence of regulated passion and reverence can thus
represent man's evolutionary hopes to build societies that, most of all, honor and protect human life.

DERIVING THIS MODEL FROM PSYCHOLOGICAL THEORY

Needless to say, these guidelines grow out of
certain fundamental positions in psychological theory; and it will be of interest to see these sources,
as well as true to our understanding of the requirements of objective work that we identify our own underlying assumptions.

First and foremost, the present proposal rests
on the now time-honored psychological principle that
the more unconsciously determined behaviors are
translated into more conscious experiences, greater
choice or mastery over powerful impulses becomes
possible. That such a mechanism of consciousness
provides man with greater mastery of himself has
been documented, all too clearly, in the area of
sexual behavior. There we are no longer afraid to
know that all men experience virtually all *impulses*,
but just what they choose to *act* on is a rather critical decision to be made in the light of all of
one's considerations. So it is with regard to aggressive impulses. These are indeed in all of us,
all the time; but how we choose to act on these impulses, and how we correlate our aggressive feelings
with our no-less-vital impulses of love for our fellow human beings, and genuine sadness for their
plight when they are hurt, are critical choices.
    The present proposal also grows out of psycho-
logical analysis of violent feelings and behaviors
in human affairs as being rooted originally in man's
most *natural* ways of protecting himself from stress.
When man must cope with stress, he activates his defense systems--among which aggression and anger represent key sources. Those who are feeling resource-
less, defenseless, threatened, and overwhelmed are
characteristically drawn to acts of violence. We
have learned to look behind even the most heinous
behaviors of people and nations to find such powerful pressures driving people to an irrational destructiveness that in many cases they do not intend.
    We also go further to see man's destructiveness
as deriving from an underlying aggressiveness that
in itself is an entirely natural, universal process
for generating energy for all life.
    However, the natural thrust of this aggression
derives in part from tapping of destructive tearing-
down forces which man unfortunately only barely
knows how to handle and channel in the "psychoatomic
reactor." So that all too often, men are pulled
along with their inexperience and lack of know-how
by this volatile energy, and flare into violent
eruptions of aggression before they are able to monitor or gauge the intensity of their reactions.
Thus, before we know it, men who did not really want
to become involved in destructiveness are acting out
a time-honored scenario of the waste of human life
that we see incessantly in culture after culture.
Note, however, that this concept of destructiveness
as springing from originally natural aggression is

far more hopeful than picturing destructiveness as an almost satanic force which lurks in the deepest recesses of man's mind waiting--almost gleefully--to be unleashed once the thin veneer of civilization is ripped away. For the implication is that someday we may learn to pace our natural aggression.

It is because of the former point of view, we believe, that too many cultural forces aim at pushing down, covering over, and avoiding release of men's underlying aggression energy lest the devil in all his fury be unleashed. But this suppression only aggravates the problem. The newer, alternative point of view from which the present model is derived sees the possibilities of men being either violent or nonviolent in the expression of their aggressiveness as much more available to choice. Men must learn how to make these choices in many areas of human experience. It is to this end that we offer the present consideration of how our newscasting services convey to us the story of our present violences and implicitly train us in our choices whether to be violent in the future.

ADDENDUM

This proposal has been reviewed with a number of professional newscasters, individually, or in a station staff meeting, and the following are their most frequent criticisms:

1. You give broadcast news professionals too little credit for the job they are doing...most are already following these guidelines.

2. From the artistic standpoint, you are mistaking emotional reserve with lack of emotion.

3. To remain objective, a newscaster must remain somewhat detached.

4. No man is capable of fully reacting to each and every story without severe damage to his psychological health--or credibility.

5. The nature of the beast makes these recommendations impractical...the newscaster has to move rapidly from one story to the next...most stories have to be shortened.

6. The good things people do to a large extent don't make news...it is inevitable that violence is featured.

On the other hand, one advertising professional who is responsible for millions of dollars of radio advertising every year suggested another novel reason why we *should* develop more humanistic newscasting:

Once the media executives catch on that people

*feel better listening to newscasts that project hope
for man's potential for nonviolence, they'll also
discover that they can really sell these shows--and
then you'll see a lot more humanistic newscasting!*

REFERENCES

1. Charny, Israel W. Regression and reorganization
    in the "isolation treatment" of children. *Jour-
    nal Child Psychology & Psychiatry*, 1963, *4*, 47-
    60.
2. Charny, Israel W. Towards confrontation of the
    naturalness of evil. *Reconstructionist*, July,
    1971, *37*(5), 7-19.
3. Charny, Israel W. Review of three volumes in
    series of Communications Arts Books, Hastings
    House Publishers, New York, 1970: William
    Small, *To Kill a Messenger: Television News and
    the Real World;* Charles S. Steinberg, *The Commu-
    nitive Arts: An Introduction to Mass Media;*
    Heinz-Dietrich Fischer, & John Calhoun Merril,
    (Eds.), *International Communications: Media,
    Channels, Functions. American Journal Orthopsy-
    chiatry,* 1972, *42*, 175-177.
4. Charny, Israel W. Introduction to a new edition
    of Luther Lee Bernard. *War and Its Causes.* In
    the Garland Library of War and Peace. (Original-
    ly published 1944) New York: Garland, 1972,
    5-13.
5. Feiffer, J. *Little Murders.* New York: Random
    House, 1968.
6. Feshbach, S., & Singer, Robert D. *Television
    and Aggression.* San Francisco: Jossey-Bass,
    1970.
7. Fromm, E. *The Heart of Man: Its Genius for
    Good and Evil.* New York: Harper & Row, 1964.
8. Gendlin, E.T. Values and the process of exper-
    iencing. In A.H. Mahrer, (Ed.), *The Goals of
    Psychotherapy.* New York: Appleton-Century-
    Crofts, 1967.
9. Ichheiser, G. *Appearances and Realities.* San
    Francisco: Jossey-Bass, 1970.
10. Kelman, H.C. *A Time to Speak.* New York:
    Jossey-Bass, 1968.
11. Mead, M. Violence and its regulation: How do
    children learn to govern their own violent im-
    pulses. *American Journal Orthopsychiatry,*
    1969, *39*, 227-229.
12. Morse, A.D. *While Six Million Died: A Chroni-
    cle of American Apathy.* New York: Random House,
    1968.

13. Osborn, R. *Mankind May Never Make It*. Green-
    wich, Conn.: New York Graphic Society, n.d.
14. Radio Television News Directors Association.
    Code of Broadcast News Ethics. Adopted January
    2, 1966. *Journal of Broadcasting*, 1969, 13(4),
    386-388.
15. Rubinoff, L. *The Pornography of Power*. New
    York: Ballantine, 1969.
16. Rudin, S. National motives predict psychogenic
    death rates 25 years later. *Science*, 1968, 160,
    901-903.
17. Sennett, R. *The Uses of Disorder*. New York:
    Knopf, 1970.
18. *The Seventh Day--Soldiers' Talk about the Six-
    Day War:* London: Andre Deutsch, 1970.
19. U.S. Government. *Report of the National Advis-
    ory Commission on Civil Disorders*. New York:
    Bantam, 1968.
20. U.S. Government. National Commission on the
    Causes and Prevention of Violence. *To Establish
    Justice, to Insure Domestic Tranquility*. New
    York: Bantam, 1970.

11. Conflict Education: A New Direction in Higher Learning

Paul Wehr, Ph.D., and Robert DeHaan, Ph.D.

We submit that the majority of Americans are
socialized with a somewhat distorted view of how
their social system operates, and particularly how
conflict shapes it. The values of conciliation and
controlled, minimized conflict are certainly prominent ones in the national ethos and do reflect the
integrative needs of a heterogeneous society--a
patchwork of ethnic, racial, economic and other disparate groupings held together in part by a delicate
modus vivendi. In the popular mind, conciliation is
the warp and woof of the social fabric.

This view of society has been given conceptual
form and intellectual legitimacy in the models put
forward by certain social theorists--notably Parsons
(13) and Lipset (11)--models which emphasize the
predominance of conciliation over the conflict process in society. This emphasis, unintentionally
perhaps, implies that major conflict is unhealthy,
counter-productive and unnecessary for the well-being of the social system. It obscures the equally
central and functional role of conflict, and in so
doing contributes to the inability of the system to
use it creatively.

Most of our students come to us having been socialized initially within this conciliation world-
view, but with increasing awareness that conflict is
more essential in the social process than that view
suggests. In the past decade, jarring movement
along racial, generational and economic cleavages
has called into question the validity of the conciliation model. The conflict-oriented model of society, presented in one form or another by Marcuse
(12), Dahrendorf (6), Baran and Sweezy (1) and oth-
ers--for all its internal contradictions and inade-

212

quacies--has assumed new relevance as students are
hit full-face with the realization that gross exploitation of certain groups and strata within the
system, opposed interests, and deep rifts in societal consensus are all essential facts. Yet the
conflict model, too, falls short because it fails to
account for the origin of conflict in the first
place and is too rigid and narrow in its conception
of how conflict is resolved.

Students enter college, then, caught in a con-
ceptual/ideological bind as these two current, major models of society--integrative and coercive,
neither of which, taken by itself, adequately ex-
plains it--present them with a confused idea indeed
of the role of conflict in social relations. Not a
great deal happens during an average student's university career to resolve that confusion. This is a
serious personal and social problem, for if students
are to be creative actors in society, they must make
substantial movement during those four years toward
an understanding of the conflict process. Our society's regeneration and survival depend on the formation of top- and middle-level leaders with some degree of sophistication in conflict analysis and some
skill in managing it creatively.

We are convinced, therefore, that conflict education must be given high priority in college and
university curricula, and that an essential component of such education is a significant degree of experiential learning of some sort--classroom simula-
tions, field-work, an off-campus semester, on-site
seminars and the like (14). The students' conception of society as a mixed conflict/conciliation
system must evolve from a reflective involvement in
it and in a way that has normative as well as cognitive payoffs for them.

Conflict educators must deal with two basic
questions--*what* a student learns about conflict, and
how he or she learns it. The content question assumes that there is an identifiable body of empirical
knowledge about conflict and its resolution to be
gained through study and reflective experience--
knowledge about the roots, settings, actors, dynamics and outcomes of various types of conflict which
students should acquire.

It is essential, however, that what students
learn becomes a part of them, integrated so to speak
with the rest of their life experience. The question of process--what educational forms can best get
the content across in a meaningful and socially useful way--can be dealt with adequately only through

the development of new methods of teaching conflict and other topics in social science.

Let us deal with the questions of content and process in turn, and within the context of the off-campus urban semester with which we have some experience.

THE CONTENT OF THE CONFLICT EDUCATION PROGRAM

Students in a program of conflict education should engage in guided testing of at least three major propositions.

(1) *Conflict is complex but analyzable and manageable.*
(2) *Conflict can be functional.*
(3) *Conflict can be creative.*

THE VARIETY AND COMPLEXITY OF CONFLICT

The view presented in this paper is based on the authors' experiences, one as director of the Haverford Educational Involvement Program, and the other as Director of the Great Lakes Colleges Association*--Philadelphia Urban Semester, in which students live in urban neighborhoods, are engaged in various supervised change-oriented types of field-work, and follow a seminar program designed to assist them in understanding both the urban environment and their field-work community or organization. They receive academic credit for their participation in the urban semester. Observations and conclusions draw upon questionnaire and interview evaluations of student participants in the two programs.

During their urban semester, participants are exposed to a wide range of conflict types, some of them more, some less personal in nature, but most of which they have not experienced previously. This "total immersion" not only educates them to the variety of social conflict--pointing up the single-cleavage fallacy--but also brings about personal growth which results from having to deal responsibly and directly with conflict.

The immersion process begins with a student's moving to a mixed or low-income urban neighborhood, as different from his/her normal environment in the

---

*Albion, Antioch, Denison, Depauw, Earlham, Hope, Kalamazoo, Kenyon, Oberlin, Ohio Wesleyan, Wabash, Wooster

case of the middle-class white as night is from day.
He/she lives most often in his/her field-work community and generally in a small living unit with his/
her fellow participants. The initial clash of
images and the subsequent period of adjustment are
the first in a series of encounters with new conflict dimensions. As the student becomes involved
in the off-campus semester, he/she often becomes estranged in certain ways from student peers and other
parts of the campus community, who understand little
of what he/she experiences or why he/she chooses to
do so. His/her priorities shift when he/she moves
out into the city and his/her new frame of reference
is often incompatible at many points with theirs.
The dominant mood on campus remains one of cool and
contemplative detachment rather than committed involvement. The off-campus participant is often
called upon to justify his/her academic and field
activity in ways that no one who remains on campus
is, and the burden of proof that he/she is doing
something educationally worthwhile is placed square-
ly on him/her. The competition for the student's
time between the demands of academic work and field-
work creates an additional tension between the participant and the campus community.

      If he/she lives with a group of fellow partici-
pants, he/she must deal with another cluster of conflicts which range from personality and racial fric-
tions, to problems with landlords, to differences
with the on-site supervisor, seminar instructor, or
field-work coordinator. More difficult to identify,
but nevertheless very real, are conflicts within
him/herself which participation creates or reveals.
The inevitable if temporary shift which occurs in
the participant/s mind away from a racial liberal
self-image toward that of white racist is a difficult one for most to deal with. Value contradictions
such as those involved in working for social conflict but valuing social harmony set up a tension in
the student's personal life as well.

      In both field assignments and the larger urban
milieu in which they exist, participants confront
another set of conflicts. Their work assignment is
often complicated by intra-community and inter-organ-
izational disputes; other complications arise from
their own differences with staff in the institution
or group with which they work, whose inertia or established patterns of action frustrate ambition for
change. Add to all of this the inter-group and
intra-organizational conflict participants observe
and experience among social units seeking to bring

or prevent change and defend interests, and one has a rich and initially disorienting mix of conflict situations.

A student's encounter with this variety of conflict planes and dimensions is not a linear one. They must deal with them not singly but simultaneously during a single semester. The student's success in dealing with one may well affect his/her capacity for dealing with the others (see Fig. 1).

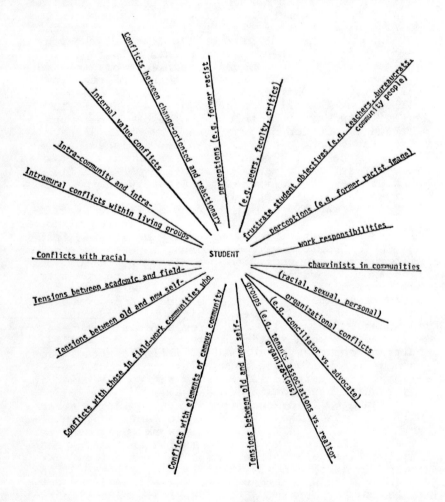

Figure 1.   Conflict Planes in Student's Experience.

The student must and does receive support in dealing with this complex of situations. The on-site seminars, field-work **supervisor**, and mutually-supportive peer relationships in the living unit all serve to increase the student's capacity to learn and grow from the reflective experience.* Coping with immediate problems which arise in these "unintentional communities" teaches much about cooperation as well as conflict. As one student observed:

> The communal life was a novel experience and one that I found rewarding. I was exposed to people from divergent backgrounds, and the give-and-take in making the house run smoothly for all was instructive. When to be compulsive, when to let things ride--questions like that came up all the time. Toward the end... our instructor threw in an intriguing exercise which involved measuring ourselves in our housemates' eyes and in our own estimation and comparing the two. This drove home the importance of obtaining feedback in cooperative institutions.

Total immersion in radically different settings, then, and a new awareness of the complexity of conflict are important aspects of the conflict education process. The relation of theory to empirical observation is another, and one which leads student participants to a methodology for analyzing conflict. Students have the occasion to test propositions in both conflict theory and the more general social science literature, and to apply those they find useful to a better understanding of the social dynamic they see operating at close range. For example, a student's field-work experience can test the validity of a number of Simmel's conflict propositions as reformulated by Coser (5). Coser suggests, for instance, that a social unit (e.g., community, organization, state) threatened by or in

*We should note here that a semester-long seminar could well be built around the analysis of conflict, and how and where it operates in the students' experience. To date, we have failed to take such a formal and systematic approach to conflict analysis on-site, although many participants are exposed to formal conflict analysis in our courses on campus.

conflict with an external force will develop greater internal cohesion as a consequence, but only if it has the necessary degree of homogeneity and value consensus to begin with. Students observe two communities in a poverty area faced with a similar problem--the threat of removal of a major segment of housing for highway construction. One is largely homogeneous in both racial and socioeconomic composition, with a sense of community and shared values. It is able, therefore, to support an effective leadership and divert the highway. The other with little homogeneity or community reacts in discord and disorganization to essentially the same threat.

Immersion in new conflict settings combines with theory-testing, then, to provide the student with new skills for understanding conflict and urban problems.

CONFLICT AS A FUNCTIONAL PROCESS

The student must become aware of the ways in which social conflict is functional. Let us return to the question of the student's view of the social system and the role of conflict therein. Through off-campus internships in public schools, community organizing, total care institutions and other assignments where substantial reform is necessary, students arrive at a conceptualization of American society more accurately reflective of it than either the integrative or coercive models, taken by themselves. Their new world-view is a mix of the systemic and the dialectic, similar to that suggested by Chalmers Johnson (10).

With his model, the social system has a tendency to move out of an equilibrium state as its division of labor--including the status and economic rewards, and life chances embodied therein--becomes desynchronized with the value system or parts of it. A case in point would be the changes leading to the equal rights and Black Power movements in the Fifties and Sixties, in which the values and self-images of black people were altered sufficiently to cause them to openly reject the inequitable division of labor and rewards and to bring on a racial revolt within a racially oppressive society. With desynchronization, the system begins to lose its legitimacy for significant elements of the population--a condition which activates a dialectical process of a sort, which in turn acts to return the system to a new and healthier level of equilibrium. The essential point is that this dynamic equilibrium depends on processes of conflict and opposition for its self-correction. Without them, desynchronization increases and the system moves further toward political oppression and massive revolution. Conflict viewed from this perspective is then, both a natural and functional element in the social system and its intensity, rate and forms will vary with the amount of change required to keep the system true to itself.(Boulding [3] in effect supports this view through his suggestions that the dialectic operates most successfully in basically nondialectic societies.)

THE CREATIVE POTENTIAL OF CONFLICT

Finally, the student should become aware of the distinction between functional and creative conflict, the former being that which contributes to the long-term maintenance and health of a system, and the latter referring to conflict which, *by the very way in which it is carried out,* contributes to the development of more positive human relationships. Creative conflict is always functional, while the reverse may not be true.

Creative conflict--a concept with deep roots in the Gandhian experience, implies a process which is self-conscious and deliberate; one in which empathy and concern for the ultimate conciliation of the antagonists are important elements; one in which means must match the desired ends; and one which insures both the realization of well-founded demands of those seeking change and the integrity of the persons or institutions called upon to make the change.

Compromise is not necessarily the outcome of the creative conflict process, but positive and healthier relations between antagonists and a new social situation meeting basic human needs of same are:

The force within any dialectical situation is derived from the clash of opposing elements within that situation. In every case of *satyagraha* the conflict is to be understood in dialectical terms. The immediate objective is a restructuring of the opposing elements to achieve a situation which is satisfying to both the original opposing antagonists but in such a way as to present an entirely new total circumstance. This is, in Hegelian terms, an aiming at synthesis out of the conflict of thesis and

antithesis. The claim for *satyagraha* is that
through the operations of nonviolent action the
truth as judged by the fulfillment of human
needs will emerge in the form of a mutually
satisfactory and agreed upon solution. (2,
p. 195)

Urban-semester students are generally in a position to see multiple aspects and phases of a con-
flict--to be able to identify not only the parties,
their goals and tactics, and their resources, but
also their motives and the true complexity of each
party. These are the necessary conditions for the
ability to empathize with all parties to a certain
degree and to develop approaches to conflict management that will reflect the Gandhian dialectical process. This is more true in some types of assignments than in others. For example, students working
in public schools could conceivably identify and empathize with children, teachers, administrators and
parents in the course of their involvement--all of
whom have some common goals, but also opposed interests which may be in constant tension. Others working as advocates for neighborhood action groups in
poverty areas find it more difficult to achieve a
multi-perspective view, since their field-work com-
mits them more heavily to one side of a conflict
situation. Even there, however, the complexity of
the conflict and underlying problems dispels the
over-simplified exploiter vs. exploited theme of the
campus radical. Student researchers find sensitive
and concerned people of good will in unexpected
places and conflicts among allies. They emerge from
these experiences with a more mature understanding
of the complexity of the urban scene and how one
needs to work with conflict skillfully to bring
about desired structural changes.

PROCESS IN CONFLICT EDUCATION

We have dealt thus far only peripherally with
the role conflict itself plays in the teaching/
learning process. Education reflects the major assumptions of society. It is not surprising, therefore, to find that until very recently the components of the educative process--from theories of
learning to actual classroom management--have been
skewed toward an associational, non-conflictual perspective of education.

In this second section, we present several alternative and complementary models of education that
can serve as theoretical bases for conflict education.

In passing, we wish to note that a false di-
chotomy is sometimes propounded between "academic
learning," generally conforming to an associational
model of learning, and "experiential learning," more
closely related to conflict education. This dichot-
omy can be resolved when placed in the context of
Guilford's "Structure of Intellect" (8) in which the
content of intellectual activity includes behavioral
(experiential) as well as semantic and symbolic
(academic) material. Further analysis of the
operation and *products* of intellectual activity
strongly suggests that the addition of the behavioral or experiential component to education brings into play more facets of intellect than does academic
learning by itself. In short, academic and experiential learning can be seen as complementary and as
enhancing each other.

MODELS OF CONFLICT LEARNING

We turn our attention to a cluster of models,
all having to do with changes in cognitions and attitudes, called "incongruity-dissonance-imbalance"
theories. These theoretical formulations reflect a
conflict-oriented model of society since they indicate that changes in cognitions and attitudes are
brought about by internal conflict which has been
stimulated by external conflict, that is, conflict
in society. Such changes in cognitions and attitudes comprise an important kind of learning and result in permanent changes in behavior.

Festinger's theory of cognitive dissonance (7)
is one such theory. It describes conditions that
cause the human being to think or take overt action.
Festinger assumes that it is possible to represent
the meanings which a situation has for an individual
by a series of elementary cognitions--statements,
propositions, or assertions that an individual
might make describing his "knowledge, opinion, beliefs."

While cognitive dissonance theory has been criticized because it is purportedly too *simplistic* to
account for all the factors in complex social situations and has yet to be *substantiated by research*
(4), it nonetheless provides a point of departure
for conceptualizing conflict-oriented education.
Since conflict education often requires that the

teacher simplify and single out the issues in the conflict as much as possible, the simplicity of the model does not necessarily detract from its value as a pedagogical conception.

What is cognitive dissonance? It can be called cognitive conflict. Cognitive dissonance occurs when one item *A* is dissonant with or contradicted by another item *B*, where *A* implies not *B*. To be more explicit, dissonance occurs when a person's cultural assumption *A* is contradicted by his/her action *B*, or when someone's belief *A* is contradicted by his/her action *B*; or when people's belief *A* is contradicted by their perception *B*. These examples, of course, are far from exhaustive.

More extensive examples of cognitive dissonance can be drawn from the lives of students. Take some students who hold the belief that "people who act friendly toward me will not harm me" (Item A). Acting on this belief, they may, for instance, invite friendly neighborhood youngsters into their apartment, actually giving them the run of the place. The students may dance, play their guitars, talk with the young people for hours on end. Students, as sometimes happens, go home for a long weekend. It has happened that upon their return they find that their apartment has been cleaned out of guitars, stereo equipment and typewriters. Suppose evidence points strongly to the neighborhood youngsters as the culprits. Cognitive dissonance occurs when the students perceive that, "People who act friendly may in fact rob me" (Item B).

Take another example: Many students believe, "I am a liberal, racially unbiased person" (Item A). Some students even assert this belief in so many words. Take a white student who holds such a belief, but finds herself as a student teacher in constant conflict with her black critic teacher. "I cannot get along with my critic teacher" (Item B). Her inability to get along, while undoubtedly a complex matter, may call into question her belief about her freedom from racial bias and result in cognitive dissonance.

Dissonance produces discomfort, and is experienced as tension. People prefer consistency and consonance among their cognitions, and will initiate a varied set of instrumental acts designed to bring about change in order to preserve the consistencies and thereby reduce tensions. Further, instrumental acts once initiated will be continued, since to discontinue them will once again introduce dissonance, which the acts were designed to overcome.

There are a number of ways of reducing cognitive dissonance. One healthy way of doing so is to change one's belief or cultural prescriptions so as to bring them more into accord with perceived reality. For example, a student who starts out believing that professionals are nothing but Establishment Lackies needs to reexamine and change this belief if, in fact, he/she sees professionals acting independently of and perhaps even counter to the establishment. A second way to change cognitive dissonance is to alter one's behavior. Take a person with a self image of a liberal who acts patronizingly toward black people. He/she needs to change his/her racist behavior if he/she is to maintain a belief about himself/herself as a liberal in the face of those who charge him/her with racism.

A third way of reducing tension, less healthy but unfortunately rather prevalent, consists of incredulity or denying one's actions that are dissonant with one's self image. A student may deny cheating on an exam in order to maintain his/her belief in himself/herself as a strictly honest person.

Some of the conflicts we spoke of earlier in the students' experience fit the dissonance model. Most value conflicts are dissonant in nature, as are tensions between old and new self-perceptions.

The value of off-campus, urban centered, experiential learning is that the richness and intensity in the urban environment are guaranteed to challenge directly the student's beliefs and cultural assumptions as well as to induce him/her to act in ways that are dissonant with his/her self-concept. In this sense, the city is the teacher because it provides the external stimuli that lead through a train of internal events to the result of changed behavior.

The theoretical weakness of the dissonance model of conflict education lies in its inability to account adequately for the interpersonal aspects of the learning-teaching process. While it accounts with some adequacy for *intra*-personal conflict, it makes little provision for *inter*-personal relationships in conflict situations.

INTERPERSONAL ASPECTS OF CONFLICT EDUCATION

A more inclusive model for conflict education can be found in Heider's theory of interpersonal relationships (9). The theory deals with triadic relationships, which for our purposes will consist of (1) the teacher or staff person of an off-campus urban program related to (2) a student, and (3) some

urban situation, state of affairs, or third person
to which both the teacher and student are related.
        For example, a student comes to Philadelphia to
participate in an urban program such as the Great
Lakes Colleges Association Urban Semester, or the
Haverford Educational Involvement Program. He/she
immediately sets up a host of relationships, among
which are his/her mutual relationship with a staff
member of the urban program, and his/her relation
ship to the city as a complex object, to which the
staff person has his/her own relationship. The
triad of relationships is depicted in Fig. 2 below:

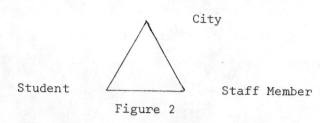

Figure 2

Heider proposed that the quality of the relationship
between each member of the triad can be expressed
with a sign--positive, negative, or a zero. A positive sign between teacher and student indicates that
they like each other, and are positively related to
each other. There is little or no tension or conflict in such a relationship. A negative sign indicates conflict, tension, discomfort or strain in
the relationship. A zero indicates no relationship,
which serves functionally as a negative sign.
        Suppose, for instance, that the incoming stu-
dent is initially frightened by the city and consequently somewhat hostile toward it (-). Hopefully
he/she finds staff persons on the urban program who
relate warmly and easily to him/her, which in turn
induces a reciprocal positive response from him/her
(+). Finally, assume that the staff person also is
committed to the city, and relates positively toward
it (+). The triadic relationship is depicted in
Fig. 3 as follows:

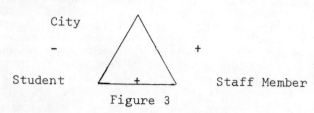

Figure 3

The combination of signs in a triad gives it a dynamic character that is so important in conflict education. If any one of the signs in a triad is negative, as is the case above, the entire triad is in a state of tension and will tend toward a stable resolution. Thus, while the student described above is in conflict with the city, he/she is induced to resolve that conflict and relate himself/herself positively to the city by virtue of the psychological pressure exerted by the staff member who relates positively both to the city and to the student. The student finds it psychologically difficult to dislike something that the staff member likes when the staff member also respects, accepts, and likes him as a person. Gradually the student's initial negative reaction to the city becomes more positive and the end result is a stable triad in which all the signs are positive.

Or the triad may move toward a less fortunate resolution. Suppose, for example, that the student perceives, rightly or wrongly, that the staff member dislikes him or has slighted him. The relationship between them may deteriorate and actually become negative. The triad then assumes the combination of signs as in Fig. 4 below:

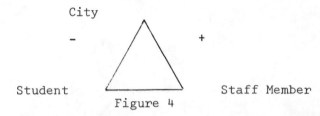

Figure 4

Such a triad is also relatively stable, but it is a broken one as well. The student rejects both the city and the staff member, and the positive relationship of the staff member to the city no longer influences him. It is a standoff. The student and staff member may physically separate themselves from each other.

Take a more explosive conflict situation. Suppose some students innocently rented an apartment that was desperately needed by a destitute family in the neighborhood; and were consequently confronted with angry members of the community demanding that they vacate the apartment. The situation can be diagrammed as below.

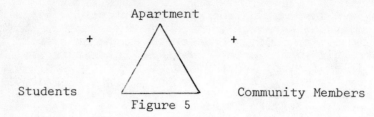

Figure 5

The possibilities for a stand-off are clearly visible. If the students reject the apartment, give it up, and move out, the triad becomes stable, but the situation remains unresolved. The same is true if a community gives up its demands for the apartment for the family. Fig. 6 and Fig. 7 depict these noncreative solutions.

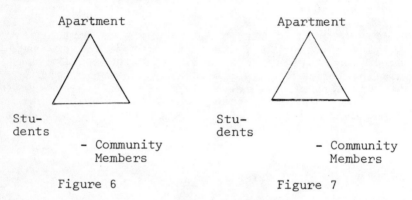

Figure 6   Figure 7

Further, merely developing a positive relationship between the students and the community--a strategy that might be followed, for example, by setting up a sensitivity training group--does not resolve the issue or bring about balance. Clearly, what is needed is a creative solution which would result in apartments for both students and the family and a positive relationship between students and community members. To bring this about, the students might go back to the housing bureau of their urban program and try to find another apartment either for themselves or for the family. Or housing might be found which neither the family nor the students could afford separately, but could if they pooled their resources.

A final conflict situation arises when a triad contains three negative relationships. For instance, a teacher may abhor the school in which he/she must teach. The pupils also dislike the school.

Suppose the teacher also fears the children who in turn despise him/her. Such a situation is explosive. Ordinarily it rapidly disperses itself, unless held together by external forces, as in school. Imbalance in triadic relationships is one model of conflict. Resolving the imbalance and restoring stable relationships within the triad can be seen as a model of conflict education. It takes energy to restore or develop positive stable triadic relationships. When such stability is attained, the members of the triad can turn their energies toward other learnings or other constructive activities.

A person's life may be depicted by a network of interrelated triads. A dissonance or negative relationship in one triad can reverberate throughout the whole network of triads. Learning how to resolve conflict and restore balance is an important and hoped for result of conflict education. Further, when a student learns how to resolve conflicts, and gains confidence that he/she has the skills and competencies to restore balance, he/she can deliberately set out to create conflict in his/ her life--that is, to enter into new untried relationships. In our increasingly urban pluralistic society, such learning--which seems to be the peculiar contribution of conflict education--is indispensable.

CONCLUSIONS

1. Social conflict must be recognized as an essential and potentially functional process in society, as important as conciliation for maintenance of the social system. Since educational processes should reflect and make use of social reality, educational theory and practice must be enlarged to utilize conflict both as a legitimate field of study, and as a valuable teaching/ learning technique. We have suggested some theoretical bases for movement in that direction.

2. One of the most promising formal contexts for conflict education is an off-campus urban-oriented learning program. Through exposure to multiple and novel conflict experiences and conscious reflection upon them, a student gains a new understanding of conflict processes. Helping him/her to resolve these conflicts and to generalize from his/her experience an approach to insuring creative outcomes, is an important function of teaching.

3. Social conflict must be made creative and this
    will occur only through the development of new
    concepts of conflict resolution such as the
    Gandhian dialectic. Students educated to the
    potential of creative conflict forms will devel-
    op more effective skills in managing conflict.
4. The field of conflict education is wide open for
    research. To insure substantial progress, we
    must build more research into present and future
    efforts at experiential learning in general and
    experiential conflict education in particular.

REFERENCES

1. Baran, Paul, & Sweezy, Paul. *Monopoly Capital*.
    Harmondsworth: Pelican, 1966.
2. Bondurant, Joan. *Conquest of Violence*. Berke-
    ley: University California Press, 1965.
3. Boulding, Kenneth E. *A Primer on Social Dynam-
    ics*. New York: Free Press, 1970.
4. Chapanis, Natalia P., & Chapanis, Alphonse.
    Cognitive dissonance: five years later. *Psy-
    chological Bulletin*, 1964, *61*, 1-22.
5. Coser, Lewis. *The Functions of Social Conflict*.
    New York: Free Press, 1956.
6. Dahrendorf, Ralf. *Class and Class Conflict in
    Industrial Society*. Stanford University Press,
    1959.
7. Festinger, Leon. *A Theory of Cognitive Disson-
    ance*. New York: Row, Peterson, 1957.
8. Guilford, J.P. *The Nature of Human Intelli-
    gence*. McGraw-Hill, 1967.
9. Heider, Fritz. *The Psychology of Interpersonal
    Relationships*. New York: Wiley, 1958.
10. Johnson, Chalmers. *Revolutionary Change*. Bos-
    ton: Little, Brown, 1966.
11. Lipset, S.M. *Political Man*. New York: Double-
    day, 1960.
12. Marcuse, Herbert. *Reason and Revolution*. Bos-
    ton: Beacon, 1960.
13. Parsons, Talcott. *The Social System*. New York:
    Free Press, 1959.
14. Wehr, Paul. *Conflict Regulation*. Boulder,
    Colorado: Westview, in press.

*PAUL WEHR writes: My interest in nonviolence
and conflict resolution began with a deep concern
about racial conflict. My family had always empha-*

sized the values of peace, racial justice and inter-
racial conciliation, and my academic interest and
value commitments in that area led me to study race
relations at the University of North Carolina.
There I became involved in the struggle for racial
justice, in particular, desegregation strategies and
the sit-in movement. I saw firsthand, in those
years, the fruits of racial hatred and the violence
inherent in oppressive social and political structures.

   Subsequent refugee relief work with the Quakers
in North Africa brought me spiritually into the
ranks of the pacifists. That experience brought me
face to face with racism and naked violence, as the
Quaker team worked with Arab refugees through the
final and bloodiest years of the Algerian War. The
images which exploding shells, shattered families,
and my first encounter with real physical insecurity
and fear etched in my memory...those images were the
major determinant of my decision to return to the
university to the study and application of nonviolent conflict management. This I did and finished
my doctoral work at the University of Pennsylvania
in 1968.

   I then taught in the areas of conflict regulation and nonviolence at Haverford College and worked
to legitimize and promote peace and conflict studies
through, first, the Center for Nonviolent Conflict
Resolution, at Haverford, and then through the Consortium on Peace Research, Education and Development
(COPRED). I am also a course director and consultant on peace and conflict studies in the short
courses program of the American Association for the
Advancement of Science.

   Recent research interests have centered in developing theoretical and practical models for creative conflict, such as Gandhian satyagraha and nonviolent national defense. My commitment is to developing alternative institutions and patterns of
social interaction which will institutionalize peace
and justice. My position is that theory and practice must develop together. I have a major concern,
therefore, that the scholar move beyond the narrow
confines of the campus and become an actionist, to a
degree.

   At present my teaching and research at the University of Colorado is concentrated in the area of
environmental and natural resource conflict resolution.

   Kent Fellow (Danforth Foundation) (1966-68)
   NATO Fellow (1969-70)

Younger Humanist Fellowship - National Endow-
ment for the Humanities (1972-73)
Director, Center for Nonviolent Conflict Reso-
lution, Haverford College (1967-73)
Director, Consortium on Peace Research, Educa-
tion and Development (1972-76)
Current Positions
Associate Professor of Sociology, University of
Colorado/Boulder
Director, Environmental Conciliation Project,
Institute of Behavioral Science, University of
Colorado/Boulder

ROBERT DEHAAN was a professor at Hope College
in Holland, Michigan from 1952 to 1968, where he
headed the Psychology and Education Departments.
Increasing dissatisfaction with the possibilities of
making changes in society through the sheltered com-
munity of a college campus, motivated his decision
to enter an urban environment. Also leading to this
decision was his long-standing conviction that high-
er education was not meeting its own expectations
for a liberal arts program. The student who spends
four years on a college campus does not directly
confront the stresses which exist in his society,
but only meets them later, generally unprepared by
his academic background to handle them effectively.
The author brought his educational interests to
bear on the problems of the city by using the city
as a laboratory--to provide a field in which the
liberal arts student could meet directly the needs
and conflicts for which their education attempts to
prepare them. At the same time, the city benefits.
Through the Great Lakes Colleges Association Urban
Semester, approximately 200 students a year come to
Philadelphia from a dozen midwestern colleges. The
students live and work (in "establishment" as well
ıs "alternative" organizations and institutions) in
the city. They are guided by supervisors in learn-
ing to function effectively and sympathetically. As
the director of the program, Mr. DeHaan attempts to
provide the cities with knowledgeable, capable, and
committed urban individuals as future citizens.

SOME OTHER PUBLICATIONS BY PAUL WEHR

- Nonviolence and differentiation in the equal
  rights movement. *Sociological Inquiry*, Winter
  1968, *38*, 65-76.
- Coleman, John R., & Wehr, Paul. Off-campus involvement programs. In Howard E. Mitchell (Ed.),

The University and the Urban Crisis. New York: Behavioral Publications, 1974, 107-120.

- Wehr, Paul, & Washburn, A. Michael. Developing undergraduate peace studies programs. *Peace and Change,* 1973, *1*(3), 4-16.
- Wehr, Paul, & Washburn, A. Michael. *Peace and World Order Systems,* Beverly Hills, California: Sage, 1976.

SOME OTHER PUBLICATIONS BY ROBERT DEHAAN

- Havighurst, Robert J., DeHaan, Robert F., Dietrich, William J., Hackanack, Henry, Johnson, LaVona, & King, Robert D. *A Community Youth Development Program.* Supplementary Monograph No. 75. Chicago: University Chicago Press, 1952.
- Havighurst, Robert J., Stivers, Eugene, & DeHaan, Robert F. *A Survey of the Education of Gifted Children.* Supplementary Monograph No. 83. Chicago: University Chicago Press, 1953.
- DeHaan, Robert F., & Kough, Jack. *The Teacher's Guidance Handbook.* Vol. I *Identifying Children Who Need Help,* and Vol. II, *Procedures for Helping Children,* Elementary and Secondary Editions. Chicago: Science Research Associates, 1955-57.
- Identifying Gifted Children. *School Review,* 1957, *65*(1), 41-48.
- DeHaan, Robert F., & Havighurst, Robert J. *Educating Gifted Children.* (Revised and Enlarged.) Chicago: University Chicago Press, 1961.
- *Guidelines for Parents of Capable Youth.* Chicago: Science Research Associates, 1961. (pamphlet)
- Detection of ability in America. Chapter 3: The Gifted Child. *The Yearbook of Education.* New York: Harcourt, Brace & World, 1961, 216-225.
- *Accelerated Learning Programs.* Library of Education. Englewood Cliffs, N.J.: Prentice Hall, 1963.

12. Children for a World Community

Children's International Summer Villages (CISV) & International School-to-School Experience (ISSE)

Doris Twitchell Allen, Ph.D.

INTRODUCTION

This chapter deals with a design for educating
for a world society, that is, a society with a per-
vading concern for the well-being of all peoples.
Thus, the field of consideration is broad, in fact
the whole world. The focus is upon people, all
people, all ages, any person anywhere. The task may
appear too vague or too large to tackle, but looking
at the broad outline of the essential forces, possible steps toward the goal become delineated. Actually these steps emerge so clearly that they appear
almost simple, and they demand action.

Millions around the world have not glimpsed the
wholeness of the world. They have had no opportunity to do so. Many--but, relative to the world population, only a few--have suggested social changes
in the direction of a world society. Groups have
urged, and in some cases have achieved, action in
world law, world trade, conservation of natural resources, health planning, world banking, control of
drugs, delinquency, and crime. Leaders urging these
social changes have emphasized, however, that change
depends upon the will and attitudes of the people
(25). Up to the present, not enough people have had
the will to work for, or to accept, a world community. Relatively few have had experiences which make
it possible even to comprehend such global relationships. Thus the need is pressing for widespread education of attitudes and motives favorable for a
sense of belonging to a world society and caring
about the welfare of its members.

The design in this chapter deals with a plan

for preparing individuals and groups for a world
community. The first thesis is that such global society is possible only when enough individuals and
groups have acquired the attitudes, the will, and
the skills of human interaction requisite for one-
worldness. The design therefore is a program which
offers education for world friendships and respect
and concern for all peoples.

The second thesis is that education, at the
depth and breadth necessary to insure progress toward a world society, must occur before adolescence.
Changes in personality can take place after that age
but the surer base for behavior which can promote
global living is education before adolescence.

The third thesis is that global relations can
be learned adequately, that is, to the point of determining behavior, only through *action*. And that
action must be in a group that is perceived as representing the whole world.

REQUISITES FOR INTERNATIONAL EDUCATION

AN ACTION APPROACH IN A MINIATURE WORLD

This design for preparation of individuals and
groups for a world society is based upon proven
principles of learning. First of all the approach
is through *action*. A person, or a group, learn
through doing. It is not enough to *talk* about
peace, or a global community. Peace must be *lived*
to be effective; and lived on a twenty-four-hour
resident basis.

Second, the practice should be in a situation
as close to reality as possible. Peace must be
lived in a "world," if that is the desired unit to
which citizens should relate. Today that is the
technological unit to which we all relate whether
we will it or not. Every place is potentially accessible. Technologically, no place is isolated.
This means that the task is to give individuals personal experience with the whole world. Since in ac-
tuality, for large numbers, this is impossible, a
whole world must be simulated. The person or group
must be given opportunity to experience *a sample* of
countries which can have the meaning of the "world."
The action must occur face-to-face with different
nationalities.

The shared experiences among the nationalities
must be varied in order to permeate the breadth and
depth of the personality: for example, from sports

to worship or meditation, from swapping coins of
their respective cultures to setting the table for
lunch with a person of another country and another
language. Each person needs to absorb, unhurriedly,
actions and attitudes of other cultures.

RECOGNIZING THE BIOLOGY OF DEVELOPMENT

The eleven-year-old. This program of education
is not beamed toward adults. The laws of learning
point to preadolescence as the formative years for
acquiring basic social relations and concepts.
These in fact are starting in infancy and developing
in early months of the first year. But this is not
the age for setting up a miniature world. To establish a world model, educators have to consider at
what age a child can leave his parents and play-
mates, and at what age he carries the stamp of his
culture to the degree that a collection of children
from different countries would indeed be perceived
as an *international* group.
    Eleven years of experience at the Children's
Hospital of Cincinnati, Ohio, with children from
three and four months to sixteen years, and my years
at Longview State Hospital, Cincinnati, with children and adults from 7 to 100 years, pointed to
eleven years as the appropriate age. Biologically,
eleven-year-olds are open and receptive to new experiences. They are not rigid; prejudices are not
too firmly set. They are free to express themselves; they are not hemmed in by the self-consciousness of early adolescence. They are not beset
by the conflicts which often characterize the
twelve-to-sixteen-year-old. On the other hand, they
do not have the dependent seeking-of-adult of the
ten-year-old. Generally they are independent enough
to be away from home for several weeks. Eleven
years stands as appropriate both for the participant
and for the needs of this educational task.
    But the eleven-year-old cannot travel alone.
Hence the design calls for eleven-year-olds to be
accompanied by an adult.

Biological factors in program building. In the
daily schedule of resident living, the times for
eating, for going to bed at night and getting up in
the morning are determined by the needs of the eleven-year-old. The same is true in planning games and
sports and other items of the day's activities.
There are physical needs and physical limits of the
eleven-year-old. He needs large muscular activity

several times a day, for example. He needs to be in
small groups part of the time, as a balance to activities in large groups. He needs some free time
to be alone, or with just one or two pals.
     And the eleven-year-old who naturally slips in-
to sign language when faced with seven to ten different languages, needs at the same time--in terms
of the goals of the program--to *hear* all languages.
He needs this opportunity to learn to *be at home* in
a multilingual environment, as is necessary, at
times, in a world society. Therefore, in the resident program, announcements in the dining room can
be given in all languages in sequence. A line-up of
the accompanying adults who speak the official language set by the host country can repeat, in turn,
the announcement first made in the official language. By this means, a child can absorb, unconsciously, the pitch, tempo, and inflexion of the
different languages and is never again a total
stranger to these languages. In fact, a teacher in
Germany has said: "It is obvious which children of
my class had the CISV international experience.
They fall into the intonation of the new language
before the others." Details such as this may seem
minor in terms of the total planning of a miniature
world but can be understood as crucial in terms of
the purposes of preparing individuals for a world
society.

INTEGRATING ADULTS INTO THE PROGRAM

     Although the long-range planning for global
living needs to start with preadolescent children,
adults can be integrated into the program. Adults
do not learn these new social behaviors of international settings as fast as the children, yet they do
learn (12), and especially when they are in a situation with children who are enjoying friendly relationships with many nationalities. The adults who
come to the miniature world as accompanists should
be those who have a love for children and who can
truly enjoy the activities along with the children.
In this kind of program, it is important that there
be no gap in communication between the children and
the adults. Experience has shown that with a first-
name relationship, eleven-year-olds can feel very
close to adults from widely-spread countries and to
adults of twenty-one to seventy-five or more years.
And the adults on their part form deep friendships
among the adults as well as among the children.
Such closeness of a broad range of ages and cultures

can make for a solid development of a global community.

PROVIDING FOR FOLLOW-UP ACTIVITIES

Starting at the age of eleven, the task includes providing follow-up activities: programs
such as reunions, seminars, and work camps for high
school and college students. These programs can
provide graduates of an eleven-year-old experience
opportunity to apply their international learnings
at older ages and to become increasingly ready for
leadership in international relations as adults (3).

CHILDREN'S INTERNATIONAL SUMMER VILLAGES (CISV)

ORGANIZATION AND STRUCTURE OF CISV

One vehicle for carrying out this design is
Children's International Summer Villages (CISV), an
international organization, conceived in 1946, with
the first CISVillage held in Cincinnati, Ohio, in
1951. It had seemed that it was enough to have
planned the design and that UNESCO or some other organization would be the appropriate agency to implement the idea. But it soon became clear that a
straight-line-to-peace action-program to be launched
worldwide was outside the comprehension even of
those who were working for improved international
relations. That eleven-year-old children could be
related to improved global relations seemed heresy
to some, even though for the previous thirty years
educators had acknowledged that the early childhood
years were the crucial formative years. However,
with the inestimable legal, financial, and general
organizational aid of the founder's late husband,
Erastus S. Allen, patent and trade-mark lawyer, and
the financial and committee aid of a widely distributed group of Cincinnati citizens, the first demonstration Village was achieved.
In 1949, Lucile Kehoe brought the dream into
operating reality. She introduced the founder to
two of her friends: James Shouse, Head of Cincinnati's largest television station; and William
Hessler, Cincinnati's leading analyst of foreign affairs. The project from that day on was out in the
community in a new way. Mr. Shouse called together
a group of citizens representing many facets of the
city who became the first CISV Planning and Policy
Board. Oliver Gale, Head of Procter and Gamble's

Public Relations, interested leading journalists
around the country, who came and reported the Village. Arthur G. Bills, head of the Psychology Department of the University of Cincinnati, and George
Kisker, Otto Klineberg, and Ronald Lippitt aided research planning. Theodore Wuerfel, with 15 years
experience as director of his own summer camp and
principal of an independent school, accepted the
directorship of this first CISVillage to be held in
June of 1951 on the outskirts of Cincinnati. Thus
the Village took shape. In the meantime, Ruth Allen
Wolkowska was setting up CISV Committees in European countries, with the result that Austria, Denmark, France, Germany, Great Britain, Norway, and
Sweden were represented along with Mexico and the
United States.

One moral and financial sponsor has to be mentioned to show the personal character that permeated
the work. The late Mary E. Johnston did not need
the demonstration of even one Village to know the
potentiality of the design. She gave her personal
friendship to the children and adults after they arrived, and for years remained a vital, personal link
in the closeness of this group. She served five
years as International, and 19 years as National
Trustee of CISV.

At this first Village, the adults from the nine
countries drew up plans for the international organization that was to be behind future Villages.
Trustees were elected from Mexico, Sweden, and the
United States. The founder was elected President.
In 1956, the original Code of Regulations was sup-
planted by a Constitution. A Swedish President and
a Swedish Executive Director were elected, and the
International Office was located in Stockholm. Subsequently, Norway and England, in turn, provided the
International President, Executive Director, and International Office. Currently the International Office remains in England. The elected officers may
be in different countries.

The International Organization is composed of
National Associations of CISV; the National Associations are composed of Local Chapters--where such
have been organized. At the present time, the administration of CISV is carried on by an International Board composed of a President, two Vice Pres-
idents, one Director chosen by each National Association of CISV, a Secretary General (non-voting), and
a Treasurer (non-voting), meeting annually; and by an
International Office in charge of the Secretary General.

RESULTS

Performance. By the end of 1978, CISV will
have held 316 Villages in 31 countries. From 5 continents, 60 countries have sent 1 or more delegations to CISVillages (starred countries have held
Villages.):

Argentina	Iceland	Nigeria
*Austria	*India	*Norway
*Belgium	Indonesia	Palestine
*Brazil	Iran	*Philippines
British Honduras	Iraq	Poland
*Canada	Ireland	*Portugal
*Costa Rica	*Israel	*Romania
Cuba	*Italy	Senegal
Czechoslovakia	*Japan	Sierra Leone
*Denmark	*Kenya	*Spain
*El Salvador	Korea	*Sweden
*Finland	Kuwait	Switzerland
*France	Lebanon	Tanzania
*Germany	*Liberia	Tunisia
Ghana	*Luxembourg	*Turkey
*Great Britain	*Mexico	*U.A.R.
Greenland	Morocco	*U.S.A.
(Denmark)	Nationalist	U.S.S.R.
*Guatemala	China	Venezuela
Guinea	*Netherlands	*Yugoslavia
Hungary	Nicaragua	

Over 13,000 children and 4,000 adults (accompanists and staff) have participated directly in the
four-week Village life. From one Village a year for
the first three years, CISV now holds around 30 Villages a year.

Research. Research was part of the originally
conceived program. Investigations were formulated
in reference to the goals. In the Handbook for
Children's International Summer Villages, these spe--
cific goals were specified (9, 1961 edition, p. 12f;
1976 revision, p. 5).

1. Individuals will make close friendships a-
round the world, that is, that countries
will become known to them in terms of close
friends rather than as abstract places on a
map, or as stereotypes built up from ignorance or limited experience.
2. Individuals will become aware of basic
likenesses of all humans, and at the same
time that they will come to know and to appreciate differences.

3. Individuals will acquire an active desire
    for world peace and a desire to work for
    it.
4. Individuals will acquire skills of commun-
    ication with individuals and with groups,
    even when many languages are represented
    and when no common language exists.
5. Individuals will begin to acquire skills of
    administration and organization.
6. Individuals will develop personalities that
    are essentially free from barriers such as
    the barrier of prejudice.

The first specific goal, to make close friendships around the world, was investigated through so-
ciometric studies. In 1951, the question was: "Who
is contacting whom?" Data were recorded from observations at a distance. This was flying right in the
face of the skeptics because they wagged their heads
and said: "Each delegation will stay to itself; so
what will you have accomplished?" What was accomplished through the research of Allen and Shepard in
1951 (11) was to present evidence that twice as many
contacts were made with "other" as with "own" delegation members. Bjerstedt of Malmo, Sweden confirmed this direction of behavior and concluded:
"No *rigid* nationality...barriers are found" (15,
p. 172).
Does the research reveal personality changes in
the eleven-year-old at the end of the four weeks of
a Village? If so, are these changes in the direction of awareness of the wholeness of the world?
The answers are affirmative.
*The eleven-year-old has stepped into a wider
world.* The child was asked in an individual interview, at the beginning and end of the camp in Cin-
cinatti in 1955 (10):
1. Who are your closest friends here at the
    Village?
2. When this Village group is invited to a re-
    union, whom would you most like to meet?
3. If next year you could travel anywhere you
    liked, where would you like to go?
At the end of the four weeks, there was a
decisive increase in the number of countries represented by those camp-mates chosen in answers to
questions 1 and 2, and in answer to question 3, an
increase in the number of countries the child would
like to visit the following year. With statistical
significance, the findings confirmed the hypothesis

that the CISV experience does expand the geographical life space of the person.

Bjerstedt (15) found similar results of an expanding world. The eleven-year-old whose core friends were of *one nationality* at the beginning of the Village held a core of friends of *multiple nationalities* at the end.

The eleven-year-old has dissipated his stereotypes of persons of different nationalities, stereotypes regarding physique, dress, manner and personality (5). Again by individual interview, the campers revealed that they had indeed corrected their images and meanings of the other nationalities which composed their CISVillage. Since stereotypes are a first step to prejudice, we have here evidence that the Village experience has formed a bulwark against the development of prejudice. This result strikes at one of the most insidious obstacles to a world society.

The eleven-year-old camper changes in his behavior in group situations. His development in the weekly Children's Assemblies is presented in *Research Remarks* (7, p. 5):

In addition to a network of close friendships around the world, friendly relations among nations depend upon the possibility of transacting business--not necessarily commercial business, but governmental and other social business--in an orderly way with adequate consideration of all points of view. Parliamentary process is difficult enough in a single culture and is manifoldly complicated in groups of multi-nationalities and multi-languages. The age of eleven is none too soon to lay the foundation for fair practices in government and other aspects of social relations among many nationalities.

A survey of the weekly children's assemblies revealed three major steps in social process:
1. presentation of self-wants, e.g., changes in menu, or in daily schedule: characteristic of the first assembly.
2. presentation of an immediate group problem, e.g., property rights ("not get into another's suitcase") or sex rights ("the boys should not push the girls into the pool"): often presented in the second assembly.
3. consideration of long-range planning,

e.g., how to promote CISV after return
home: usually not arising until the third
or fourth (last) assembly.

To pass through these social steps does indeed
result in a changed eleven-year-old by the end
of four weeks. The tedium and frustration of
working through the Declaration of Human
Rights, experienced by Chairman Eleanor Roosevelt because of many languages and because of
discomfort and suspicion among committee members from different countries, could never be
the same problem for a CISV child grown to
adulthood. These assemblies which treat problems of the age of eleven and immediate problems in the Village, and which are without
preachment by the adults, can reach deeply into
the personality and yet set up a practical pattern of action.

This is one area of development that can be
transferred almost bodily into adult international situations. Therefore, the parliamentary assemblies are recommended in the CISV
Handbook for all the campers, not for just a
council of representatives. Every child needs
opportunity to pass through each of three so-
cial-interaction steps as a solid background
for functioning in the future.

To assess the efficacy of the program of CISV
for preparing individuals and groups for a global
community, the question was asked: "Are CISV youth
distinguishable from non-CISV youth?" (5).

Bjerstedt (14), in an introductory study,
worked with three groups: non-CISV Swedish boys
(12-14 years) and non-CISV Syrian boys (14-16 years)
at a non-CISV Czechoslovakian camp at the time data
were collected, and CISV boys (14-19 years) who had
attended CISVillages when they were eleven years
old. The CISV boys were contacted shortly after
they had attended a CISV Reunion Camp in France.

In their responses, the three groups were
sharply contrasted. The non-CISV Swedish boys gave
diffuse or simple answers with very little international awareness. The non-CISV Syrians showed
strong international awareness but were *chauvinistic*
in their answers. The CISV Reunion boys reflected
objective, differentiated thinking, with strong international awareness which was directed toward global friendship.

A comparison of CISV youth and comparably out-

standing non-CISV youth in Vienna, Helsinki, Stockholm, and Oslo was made by Cormack (18,5) with the
use of an Opinion Questionnaire. At the end he
asked what kinds of conditions would make them
change their opinion. Answers to this last question
were analyzed into three types:

1. Nothing would change their mind.
2. Only impossible, unrealistic situations of
    obvious fact distortion would change their
    mind.
3. The person states conditions under which
    his answer holds: demonstrates analysis of
    his answer, or presents introspection into
    the basis for his answer.

Scoring was done without knowledge of whether
the papers were from a CISV or non-CISV youth.
Three judges showed high consistency of scoring.
Cormack commented:

The person with highly prejudiced views will
not accept any evidence as really contradictory
to his ideas and will often reinterpret the
most improbable data as support for his hypotheses. It was predicted that the CISV group
would give a larger proportion of responses
which were objective and which analyzed their
own attitudes (type-C responses). Results were
as predicted: the CISV youth gave a preponderance of the analytical type of response in contrast to the non-CISV youth, who employed a
high percentage of rigid, dogmatic answers
(type-A response) (7, p. 3).

Thus Cormack and Bjerstedt, even with their introductory studies, found similar results. The CISV
youth who had had the CISVillage experience at the
age of eleven revealed more objective, differentiated, non-rigid, analytical thinking--a most important component of human behavior for a world society.
A common question always has been: "What are
these CISV eleven-year-old graduates of the Village
experiencing when they are adults?" In 1968, CISV
research leaders (24) asked even more specifically:

1. Does the behavior of young CISV adults tend
    to reflect a continuing *interest* in people
    of other countries?
2. Does the behavior of young CISV adults tend
    to reflect a *concern* for the welfare of
    people in other countries?
3. Does the behavior of young CISV adults in
    regard to interest and concern for people
    in other countries vary significantly from
    that of a comparable group of young non-
    CISV adults, selected on the basis of their
    school performance academically and social-
    ly at the age of eleven?

    The Village program had been planned to make it
seemingly reasonable to predict an affirmative answer to all three of these questions. However, results needed to be evaluated.
    A questionnaire was devised by Fred H. Wright(24)
Through the cooperation of W.P. Matthews, Jr., Secretary General in the CISV International Office, the
questionnaires were sent to the National CISV Association headquarters in the different countries with
a request for them to mail them to the individuals.
There is no way of knowing how many of the CISV
group received a questionnaire. Even so, the return
from 172 individuals was 24.5%, almost 2½ times the
10% return which many researchers consider good.
    The sample that did respond seemed adequately
representative of the total group to warrant consideration of the findings. The group of respondents
was balanced by sex and by number of years' lapse
between attendance at a Village and answering the
questionnaire. The age-range was from 20 to 30.
    The control study was not carried out because
funds were not available. Yet it seems important to
report the results for the CISV respondents. Hopefully a control study can be made at a later date.
    An attempt to sample continued interest in peo-
ple of other countries was the reason for asking
such questions as: "Have you been in other countries *since* you attended your CISVillage? If yes,
what countries? How long? At what age?
    A third of the scorable responses indicated 1
to 3 trips to other countries; one-third, 4 to 6
trips to other countries, and one-third, more than
that. One individual had taken 62 trips and another, 72 trips. These are not just excursions
across a boundary for an ice-cream cone or a movie;
the average length of time in other countries for a

majority of the respondents was a stay of over 7 months. As to the spread of countries represented in these trips, more had visited 4 to 6 countries than had visited just 1 to 3. And as many had visited 7 to 9 countries as had visited 1 to 3.

Interest in people of other countries was tapped also by this question: "Estimate the number of persons who live in other countries to whom you have written two or more letters or cards during the past year." About half have written to 1 to 5 persons. Ten percent have written more than twice to 21 to 55 persons. Data on degree of crossing over boundaries of native languages in this correspondence is not yet available. The number of native languages represented by those to whom letters or cards were written is 16.

To the question, "Do you know any language other than your own native language?" 96 percent of the scorable responses were "yes." Five of the 7 "no" responses were from the United States. Five percent of the 172 respondents knew 6 non-native languages. Even without the control group, these data point to the fact that in travel, correspondence, and knowledge of languages, the CISV group is outstanding in its interests and contacts with persons of other countries.

To glean information on their concern for the welfare of people of other countries, an analysis was made of responses to four questions. A reply was examined to ascertain whether the answer contained an "international" or a "domestic" component, and whether that component was "with" or "without social significance." Items were scored as socially significant only when so specified by the respondents, e.g., "Go to an undeveloped country and help solve agricultural problems." Grouping replies to four questions regarding "current occupation," "occupation the person hopes to enter," "main ambition," and "organization to which the person belongs" (avocational interests), the "domestic" component far outweighed the "international," 375 responses to 70. Thus interest in, and concern for, people of other countries is not expressed in answers to these vocational-avocational questions.

But whether these young CISV adults have concern for humans--whether domestic or international-- the answer is strongly "yes." Of those 70 responses with an "international" component, 6 times as many are "socially significant" as "not socially significant." And of the 375 responses which are "domestic," more than twice as many are "socially significant" as "without social significance."

The program emphasis of CISV which is without preachments of attitudes and motives emphasizes, by *action,* a "living together in one world." There is no action example of going into other countries to do good works. There is no apparent awareness in the Village that certain persons are from underdeveloped countries and others are not. The children themselves use the phrase,"We were a family." One of the delegates to the first Village of 1951, Ingolf Stahl, of Stockholm, then editor of the CISV News, at the age of 13 wrote: "We must all work to have a world in every place." These research figures of preponderance of "social significance" in vocation and avocation and ambitions, whether domestic or international, seem to reflect these words. In a world community, the importance is not whether the person is in this place or that, but rather that his outlook be humanitarian and that his field of awareness be the whole globe--in other words, that there shall be "a world in every place."

The last item on the questionnaire was a non-fact question: "If whatever I wished could come true, then above all I would wish that:" These replies, like previous questions, were analyzed for an "international" or "domestic" component and for "social significance" or "no social significance." In the replies, over twice as many carried an "international" as a "domestic" component; and of these international replies, 96 percent had "social significance." Of the "domestic" answers, three-fourths were "socially significant."

These are merely samples of the CISV research. A 71-page *Summary of CISV Research 1951-1969* is available from the CISV International Office.

INTERNATIONAL SCHOOL-TO-SCHOOL EXPERIENCE (ISSE)

However effective CISV may be, it is not sufficient to prepare only a selected group of children for a world society. "*All*" elementary school children need to be given opportunity for face-to-face contacts with many nationalities. "*All*" elementary school children need to build close personal friendships around the world, and have opportunity to develop feelings of responsibility for contributing to the shaping of a global community. International School-to-School Experience, ISSE, is presented as one way to meet this societal need.

THE ISSE PROGRAM

International School-to-School Experience (ISSE) sets up partnerships between an elementary school in one country and an elementary school in another country. This gives opportunity for total school involvement. ISSE brings four eleven-year-olds and an accompanying adult from another country into a host school for a four-week period. These visiting children teach their native songs and dances, arts and crafts, games and sports, and perhaps simple sicence experiments to the children of their host school. These eleven-year-olds, two boys and two girls, meet with each group from kindergarten through sixth grade, according to a schedule agreeable to both hosts and visitors. The hosts in turn demonstrate *their* activities. All participate in one another's programs. They come to make friends, share their culture and learn from the host's culture.

The visiting adult also has a school schedule. Some period each day might be devoted to summarizing the adult's observational notes. Some time might be given to teaching in the host school. The "teaching" might be informal talks, demonstrations in the special field of the adult, or teaching his (her) native language. At times, the visiting children need their adult as interpreter--but perhaps not for their regular sharing periods in classes. Sometimes the visiting children are more free and creative when they are "on their own."

Language. The visiting children usually do not know the language of the host country. But all understand one another through the action character of the shared activities, and through sign language which is spontaneously used by children of eleven. And part of the interest is to learn words and phrases of one another's language.

Living Arrangements. Each visiting child lives in a home where there is a same-age, same-sex child who attends the Host School. The visiting adult lives in a fifth host family.

Finances. The visiting adult and children do not have any living expenses during their stay. Their own school community pays for their travel expenses. In some cases, the family might pay all the expenses. But selection should not be made on the basis of ability to pay. The visiting child's family may contribute according to its means.

Reversal of Host and Visitor. The Visiting School becomes the Host School some months or weeks later. For example, if a school of Iran visited a United States school in March, that United States school might send four eleven-year-olds to their partner school in Iran in May, according to a schedule worked out between the partner schools.

Maximum International Contacts. Every year a host receives children from a country that has not visited them previously--as far as rate of expansion of the program permits. With such plan, by the time a kindergartener has completed fifth or sixth grade, he has had opportunity for face-to-face contacts and friendships with children from six or seven countries. In this way the elementary school experience is multinational.

Selection. A good principle is that selection of the children and the adult be based on some criteria other than ability of the person or the person's family to pay travel expenses. A child representing his school should be:
1. Eleven years old at the time of departure for the host country
2. Sufficiently independent and emotionally stable to be away from home for four weeks
3. Sufficiently advanced in his studies to be absent from his school for four weeks
4. Interested in becoming friends with children of other countries
5. Interested in sharing his native songs and dances, arts, sports, costumes, and language, and in turn learning from the host children
6. Interested in adapting to foods, schedules, and family and school living which may be very different from his own
7. Able to transmit his experiences to his school and to his community, upon return home, by radio, television, talks in person, exhibits, demonstrations, and so on

The adult accompanying the children should be:
1. A person who enjoys working with children and is well accepted by them
2. Interested in contributing to the goals of ISSE for a world community
3. Prepared to teach some specialty, if so arranged between the adult and the host-s school principal
4. Prepared to keep observational or other

notes on the process of the project

RESPONSIBILITIES OF PARTICIPATING SCHOOLS

Schools as visitors. Two major responsibilities of visiting schools are:
1. Selecting a team of eleven-year-olds, two boys and two girls, and one adult to represent their school in a host country
2. Arranging for the payment of round-trip travel expenses of the school's five representatives. (Such payment sometimes comes from civic groups, or from government, or some special grant, or some other source or *combination* of sources including the child's family.)

Schools as hosts. Two major responsibilities of hosting schools are:
1. Arranging for each of the four visiting children to live in a family which has a same-age, same-sex child who attends the host school; and arranging for the adult to live in a fifth family
2. Arranging for these host families to provide the visiting children and adult with all meals, except any provided by the school, local transportation, and with incidental spending money such as entrance to the zoo or an entertainment.

REPORT OF RESULTS

Records are kept in a way to report objectively regarding the results. The participating schools contribute to these records and aid in the interpretation and the resulting recommendations. Such record-keeping is conducted in a way to give priority to the *process* of the project. No value ensues from killing a process through attempts at measurement. This fact has been met in CISV. There are ways to maintain the "process" and yet to record and report. Research experience from CISV is available as one guide.

ORGANIZATIONAL STRUCTURE OF ISSE

This is being worked out gradually by the participating countries. Temporary leadership is by an International Committee composed of a Chairman, Vice-Chairman, and Secretary-Treasurer, elected by

the International ISSE Annual Conference Workshop.
Regional Coordinators have been chosen at this same
annual meeting.

RELATION OF ISSE TO CISV

ISSE is a companion organization to Children's
International Summer Villages, CISV. The program of
ISSE has grown out of CISV. The basic elements are
the same: face-to-face international contacts in
everyday living, the age of eleven, two boys and two
girls representing each country, one accompanying
adult, a period of four weeks, the teaching of native activities to children of other countries, and
learning from the others. All of these have yielded
positive results in CISV for more than a quarter
century. CISV may be viewed as the program for *intensive* international experience for selected children; ISSE, as a positive and practical way to give
at least, *some* international experience to any and
all elementary school children.

SUMMARY AND EXPECTATIONS

To meet the need for educating the attitudes
and the will of people globally, two designs for
preparing for a world society have been presented.
One, Children's International Summer Villages, CISV,
has been developing and enlarging steadily for twenty-seven years, since 1951. Research supports an
interpretation of personality growth within the program of attitudes, motives, and habits of thinking
which are favorable to a world community. The other
program, ISSE, stands as a necessary companion organization to CISV in order to extend education for
a world society to any and all elementary school
children.
In both CISV and ISSE, it is expected that
typically--as learned from CISV's twenty-seven years
of experience--these child graduates from the preadolescent experience will engage in a variety of
teenage and adult international experiences. *It is
predicted that those children of CISV and ISSE who
as adults come into positions of international influence will tend to serve the governance of a world
society with efforts toward equity.* And it is expected that, in general, all of these participating
children will:
    1. Become aware of the *possibility* of a world
        society;

2.   Develop a sense of *individual responsibil-ity* for such oneness of the world;
3.   Develop a *desire to act* to achieve global respect and concern for all men everywhere.

REFERENCES

1.   Allen, Doris Twitchell. Twenty-five years of CISV: Past and Future. *CISV NEWS*, July 1, 1976, 3-4.
2.   Allen, Doris Twitchell, & McKay, Peter. *A History of CISV 1951-1976*. Newcastle Upon Tyne, England: International Association for CISV, 1976, 34 pp.
3.   Allen, Doris Twitchell. Social Scientists Examine the Middle East conflict: a symposium. *International Understanding*. Monograph Supplement to *The International Psychologist*, 1971, *12*(2). *International Understanding*, 1971, *8*, 31-33.
4.   Allen, Doris Twitchell. *Children's International Summer Villages: Summary of Research 1951-1969*, Newcastle Upon Tyne, England: International Association for CISV, 1969, 71 pp.
5.   Allen, Doris Twitchell. Measurements of effectiveness of a program for peace: Children's International Summer Villages. *International Mental Health Research Newsletter*, Summer, 1968, *10*(2), 13-15.
6.   Allen, Doris Twitchell. Communication--cornerstone to peace. *Research Remarks*, 1966, *3*, 1-7.
7.   Allen, Doris Twitchell. Part I: Are CISV youth distinguishable from non-CISV youth? Part II: Is the eleven-year-old different at the end of four weeks of a CISVillage? *Research Remarks*, 1965, *2*, 1-11 (including an annotated bibliography).
8.   Allen, Doris Twitchell. Growth in attitudes favorable to peace. *Merrill-Palmer Quarterly Behavior and Development*. 1963, *9*(4), 27-38.
9.   Allen, Doris Twitchell, & Matthews, W.P., Jr. *A Handbook of Procedures for Children's International Summer Villages*. Chambery, France: Impremeries Reunis, 1961, 146 pp.; 1976 Revision of Second Edition. Newcastle Upon Tyne, England: International Association for CISV, 1976.
10. Allen, Doris Twitchell, & Miller, C.B. *Social expansiveness and change in a Children's International Summer Village group on a single criterion*. MS. Cincinati, Ohio: CISV Research Center, University of Cincinnati, 1961, 1-33.

Annotated in *Children's International Summer Villages: Summary of Research, 1951-1969 (ibid,* no. 4), p. 27.

11. Allen, Doris Twitchell, & Shepard, R.H. *Cincinnati's 1951 International Summer Village.* MS. Cincinnati, Ohio: CISV, 1952, 38 pp.

12. Allen, Doris Twitchell. Children's International Summer Villages. *Educational Leadership,* 1951, *9*(2), 110-114.

13. Bjerstedt, Ake. Informational and non-informational determinants of nationality stereotypes. *Acta Psychologica,* 1961, *18*(1), 2-5.

14. Bjerstedt, Ake. "Ego-involved world mindedness," nationality images, methods of research. *Conflict Resolution,* 1960, *4*(2), 185-192.

15. Bjerstedt, Ake. Reduction of "barrier tendencies" during experience of international co-living. *Acta Psychologica,* 1958, *13,* 329-346.

16. Bluestien, Venus. Characteristics of children selected for CISVillages. *Research Remarks,* 1967, *4*(3), 1-4.

17. Cass, James. Catch them while they're young. *Saturday Review,* 1975, 11 January, 53.

18. Cormack, R.H. *CISV evaluation study.* MS. Cincinnati, Ohio: University of Cincinnati Department of Psychology, 1961, 24 pp.

19. Handler, Leonard, Shrader, Raymond, & Simpkinson, Charles. Relation of personality variables to peace. *Research Remarks,* 1968, *5*(2), 2-3.

20. Robbins, Nancy. Love, learning, and Leeds. *Daisy,* 1977 Summer, 13.

21. Schurian, Walter. Contributions of CISV research to the planning and operation of CISVillages. *Research Remarks,* 1966, *4*(1), 1-8.

22. Spaander, J. Plans for developing the potentialities--tolerance as one of man's potentialities. In: What are man's potentialities for peace: a symposium. *International Understanding,* 1968, *6* (Autumn), 19-25.

23. *The Enquirer.* "Too Young to Hate." *Cincinnati Enquirer,* 1976, 7 August, A-4. ("Too Young to Hate was the title of a CBS film narrated by Walter Cronkite, aired in 1963 and repeated thereafter).

24. Wright, F.H., & Allen, D.T. A follow-up study of former child delegates. *Research Remarks,* 1969, *6*(2), 3-12.

25. Yost, Charles W. World peace is possible. *World,* 1972, 12 September, 17-21.

26. Zucker, K.B., & Jordan, D.C. The Paired Hands Test: a technique for measuring friendliness.

Journal Projective Techniques & Personality Assessment, 1968, 32(6), 522-529.

DORIS ALLEN writes: *I was born in Old Town, Maine in 1901. In retrospect my education in psychology began in my earliest years, well before I started school. Riding in the buggy with my physician father whose specialty was children, I learned how he brought a six-year-old child out of a tantrum of protest against her prescribed medical regime to a rational state of responsibility. By the time he had left she had understood what medicines she was to ask the nurse to give her. I learned about the therapeutic touch when I went with him to see an infant who reportedly had been screaming for two hours. We heard the child a block away as we drove up. A moment after the door closed behind my father, the crying ceased. He later explained how he had placed his hand on the infant's stomach. I knew the kind authority of that hand, and understood.*

My mother who had taught primary school before her marriage often told stories of how she helped those who were slow in learning to read. And she made a point of getting my next older sister and me into the parlor when a salesman called: "They know just what to say and if you are not careful, you buy something you don't need." When as an undergraduate at the University of Maine, I was introduced to James' Principles of Psychology, *I seemed already to know the principles and had only to learn the detail.*

At the end of my doctoral studies in psychology at the University of Michigan, I was at the crossroads, whether to get post-doctoral experience in nerve impulse research with Lashley at Chicago or to get new approaches to analysis of the total behavior of humans with Lewin at the Psychological Institute of the University of Berlin. I chose the latter.

Upon return from Europe in 1932, I applied my Lewinian experience at the Child Education Foundation in New York City as Director of Field Laboratory and focused on the nursery and primary school child for three years. With marriage, I came to live in Cincinnati (Glendale) and introduced psychological services into the Children's Hospital, and into the Children's Convalescent Home in 1936. In 1944, I started thirteen years as Chief Psychologist at Longview State Hospital, and in 1949 started giving part time to the University of Cincinnati Department of Psychology. With my resignation after twenty-three years, I received the status of Pro-

fessor Emeritus of Psychology of the University of Cincinnati.

In 1946, I conceived the idea of Children's International Summer Villages (CISV). With the aid of my late husband, and citizens of Cincinnati, the first Village was held in 1951. I am now an Honorary Counselor to the CISV International Board of Directors. In 1972, I founded International School-to-School Experience (ISSE), as a companion organization to CISV.

Currently, my base is in Trenton, Maine, from which I take off to give courses and workshops in psychodrama. I am part-time Professor of Psychology at the University of Maine at Orono. Half of my time, I give to the work of CISV and ISSE. In my home on the sea, with the blue heron and seals, I enjoy visits from my son and his family and from friends.

Section Three

The World: Design for Nonviolent International Relations

13. Dealing with Collective Violence [with Examples from India and Kent State]

A. Paul Hare, Ph.D.

By October 1971 the problem was clear. It had become the talk of the town. The killings at Attica prison had provided the most recent evidence. The lead comment in the *New Yorker* (4) in the "Talk of the Town" summarized the recurring themes which had been previously outlined by Tom Wicker in a column in the *New York Times* (5). The *New Yorker* noted that, right down to minute details, the Attica massacre followed with uncanny faithfulness a script that had governed many other recent American tragedies: the Chicago convention, Jackson State, Kent State, My Lai, and the Newark and Detroit riots. In the first stage of the tragedy, some form of disorder--almost any form of disorder, from a student sit-in to a civil war--breaks out. The authorities receive, and believe, exaggerated reports of the trouble. The authorities then invest the disorder with symbolic importance so that each outbreak, however small, is seen as a perhaps fatal crack in the structure of constituted authority. Usually, "outside agitators" are blamed, in order to give the impression that a perfectly good lot of students or prison inmates have been corrupted and used by evil forces. In the second stage, the authorities employ overwhelming, indiscriminate force to restore "order," usually killing and injuring people other than the ones they meant to kill or injure. In the third stage, the authorities publish accounts of the event from which the brutality and lawlessness of their own people have been expurgated. Soon others--the press, the victims, investigating committees, or sometimes lone individuals--publish accurate accounts. But a large part of the public goes on believing the official version. What can be done to

break into this cycle of events with some form of
nonviolent intervention? Part of the answer comes
from India, where the Shanti Sena (Peace Brigade)
has successfully intervened in communal riots.

THE ROLE OF THE SHANTI SENA IN THE HINDU-MUSLIN RIOTS IN INDIA, 1969-70

Narayan Desai is the head of the Shanti Sena
(Peace Brigade) in India. Narayan grew up in
Gandhi's ashram, where his father, Mahadev Desai,
was Gandhi's secretary for many years until Mahadev
died in prison. Gandhi had called for the formation
of a Shanti Sena during his lifetime but was assas-
sinated a few weeks before the first meeting was to
be held. The regular service of the Shanti Sena is
similar to the U.S. Peace Corps and VISTA programs.
Individuals or groups of volunteers, primarily young
adults, live and work in communities where there is
a need for a school teacher or some type of community organizer. Once a month the volunteers in the
same region come together to discuss problems of
common concern. If there is a social issue which
they feel should be supported through public protest, they take to the streets with banners and
songs. If there is some natural or human disaster,
such as the problem in 1971 of over nine million
refugees from East Pakistan, they leave their villages temporarily and work in the disaster area in
relief and reconstruction or join forces with the
refugees in the maintenance of their camps. In
these ways they are much like members of other service organizations, such as the Red Cross. They
differ in that they are also willing to intervene
directly and nonviolently in violent situations.
Narayan Desai has described two of these occasions:
the communal riots in Baroda and Ahmedabad (1).

RIOTS IN BARODA

The Shanti Sainiks of the Gujarat area first
heard about the outburst of violence in Baroda at
their monthly meeting. Although there was also violence in other cities, they decided to go to Baroda
because there were some volunteers already working
in the city and one of the Gandhian journals was
published there, so that there might be some sympathy and cooperation from the readers of the journal.
First they announced their position on the issue which had led to the violence, showing their

allegiance to the common man and their disapproval
of the use of violent means to settle the issue.
Within a few days some 32 volunteers had joined together and had elected one of their members the
leader for the specific purpose of working in the
riot situation. The discipline was made clear to
every member that the Shanti Sena would be meeting
at least once a day and all important strategic decisions would be made at that meeting. The minute-
to-minute instruction would be given by the leader.
The instructions of the leader could, however, be
discussed or challenged in the daily evening meetings.

The work of the Shanti Sena was divided into
three groups:
1. Meeting the leaders of public opinion--2
    members
2. Rumor fighting--4 members
3. Patrolling--26 members

The two persons selected for meeting the leaders of public opinion in Baroda were workers of good
reputation, known for their nonpartisan attitude and
respected for their past services. They were both
in their early thirties. The city police, the Congress political party, and the opposition were first
contacted by phone. It was fortunate that the team
got an appointment with the police office first.
The officer knew both the workers by their names and
may have also read their articles in the Gandhian
journal. "The purpose of the Shanti Sena at this
present juncture," the Shanti Sainiks explained to
the police officer, "is to establish peace in the
city. We would like to have official information
about the situation and would love to cooperate in
whatever way we could. We would also like to make a
request, that you please do not use firearms in
dealing with the people."

"You are the first person to make this kind of
request," said the police officer. "Everybody else
has been pressing on me to resort to firing but I
have been struggling to avoid it."

"Then we are allies. This also gives us a
field of cooperation; we would like to persuade otherwise those citizens who are pressing you to resort
to firing."

"You alone can do it. I will tell you whom you
should meet." The police officer was voicing his
confidence, because the nonpartisan attitude of the
Shanti Sainiks was well established. The officer's
confidence encouraged the Shanti Sainiks too. They
did not leave the police station, however, before

discussing what alternative tactics could be applied
in order to handle the crowd instead of resorting to
gunfire. They also obtained permission to go out in
the city where the curfew order was imposed.

The first political leader whom they met after
leaving the police station was the leader of the local Congress party, the ruling political party. He
was well known and well-to-do. Both the Shanti
Sainiks had known him from their childhood. There
was a gap of a generation between them and the political leader. This would naturally make him a man
to be respected by the Shanti Sainiks; conversely
the Shanti Sainiks would expect to be treated with
some amount of affection.

But the political leader was in no mood of affection. As soon as the Shanti Sainiks entered his
crowded room, he almost shouted: "Here come
Vinoba's men." (Vinoba is a venerable leader in the
Gandhian movement, the organizer of the land-gift
program.) "They will now talk about peace and nonviolence. Let nonviolence be damned. What we need
now is stricter police action. Those who talk about
nonviolence are cowards and they shold be given
Sarees and Churees (women's dress and bangles) to
wear." The Shanti Sainiks accepted the wrathful
welcome smilingly. They knew that it was always
good to let the steam of the other party off in such
circumstances. Before coming to see this leader,
the Shanti Sainiks had already discussed among themselves what would be the crux of the argument with
him. The leader was proud of being the head of several civic organizations and had been responsible
for building up new institutions in the city. They
had remembered Vinoba's advice to them when going
out to ask for land from the landowners. "I will
tell you how to approach the landlords," Vinoba had
taught them. "When you meet them, try to find out
the good qualities in them. The good qualities in
man are like the doors in a house, while the evil
qualities are like the walls." You can enter the
hearts through the doors, but are likely to break
your own head if you try to enter through the
walls." So the Shanti Sainiks had considered what
good qualities in this leader could be approached.

"Thank you for calling us Vinoba's men," said
one of the Shanti Sainiks. "That reminds us that
Baroda is a city which Vinoba loves, as indeed you
love it yourself. Isn't it true that you love the
city as nobody else does? You are among the builders of the city which is known throughout the country for its cultural activities, its music, its art,

its literature.   Would you allow the name of the
city to be blemished with blood?"

"Blood?   Who talks about blood?   Go and talk
about that to your friends in the opposition parties
who are bent upon having bloodshed in the city.   I
am not talking about blood."

"That is exactly where we are planning to go
from here.   But we are reassured to hear that you
are not for the shedding of blood in this beloved
city of ours.   Could you suggest any ways of doing
that?"

"Ask those who indulge in violence this question."

"Please believe us that we are as much pained
as you are because of the burning of houses and
looting of shops.   But you will agree that the blood
is shed more by police firing than by anything
else."

"What can the police do?   They have to maintain
law and order.   Can you suggest means other than
firing to maintain peace in this city now?"

"We have been walking in various parts of the
city, and we feel that there is more lawlessness in
those areas where the curfew order is not imposed.
How about imposing curfew order in the rest of the
city for a day or two?"

"That seems to be a good idea."

"Why not call the police officer and see if
your advice is acceptable to him?   I am sure he will
be willing to accept the advice of an experienced
and respectable man like you."

The Congress leader immediately telephoned, and
of course the police officer was ready to accept his
advice as an alternative to firing.

The opposition was a united front of several
political parties.   The Socialists probably had a
larger following; the Communists were better organized.   They did not trust each other.   The Socialists were good friends of the Shanti Sainiks who
went to see them next.   Luckily it turned out that a
leader of the Communists was once a classmate of one
of the Shanti Sainiks long ago, but had not had the
opportunity to meet him since then.

The Socialists were aware that the leadership
could be in their hands only if the struggle did not
become totally violent.   One of the state-level
leaders of the Communists had gone on an indefinite
fast as a measure of protest against the decision of
the government as well as the violence following the
decision.   It was not very difficult to explain to
the Communists that the life of their leader could

be saved only when the violence would stop. Both
the socialist and the communist leaders were also
persuaded to sign an appeal for peace within the
city.

The four Shanti Sainiks who had the task of
fighting rumors issued a daily bulletin. This bulletin requested the public not to believe in exaggerated figures of casualties. They also published
incidents of bravery and nonviolence among the people. They could collect and edit the news from the
Shanti Sainiks who were moving freely in the city,
the police, and the political parties. On the third
day after the Shanti Sena arrived in the city, they
organized a peace procession. This was a silent
procession with placards and signs. Many citizens
of Baroda joined the silent procession. It marked
the beginning of normal activities in the city.

The group of Shanti Sainiks responsible for
patrolling, with the largest number of volunteers,
distributed itself into several groups. Some of
these groups were posted at potential points of violence. One group moved from place to place keeping
in touch with every other group. Some of these volunteers had to enter into arguments with crowds who
had collected heaps of rocks to hurl at the police.
Others had their arguments with the police for using
their "lathee" sticks.

It was one of these groups that heard the rumor
of a boy being dragged to the police station and
beaten there. The police superintendent was immediately contacted. He made arrangements for a deputa-
tion of citizens to go inside the police station and
meet the boy. He also issued orders not to beat up
anyone after being taken into custody.

Sometimes the patrolling volunteers had to intervene directly between the police and the violent
crowds facing both the lathees and the rocks.

As the situation began to return to normal,
some of the Shanti Sainiks wanted to go to other
places where violence had spread. But they were requested by both the police officer and the political
leaders to continue to function in Baroda because
they found their services to be useful for the maintenance of peace.

In cases of collective violence, the Shanti
Sena usually takes up relief activities as soon as
violence has subsided. Relief activities may be one
or more of the following:
1. Visiting the wounded victims in hospitals
2. Organizing medical relief for those who did
    not manage to go to hospitals

3. Distribution of food and clothing to the victimized families
4. Sanitation campaign in places where the sweeping was neglected owing to the disturbances.

These activities were not carried out in Baroda because they were organized locally by the citizens.

One important post-riot activity of the Shanti Sena is to organize small or large group meetings and discuss with people the causes and effects of the riot. This again needs very careful planning and leadership, because it is not very easy to organize these meetings when the minds of the people are still tense. But these meetings are very useful in organizing peace committees for action in possible future violence.

Some important techniques of the Shanti Sena which were not used in the particular case at Baroda are:

1. Fasts by well-known Shanti Sainiks
2. Organization of citizens peace committees
3. Taking the collaboration of other social work organizations, especially women's organizations
4. Use of the radio for public appeals and fighting of rumors, etc.
5. Relief activities among refugees
6. Organization for building new houses for the victims of the riots.

RIOT IN AHMEDABAD

Ahmedabad, with 1,600,000 people, is a much larger center of population than Baroda. In March of 1970, after four months of work in the riot-affected city, Narayan Desai was able to report that although the work was by no means complete, the machinery had been set up to continue the work of the Shanti Sena through local people. The Shanti Sainiks had begun their service at a point of high tension between Hindus and Muslims, when almost everyone they met was surcharged with the wrath of communal frenzy. Over a period of months this situation gradually turned into an atmosphere of mutual good will and trust. Narayan notes that he was tempted to write a book about the Shanti Sena in Ahmedabad but he lacked the time. "It was easier for the people of my father's generation to write books," he said, "because they had plenty of leisure in prisons, but that fortune is not ours now!"

There was a definite pattern in the riots,

Narayan Desai observed. The deliberate rumor mon-
gering, the small incidents followed by big rumors
culminating in big incidents. Looting followed by
arson, furthered by rumors once again, ending with
killings on a mass scale and brute acts of the most
unthinkable nature. All this was in a very systematic pattern. Each phase could, perhaps, have been
avoided, if proper measures were taken prior to the
phase. The bigger incidents could have been avoided
had proper action been taken after the smaller incidents; the arson could have been avoided if some immediate steps had been taken after the bigger incidents, and most of the killings could have been
avoided had the rumors been counteracted instantane-
ously. The government and the police might have had
their own reasons for not resorting to sterner steps
earlier. But the damage was done in no time.

During the first days of their work the Shanti
Sainiks tried to stop the riots wherever they could.
They succeeded in some cases in saving some individuals from being killed and some areas from being attacked by mobs. But on the whole, the riots were
too large for a handful of Shanti Sainiks to prevent
them from spreading. As an organization, the Shanti
Sena functioned only from the fourth day after the
outbreak of the riots.

The initial work of the Shanti Sena was, naturally, that of visiting the riot-affected people.
The saffron colored scarves of the Shanti Sainiks
were seen everywhere in the city. They inspired a
mixed response among the people. The positive reaction was of relief and appreciation, the negative of
resentment and ridicule.

The Shanti Sainiks began the work of reconciliation and tried to persuade the riot-stricken people
to return to their homes from the refugee camps. It
was a three-way process. One one side they had to
persuade the majority community to be willing to
welcome the people back in their midst. On another
side, they had to persuade the minority community to
be brave enough to forgive and forget what had happened. On the third side, they helped the government to hasten reconstruction of houses that had
been razed during the riots. Slowly the situation
began to show some signs of change. The major work
of Shanti Sena was to listen and talk. They had to
listen patiently to the bitter language of both
sides. They had to make house-to-house contacts,
participate in group discussions of all kinds, organize street corner meetings, and sometimes address
large gatherings inside mosques and temple compounds.

In itself, talking to the riot-stricken people was a service. But there were other acts of more concrete service, such as clearing debris from gutted houses and preparing to build new houses, dispensing medicines, collecting and distributing blankets and utensils to those who had lost theirs. This could not have been done without the preliminary work of creating a favorable atmosphere by persuasion. In all, the Shanti Sena distributed blankets to about 2500 families and utensils to about 100. They treated approximately 1200 patients. They were instrumental in relocating about 500 families to their new homes. In later stages both physical and psychological rehabilitation activities went on simultaneously.

One of the things that had troubled the Shanti Sainiks very much during the earlier months was the apathy of the intellectuals. Meetings and group discussions had, therefore, to be organized in colleges, hostels, clubs, and associations with a view to make intellectuals interested in the problem. This work bore fruit within a few months when a number of intellectuals came forward to offer their cooperation in the work of the Shanti Sena. A biweekly called "Insan" (Human Being) was also published regularly from Ahmedabad and was distributed freely in the city. Students of various colleges volunteered to help distribute "Insan." Students also helped in collecting blankets for the riot-stricken.

Two special activities of the Shanti Sena were the rehabilitation of women and children and the economic rehabilitation of the poor, who had lost their means of livelihood during the riots. After much hard work, the Shanti Sena was able to start a program for the welfare of women and children rendered destitute during the riots. It organized a transit camp for these women and tried to help them by teaching them handicrafts and ways of better living.

The Shanti Sena also prepared a scheme for the economic rehabilitation of those persons whose total capital was less than 250 rupees (about 35 dollars) and whose possessions were destroyed during the riots. The Shanti Sena gave loans without interest to such people. Some leading citizens of Ahmedabad were persuaded to take an interest in this problem.

Most of the activities of Shanti Sena were centered around the relief, economic rehabilitation, and reconciliation work in the months of October to December. In January, preparations for organiza-

tional follow-up began. The last week in January
was observed as peace week; massive efforts were
made to bring the message of peace to everyone in
the city. Nearly 500 volunteers from teacher-
training institutions went from house to house carrying the message of peace. They estimate that
about 20,000 houses were reached in this way. On
January 30 (the day of Gandhi's assassination) World
Peace Day was observed. Six peace processions
formed in different parts of the city covered over
30 miles, carrying placards and singing songs. Hindus and Muslims by the thousands walked together for
the first time after the riots, shouting "We may be
Hindus, we may be Muslims, but first of all we are
human beings!" Thousands of people were moved by
the sight of this sea of human brotherhood trying to
wash away all the stains of the bloody riots. After
the six processions met at a central place in the
city, they walked together for about a mile before
turning the march into a mass prayer meeting.

NOON RALLY AT KENT STATE UNIVERSITY

Some of the participants in the nonviolent
movement in the United States are aware of the activities of the Shanti Sena and are trying to adapt
their methods to situations of violence or potential
violence in America. One set of persons is of students and faculty at Kent State University who had
responded to the killing of four students during a
campus protest on May 4, 1970, by forming several
groups dedicated to nonviolent action and nonviolent
intervention in conflict. One group operated primarily as unofficial marshals at rallies and other
campus events; the other group set up a Life Center
as a basis for promoting nonviolent action and life-
style. Throughout the year following the May 4 incident, there was an almost continual threat of major violence on the Kent State campus. One occasion
which might have turned into a major confrontation
between students and administration was the rally
which was held after the U.S. announced its plans to
invade Laos.

As a dramatic presentation, the noon rally on
February 4 at Kent State included almost all of the
techniques of mass protest. Several thousand students assembled, marched, listened to speeches, and
chanted slogans. Individuals or small groups carried flags and engaged in symbolic attacks on objects of protest such as ROTC or the American gov-

ernment.

However, the performance received no applause
from the university administration nor from the student newspaper. An editorial on February 9 in the
Kent Stater was headed "Rally, really?" It said in
part:

> Friday's "rally on this campus has left us cold.
> What was to have been justified outpouring of
> feeling and frustration over the American spon-
> sored invasion of Laos quickly was perverted
> into another session of haranguing and violence
> sponsored by Kent State's "radical" community...
> We cannot be convinced that the march to the
> Administration Building was a spontaneous thing.
> We believe the whole thing to have been planned
> to bring Kent State to its knees once more. And
> that disgusts us.

The editorial went on to point out that there
are no "innocent bystanders" under current rules and
that this type of rally could well lead to another
confrontation with the Ohio National Guard. It concludes:

> Just keep the action between the officials and
> the participants. And leave the rest of us out
> of it. And keep the whole mess off this campus.

Clearly the editors of the Kent paper could see
only the dysfunctional aspects of the rally. If, as
they feared, the rally had led to closing the university, it would indeed have been completely dysfunctional for the university in its present form.

The problem for the university and for the nonviolent movement is to discover how this rally and
other rallies can become a functional part of the
university life. Not by preventing rallies or de-
fusing them so that they sputter and die, but by
acknowledging the problems they dramatize and using
the commitment they generate in the participants to
work toward solving the problems.

Following an analysis based on functional theory (3) we can see the rally on February 4 as the
first step in a four-step process of problem solving
where the first step is to state the problem, the
second to gather facts, the third to organize for

action, and the fourth to carry out the action. In
this case the problem was moved to the second stage
by a teach-in held in the week following the rally.
However, the teach-in was not planned by the rally
organizers. It represented a creative intervention
by one of the university faculty members. As we
look at the record of the rally in more detail, we
will see other attempts at intervention, some more
creative than others.

EVENTS PRIOR TO FEBRUARY 4

The Friday rally had been planned during the
preceding week by representatives of some 15 campus
groups who had called a press conference to announce
a rally at noon Friday to protest the invasion of
Laos. The head of the Kent Medical Fund (a fund
formed to pay medical expenses for students wounded
at Kent and Jackson State) read a statement which
said in part:

> We call, rather we demand, that the President
> recall the Saigon mercenaries from Laos, stop
> all the bombing...recall all American troops
> ...(*Kent Stater,* February 5, 1971, p. 1)

He went on to say that the conditions in Indochina
were the same as those last May, when four students
were killed at the Kent rally protesting the invasion of Cambodia.

At the news conference there was some question
whether the rally had been registered with the university administration. To hold an unregistered
rally would have violated university rules and subjected the students who took part to expulsion from
the university under the new Ohio law, House Bill
1219. Ever since the law was passed the previous
September, some students had been looking for ways
to test the legitimacy of the law. On Thursday
night one of the planners of the rally thought that
Friday's rally might provide the occasion to test
it. However, by Friday morning a rally spokesman
said that the rally would be registered by noon Friday. Further, the Director of Student Activities
for the university was quoted as saying that the
rally didn't have to be registered. Thus, registered or not, the rally would apparently not be seen
as an actual test of House Bill 1219. Nevertheless,
it did have significance as the first dramatic event

of the current "season" of protest. A member of the
Student Mobilization Committee noted that the rally
was "a reassertment of the tradition of free protest" (*Kent Stater*, Friday, February 5, 1971).

THE RALLY

The tolling of the bell on the commons at noon
signals the time to begin. As the rally moves from
point to point across the campus, it seems as if the
students are proceeding through the "stations of the
cross" as at each stop they speak about or enact
some important social or psychological event in the
recent history of Kent. Beginning on the hillside
near the place where students were killed during a
demonstration related to the invasion of Cambodia
some months before, the students seem to be saying
that once again the United States government is
about to invade a country in the Indochina area and
that once again the students feel powerless to prevent this action.
Next, the crowd, following the leaders with a
portable sound system, moves to the site of the former ROTC building which had been burnt to the ground
in the protests of the previous May. Here the leaders burn a replica of the ROTC building made from a
cardboard box. The message seems to be that if someone had intervened at an earlier point in the control
of the ROTC and the army, perhaps the war would not
have come about. But again the students seem powerless to change that.
At the next point, in front of the Student Union, student leaders speak of the problems of the
black students and their attempts to obtain money
for a black student program. Here the message seems
to be that there are basic problems which divide us,
such as the problem of race, which could be dealt
with even within the university, but here too we
find it difficult to find a solution. One of the
speakers, a white student, reviews the problems as
follows:

On this campus and on campuses across the country, the universities are still complicit with
the war in Vietnam. They are sending men from
this campus to fight in Vietnam. We have been
fighting against them for two years and we are
not going to stop. Last spring two or three
thousand people, and maybe more, decided what
they felt about ROTC on this campus. They de-

cided right over there by burning that place
down....ROTC is not going to stay on this campus, it is going to go. (The speaker goes on
to list the numbers of students who have been
killed at various colleges during the past
spring while protesting the war. He cites the
repression by the state of Ohio with new laws.
He notes that black students went through all
channels to try to get money and that one black
student was arrested at gunpoint for chalking
the figure $40,000 on the sidewalk.)

Next a black student comes to the microphone:

I just got out of the Portage County jail. I
want to organize a coalition...It is about time
that Kent State woke up from the dead sleep the
administration has been trying to put on us.
(He calls for support from the student body for
the Black United Students--BUS.)

A white student follows at the mike:

We have been asleep every winter, but this winter we are going to move. There are people all
over the country who are watching us....I saw
the president get out of his car and go into
the administration building. Last fall when we
marched he was not there, but today he is there.
I say let's go to President White and talk to
him again.

    The crowd moves to the front of the administra-
tion building. It seems to express the hope that
someone in authority at the university will surely
have some answer for them. But as they probably expect, they once more face locked doors and guards.
No communication and no direction seem to be coming
from that source, at least for the moment. A student speaker reports that someone from the administration said that there will be no discussion because the students are too emotional. Indeed it is
an emotional scene, but the task for the students
and faculty and administration at that moment is to
be able to understand and deal creatively with the

emotions that are present.
    A white student is speaking:

> Black students are the field niggers, we are
> the house niggers. And we ain't happy niggers
> at Kent State. We want to see our master. We
> want him to cut our chains off. We want him
> to help free the Kent 25. We want President
> White to align himself against House Bill 1219
> ...We want President White to give $40,000 to
> BUS...He built a new stadium for the football
> team when they needed it...I just talked to a
> couple of administrators and President White
> seems to have disappeared.

(Crowd chants: "We want White." At this point
faculty and student marshals are moving about, preparing to attempt to prevent violence if it should
erupt. However only a few of them, including Jerry
Lewis, a professor sociology, have armbands.)

> Not once have we been able to talk to President
> White. We had many rallies at Kent State and
> always President White unbelievably disappears
> ...We demand to see our master...We demand to
> see President White.

During this speech two students are having a
contest at the foot of the flagpole in front of the
administration building. The long-haired student
attempts to uncleat the halyard so that he can bring
down the American flag. The short-haired student
tries to wind up the halyard as fast as it is un-
wound. The long-haired student moves away as about
six large, short-haired students take up positions
in a circle around the flagpole. One of the student
marshals suggests that I take a picture of the group
around the flagpole since it contains "half of the
undercover agents on campus."
    By this time the frustration of the crowd has
reached a peak. Some action is sought which at
least symbolically will show some intervention on
behalf of the students. One leader calls for someone to lower the flag to half-mast. This is in effect a call for some students to struggle with the
men who are obviously guarding the flagpole. Tension is rising. Such a scuffle might turn into a

major confrontation which might include an attempt
to break down the doors of the Administration Building. At this point the student and faculty marshals
move into action. They discuss whether to place
themselves in a human chain between the demonstrators and the front door of the Administration Building, and seem to be prepared to do this if the situation warrants it. Meanwhile the speaker at the
mike is saying:

> The corridor in that building is crawling with
> police. They have night sticks. They have
> guns and they have helmets...Violence origi-
> nates from the establishment. If we the people
> use violence, it is only to counteract our
> frustration as a last resort. Violence is
> wrong. That is true. But they use violence
> against us all the time. If students resort to
> violence, it is by necessity.

Now the crowd turns to watch the struggle for
the flag. Someone is trying to cut the halyard
while others struggle with the defenders. The focus
now shifts from the door of the Administration
Building to the struggle for the flag. The marshals
move down to the scene of the struggle and place
themselves between the plainclothes agents and the
demonstrators. One of the women in the group of
marshals taps a tall male demonstrator on the shoul-
der and asks him to "cool it." Now the struggle
subsides and major violence has been averted by the
intervention of the nonviolent marshals. However,
one of the demonstrators is able to cut the halyard,
allowing the American flag to slide slowly to the
ground as it is blown free by the wind. The speaker
continues:

> Let's not have any more busted now on some hum-
> bug charge like walking in to our own building
> ...There are some good things that have hap-
> pened so far. That is the first American flag
> I have seen in weeks that has really flown free.

(We note the ability of the leaders to give new
meaning to old symbols.)

We have shown that students are no fair weather
radicals...Instead of going in there to fight
those armed cops we can wait here...The weather
is not too bad.

(Actually it was quite windy and cold. After an
hour or so outside I was ready to go into an un-
locked part of the Administration Building to warm
up. Many students had left the rally by this time
to go to class. Those who remained were certainly
not "fair weather" radicals.)

PROPOSAL FOR A TEACH-IN

Just before the flag incident, which ended with
an NLF flag being raised and later taken down, one
group split off from the main rally and moved down
the hill to the new ROTC headquarters in the old library building. Not long after this, one of the
student leaders called for a strike. At this point
Jerry Lewis, a sociology professor and third party
marshal, spontaneously suggested the possibility of
a teach-in on the various issues raised by the rally. It is important to note that Lewis and the other marshals are not appointed by the administration
or by any other group. They are volunteers who are
committed to nonviolence and who have been trained
in techniques of nonviolent action and marshaling.
The group was formed as a response to the May 4
shooting. The present activities are coordinated
through the Life Center formed in the fall of 1970
to sponsor and facilitate a variety of activities
devoted to nonviolence.
Some of the more active students rallied around
the idea of a teach-in and spent some hours with
Lewis on Friday afternoon planning for a set of lectures and discussions to be held the following week
to provide information about the problems facing the
students, the problems which had been so dramatically presented in the course of the rally.
These discussions were held in and around the
Life Center at the Honors and Experimental College.
The discussions involved some of the same people who
had met that morning to consider a proposal for a
summer institute on nonviolence at Kent. It involved people who had become accustomed to meeting
in the Life Center to talk about creative nonviolent
actions such as establishing a cooperative store or
satisfactory ways to introduce students to responsible community government. Some of those who were

most active as marshals at the rally had spent some time the evening before at the Life Center in a seminar on nonviolent action, learning together about theory and practice in other situations.

In sum, Friday's rally was not as spontaneous a as it might appear to the casual observer. On the one hand, those students who were able to create this very dramatic form had been practicing in various ways at Kent for some months and had an intimate sense of the problems and issues which would capture the imagination of the students. On the other hand, the students, faculty, and administrators who acted as third party marshals in promoting a nonviolent rally were also schooled. They had engaged in training sessions for marshaling, in seminars on nonviolence, in informal get-togethers and endless encounters with resource persons from all over the United States and indeed other countries as well. They managed to carry off an organized activity without the appearance of organization. This too is one of the goals of the current nonviolent movement.

THE TEACH-IN

Ideally the teach-in held the following week would have provided the information needed to understand the issues presented at the rally. The next week might have been given over to the development of some form of social organization, such as a set of "task forces" which would contain members with the skills and authority necessary to deal with the various problems. The third and following weeks might have seen the implementation of creative solutions to the problems.

However, by the time the teach-in was over it was not apparent that social change was progressing in so orderly a fashion. A series of discussions on the various issues had been planned for Monday through Wednesday with a final "bitch-in" on Thursday night in a large hall at which anyone could take the microphone and state his grievance.

Unfortunately the police chose a session on "repression" as the occasion to arrest one of the students on a previous charge. This touched off a march to President White's house that night. The third party marshals were once more on the scene. This time they were joined by other students who noted that only a few marshals were visibly identified by armbands and were concerned that the yelling and screaming might turn to violence. At the president's house the students demanded an open forum on campus problems within 24 hours. This demand was later extended to a week's time limit. At that time the students asked that the president and other key administrators appear to answer questions.

The increased tension moved the Faculty Senate to appoint nine faculty members as official "observers" at future mass events. Professor Lewis was reprimanded for missing his 1:10 class on the day of the rally. He had told his students he would make it up later but it is an offense under House Bill 1219 to use class time to participate in nonteaching activities of this type. The state police radio had announced at one point that he was "leading the rally."

The events at Kent continue to crowd in upon each other. The progress is something like that of the frog in the well. For every "great leap forward" there is some slipping back, or perhaps leaps in other directions. But there is also evident progress in the direction of nonviolent social change. The problems at Kent are not only real but shared to different degrees by universities throughout the world. Any solutions can also be shared.

A FUNCTIONAL ANALYSIS OF NONVIOLENT REVOLUTION

Both the Shanti Sainiks in India and the students and faculty at Kent State who are involved with third party marshaling and the Life Center are consciously and conscientiously involved in a nonviolent revolution. It is a revolution in two senses, first because they hope for an extensive change in the social system (India or Kent State) in the relatively short run, and second, because they have an image of the way the society might look when the new order has arrived. Following the theoretical framework of Parsons, Effrat, and others, this revolutionary activity can be described in functional terms (2). In brief, the functional approach suggests that all social systems, no matter how large or how small, have four basic functional problems to solve:

Problem	*Substructure of Society*	*Functional category*
1 - Provide basic values and bring new members into the system	Religion and the family	L-Latent pattern maintenance and

		tension management
2 - Provide facilities	Economic system	A-Adaptation
3 - Provide solidarity and norms	Informal friendship groups and law	I-Integration
4 - Provide direction for attainment of group goals	Political system	G-Goal attainment

That is, every group must have a set of values which defines its basic purposes (L), the facilities and information necessary for the task (A), an appropriate set of roles for members to play and enough feeling of solidarity between members to carry them through the task (I), and enough coordination of activity to bring the task to a successful conclusion (G). Members of groups dedicated to social change or social revolution have functional problems to solve at two system levels, within their own group and within the society as a whole. The problems within the group are often dealt with in some form of living arrangement such as a commune or intentional community. In India the Gandhians often live together in a small community (ashram) or at a training center (kendra). At Kent State some students live together in communes while much of the organizing activity takes place in the Life Center, a room on the university campus. The activities at each system level for the Shanti Sena and the Life Center are represented in Table 1.

Thus within the ashram or kendra the Shanti Sainiks deal with their internal problems of pattern maintenance, adaptation, and integration. Their work (or goal attainment) is their attempt to bring about change in Indian society through protest (L) to affirm their dedication to the cause of human rights, through the promotion of village industry (A) as they continue "constructive programs" involving spinning or the manufacture of clothes from homespun materials (khadi), through direct intervention in conflict situations (I) as they help control riots such as those in Baroda and Ahmedabad, and finally through long range programs of community development (G) such as the land-gift movement (bhoodan) where landlords are asked to give a portion of their lands to the landless peasants and the organization of villages on a self-governming basis (gramdan).

In a similar way the students in the Life

Table 1.   TWO CURRENT EXAMPLES OF REVOLUTIONARY
SOLUTIONS TO FUNCTIONAL PROBLEMS

Country and Organization	System Level				
	Organizational (L,A,I)	Societal			
		Latent Pattern Maintenance and Tension Management	Adaptation	Integration	Goal Attainment
India Shanti Sena	Ashram, Kandra	Protest	Constructive program: khadi, spinning	Riot control: Baroda, Ahmedabad	Bhoodan, Gramdan
U.S.A. Kent State	Life Center	Protest: Noon rallies	Coops, Student housing	Third party marshals	Student government, new courses

Center do their work as agents of change on the Kent
campus by taking part in protests, such as the noon
rallies, to affirm basic student rights (L), by
helping to develop cooperative stores and better
conditions for student housing (A), by intervening
at times of conflict as third party marshals (I),
and by promoting new forms of campus government and
initiating new courses on nonviolence and social
change (G).

In sum, it is not enough to deal only with the
overt violence in a social system. A group devoted
to nonviolent social change, especially revolutionary social change, must also be willing to deal with
"structural" violence, those traditional ways in
which people have dealt with each other, with profit
to some at the expense of others whose human rights

were being denied.   They cannot simply protest, or
even simply intervene nonviolently in situations of
high conflict.   For one cannot engage in peacekeep-
ing without asking the questions: whose peace?
and who is being kept?   Gandhi urged that men create
social systems in such a way that all men would be
freer than they were before, that all would realize
the value of being a human being.

REFERENCES

1.   Desai, Narayan.   *Towards a Nonviolent Revolu-
     tion*.   Rajghat, Varanasi, India: Sarva Seva
     Sangh Prakashan, 1972.
2.   Effrat, Andrew.   Editor's introduction.   (Appli-
     cations of Parsonian theory.)   *Sociological In-
     quiry*, 1968, *38*(2), 97-103.
3.   Hare, A. Paul.   Theories of group development
     and categories for interaction analysis.   *Small
     Group Behavior*, 1973, *4*(3), 259-304.
4.   *New Yorker*.   "Talk of the Town."   October 2,
     1971, pp. 29-30.
5.   Wicker, Tom.   "Parallels."   *New York Times*,
     September 21, 1971.

*After a dozen years at Haverford College where
he introduced the Computing Center and the Center
for Nonviolent Conflict Resolution, PAUL HARE moved
on to South Africa in 1973 where he holds the Chair
of Sociology at the University of Cape Town.   During
1972-74 he also coordinated a working party to find
a solution to the problem of displaced persons on
Cyprus at the request of the Government of Cyprus.
Some of his time at Haverford was spent overseas in various activities including: Deputy Representative for the U.S. Peace Corps in the Philippines, Visiting Professor at the Institute for Advanced Study in Vienna, and Co-Director of the An-
tillean Institute of Social Science in Curacao.
In the U.S. he was principal investigator of a
four year NIMH grant to study nonviolent direct action.   Together with a multidisciplinary research
team he took part in and observed many varieties of
nonviolent action.
His academic background includes undergraduate
degrees from Swarthmore College and Iowa State College (Ames), a Master's from the University of Pennsylvania, and a Ph.D. in sociology from the University of Chicago.   For several years he was a post-
doctoral fellow in mental health at Harvard Univer-*

sity.
       In addition to nonviolence, his special field
is the study of social interaction in small groups.
He is an editor (with Edgar F. Borgatta and Robert
F. Bales) of SMALL GROUPS (rev. ed., 1965, Knopf);
author of HANDBOOK OF SMALL GROUP RESEARCH (rev.
ed., 1976, Free Press), author (with Michael S.
Olmsted) of THE SMALL GROUP (rev. ed., 1978, Random
House), editor (with Herbert Blumberg) of NONVIOLENT
DIRECT ACTION (1968, Corpus); and LIBERATION WITHOUT
VIOLENCE (1977, London: Collings). He was editor
of the journal SOCIOLOGICAL INQUIRY and has pub-
lished articles on social interaction in the socio-
logical and psychological journals.

SOME OTHER PUBLICATIONS BY A. PAUL HARE

- Nonviolent action from a social-psychological per-
  spective. *Sociological Inquiry*, 1968, *38*, 5-12.
  Also pp. 513-530 in A.P. Hare, & H.H. Blumberg,
  (Eds.), *Nonviolent Direct Action*. Washington,
  D.C.: Corpus Books, 1968.
- Social-psychological analyses of nonviolence. In
  A.P. Hare, & H.H. Blumberg, (Eds.), *Nonviolent Di-*
  rect Action. Washington, D.C.: Corpus Books,
  1968, pp. 1-30. In W. Moss, (Ed.), *Violence*.
  Williamsburg, Virginia: The College of William
  Mary, 1968, pp. 46-66.
- Groups: role structure. In D.L. Sills, (Ed.),
  International Encyclopedia of the Social Sciences.
  New York: Macmillan & Free Press, 1968, Vol. *6*,
  pp. 283-288.
- The nonviolent alternative: research strategy and
  preliminary findings. In J.F. Short, Jr., & M.E.
  Wolfgang, (Eds.), *Collective Violence*. Chicago:
  Aldine, 1972, pp. 355-369.
- Group decision by consensus: reaching unity in
  the Society of Friends. *Sociological Inquiry*,
  1973, *43*(1), 75-84.
- With H.H. Blumberg, C. Fuller, C. Walker, &
  H. Kritzer. Evaluation of training for nonviolent
  direct action. *Mental Health and Society*, 1974,
  1, 364-375.
- A third party role in ethnic conflict. *Social Dy-*
  namics, 1975, *1*(1), 81-107.

14. Intercession in Violent Intergroup Conflict

Bryant Wedge, M.D.

On 1st September, 1965, I received a telephone call from a State Department official in the Dominican Republic. The connection was poor, but I gathered that he was asking me whether I would be willing to come to the Dominican Republic to establish contact with young Dominican revolutionaries in order to determine whether there was any way, satisfactory to them, to open communication between them and the United States diplomatic mission in that country, and, possibly, even to reduce the violence and killing that was taking place in the country. I accepted the invitation, provided that I would be able to act as a wholly independent consultant, and thus began a real-life experiment in psychiatric intercession in violent intergroup conflict.

Before I report on the outcome of this particular case, it may be useful to outline some of the considerations that went into this decision to intercede, to engage in a form of mass therapy. Let me begin by suggesting that the principal function, the *raison d'être* of the psychiatric profession, is the reduction or elimination of human suffering that arises from the alienation of men from their fellows; that, at least, is one principal element in any definition of mental ill-health. Over the years, the psychiatric profession has gradually acquired and elaborated a body of knowledge and methods designed to reduce alienation of the individual from his family, friends and society, and even himself. We have learned to identify, and to some extent to correct or prevent, genetic, metabolic, and biochemical disorders, have learned to recognize and sometimes to intervene in faults of personal psychological development by methods of psychotherapy, and we are even learning to help the individual come to

terms with his family and social environment. The
object, then, of psychiatric effort is human relationships, and we intervene at whatever level best
facilitates well-being in those relationships. Only
recently, the psychiatric profession has turned some
attention to still another source of alienation and
destructiveness in human relationships--the level of
relations between groups of men.

There is no doubt that intergroup conflict is a
prime source of untold human alienation, suffering
and destruction. Domestically and internationally,
unbridled intergroup conflict leads to massive distortions in the lives of men, even to killing in institutionalized war and intergroup violence. In his
last address, which he did not live to deliver,
President Franklin Roosevent wrote that, "We are
faced with the pre-eminent fact that if civilization
is to survive, we must cultivate the science of human relationship--the ability of peoples of all
kinds to live together and work together in the same
world, at peace." It has often been suggested that
psychiatry as an applied science directed to the
amelioration of human relationships could bring useful insight and method to the understanding and
treatment of destructive intergroup conflict.
(Here, I use the term psychiatry in the generic
sense to represent professional concern with the diagnosis and treatment of psychological disturbances,
rather than in the narrower definition of a medical
discipline--professionals such as social psychologists and anthropologists who apply their methods to
similar purpose can be said to be exercising psychiatric functions (15,16). For example, Harold Lasswell (7) has written of the possibilities of "mass
therapy of destructive prejudices" by applied psychiatry, and a whole body of literature has developed on the theme.

Two significant experiments in bringing together persons from the two sides in intergroup conflicts in which violence had occurred have been reported recently. John Burton (1), using a method of
"controlled communication," invited representatives
of groups in violent conflict into discussions directed by academic third parties and carried on in
neutral settings, in the course of which scientific
exercises and propositions were introduced that were
intended to help participants in understanding and
objectifying the issues. Doob *et al.* (3) brought
prominent citizens of Kenya, Somalia, and Ethiopia--
which were involved in sometimes bloody border dis-
putes--together in a workshop conducted on group dy-

namics and sensitivity-training lines. In each experiment, there was convincing evidence that third-
party intercession can greatly improve communication
and understanding between members of groups that are
at sword point, but the most important outcome is
the demonstration that such intercession, a kind of
private or informal diplomacy under scientific auspices, is possible and acceptable to the governments
concerned.

The intercession that I am about to describe
was somewhat different in character; it was not under any kind of experimental control, but involved
careful and circumscribed initiatives taken in the
context of a complex and many-sided social reality.
Nevertheless, many of the same phenomena were observed as in the more experimental circumstances,
and some of the same techniques--mainly those of
bringing about direct contact between the parties on
relatively neutral ground--were useful in altering
attitudes that fed the conflict. I believe that
this is the first reported psychiatric intercession
in large-scale social conflict, and is significant
for the demonstration of the possibility as well as
for the outcome.

I will outline some of the main characteristics
of groups in interaction, and a general model for
third-party intercession in intergroup conflict.
Then I will describe observations that I made in the
Dominican Republic while carrying out the consultation that I had so eagerly accepted.

A SIMPLIFIED MODEL OF INTERGROUP INTERACTION

Since interaction between groups in real-life
circumstances is invariably complicated by a multi-
plicity of actors and factors that influence the relationship, it is useful to conceptualize the process in the most essential terms--those of the natural history of group formation and interaction.
This helps the observer to distinguish between the
basic issues in the interaction and those numerous
accidental and adventitious factors that bear upon
it; it is helpful in maintaining perspective.

The famous Robbers Cave Experiment, described
by the social psychologist, Muzafer Sherif, and his
colleagues (11) provides a classical simplified model of the development of intergroup conflict and its
subsequent reduction. The principal propositions
demonstrated by the experiment probably hold true
for all human groups, including nations; in any

event, they accurately describe the events that un-
folded in the present case study.

The first proposition is that when individuals
are brought together under conditions that require
cooperation for the attainment of goals which have
common appeal, a group will be produced with definite social structure, customs, and patterns of communication. In the Robbers Cave Experiment, 11-
year-old boys were brought together in two separate
and isolated groups in a summer camp. Each group
was provided with camping adventures that required
working together; and each rapidly developed its own
hierarchy, and adopted names--the Eagles and the
Rattlers--and distinctive behavioural norms; indeed,
what could be described as group micro-cultures that
to a large degree determined the activities of the
members.

The second proposition is that competitive and
frustrating relations between two groups stimulate
the development of unfavourable images of each other
while increasing in-group solidarity. The Eagles
and the Rattlers were ready enough to be suspicious
of "those other guys" at first contact, but when
they were exposed to contests such as tug-of-war in
which the success of one group meant the defeat of
the other, they each quickly developed attitudes and
stereotypes denigrating the other and glorifying
their own virtues and champions. Indeed, they began
to harrass each other and ultimately to fight.
Group members who attempted to make peace were os-
tracized by their own as well as the opposing group.

The final main proposition is that intergroup
friction and tension tend to diminish when communication and contact are opened between the groups,
particularly when the groups must cooperate to attain "superordinate" goals desired by each. Furthermore, a series of such occasions for cooperation
tends to have a cumulative effect in reducing tension. In the Robbers Cave Experiment, the two
groups of boys were confronted with problems which
neither group could solve alone--fixing the camp
water supply, obtaining a movie, starting a stalled
food truck--and there was a rapid dissolution of the
intergroup tension and a shift in the unfavourable
images held by each group for the other.

Each of the propositions of this model has been
shown to hold true for a wide variety of experimental and natural groups in interaction. The development of stereotyped misperception between groups and
nations in circumstances of competition and conflict
has been demonstrated repeatedly, and the role of

such misperception in sustaining conflict or at
least impeding its reduction has been shown (4,12).
The final proposition, that friction between groups
can be reduced by cooperation in attaining superordinate goals, has not received so much attention except, perhaps, in experimental games (13). It is
precisely this proposition that provides the basis
for efforts at sociotherapeutic efforts to reduce
friction between groups.

The Robbers Cave Experment has two particularly
importnat implications for theories of intergroup
relations. First, the development of intergroup
friction does not depend simply on individual psychopathology but, rather, springs from the psychological characteristics of group life. I think this
is generally true of intergroup conflict, and that
theories that such conflicts, including their manifestation in war, arise from the psychological needs
of individuals are not tenable (5). This is not to
argue that individual motives are not expressed
through group conflict, or that psychopathology, es
pecially of leaders, may not contribute to conflict,
but that, for the purpose of reducing intergroup
conflict, it is necessary to approach the fundamental issues on the group and intergroup level. In
fact, there is a good deal of evidence that those
persons who are most inclined to question the perceptions that their own group develops are apt to be
poorly adjusted socially and psychologically. Good
mental health within groups, then, may actually be
manifested by sharing misperceptions of and hostility toward other groups.

Second, shared misperceptions of the character
and the intentions of the outgroup appear to be the
effect of competitive group interaction, as well as
a contributing *cause* of continued conflict. This
helps explain the resistance of such misperceptions
to correction by evidence; indeed, as every ambassador knows, a nation's own representatives risk their
credibility at home when they report first-hand
facts that run counter to their society's perceptions (10). It follows that direct attack on group
misperceptions, attempting to counter them with evidence, is apt to be ineffective; approaches to conflict reduction that do not directly challenge group
perceptions of the other are more likely to succeed
--even in changing misperceptions--than those that
try to correct such misunderstandings.

The interaction between the United States diplomatic mission to the Dominican Republic and Dominican "revolutionary" youth reproduced the elements

of the Robbers Cave Experiment, despite substantial differences in the complexity of the context.   For example, neither group was the primary concern of the other in this case--each had many other groups and issues to deal with--nor was the interaction one of direct and competitive confrontation, but rather one of mutual, wary anxiety about the other.   Each of these two groups was well structured internally, each found the other's action important to its purpose and felt frustrated by the other--especially in terms of its perception of the other--and each developed well-defined and widely shared stereotyped opinions of the other that strongly influenced their interpretations of unfolding events.

Before developing the theory further, I will present a model for intercession and then describe in more detail my own experiences in the Dominican Republic.

METHOD: THE INTERCESSION MODEL

Psychiatric intervention in states of alienation always involves an effort to establish communication with the alienated person.   For this purpose, the psychiatric interview has been developed and extensively elaborated with the central purpose of communicating with and understanding the other person in his own terms, as he views the world around him.   This does not mean that the psychiatrist necessarily agrees with the patient, but only comprehends his point of view.   This allows the psychiatrist to identify sources of alienation and to intercede between the alienated person and his environment, correcting any sources of disturbance that he can in the evolving state of the scientific art, whether the sources be biochemical, psychological or social.

A dozen years ago, in the course of travel to nations that were in conflict, I observed alienation between whole groups and nations, including persistent misperceptions, and action based on misperceptions, which often contributed to dangerous and destructive conflict.   I found that, as one listened with the suspended judgment typical of the psychiatric interview, it was sometimes possible to identify the sources of what can be called psycho-political alienation.   It was hypothesized that this condition could be altered through deliberate attempts at fostering communication between the alienated parties.   I thus began the study of the application of psychiatric method to groups of men that were estranged from one another (14).

The techniques and interpretations that evolved
from the systematic interview of members of national
groups were then tested and elaborated by students
of communication and diplomacy. The method involved
instructing students to choose subcultural groups
strange to them, and to undertake to establish,
maintain, and terminate acceptably processes of dialogue with their members--groups such as convicts,
motorcycle clubs, drug-users, radical political
groups and the like. The essence of the system that
evolved from this work is the iron necessity for
careful phasing of the experience, much as in a psychiatric interview (17). One of the first lessons
that my students and I learned is that mediation is
useful mainly when the parties are already agreed on
the points to be mediated.

Groups in mutual conflict can be approached in
the same way, and a dialogue established with each
group on *its own terms*. When dialogue with both
groups has been established it becomes possible to
begin to identify points of common or joint interest
between the groups. Here, the classic mediation
technique involves the mediator in moving back and
forth between the groups to negotiate agreements acceptable to both; this method is sometimes brilli-
antly successful in highly structured circumstances
(6). In our real-life experiments, we have found
that it is often possible to find some occasion to
bring representatives of the groups together on some
common ground, and to assist them in identifying
their common interests.

As in the case with experimental groups, direct
contact and communication between groups in conflict
initiate some change in attitude; enough, in many
cases, to allow some members or leaders to envisage
the possibility of working together on common problems. Once a programme of cooperation has been established, it is wise for the intercessor to bow
out; otherwise he is apt to be seen as interfering
in the interests of the groups himself, even as em-
pire building for his own purposes. He should, we
have found, be quite firm in his termination. The
complete model for intercession in intergroup conflict can be expressed in five stages:

1. The intercessor (an individual or group)
    establishes contact with each of the par-
    ties through a process of dialogue as an
    interested outsider;
2. Interests of the parties are defined
    through the dialogue and possible mutual
    interests are tentatively identified.

3. Members of the conflicting groups are
    brought together on neutral ground to es-
    tablish contact and communication;
4. Assistance is given in considering pro-
    grammes of cooperation between the groups;
    and
5. The intercession is terminated when cooper-
    ative programmes are established.

There is a very striking difference between the
small, experimental groups that Sherif and others
have worked with and the large-scale, naturally oc-
curring groups that come into social conflict. In
large groups, there is no disposition whatsoever to
blur the boundaries of the groups or to engage in
across-the-board attempts to integrate the interests
and efforts of the groups. Instead, what is sought
is the development of *some* areas and means of cooperation, often quite limited at first. Ideally,
this results in the establishment of programmes that
engage some of the members of each group in working
with the other; some colleagues and I have termed
this an "inter-system system," and we believe that
such systems restrain larger scale intergroup conflicts. Rather than the global superordinate goals
of small groups, the purpose is the establishment of
what I term "partial superordinate goals" (5). The
reasons for this are clear. In large and enduring
social groups, powerful interests and institutions
have grown up, there are always shared beliefs and
attitudes among the members that are highly valued
and unique to the group, and identification with
group distinctiveness is important to the members.
Consequently, any effort to blur boundaries, to
bring groups together in a sweeping way, is certain
to be fiercely resisted.

The foregoing considerations determine, to a
large extent, the requirements for the third stage:
bringing group representatives together. Members,
and especially leaders, of adversary groups resist
meeting their opposite numbers for explicit negotiation, most especially for the kind of general peacemaking which offends social militancy.

I have found that opportunities arising out of
the flow of circumstances can be developed into occasions for meeting on some neutral ground. While
Burton and Doob both provided an agenda of experimental exercises designed to enhance the participants' self-examination, I have proceeded with no
agenda whatsoever; in my experience, bringing members of adversary groups together for purposes not
directly related to their conflict is most effective

in opening contact and communication between them.
    If the intercessor has been correct in identi-
fying the possible areas of mutual interest between
the groups, he can rely on these interests to assert
themselves in the processes of contact. There is no
manipulating of large-scale groups in conflict--at
least from the powerless position of a psychiatric
intercessor--and the representatives of each group
must be allowed to work out their areas of cooperation in their own way. In particular, the participants from each side have to consider the timing and
method of communicating their impressions to their
respective groups; these announcement policies are
often quite dissimilar, as they depend on the particular political temper and communication habits of
their reference groups. In short, for such inter-
cessions to succeed, it is necessary for participants to maintain the highest credibility as loyal
members of their group of origin; generally, they
can persuade their group to support a programme of
limited cooperation with the adversary only when
they are convinced that such cooperation is in the
self-interest of the group.
    We are now in a position to examine a specific
instance of intercession in intergroup conflict.

A CASE STUDY IN THE DOMINICAN REPUBLIC

BACKGROUND: THE FORMATION OF THE GROUPS

    On 24th April, 1965, a group of young military
officers in the Dominican Republic attempted a *coup
d'état* against a government which they suspected of
intending to perpetuate itself in office by imposing
military-oligarchic rule. They were opposed by senior officers in control of the regular military
forces. When the regular forces attempted to suppress the uprising by force, massive violence erup-
ted in the capital city of Santo Domingo as large
numbers of citizens, especially youths, rallied to
support the revolution. An armed and angry mob was
organized in the city, and the armed forces were
brought to a stop; at least 700 people were killed
in four days, and the country verged on civil war.
At this point, the United States intervened and
troops were interposed between the warring parties,
but hostilities continued for some time.
    These events mobilized and crystallized a num-
ber of groups, among them a Revolutionary Dominican
Youth Movement, and a deeply concerned and thorough-

ly challenged United States diplomatic mission.
This study is concerned with intercession between
these two groups.

The group self-identified as the Revolutionary
Youth Movement was brought into being by the April
uprising. While a number of conspiratorial groups,
especially communist and Castro-communist groups,
had arisen even before the assassination of the dictator, Trujillo, in 1961, and while there were various loose political groups in the schools and universities, none of these had gained any broad support, nor were any of them able to lead or control
the movement that was mobilized by the uprising.
Instead, thousands of young Dominicans, infected by
democratic and reformist ideals, deeply frustrated
in their aspirations by the chaos into which the society had fallen after the downfall of the dictator,
and especially disgusted by the manoeuvrings for
power and advantage by a privileged oligarchy in
league with a corrupt military, had flocked to the
centre of Santo Domingo in response to the call of
the young military rebels (18). By the time they
had been attacked by the regular military and had
themselves become armed and organized in the defence
of the city, they were fully mobilized as a group.
Among them were virtually all of the rising young
leaders of the nation.

The political culture of the young revolutionary group was entirely new to the Dominican Republic. There were no dominant leaders and no structure of authority, but instead a powerful consensus
process developed among them. Every succeeding
event was discussed widely until an interpretation
and a position was agreed on--sometimes in hours,
sometimes over several weeks--after which the decisions reached became a permanent part of the group
belief system and deviation led to isolation of the
deviant. Their primary concern was negative, to
prevent the dominance of the old military-oligarchic
alliance in Dominican life; beyond that, they sub-
scribed to reform of the social structure, constitu-
tionalism, and the idea of progress through work.
As a secondary issue, they were critical of the
United States military intervention, which many of
them thought had prevented the victory of their revolutionary forces and which they saw as an intervention on the side of the old style régime.

Towards the United States mission, the young
revolutionaries were unremittingly hostile; they
felt that the mission had recommended the intervention in order to crush the revolution, and they

strongly resented the imputation of a communist
character to the revolution in official statements,
especially by the President of the United States--
although they were ready to proclaim that there were
a number of communists among them, and that they accepted communist leadership for practical purposes of
of organizing their military defence. They asserted
that they would never follow this leadership politically, and would control their own communists. This
attitude was not helped by a press critical of the
United States, which they followed carefully. Towards the United States as a nation, they were more
friendly; they believed that assistance from the
United States would be absolutely necessary for
their reform programme to succeed. They were frustrated by their inability to communicate with the
United States, and yet distrusted the Embassy and
would not approach it.

     For its part, the United States diplomatic mis-
sion had, as a group, suffered what can be characterized as a traumatic experience. At the time of
the uprising, the mission had numbered something
less than fifty officials, headed by the Ambassador
and organized on standard bureaucratic lines. This
group of men had striven exceedingly hard to encourage the stabilization, democratization, and development of Dominican society, which was just emerging
from a radical dictatorship, when they were overtak-
en by events (18,8). The uprising surprised the Embassy as it did all Dominicans, including the participants. Long-established friendships with Dominican people were broken, the bloodshed in the streets
was appalling, and the Embassy came under sniper
fire. Worst of all, from the Embassy's viewpoint,
all of their intelligence reports indicated that
many foreign-trained communists were actively involved in the uprising.

     The decision to intervene in a Latin American
country with combat troops for the first time in
nearly 40 years brought a storm of protest from almost every Latin American country, and from some
countries outside of the hemisphere, while significant sectors of the American press were strenuously
critical. The President of the United States had
taken the decision, but the Embassy was involved and
was, of course, forced to defend its recommendations.
The shooting went on, troops poured in to a high of
28,000, the President constantly sought information,
advice, and justification, high-level diplomatic
missions from the United States and the Organization
of American States descended on the Embassy, the

press corps made demands, and all the time confusion
reigned in Dominican politics with a whole series of
claimants to leadership rising and disappearing from
public view. The members of the Mission literally
worked day and night and established a group-belea-
gured solidarity into which newly-arriving members
were rapidly recruited.

It was only when truce lines were established
and the violence diminished that it began to become
evident to concerned members of the United States
mission that most of the rising young leaders of the
country, especially those from the universities,
were somehome associated with the uprising. It was
not at all clear how they were organized or who
their leaders were, although they supported the rebellious young officers and certainly had a number
of communist personalities among them and vast quan-
tities of communist literature available to them.
With this knowledge, and in the absence of any direct contact or discussion, the mission was naturally wary, especially as such public statements as
newsmen brought from the scene included vigorous
condemnation of United States policy in general and
of the Embassy in particular. However, the significance of these young leaders to the future of the
country was obvious, and the mission became concerned as to how to establish contact with them to
explore the possibilities of offering encouragement
and cooperation in building democratic institutions
within the Dominican framework.

It was at this point, some four months after
the uprising, that a Youth Affairs Officer from the
State Department who knew of my previous work in establishing dialogue between hostile groups suggested
that I be invited to consult on the matter; the Ambassador, somewhat reservedly, agreed.

ESTABLISHING CONTACT

Before going to Santo Domingo, I negotiated the
terms of consultation with the sponsors--I would act
as an independent consultant, neither representing
the United States Government nor subject to official
control, while the mission was entitled to disavow
any responsibility for my work or findings. I would
not, it was understood, identify any of my infor-
mants among either the revolutionaries or the United
States Government. I decided to establish dialogue
with Dominican youth before engaging with the Embas-
sy--I wished to avoid any partisan preconception
that might interfere with perception. I familiar-

iarized my ear and tongue to the Spanish language
and consulted a wide variety of sources as to the
history and circumstances of the uprising. I read
books of history and back-files of the newspapers.
I consulted scholars and newsmen and was briefed by
State Department experts, and I studied maps. Very
little was known about Dominican youth since the uprising, but I at least learned something of the
background.

Scouting, in the dialogue model, continues until communicative contact is made with the group being approached; that is, continues during on-site
observations without participation. By chance, I
arrived in Santo Domingo on 25th September, a few
minutes after deposed President Juan Bosch had
landed after his return from exile, and a day of
great tension in the constitutionalist zone. I established myself in a local hotel near the demarca-
tion line--in itself a statement of nonofficial
identity--and entered the zone dressed as an American scholar. As I walked among the tense crowds for
several hours, I approached no one nor they me. I
observed the grimness, the tension, the determination. Guns were everywhere, in the hands of patrols
of young men who carried them proudly and professionally. Deadly seriousness was the order of the
day.

I was, of course, profoundly interested in attitudes toward me as a conspicuous American, the only one in the zone that day. It was apparent that I
was observed, but no look or gesture, friendly or
hostile, was directed toward me. This was a community that would not engage in radical stereotyping
but would wait for evidence; these were serious and
dignified people.

After six hours, I felt that I had absorbed
enough "feeling" for the community and knowledge of
its styles of communication to initiate contact with
some of its members. Since it was evident that any
approach on my part would not be welcomed and also
clear that the organization of the groupings was
very diffuse with no clear channels of access, I
could not risk singling out any particular persons.
I decided to invite an approach to me, and did so by
joining a crowd in raising my arm in the clenched
fist "salute of the oppressed" at some high point in
the speech which former President Bosch was making
from a balcony. Within minutes, three young men approached me and asked, "who are you?" When I answered, the dialogue was started, and I was soon being instructed in the organization and articles of

faith of the revolutionary movement and introduced
to a wide range of participants. "What is your purpose here? How long are you going to stay?" I explained that I was a psychiatrist interested in the
political psychology of revolution, and that I had
come to study their revolution and planned to stay
for three weeks. They supplied me with the Spanish
words to describe this role and, during our exchange,
sharpened the definition, which was helped by my
calling card identifying me as the Director of the
Institute for the Study of National Behavior--
conducta nacional, as this became translated. But
the real test followed very quickly with a vigorous
criticism of the United States intervention. I said
that I would try to understand their point of view
but that I might not agree with it. This led them
to extensive elaborations of their complaints and of
their understanding of and participation in the revolution. They then took me into their counsel as
they criticized the speech that Bosch was making,
supporting some points and disagreeing with others.
Clearly, this was a thinking audience, not blindly
accepting any leadership, and even reexamining their
own ideas. Indeed, they soon asked my opinion of
their theories and I responded with absolute frank-
ness.

     Before we ended this episode, my informants had
described their own involvements in the uprising and
insisted that they, and Dominican youth generally,
were dedicated to the democratic reform of their society. They would deal with issues as they arose in
practical terms and would accept no ideological or
personalistic leadership. They would examine the
ideas of communism as any other but, frankly, Dominican communists were unsympathetic. They recommended that I become acquainted with the 14th June Movement, a Castro-communist organization that was sometimes practically helpful, as when it supplied the
know-how to organize the armed defence of the revolution. They recommmended that I observe an attempt
to reopen the Autonomous University of Santo Domingo
under revolutionary auspices which was to take place
in two days. "We can transform our society," they
said, "only if we have the knowledge and technical
skills, and we can acquire those only in the university."

     During the next three weeks, all of the obser-
vations of these first dialogue partners were borne
out. Most important, of course, was the discovery
that there was a genuine group or movement with
which some thousands of young Dominicans identified

themselves, and that it was possible for the intercessor to enter into serious dialogue with its members. I recorded 33 interviews-in-depth with individuals, and 18 extended exchanges with groups
that included 248 participants. These exchanges always involved a certain amount of testing of me and
my views; the question really was whether I could
recognize the personal and social concerns and aspirations of their group. But, mainly, both my dialogue partners and I became concerned to define what
they meant by "revolution" and how they could proceed toward their goals. There were subvarieties of
dialogue, including friendly debate with groups and
vigorous dialectic argument with young communists,
but for the most part we became jointly engaged in
diagnosing the social-political realities of the nation. I refused to criticize or defend the United
States intervention.

    One particular problem was that of political
language. Youth who had been mobilized into political consciousness by the uprising generally lacked
the concepts and words to discuss their purposes.
They seized on the most generally available formulation, which happened to be a Marxist pamphlet, Leo
Huberman's *Principles of Socialism*. From this, they
learned to speak in terms of the "necessity for
transformation of the political, social, and economic bases of national life." While a few communists
among them may have meant to achieve this through
class warfare and revolution in the Marxist sense,
the great consensus saw the issue as one of reform
of existing institutions to provide broader social
justice. Still, the democratic aims concealed in
Marxist language might make for nervousness on the
part of the United States mission until one could
get at the intentions behind the jargon.

    A second problem was my own credibility. In
the circumstances of conspiracy and announced intelligence activities of the United States Government,
it is not surprising that many of the revolutionaries suspected that I was an intelligence agent.
When we were well acquainted, they would tell me of
this suspicion. My answer was that I was a thoroughly independent scholar, but that there was no
way I could possibly prove that I was not from the
Central Intelligence Agency. But, what if I were?
Did they not insist that they wanted the United
States to understand them? This sort of exchange
almost always ended with their extracting a promise
from me to do my level best--whether I was such an
agent or not--to convey my understanding of them to

the United States Government. In any case, I did
not conceal the fact that I was having discussions
with the United States Embassy and this, of course,
stimulated comments on their views of the official
United States mission which, as we shall shortly
see, included a high component of hostile stereotyping.

My dialogue with the mission took an entirely
different form. The Embassy had consented to my
consultation and had been informed of my arrival.
My role was well defined, although novel and a little unsettling to the officials. The approach was
formal and respected bureaucratic structures. I
called on the Ambassador several days after my arrival, after I had established dialogue with the
young Dominicans. I was briefed on the Embassy's
judgments concerning political events. Then, I systematically introduced myself to every section of
the Embassy concerned in any way with youth affairs,
some nine sections in all. In each case it was necessary to lay out my credentials as a consultant,
and to indicate my knowledge of and sympathy for the
rigors of the Foreign Service.

The stimulus to dialogue was my acquanitance
with the young revolutionaries; every member of the
mission was keenly interested in what was developing
in the Constitutionalist Zone or, as some of them
called it, the Rebel Zone. (I find this regularly
true, that whenever a group is defined as a potential adversary, interest is very high in that group,
especially in the absence of contact.) However,
here too, considerable stereotyping had taken place
and I found that it damaged my credibility to challenge the stereotypes with my facts or opinions; I
neither criticized nor defended the revolutionaries.

Now, while these discussions covered a great
range of topics, I will confine myself to summarizing the views that these two groups held of one an-
other--a subject on which I gathered a vast amount
of data since knowledge of my acquaintance with the
"other" group naturally elicited opinions concerning
it from each side. There was some variety of knowledge and viewpoint in each group, but there was also
a modal or dominant image of the other, each group
manifesting elements of what Ralph White has termed
the "hostile enemy image" (22).

One startling aspect of these hostile images
was the degree to which they were compounded of
proven or believed facts. Each group had extremely
accurate information about the other side; the Embassy was entirely correct about the presence, ac-

tivities and purposes of Dominican communists--many
of whom I came to know quite well--and the revolutionaries were correct when they reported Pentagon
contingency plans that were closely held secrets
(and which I did not learn of until some months later). It was soon evident that my firsthand knowledge of each side carried very little weight with
the other, and any challenge to the stereotypes was
rejected, and it was clear that if I were to urge
contrary facts and interpretations concerning either
group on the other I would soon lose all credibility.

IDENTIFYING COMMON INTERESTS

What I have reported so far are the attitudes
that were expressed during the first phases of dialogue with the two groups, each group asserted its
belief that the other was unmitigatedly hostile to
its purposes. As the dialogues progressed, however,
each group began to enquire whether I thought the
other would be willing to assist toward the realization of its purposes in limited and acceptable ways.

The United States mission was vitally interested in the reestablishment of political stability
in the Dominican Republic and the resumption of democratic institution building. Quite obviously, this
shaky young republic would need substantial American
technical and economic assistance to achieve this
end; just as obviously, the leadership, technical
manpower and intelligentsia to build democratic institutions would have to be drawn in large part from
the generation of youth, especially those in the
universities. The United States could hardly risk
supporting institutions that were communist in their
leadership and character. But the matter was still
more complicated; if the United States did not recognize and help with the development of democratic
reform, would this not throw Dominican youth into
the arms of the communists who promised radical revolution?

The revolutionaries for their part, while they
sought radical reforms in Dominican society, also
recognized that hard work and technical skill would
be needed and, after five months of intense political education in the Constitutionalist Zone, were
turning their thoughts to preparing for these tasks
by returning to their studies. They knew, moreover,
that their nation would need external assistance
from the United States, but they were extremely wary
of political conditions attached to such assistance.
Whatever institutions were built, they wanted to be

Dominican institutions; whatever assistance they received should be on Dominican terms.   In particular,
they applied this formula to their hopes for the
great university of their country, the Autonomous
University of Santo Domingo.

The Autonomous University had been the centre
of a great deal of controversy ever since the assassination of Truijillo; indeed, it had been shut down
by strikes or government action much more than it
had been functioning. It was closed again at the
uprising, but faculty sympathetic to the revolution
called a formal council and elected a reform-minded
rector and administration. The Council was boy-
cotted by about one-third of the faculty who prompt-
ly founded their own university on conservative ped-
agogic lines. While there was considerable controversy about the legality of this action, the administration announced that the university would be
opened on 27th September, and despite many provocations and difficulties it was. The Provisional Government refused to pay salaries, but the faculty
taught anyway. It was soon evident that the new
university administration had the complete confidence of the revolutionary youth and would take care
to keep it. At this point, my diaogue extended to
the professors and administrators and their interest in recognition and technical support in organizing the university became sharply clarified.

Now, as I alternated between the two groups.
with the knowledge of each, they both sharpened
their statements of interest in cooperation, and
they both emphasized the conditions. These conditions, I should emphasize, were incompatible with
mediation; the university administration could not
afford to deal directly with the Embassy for it
would lose credibility with the young revolutionaries, while the Embassy could not deal with a very
controversial institution which might, after all,
prove to be communist controlled. Instead, as my
announced departure date approached and I emphasized
that this would terminate our contact, both the Embassy and the revolutionary youth-university administration complex pressed me very hard to advocate
their interests. The Embassy asked for concrete
programme recommendations that would open up some
channels of communication with Dominican reformist
(as I would term them in American political language)
youth and, of course, hoped that my analysis would
support its own judgments. The youth-university
group urged me to encourage the United States government to stop worrying about the dangers of commu-

nism and to support their reforms, but they always
attached the provision that any assistance would
have to be completely without political conditions.
Although I explored the possibilities thoroughly,
neither side would agree to direct contact with the
other.

BRINGING THE GROUPS TOGETHER

The first copy of my report to the State Department was sent directly to the American Ambassador in Santo Domingo; he endorsed its findings generally. In the report, I outlined the development
of the new political culture among Dominican youth,
emphasizing its complete lack of communication with
the United States and its conditional interest in
establishing contact. I recommended that maximum
attention be given to establishing contact, through
sponsorship of a variety of programmes which would
bring nonpolitical American groups and individuals
into contact with the young Dominicans, but I specified a range of programme possibilities. I expressed the view that the Autonomous University
would become the principal instituional expression
of reformist aspirations.
    I was asked to outline specific recommendations
for developing a programme of assistance to university development in the Dominican Republic. I recommended a carefully phased approach with the first
step being confined to the sponsorship of expert-to-
expert and institution-to-institution contact. Out
of this, I expected would grow a phase of joint programme exploration with emphasis on the Dominican
character of the institution, and from this process
I anticipated the development of specific projects
suitable for international development assistance.
    Here the matter rested from the end of October,
1965, until April, 1966. Meanwhile, a fragile peace
had come to the Dominican Republic; American troops
were officially withdrawn and preparations were under way to internationally supervised free elections.
The university continued to function while the more
conservative, private Universidad Nacional Pedro
Henrique Urena was planning to begin its classes. I
had predicted that the Movement of Reformist Youth
would remain cohesive, that the autonomous University would continue to operate under its reformist
administration and that the Provisional Government
would eventually recognize the administration.
    All of these predictions were based on direct
acquaintance with the persons involved and were at

some variance with the official estimates based on
secondary sources. When elections were held in the
university at the end of March and the reformist administration was confirmed in office, the Provisional Government resumed its recognition and financial
support. I received another call from Washington
asking if I could put my recommendations concerning
the university into effect.

At my suggestion, an extremely competent research organization was asked to administer this experiment in international contact while I continued
as consultant.* In May, the Project Director and I
visited the Dominican Republic and offered to sponsor the visits of ten expert consultants to the two
universities in Santo Domingo with the support of
the United States Agency for International Development. We were formally invited by both.

We offered to attempt to recruit any experts
that the universities designated. The administration of the Autonomous University asked us to invite
a professor of chemistry from Mexico, a professor of
agronomy from Puerto Rico, and a professor of higher
education from the United States; in addition, there
were requests for experts in university administration, pharmacy, engineering, architecture and city
planning, economics, and teacher training. Both the
Embassy and the Agency for International Development
in Washington approved these plans and, to their
very great credit, agreed to our inviting consultants solely on the grounds of technical expertness,
without any consideration of nationality or political status. One of the most inspiring aspects of
this project was the readiness with which outstanding experts recommended by professional organizations accepted our invitation, despite the dangers,
uncertainties, and token compensation.

The consultant group was gathered together and
was thoroughly briefed on the background of the project, the session being joined by a principal official from the Autonomous University; they were asked
to act as purely technical consultants and to develop recommendations in joint consultation with their
Dominican counterparts, the visits being in July. I

---

*This program was administered with extraordinary
patience and skill by Dr. Henry P. David as Project
Director for the International Research Institute of
the American Institutes for Research. Neither Dr.
David nor the American Institutes for Research bear
any responsibility for this report.

accompanied the first consultant group of three experts, later joined by two others.

As the consultations began, there was an immediate crisis of confidence when newspaper articles appeared suggesting that the experts had come solely to assist the conservative university. The expert consultants were each individually subjected to accusations of perfidy or puppetry to an alleged United States policy of supporting "reactionary" forces, and each of them asserted his personal neutrality towards Dominican political questions and his sole interest in better education. This testing reached its height at a luncheon given by the administration of the Autonomous University for the visiting experts, when the Mexican professor spontaneously made an impassioned speech to the effect that he was certainly no puppet and that he believed the project to be nonpolitical in character. He pointed out that the life or death of the university depended on the quality of its work and that it needed every assistance it could get, regardless of the source, just so long as there were no political conditions attached. Each consultant declared his readiness to provide his best technical judgments, regardless of any other concern.

After this crisis, the consultations soon settled into a steady and intensive process, with the professional quality of the experts overriding any other consideration. Within a very few days, a genuine joint working relationship had developed and administration and students both recognized the complete seriousness of the project. A few provocations from splinter parties of the extreme right and extreme left completely failed to mobilize any support in the face of this working relationship. Soon, too, social relations began to develop, climaxed by a magnificent feast in the open at the university's experimental farm.

In the course of this visit, the consultants were invited to have lunch with the Ambassador who was interested in the progress of the project, and judged that this would not disturb the relationship in the university any more than did our continued consultation with the more conservative university.

These developments opened an opportunity to bring members of the two groups together; both groups were pleased to honor the consultant group. After considerable consultation on all sides, the rector of the Autonomous University invited twenty leading members of the Embassy, exclusive of the Ambassador for protocol reasons, to join twenty lead-

ing members of the university administration and
faculty, including members of the important Reform
Commission, in honoring the visitors. To the guest
list were added the Mexican Ambassador, the Papal
Nuncio and two bishops who, added to the five consultants on the scene and myself, were expected to
act as neutral buffers. The rector of the conservative university was also invited but did not think
it wise to attend, although the rector of the Cath-
lic University from the second city of the Dominican
Republic, Santiago de los Caballeros, did make an
appearance.

For over fifteen months, the two groups had
been watching each other at a distance without direct contact. I have outlined the images that were
held by each side of the other, but there was also
great interest and curiosity on each side. Did the
others really have horns? Were the Embassy officials really reactionary capitalists? Were the university officials really communist puppets?

As the guests arrived, they tended to pair off
quickly, or rather to form triangles with one of the
buffer groups as the third member. Prototypical was
the pairing of the rector with the Public Affairs
Officer of the Embassy. These two senior members of
their parties stood for two hours in earnest dialogue, an open space having formed around them which
only I and the servant with drinks entered. Each
partner in this dialogue reviewed his side's case
with a good deal of ardour; the rector asserted that
he could never accept United States intervention in
Dominican affairs, and the Public Affairs Officer
argued just as heatedly that the interventions had
probably saved the Dominican society from tearing
itself to peices. Both agreed, however, that the
task of rebuilding and modernizing the society was
immense, and that each side had a role to pay in
this great effort.

The same sort of event was taking place in every corner of the rector's spacious house. The next
day, I met with a sizable sample of the participants
from each group and observed a very striking change
in the attitudes which they held toward each other.
There was no change whatsoever in basic beliefs, nor
would any participant from either side admit that he
had learned any new facts or changed his interpretation of the facts which he had. But the members of
each group now recognized their counterparts as
serious and dedicated men who were sincere in their
commitments to the development of a better society,
no matter how much they might differ in social phil-

osophy and ideas as to method. In brief, the two
groups kept their identities distinct and intact,
they remained at odds on many issues, but they now
perceived the other group as consisting of "men that
you can work with" in limited ways. Two days later,
the Ambassador invited the Rector for lunch.

Five days after this first meeting, I returned
the Rector's hospitality with a party at the house
of an American friend. This time, however, we invited somewhat different guests; persons from the
university and the mission who were less concerned
with policy and more involved in programme administration were included and, except for the expert
consultants, no neutral buffers were present. While
some of the characteristics of the first meeting
were repeated--a certain amount of assertion of
one's own position and feeling out of the other--
this process was much reduced in intensity. Rather,
the principal focus of discussion was quite practical: by what administrative arrangements might some
of the programme recommendations which were emerging
from the consultant's joint discussions with their
counterparts be effected?

PROGRAMMES OF COOPERATION

Although substantial contact had been established between the leadership of the two groups, and
the possibilities of limited cooperation had been
recognized, there were still impediments to the actual development of projects. First, the projects
had to be carefully specified; there was no possibility, for example, that the mission could just ap-
prove a shopping list of the needs of the university
for external assistance. And each group had to consider the effects of any programme on the overall
development needs of the Dominican Republic. Moreover, neither leadership group had a free hand. The
university administration had to walk carefully and
justify any cooperation with the United States in
order to maintain its good relations with the students. The United States mission had to go through
the difficult process of allocating technical assistance funds to this purpose in the face of overwhelming demands from other sectors of the society; then,
it had to justify such allocations to the Washington
headquarters of the Agency for International Development. And, throughout all of this, great care had
to be taken to maintain even-handedness in terms of
other Dominican domestic institutions.

As the experts' visits continued through the

summer, each consultant spending about two weeks in working consultation, there was a consolidation of working relations and further definition of conditions of possible future cooperation. The most important consensus that emerged from these joint considerations was that cooperation would be most useful if it were sharply limited, and initiation of proposals would rest entirely with the Dominican Institution. The volume on *Higher Education in the Dominican Republic* which resulted from the consultants' reports was distributed to the Dominican institutions, United States mission, and the State Department; its recommendations focused on steps which could be taken with Dominican resources (2). However, it was agreed that continuing consultation would be extremely helpful in upgrading the university's offerings and that some visiting professors could fill in in special fields of study until Dominican students had gained competence in those subjects; moreover, it was thought that assistance could be given to promising students to obtain foreign training in needed fields.

TERMINATION

The experiment in intergroup intercession was substantially completed when cooperative mechanisms began to be worked out between the groups, but there were still a good many problems in programme development. It seemed to me that their solution could be facilitated by continued consultation on programme development, but it soon became evident that both groups preferred to work directly with each other, and that continued activities of third parties would be unwelcome and, indeed, superfluous. With some regret, I resigned from my consulting relationship.

Almost the last episode of this experiment was stimulated by the appearance of an attack on the programme of cooperation in a communist newspaper in Santo Domingo. I was accused of being "an agent of cultural penetration who, by clever psychological means, has weakened the true (i.e., communist) revolutionary spirit." I was also represented as having been a friend of President Kennedy, which was regrettably untrue but which certainly increased my popularity, for President Kennedy was the popular ideal of most young Dominicans, including reformists. The article called on students to rise and reject this cooperation. By this time, however, the programme was so well established and accepted that the

rector was able to reply on a TV programme. He cat-
egorically denied cultural penetration, but pointed
out that the university was happy to receive economic and scientific help from such international programmes as this had been. After that, the attacks
died down. But this event, in November, signalled
the completion of the intercession.

Retrospectively, it would have been technically
better to have terminated the intercession experiment as soon as direct contact and the beginnings of
working relations had been established between the
two groups; in fact, I think that termination intentions should have been announced immediately after
the very first group of academic visitors had
brought members of the groups together, and that we
should have ended the project with the completion
of expert visits and presentation of their reports,
leaving the groups to work out their own programmes.
That I did not do so arises from a counter-transfer-
ence problem; after nine months of effort in bringing groups together, I had acquired a deep personal
interest in the outcome and did not altogether trust
the strength of the cooperative ties.

More than five years have passed since this experiment, during all of which time some level of
contact and communication has been maintained between the United States mission and the universities
of the Dominican Republic. The new reformist culture of young Dominicans has maintained its nationalist thrust and has often been extremely critical
of the United States, some groups quite violently
so. But at no time has there been a mass demand for
a break in contact between the institutions, even
when a second national election was conducted in a
heated climate. The two groups have proceeded very
carefully but have continued to cooperate.

CRISES, PROBLEMS AND ACCIDENTS

In reporting on this experiment in intercession, I have limited my description to the most essential events involving the two groups and the intercession process. It would be misleading, however, were I not to add that a whole multitude of
crises, problems, and accidents arose in the course
of the experiment that materially affected the process; this, of course, is always the case in circumstances of social turmoil and intergroup conflict of
any magnitude. It is just for this reason that a
strong and simple model of the process is necessary
in order to proceed, otherwise one would become lost

in the forest. Plans and next steps have constantly
to be adjusted to the flow of circumstances and correction has to be made for their consequences.

At the very outset of my on-site dialogue, for
example, an episode occurred that forced me to break
my own rule that the intercessor should never intervene in the events taking place, but should limit
himself to developing his own dialogue. While I was
talking with students and faculty who had gathered
to try to open the Autonomous University, an American military vehicle came driving down Alma Mater
avenue. The students went into an uproar and
stopped the vehicle, whose two soldiers warned the
crowd back with their weapons and drove on. Some
students were preparing to attack the soldiers with
stones and bottles when they returned, and serious
bloodshed appeared imminent. I intercepted the vehicle and persuaded the soldiers to report to their
commanding officer before continuing their patrol;
meanwhile, cooler heads prevailed among the students
and it was realized that bloodshed would certainly
cause the university to be closed indefinitely.
When the patrols were resumed, they were resentfully
ignored.

Subsequently, I learned that the patrol was
routine and had been ordered in complete ignorance of
its affront to the hard-won and deeply-cherished
principal of *fuero*--freedom from police or military
interference in the universities. I urged the Embassy to have the patrol halted but it continued for
two weeks as the military commanders thought it a
bad precedent to back down in the face of protest or
force. This episode disturbed my dialogue with students who naturally thought that anyone who could
send troops away must have great power. Only the
intervention of a leftist professor trusted by the
students restored my standing with them. Nor was
this a good footing on which to approach the Embassy, as my urgings put it in a difficult position.
Despite these difficulties, however, I would have no
choice but to act the same way again, and the fact
is that the dialogue was able to continue with both
groups.

Again and again, events occurred that impinged
on the dialogue. In these complex and shifting circumstances, the chief technical challenge was to
keep my independent role absolutely clear to both
groups at all times. As is always the case when one
intercedes between conflicting groups, each makes
very strong efforts to co-opt the intercessor to its
camp; failing that, the groups are apt to ostracize

the outsider. The problem is to define and redefine
one's role as an outsider who truly appreciates and
respects the group outlook while remaining thoroughly neutral with respect to the conflict. This role
is accepted for two reasons; every group in conflict
develops an intense wish to be understood in its own
terms, particularly by outsiders. And at some level
of self-concern, the members of such groups want to
find a line of communication with their adversary to
a less hostile attitude--the threat to group values
or even to life from hostile action of the adversary
is too great to be ignored if there is any chance of
mitigating it. In any event, the final guarantee of
the neutral role was my own determination to terminate the intercession at any time if either party
should wish to terminate their contact, or if either
group should insist on any action that I believed to
be unacceptable to the other.

DISCUSSION

Third-party intercession in intergroup and international conflict is scarcely new in the world;
it is an ancient function of professional diplomats
and concerned private persons. Not new, either, is
the idea that finding some way of getting representatives of conflicting groups together may somehow
contribute to peaceful resolution of conflict. The
Quakers, for example, have a long experience in just
such activity, growing out of Quaker values and
moral commitment. What is new in the experimental
approaches of Burton, Doob, and others is the theoretical basis of the approach and the development
and testing of new procedures and techniques based
on theoretical-empirical analysis. Such approaches
permit the more precise specification of the problems and the development of systematic procedures--
rules of the game--for their alleviation. We can
begin to build a science of what I would unashamedly
call peacemaking.
The real-life experiment that I have reported
generated considerable first-hand data that suggests
that the broad dynamics of group formation and intergroup conflict which have been so carefully examined in small group experiments also hold true for
much larger groups in the context of complex social
reality. Certainly, the two groups examined each
developed a distinctive micro-culture with radically
disparate cognitive structures. Certainly the phenomena of stereotyping and enemy-image formation

were thoroughly in evidence, as was the cyclic nature of the hostile interaction between them. And, finally, the profound effects of direct contact and communication on those images and the hostile cycle was observed in the experiment.

Obviously, one case is not an adequate test of a theory, the single case cannot define the limits within which the theory is applicable. We do not yet know to what size of group the model may be applied, although there is considerable evidence that large nations behave in the predicted manner. Nor do we know the effects of more historically established and deeply entrenched structures of shared belief and language on the interaction. What, for instance, is the effect of racial identity? Do the same dynamics obtain between such long-established groups as the Flemings and the Walloons? Such questions can be answered only by compiling a number of case studies drawn from real world observation.

Beyond the scientific study of social behaviour, however, such studies are experiments in social action. The first hypothesis, that contact and communication between members of groups in conflict will favourably alter the images which they hold of one another was strongly supported, although in rather unexpected ways--the images changed less than the judgments about qualities of the other side that had not been central to the images. The second hypothesis, that programmes of limited cooperation in the pursuit of partial superordinate goals would result in even further movements toward less hostile images was also supported, but the finding that such cooperation blurs the boundaries in small groups did not obtain for these larger groups embedded in distinct national contexts. Here, then, may be one of the limits to which the findings of small group experiments are applicable to large group interaction.

It is still harder to judge whether the third major hypothesis--that the development of limited cooperation and favourable changes in the images between two groups playing subordinate roles in circumstances of violent social conflict would diminish the degree of violence--was supported by the experiment. After all, the violence in the Dominican Republic was essentially that of a civil war to which the United States and its diplomatic mission were not a party. It is my judgment, however, that the alienation between these groups and the unfavourable opinions which they held of each other did impede the construction of civic order and that the reduction of alienation contributed to a return of domes-

tic peace. I am quite certain that the young Dominicans were less inclined to feel desperately isolated when some channels of communication were
opened and I am positive that the United States mission was less anxious about the political dangers of
the reformist youth movement after contact was established.

Technically, the requirements for third party
intercession in intergroup conflict can be tenta-
tively specified. The most difficult, of course, is
the definition and maintenance of one's role as a
genuine third party. Here, the model of psychiatric
interview technique was indispensable, for the daily
task of the psychiatrist is to communicate with
alienated persons on their own terms without joining
them in their alienation, and he must make it clear
that that is precisely what he is doing. Succeeding
in this task requires the psychiatrist to maintain
constant consciousness of his role and of how it may
appear to others.

As I have outlined, the testing of this role was
severe in this case. And one source of difficulty
on all sides was the sponsorship of the United
States Government. While this had the advantage of
securing access to the mission and to policy councils, it had the disadvantage of requiring scrupu-
lous vigilance to avoid the entirely understandable
wishes of the foreign service bureaucracy to exercise some control over my recommendations or to
elicit information from me about my private contacts
with the young revolutionaries. It was necessary
for me to emphasize over and over that I was an independent consultant and to set very careful limits
on my involvement.

Obviously, however, an identifiable neutral and
disinterested sponsorship for such intercession
would provide a much better base. I searched dili-
gently for such sponsorship without success. The
foundations are generally unwilling to sponsor projects that may touch upon national interests, the
United Nations was limited to a very peripheral role
at high diplomatic levels, and private funding was
impossible to find. There are cases in which the
United Nations Institute for Training and Research
or UNESCO might provide sponsorship, but not where
there is great power involvement. I have to conclude that there are two broad possibilities for developing such roles: the further development of a
rigorously professional consulting position of which
this case is an example, and the very considerable
strengthening of private peacemaking institutions.

The technical heart of the intergroup intercession model lies in the capacity for controlled involvement with persons and groups whose interpretations of reality are at radical variance with each
other. The dialogues are conducted so as to recognize each group's purposes and interpretations of
reality. One listens and communicates within the
system of the group's assumptions, while making it
clear that one does not necessarily share those assumptions. Groups, as do patients, want to be understood and recognized more than they demand agreement. After all, every human person and group is
guided in action by a unique mixture of assumption,
myth, fantasy and feeling that has arisen out of its
particular experience and circumstances. The technical task is not to challenge or change these
views, but to find within them a basis for contact,
communication, and possible cooperation between conflicting parties.

The final technical contribution from this experiment lies in the arrangements for bringing the
parties together. There need to be enough participants from each side to validate one another's reports when they return to their larger group. They
need to include persons from sufficiently high levels to have policy access, but generally should not
include the ultimate decision makers. Third party
buffers should be present: persons that both sides
respect and whose good opinion they want to maintain. And there should be no formal agenda. All of
these propositions can be tested in other cases, but
have been useful guidelines in experiments in intercession in domestic intergroup conflict. Timing is
a vital question but all that can be said from this
case is that timing was determined very largely by
the flow of larger circumstances; the possibility of
some kind of meeting was established in the first
round of dialogue, and both groups kept this on
their agenda of priorities although it was nine
months before the circumstances were ripe.

Probably the most significant technical procedure is the rigorous phasing of the intercession
process. The aims and procedures of each phase are
distinctive, and any departure from them disrupts
the process. The two major departures from the mod-
el--my intervention with the military patrol and in-
decision in termination--serve to illustrate the
problems which arise from deviation from phase-spe-
cific procedures.

CONCLUSION

I began this discussion by wondering whether psychiatry might have something to contribute to the reduction of alienation between groups of men, especially to the ultimate product of extreme alienation, intergrou⸗ violence, and war. I have reported on an attempt to apply psychiatric methods, suitably modified, to one instance of conflict between groups and have specified a procedural model for such intercession.

The outcome suggests that propositions about the nature and dynamics of intergroup conflict can be tested by systematic observation, and that it is possible to develop and apply systematic procedures to the reduction of the severity and violence of such conflicts.

In my judgment, we can "cultivate the science of human relationships" at the intergroup level as President Roosevelt appealed to us to do. One of the principal strategies for the psychiatric sciences is to experiment with techniques designed to establish contact, communication, and cooperation between conflicting groups. Such a strategy will not only allow us to refine theory and technique, but may also contribue substantially to more peaceful relations between the groups. The process may be likened to "tying down Gulliver," that is, establishing threads of restraining influence on the forces in group life that lead to destructive conflict (19). Eventually, perhaps, an evolved and tested body of scientific knowledge and procedure will emerge that can tame the excesses of group behaviour that threaten the survival of mankind.

REFERENCES

1. Burton, J.W. *Conflict and Communication*. New York: Free Press, 1969.
2. David, H.P. (Ed.), Higher Education in the Dominican Republic: A Report of Academic Visits. Washington, D.C., American Institutes for Research, 1966. (mimeo)
3. Doob, L.W., Foltz, W.J., & Stevens, R.B. The Fermeda workshop: a different approach to border conflicts in Eastern Africa. *J. Psychol.*, 1969, *73*, 249-266.
4. Frank, J.D. *Sanity and Survival*. New York: Random House, 1967.
5. Glenn, E.S., Johnson, R.H., Kimmel, P.R., &

Wedge, B. A cognitive interaction model to analyze culture conflict in international relations. *J. Conflict Resolution,* 1970, *14,* 35-48.

6. Lall, A. *Modern International Negotiation.* New
York: Columbia University Press, 1968.

7. Laswell, H.D. *Power and Personality.* New York:
Norton, 1948.

8. Martin, J.B. *Overtaken by Events.* Garden City,
New York: Doubleday, 1966.

9. North, R.C. Perception and action in the 1914
crisis. *J. Internat. Affairs,* 1967, *21,* 103-122.

10. Pinderhughes, C.A. Understanding black power:
processes and proposals. *Amer. J. Psychiat.,*
1969, *125,* 552-1556.

11. Sherif, M. *et al. Intergroup Conflict and Cooperation: The Robbers Cave Experiment,* Norman,
Oklahoma: Institute of Group Relations, 1964.

12. Stagner, R. *Psychological Aspects of International Conflict.* Belmont, Calif.: Brooks/Cole,
1967.

13. Stoessinger, J.G. *The Might of Nations.* 2nd
Edition. New York: Random House, 1969.

14. Wedge, B. Toward a science of transnational
communication. *Symposium No. 7, Application of
Psychiatric Insights to Cross-cultural Communication.* New York: Group for the Advancement of
Psychiatry, 1961.

15. Wedge, B. Psychiatry and international affairs.
Science, 1968, *57,* 281-283.

16. Wedge, B. Training for psychistry of international relations. *Amer. J. Psychiat.,* 1968,
125, 731-736.

17. Wedge, B.   Training for Leadership in Cross-
cultural Cialogue. San Diego, Calif.: Institute for the Study of National Behaviour, 1960.

18. Wedge, B. The case study of student political
violence. Brazil and Dominican Republic, *World
Politics,* 1965, *21,* 183-206.

19. Wedge, B., & Rohrl-Wedge, V.J. Tying down Gulliver. *Attitude,* 1970, *1*(6), 2-71.

20. Wedge, B. Mass psychotherapy for intergroup
conflict. In Jules Wasserman (Ed.), *Man for
Humanity.* Springfield, Illinois: C. Thomas,
1972, 307-323.

21. Wedge. B. The individual, the group, and war.
In H.Z. Winnik, R. Moses, & M. Ostow (Eds.),
Psychological Bases for War. New York: Quad-
rangle/New York Times, 1973, 65-82.

22. White, R.K. *Nobody Wanted War: Misperception
in Vietnam and Other Wars.* Garden City, New
York: Doubleday, 1968.

BRYANT WEDGE harbors the notion that a condition of dynamic peace can be attained through a process of continuous conflict resolution at all levels of social encounter; the problem is to implement mechanisms and institutions to this purpose. Currently he is Co-Chairperson of the National Peace Academy Campaign which is mobilizing people in the United States to compel their government to establish a research and training institution at the Federal level.

Bryant Wedge came to this commitment from a conventional career in psychiatric medicine; born in 1921 in Coldwater, Michigan; educated at Kalamazoo College and the University of Michigan Medical School; trained in psychiatry at the Queen's Hospital, Honolulu, Hawaii and the University of Chicago, and in psychoanalysis at the Chicago Psychoanalytic Institute. He was Psychiatrist-in-Chief at Yale's Department of University Health from 1954 when he was was invited to exchange views in a number of other countries as U.S. Eisenhower Exchange Fellow in 1958. This experience exposed him to the uncertainties of high-level diplomacy and to the frightful human costs of unbridled conflict and war. Since it seemed to him that there was a profoundly psychological dimension in these conflicts of groups and nations, he says that he "had no choice" but to pursue an understanding of the theory and therapy of group conflicts in as practical a way as possible.

After a long search, Dr. Wedge found a true working partner in the late Hadley Cantril who was also pursuing the human dimension in international affairs. He founded the Institute for the Study of National Behavior in Princeton, N.J. in 1962, and began a series of practical studies of various international problems as an independent researcher contracting with foreign policy agencies of the U.S. Government. For example, one study of international communication was based on interviews of a hundred professional interpreters and then by interviews of citizens of other countries as to the images they held of the world. As this work evolved, he began to see the possibility of therapeutic intervention in some conflicts, peacemaking or mass psychotherapy; the intervention in the Dominican Republic described in this volume represents the first opportunity to begin to apply these ideas and may be one of the first successful applications of impartial non-power mediation to a conflict of such scale.

It isn't easy to obtain a hearing for zero-power approaches to conflict in a power-obsessed world.   It dawned on Dr. Wedge and a number of his friends and associates that the sanction and legitimization of such efforts would require institutional manifestation at the national level in all countries, including, of course, the United States. Starting in 1975, a national campaign to organize popular understanding and support for a peace institution in the United States was begun to gain popular support.   A bill to establish a study commission for a national academy of peace and conflict resolution has been passed by the U.S. Senate and is expected to pass the House in 1978, and, more important, there are now a good number of people who really understand the idea and are working practically for its implementation.

Bryant Wedge keeps touch with the basic human issues by maintaining a psychotherapeutic practice, which also supports this peace-building work.   Since he has now met many people in all parts of the world who are like-minded, he is optimistic that the habits of 6,000 years of human history can be altered.

SOME OTHER PUBLICATIONS BY BRYANT WEDGE

- Editor, *Psychosocial Problems of College Men*.   New Haven, Conn.:   Yale University Press, 1958.
- *Visitors to the United States and How They See Us*. Princeton, N.J.:   Van Nostrand, 1965.
- International propaganda and statecraft.   *Annals Amer. Acad. Political & Social Science*, 1971, *398*, 36-43.
- With Frank M. Ochberg, John P. Spiegel, T.L. Kostrubala, B. Eichelman, & D.J. Scherl.   In H.M. Gant (Ed.), *Intervening in Community Crises: An Introduction for Psychiatrists*.   Washington, D.C.: Task Force Report, American Psychiatric Assoc., 1975.   (pamphlet)
- Intercultural communications: an interview. *Peace Corps Training & Program Journal*, 1975, *3*(5), 17-24.
- *Strength through peace: the need for a United States Peace Office*.   Report of Hearing.   Subcommittee on Education, United States Senate, May 13, 1976, pp. 71-96.   (GPO72-026 0)

15. Mundialization: World Community at the Doorstep

Citizen Taxes for the U.N., Mundialization, and Town-Twinning as a Way to Peace

Alan Newcombe, Ph.D., and Hanna Newcombe, Ph.D.

> "Most people would succeed in small things
> if they were not troubled with great ambi-
> tions." - Longfellow

World Federalists have the greatest ambition of
them all, namely, to establish a world federal government to create a world in which war does not and
cannot occur. This world would continue to experience disputes, but differences between men would not
be resolved by armed fratricide. Unfortunately, not
everyone enjoys activities directed toward the long-
term and major objectives of World Federation. One
major difficulty with the World Federalist movement
is that there are too few activities capable of early success.
 *"Mundialization" is a political process in the
here and now which can bring local and early success.* As it has been modified in Canada, it involves people in a variety of activities, gradually
exposing them to the idea of world government.
 In 1967, the town of Dundas, Ontario (pop.
16,000) declared itself mundialized, thus becoming
the first community in the Western Hemisphere to
carry out this symbolic act of world citizenship.
Since then, other Canadian towns have done the same,
raising the possibility that Canada may be the scene
of a third wave of mundialization, following those
that took place in Japan and Western Europe beginning after World War II.
 By becoming mundialized, Dundas pronounced itself a "world city"--a fragment of world territory
linked to the community of man. It did this by a
unilateral act, which, while without legal status,

demonstrates its world allegiance, given voluntarily prior to the existence of a "one world" institution requiring such allegiance.

The mundialization movement was born in Hiroshima, in 1945, when the surviving citizens declared their resolve to work for a world federation that would make impossible any repetition of the tragedy that their city had undergone.

Independently of this, mundialization was also begun about the same time in France, where it was first conceived by Colonel Robert Sarrasac-Soulage, and then extended to other countries, including West Germany, Britain, Denmark, Belgium, Italy, and India. The peak of success of the mundialization movement in France was in 1949.

Japan has witnessed the most rapid and extensive growth in mundialization. The city of Ayube, Kyoto Prefecture, was mundialized in 1950. The village of Hozumi, Nagano Prefecture, followed. Okayama Prefecture was mundialized in 1957, followed by Ishikawa and Kyoto, and in 1963, Tokyo, the world's largest city. By 1965, the mundialized local governments of Japan embraced 21 prefectures and 267 cities, towns and villages, representing a total population of 54 million, which is more than half the total population of Japan. The mundialized local authorities are organized into the Japan Council of Local Authorities for the Realization of World Federation. Since 1965, there has also been a World Council for Mundialization, with headquarters in Tokyo (now in Hiroshima), which seeks to unite all the mundialized communities in the world.

In all of these places, mundialization involved persuading the City Councillors to pass a By-Law* stating that the community wished to live in peace with other communities in the world under a World Government or a system of World Law or some other synonym. With the passage of time this By-Law may be forgotten, as there is no action stemming from it to remind citizens of its continuing application.

MUNDIALIZATION, WORLD TAXES, & TOWN-TWINNING

How did the new impetus for mundialization develop in Canada? If we may be immodest, let us say that it all started with two people, namely, the authors of this article.

As long-time World Federalists, we had known

---

*an ordinance in the U.S.A.

about mundialization for some time, but it came to
our attention emphatically in late 1966. As co-edi-
tors of *Peace Research Abstracts* and *Peace Research
Reviews*, publications of the Peace Research Institute
- Dundas, we were compiling for the first issue of
the latter publication a review of "Alternative
Approaches to World Government." Mundialization was
one of 15 approaches discussed. Late one evening as
we sat in our kitchen, we wondered if and how the
immensely successful Japanese mundialization approach could be adapted to North American conditions.
Out of this brain-storming came the marriage of
three existing efforts: mundialization as it had
been practiced in Japan and France, citizens' contributions to the United Nations, and the town-twinning (or sister towns) program. To this was added
the symbolic act of flying the United Nations flag
at the city hall throughout the year.

   With the help of others we have since persuaded
the Councils of several communities in Canada and
the U.S. not only to pass the By-Law, but also to
incorporate in it the decision to:

1) *Fly the United Nations flag daily beside
   the national flag at City Hall.*

2) *Raise each year, by voluntary subscription,
   a sum of money, equal to 0.01% of the total
   taxes raised by the city, to be given to
   the United Nations Special Account.*

3) *Twin with another community in another
   country which is mundialized according to
   the original concept, or is willing to mun-
   dialize.*

   Flying the United Nations flag has a certain
psychological effect, in that it reminds citizens,
each day, that there is a world outside local confines. There may be many things wrong with the
United Nations, but it remains the *only world* organization now in being. Once a gambler complained he
had lost money at roulette and that the wheel was
"fixed." Reminded that he had known this before he
began to play, he replied, "Yes, but it is the only
game in town." So the United Nations, with all its
faults, has the only flag recognized in the world as
being that of a *world* organization.

   The approach of collecting contributions for
the U.N. was based on the desire of many people to
express their moral support for the United Nations
in some tangible and concrete way. Although the
Charter speaks in its Preamble of "We, the people of
the United Nations...," in practice, the U.N. is a
"league of nations," that is, of governments. This

is true both with respect to financial support and
decision making. The ordinary person in the world,
longing passionately for a permanent peace and amity
among nations, has no direct link to the world organization. Many people have felt this need over
the years, and in 1965 machinery was set up at the
U.N. (the U.N. Special Account), so that citizens or
organizations other than national governments can
make contributions without having them merely sub-
tracted from the U.N.'s assessment on their own nation. The act of contributing is far more a moral
gesture of support than a real financial help, but
this is of tremendous importance. It could, of
course, also become financially significant if the
movement grows, and if cities like Tokyo (which has
not contributed to the U.N. in spite of its mundialization), London or New York were to contribute .01
percent of their income from taxes, as Dundas has
done. The reasons for setting a percentage is not
merely to obtain these larger amounts from the big
cities, but to give guidance to newly mundialized
cities on what their fair share might be. The payment to the U.N. represents an attempt to establish
the principle of world taxation, and a hope of
reaching the point where people pay the U.N. a portion of their income for protecting their homes and
families against the ravages of war far more effectively than any national government is any longer
capable of doing. This desire to establish the
principle of world taxation also led us to prefer
contributing to the U.N. Special Account, which
leaves the U.N. free to use the money as it sees
fit, rather than earmarking it for refugees or other special welfare projects, as we also had the option of doing. After all, a citizen of a country
does not designate whether his taxes should go to
education, highway building or other purposes.
     Persons in our city are reminded of the fact
that we are mundialized when we raise funds by
"side-walk solicitations." Not everyone can read
Clark and Sohn or talk with a member of the Foreign
Office, but even 13-year-old children can enthusias-
tically sell "tags for peace." People learn that
they are living in a mundialized community and find
out about world government when they are asked to
sell "tags" or to buy them.
     The third approach--town-twinning--is actually
more widespread than mundialization, and has been
carried on for years in many parts of the world
quite apart from mundialization. There are mundialized towns which are not twinned, and twinned towns

which are not mundialized; if the two streams would merge, each would gain greatly in strength.

Town-twinning. Town-twinning, a program of international exchange and cooperation between two towns in different parts of the world, is a people-to-people program, with projects carried out not only by the municipal governments, but by schools and citizens' organizations of all types. Town-twinning has been approved by the United Nations and by UNESCO. The United Towns Organization (U.T.O.), which a town joins when it undergoes twinning, was founded in 1957 in France by Jean-Marie Bressand, the former French resistance leader, in an effort to combat the kind of intolerance and prejudice that led to World War II and the Nazi oppression. There are now 600 towns from 46 countries in the West, the East, and the Third World involved in twinning. Dundas is twinned with Kaga in Japan.

Twinning is an operation that people like and enjoy. Almost anyone can become involved in the various twinning activities. We have exchanges of children's art, slides, homemade movies, tapes of choirs, letters and people. The twinning operation has three advantages which were not foreseen:

1) In dealing with a super-ordinate goal, the divisions between groups *within* the community became less. Both religious and government school systems have worked together to present the Dundas School system to Kaga. The divisions between Catholic and Protestant or Christian and Jew are minimized when one is dealing with a sister city whose inhabitants do not belong to the Judaic-Christian tradition.

2) The Canadian Ambassador to Japan now takes care to include Kaga on the route of travelling exhibits of Canada. Thus, Canada as a nation is involved with the mundialization program.

3) Visits between the sister cities bring prestige and honour. The authors have examples of people opposed to the idea of world government who changed their minds after visiting Kaga, our sister city.

The "twinning" project also produces publicity. Each time a visitor returns from Kaga, the Dundas newspaper celebrates the event. World government and the ideas of mundialization are mentioned.

Twinning, to be effective, must have the active support of local organizations *before* civic endorse-

ment. The idea must be explained to as many groups
as possible. These groups, in turn, are encouraged
to meet privately with each member of Council. It
is one thing to have a person opposed to an idea
which he understands, but it is a tragedy to have
him opposed to an idea which he does not understand!
Support by many local groups will help persuade some
Council members that mundialization is a good thing.

Twinning of mundialized towns has potential
political significance: if enough "world cities"
were to group together, eventually the world might
be put together in a different way. This is especially true of "chain twinnings": if each town has
two twins rather than one, we can build chains of
mundialized towns around the world. Or even better,
if each town has at least three twins, we can build
networks.

The beauty of this approach is that this new
grouping, the United Towns, would be nonterritorial
(since the twinned towns are separated in space) and
introduce no new lines of natural cleavage (nationality, race, religion, class, or ideology).

This satisfies the requirements of Margaret
Mead when she says: "Our organizational task, then,
may be defined as reducing the strength of all mutually exclusive loyalties, whether of nation, race,
class, religion, or ideology, and constructing some
quite different forms of organization, in which the
memories and the organizational residues of these
former exclusive loyalties cannot threaten the total
structure. The difficulty of arriving at such a
conception only attests to the dangerous hold of
past models on our imagination" (1).

Lines of fission in the town network are difficult to conceive: How could towns A and B gang together to attack a group of other towns, when A and
B are geographically separated and so is the other
group of towns: and when, as likely as not, the other towns are parts of the same network, and therefore more or less distant "relatives" of A and B?

However, so far this is mere futuristic speculation. Chain twinnings are still rare,* and networks nonexistent. On the more mundane level, the
best argument for mundialization is that it starts
people thinking about a world in which wars do not
and cannot occur, and the need for world government.
When Catholic school children enter a government

---

*Hamilton, Ontario, now has two twins--see list at
end.

school for the first time in a 100 years to help
decorate for the Kaga-Dundas Day, more new friendships may be formed. When the representative from
the Chamber of Commerce finds himself sitting with
the representatives of two rival trade unions, they
may each find that there are more things which bind
humanity together than lines of division with which
they are most familiar. When conservative farmers
of the adjacent community attend an "international
day" and can taste strange and exotic foods, their
attitudes toward another culture change as do their
attitudes towards peace and world government. One
day perhaps both Kaga and Dundas will twin with other towns.

Mundialization, modified to include the flying
of the U.N. flag, voluntary subscriptions (town taxes) for the U.N. and town twinning, could become
part of a chain reaction for peace to bind the world
together. If this practical day-to-day involvement
in cross-cultural cooperation, both on a local and a
world level, contributes even a little to world
peace, it will have been worthwhile.

Gandhi said, "Let there be peace on earth and
let it begin with me." We have changed this slogan
slightly and say, "Let there be peace on earth and
let it begin with us," where "us" includes the people in the community where we live. There are some
people in the anti-war or peace movements who spend
a great deal of time organizing national committees
for this or against that who seem to be incapable of
talking with their fellow citizens and starting a
small step for peace with a majority of the people
in their town.

In the paragraph above we have referred to the
"peace movement" as distinct from the "anti-war
movement." What many Americans do not realize is
that Canada, as one example, does not have a draft
for military service and has not had a recent war
(we might be called an "underprivileged nation"),
and thus for the last decade we in the Canadian
peace movement have been looking for positive steps
to take towards a world at peace. On the other
hand, peace-minded people in the U.S.A. have been
involved in protesting the draft and the Viet Nam
war and have thus been reacting to initiatives from
the military and have been engaged in what we call
the "anti-war" movement; this movement has a different goal to our peace movement and uses different
techniques.

SOME UNDERLYING THEORY

The mundialization process, as outlined above, raises several questions:

1) Can such a modest step really contribute *significantly* to world peace? Admittedly, it points in the right direction, but can it make a dent towards the creation of a warless world?

2) By what psychological mechanism will war be eventually abolished?

3) Can radical changes, such as the abolition of the all-powerful sovereign nation-state, be achieved by very nonradical means, or are they perhaps *better* achieved that way?

4) To what types of people, of what ideological persuasion and mental makeup, does mundialization appeal, in contrast to such anti-war actions as demonstrations?

5) What types of people *need* to be influenced to create a warless world? Obviously these questions are interrelated. It seems best to begin with the question--*By what psychological mechanism will war eventually be abolished?*

We have in mind here two alternative mechanisms which are possible: a) Peace by proscription of violence: "Thou shalt not kill" taken literally. b) Peace by enlarging the in-group until it encompasses all mankind.

Since mundialization obviously belongs to the second type of mechanism, we will enlarge upon it somewhat. Whether the causes of war are economic, religious, nationalistic, racial, ideological, or dynastic, one condition obtains in the mind-set of the belligerent: the division of the world into the "we" and the "they," the in-group and the out-group, our friends and our enemies. Particular conflicts, either real or imagined (conflicts of interest, or misunderstandings and escalated misperceptions) sharpen and solidify this division, but do not usually create it. The division precedes the conflict, and provides a nucleus for conflicts to grow on, even if the division itself is originally conceived in a merely functional and not a hostile way (e.g., labor and management).

Margaret Mead, trying to elucidate the differences between the behavior of animal groups and human groups with respect to killing their own and other species, compares the human in-group to "conspecifics" (members of the same species) and the

out-group to "non-con-specifics" (members of other
species). Moral codes in human groups forbid the
killing of members of the in-group (just as animals
will not in general kill their con-specifics except
as an accidental result of sexual rivalries), but
under warfare conditions encourage the killing of
the enemy (just as animals will kill members of other species, as either rivals or prey).

Many writers have pointed out how the size of
the human in-group (the "security unit") has grown
through history and pre-history. The progression is
usually expressed as: family, clan, tribe, nation.
Often the conclusion is reached that the progression
is unfinished, and that "continental region" and
"world" are obvious next members. As the size of
the in-group grows, there are fewer and fewer external "enemies" left, and the hope is that war may be
eliminated as a result. The growth of the security
unit is certainly encouraged by the development of
modern weapons, since the nation-state as a security
unit is no longer able to give its members security.
It is also encouraged by the development of means of
communication and transportation which has made the
world smaller.

A hint at another pair of alternatives, this
time in the mental orientations of peace-minded people, was glimpsed in some very preliminary empirical
observations made recently by the authors. There
seem to be two somewhat distinct groups, one tending
toward such values as nonviolence, reconciliation,
humanism, supporting the underdog; and the other toward such "colder" values as world law, utilitarian-
ism ("do what produces best results"), and democratic participation. This might well be the difference
between the religious and the political orientations
in peace thinking, or between the pacifists and the
world federalists; here mundialization seems to line
up with the latter, more politically inclined, sen-
timents.

But there is a difference. Mundializers do not
talk in either institutional terms, like the world-
constitution drafters, or large-scale functionalist
terms, like the economic integrationists. The appeal is largely to *symbols* of the gradually emerging
world community (world flag, world tax), and therefore represents an attempt to influence *attitudes*
rather than institutions, to build the climate of
world community which must necessarily form the
background of future world *institutions*. This emphasis has long been lacking in World Federalist
thought and practice, and hopefully will supplement

and reinforce the older, more coldly rational tendencies.

Can radical change be achieved by nonradical
means? It is obvious that the change from a nation-
state system, in which "war is just a continuation
of politics by other means" (Clausewitz), to an organized world political community, in which war is
impossible, would be a radical, indeed revolutionary
change. It is a fundamental, comprehensive change
(from the roots up), but it does not involve the
displacement of one social class by another.

There is another sense in which World Federalists are normally not considered as radicals. Even
if their ends are classified as radical, their means
definitely are not. Their approach is usually elit-
ist, although there are exceptions, such as the
World Constitution and People's Parliament Association. Demonstrations are usually frowned upon,
marches are rare; delegations to government and public lectures and literature distributions are the
usual forms of action.

Mundialization, too, uses mild rather than
drastic means. It does not seek confrontations, but
does seek involvement at the grass-roots level. It
goes to the people where they live, offers them activities they like to do; but in this pretty, be-
ribboned package, there is the invaluable gift of
planetary citizenship and planetary responsibility.

Before we can decide whether such mild means
can really move the world toward a comprehensive
change, we need to look at two questions:

a) To what types of people does mundialization
    appeal?
b) What types of people need to be influenced
    to create a warless world?

The answer to the first question is known from
personal observation of the experience of Dundas,
Hamilton, and other Canadian cities. First of all,
the people influenced tend to be people in organizations, those already concerned with other problems,
those who are aware and civic-minded. But this is
not exclusively so. When the Mayor of Richfield,
Ohio, travelled through Dundas, he asked a service
station attendant about mundialization and received
an answer. The school children who sell tags for the
the U.N. Special Account, their parents who attend
Dundas-Kaga Day exhibitions arranged by the Home and
School Association, the citizens who host visiting
Japanese children or the Canadian children who visit
Japan, the poster painters, bake sale bakers, tag

stringers, and envelope addressers are not elites of any sort, not even knowledge or information elites, they are just "Middle Canada" types of people who got caught up in interesting activities. But they do learn that people in other countries have interesting things to offer or send or show; that they are interested in what we show or send them; that other cultures are different in many ways, which is what makes them interesting, but terms like "inferior" and "superior" are meaningless; that foods, dress, dances, art forms, school terms, child-rearing practices, and the position of women do differ, but that many problems are similar, and many habits quite alike. Kids play baseball in Japan, and they have snowball fights, though under somewhat different rules. But the main lesson that comes shining through is the old cliché about the brotherhood of man--except it somehow ceases to be a cliché and becomes a living reality.

A sceptic once asked us: "If Canada and Japan ever went to war, don't you think that Kaga and Dundas kids would fight each other?" The answer is yes, of course. Once war starts, all is lost. But the change in public opinion may be such that it will just never happen. We will never even know what was prevented, because we cannot know alternate futures; but there is evidence, from studies of other transnational bonds (international nongovernmental organizations) that transnational bonds do strengthen world society to an extent that it can withstand the pressures and strains of international (really intergovernmental) conflict without breaking up. These bonds were not strong enough before World War I or II; they just *may* be strong enough now, but adding a bit more to that strength may add the vital extra safety factor to keep World War III away (2). Just as love in a good marriage can be strong enough to withstand even violent arguments without a breakup, so that largest of all social units, mankind as a whole, needs "the tie that binds," for we cannot hope to do away with the conflicts that will continue to test that strength.

The people influenced by mundialization are both organization people and ordinary people, although perhaps the former are more influenced. What about differential effects on the political spectrum? It has been our experience that the extreme right and the extreme left both reject mundialization. The extreme right abhors the "one world" theme and suspects vile plots to subvert the nation. For the extreme left, mundialization is too bland

and mild, does not "attack" social "evils," is not
sufficiently "against" anything. The moderate left
and centre is perhaps the most enthusiastic. The
moderate right (conservatives) is usually somewhat
reservedly willing to go along, and then discover to
their surprise that they *are* different from the far-
out conservatives who are opposed--who they previously felt were the same type of people as themselves.

Now we are ready to tackle the further question: Who *needs* to be reached? The simple answer
to this is "the majority, or at least a sizeable
minority so that the politicians take notice." Now
the majority of people are (by definition) at the
centre of the political spectrum. The people on the
extreme ends, both left and right, make a lot of
noise, are articulate, and work very hard to be publicly visible; but they are, after all, only a tiny
minority of the population, and any wise politician
knows that. They cannot move society without persuading or co-opting the great middle, as indeed nobody can, except by use of force.

And so our conclusion has to be that mundialization reaches precisely those people who need to be
reached in order to move the world toward a world
community. These people tend to be alienated by
demonstrations or other forms of confrontation politics, but the associative, unifying, integrationist,
participatory type of activity associated with mundialization appeals to them. They don't have to be
against anything, don't have to get angry or ex-
cited, but merely to enjoy warm friendships and enlarge their circle of interests and thereby enrich
their own lives.

It remains to be shown whether mundialization
affects these people deeply and lastingly enough.
The effect, though quite real and visible, has not
yet been proved to be strong enough to resist adversity, or persistent enough to remain in memory and
form a habit. To obtain this evidence, we will have
to observe mundialized communities for a longer time.
It is, of course, necessary to keep mundialization
activities going to prevent public forgetting, which
is only too easy. An active Mundialization Committee is a *sine qua non*.

And so, finally, we find that we cannot yet answer the primary question, *"Can mundialization contribute significantly to world peace?"* In all
truthfulness, we cannot possibly know the answer;
nor do we know it about any other peace action,
peace politics, peace education, peace research, and

so on. No one has yet attained permanent world
peace; so that in a sense we have all been failures
so far. Possibly we are moving in the right directions (some of our peace activities are), but we
have as yet no measuring sticks to determine rates
of progress or even directions of motion.

Kenneth Boulding once said (private communication), that he is more interested in peace dynamics
than in peace actions. If we take this to mean that
an understanding of what brings about peace followed
by responsible, deliberate actions based on that understanding, is more important than loud proclama-
tions or silent witness of our emotional or moral
commitment to peace, we fully concur.

If our tentative analysis is correct, mundialization can contribute to peace dynamics. It is
part of an emerging pattern of world integration, a
strand in the pattern of peace which is being woven,
slowly and patiently, before our eyes.

APPENDIX

The following is a list of towns and cities
which have mundialized in Canada (up-to-date to the
end of 1976); where there is a twin town it is
listed in brackets.
   Aurora, Ontario
   Brantford, Ontario (Osijek, Yugoslavia).
   Calgary, Alberta (Jaipur, India)*
   Courtenay, British Columbia (a town in Yugo-
     slavia)
   Dartmouth, Nova Scotia (Tema, Ghana)
   Dundas,Ontario (Kaga, Japan)
   Halifax, Nova Scotia (Accra, Ghana)
   Hamilton, Ontario (Mangalore, India) (also
     Fukuyama, Japan)

---

*The story of Calgary-Jaipur is an inspiring one
and should be included here. Professor T.K.N.
Unnithan, now at the Department of Sociology at the
University of Jaipur, spent some time in Calgary a
few years ago, and there heard about mundialization. After his return to Jaipur, he succeeded in
mundializing that city. He had also cooperated,
earlier, with Jim Nielsen in Calgary in mundializing Calgary. Now the two mundialized cities
twinned.
Unnithan reported that the rich of Jaipur are so
inspired by the generosity of the Canadians that

Kitchener, Ontario
London, Ontario
North York, Ontario
Oakville, Ontario (Popayan, Columbia)
Ottawa, Ontario (Georgetown, Guyana)
Paris, Ontario
Richmond Hill, Ontario
Rock Island, Quebec
St. Catharines, Ontario (Port of Spain, Trinidad)
Toronto, Ontario (Amsterdam, Netherlands)
Victoria, British Columbia
Waterloo, Ontario
West Flamborough, Ontario (St. Vincent in the Caribbean)

REFERENCES

1. Mead, Margaret. Alternatives to war. *Natural History*. Special Supplement, Dec. 1, 1967, 65-69.
2. Smoker, Paul. Nation-state escalation and international integration. *Journal Peace Research,* 1967, *1,* 61-75.

Since this article was written, we have had more time to observe and evaluate the activity. Originally we began mundialization as peace activists who had an idea that intuitively looked good; we rushed into mundialization activity without first developing a theory and found that it worked. We are now at the stage where we can say that it works well in practice, but will it work in theory? Here are some of our further thoughts about mundialization at this writing:

Richard Borden of Purdue has repeated the

---

they are donating money to purchase eye glasses for the poor, to pay for food for poor patients when they are in the hospital, and the hospital is donating its services. Other Indians were amazed to hear this. Apparently the rich tend to ignore the plight of the poor on the grounds that they are being punished for sins in a former life. Unnithan says that he thinks the value of this program to the esteem in which Indians hold Canada is the equivalent of a conventional foreign aid program worth a couple of a million dollars.

shocking experiments of Stanley Milgram and has
found that if a man or a person known to be in favour of violence is present as an observer of the
experiment (a woman who is in *uniform* is also perceived as being in favour of violence) then high
shocks are given by the subject. If the observer is
a woman or a person known to be opposed to violence
(a statement that the observer is a Quaker is sufficient stimulus), then smaller shocks are given.
However, the effect of any observer disappears as
soon as the observer leaves the scene. But so long
as the observer is present, the unspoken social approval or disapproval of violence acts as a catalyst
which influences the extent of violent behaviour.
We now think of the possible passage of laws in favour of peace and world law as adding to the possibilities for reducing violence *within* the mundialized community, especially if every year the citizens remind the community that it is mundialized by
having a tag day to raise money for the U.N. Special
Account.

Milgram has also done another experiment
("Small World") in which he found that when a student was given a letter to transmit to a stranger
some hundreds of miles away and told that it had to
pass from one friend to another, it took only three
or four intermediaries to get the letter to its destination. Without knowing of this experiment, we
used the technique in approaching members of City
Councils; we always asked members of the mundialization committee either to approach council members
whom they knew personally or to find someone else
who knew the council member; we had very little difficulty in finding such people.

We have found that if many people are to visit
the sister city, the airline economy round-trip
fare should be less thatn $1,000. If the sister
city has a different climate, such as St. Catharines
and Port-au-Spain, then many people will become involved in visits. St. Catharines charters 150 seats
on an aircraft in order to visit Trinidad at the
time of carnival and people from all walks of life
become involved. This is particularly valuable in
building a climate of opinion in favour of peace.

Individuals who have visited sister cities have
reported that their attitudes have changed as a result of such visits, and that they have become less
ethnocentric and more peace-minded. Twinning is
thus not just the icing on the mundialization cake,
but is also a very important vehicle for helping
people to change their attitudes at the speed that

people want to change and when they are ready to change.

One way of gauging just how much attitude change is needed in our various communities is to assume that a treaty for General and Complete Disarmament has been signed by our government but awaits ratification. The question to put to people then is, "Do you believe that your government would ratify the treaty?"

HANNA NEWCOMBE was born in Prague, Czechoslovakia in 1922 and came to Canada with her parents in March 1939. She graduated from McMaster University in Hamilton with a B.A. degree in chemistry in 1945; she was awarded the Chancellor's Gold Medal for academic achievement. She received her M.A. and Ph.D. degrees from the University of Toronto in 1946 and 1950, both in inorganic chemistry.

She was married to Alan Newcombe in 1946. While raising a family, she did part-time abstracting for Chemical Abstracts and conducted a scientific translation service. She taught chemistry part-time at McMaster University for four years.

Her understandable interest in international relations expressed itself in membership in the Women's International Relations Club as an undergraduate, and then from 1947 in membership in the World Federalists of Canada, and from 1960 in membership in the United Nations Association, and the Voice of Women, and the Chairmanship of the International Affairs Group of the University Women's Club of Hamilton.

In the spring of 1962, she took part in the campaign for funds for the Canadian Peace Research Institute. In April 1962, as a volunteer she began abstracting the peace/war literature for the Canadian Peace Research Institute, and in October 1962 she joined the staff of the Institute as editor of the Peace Research Abstracts Project, an endeavor which came to be shared with her husband in February 1963. In June 1964, the abstracts produced by this project were made available to the public in the form of PEACE RESEARCH ABSTRACTS JOURNAL. In January 1967, after some months of preparative work, this husband and wife team produced another journal--PEACE RESEARCH REVIEWS.

Hanna is also National Vice-President and Co-Chairman of the Policy/Political Action Committee of World Federalists of Canada, and President of the World Law Foundation (Canada). She is a member of the Emergency World Council, the World Federal Au-

thority Committee, an alternate delegate to the Peo-
ples Congress, a delegate to the World Constituent
Assembly (Innsbruck, June 1977), and a registered
World Citizen.

She has taught peace research at York University (Toronto), McMaster University (Hamilton, Ontario), and Mohawk College (Hamilton, Ontario).

She and Alan were awarded the Lentz International Peace Research Award in 1974. She also received a Peace Hero award from the World Federalists in 1973.

Hanna has served for many years as Treasurer of
the Canadian Peace Research and Education Association, and for a time served on the executive of
COPRED (Consortium on Peace Research, Education and
Development).

(See Chapter 1 for biographical note of Alan
Newcombe and for some other publications by Alan &
Hanna Newcombe.)

16. Transition from Violence in the International System

J. David Singer, Ph.D.

Confronted with the question of world peace, the concerned observer usually comes face-to-face with the need for "system transformation." That is, we come to recognize that the organization of peoples into nations and the patterns of interaction among those nations have given us unacceptable amounts of poverty, exploitation, and indignity, as well as an average of two international wars every three years. The possibility of system change, however, brings with it the probability of violence. We now have a global system in which almost all important change either rests upon, or leads to, violence. Whether it is the redistribution of wealth, power, or status, and whether the protagonists are individuals, ethnic groups, classes, or nationalities, we seem unable to achieve the desired changes without a high level of associated violence. Clearly, any global system that is so impervious to change without violence *must* be radically transformed.

But this is only half--and perhaps the easier half--of the problem. More difficult is the way in which such transformation might be brought about. One "lesson from history" is that the only things that are resisted more vigorously than changes in the *distribution* of wealth, power, and status within and among nations are changes in the *rules* and arrangements by which these valuables are distributed. As we look for ways in which we might accomplish, in a nonviolent fashion, the transformation of those arrangements (i.e., the structure and culture of a global system), we must cope with the problems of *positive feedback*--or self-amplifying feedback through which new changes are initiated. But once we arrive at that new state of global affairs, our preoccupation must be with the problem of *negative feedback,* or that which serves to maintain a relatively unchanged system. (The meanings of positive and negative feedback, as well as homeostatic mechanisms will become clearer in due course.)

When a social system--be it the family, the city, or the global society--is functioning in a reasonably satisfactory fashion, our objective is to keep it that way. More specifically, we want to be sure that the system can *adapt* to a wide variety of internal or external perturbations, rather than be sent off into a markedly different state by such minor stimuli. To put it another way, once a system is performing reasonably well for most of its inhabitants, it is desirable to keep it from either changing radically or from being so rigid that no changes at all can occur. To achieve and maintain such an appropriate equilibrium condition, the system must be dominated by the *negative*--or self-correcting--feedback that is provided by homeostatic mechanisms. When these self-correcting mechanisms are dominant, we experience a fair amount of flexibility and responsiveness in the system, but it never goes "too far." As one party or faction or nation gains too much power, for example, others tend to coalesce and redress the imbalance. Or as the supply of a desired commodity dwindles, its selling price goes up, and (in principle!) that leads to an increase in production and thence a decline in price, thus making for a reasonable relationship between supply and demand.

Nineteenth century liberals believed (with some justification) that the invisible hand of the self-correcting, negative feedback mechanism was actually at work within and among nations. But to believe that in the mid-twentieth century, one must be quite naive. Things have, as they say, gotten out of hand. In today's global system, the negative feedback mechanisms--political or economic--are just not performing very well. Thus, we must effectuate some radical changes in the system so that it once again becomes more self-correcting. In order to do so, as noted above, we need to initiate a number of self-amplifying, *positive* feedback, processes.

However, we have little knowledge regarding the best place to start, or which system characteristics to work on first, or how to mobilize the forces necessary to get started. Partly, this is because it will be a new experience if we *do* try to modify the global system in a conscious way. Also, it is safe

to assume that we will not only prefer different
strategies, but different outcomes. But an equally
serious handicap is that we have done little serious
research on system transformation at *any* level, from
the global down to the familial.

As depressing as this may be, it need not para-
lyze us. First of all, social scientists have made
a good many smaller discoveries, and some ingenious
yet careful synthesis of these might add up to a
modest "theory" of system transformation. Secondly,
if our most creative and competent social scientists
were to address themselves to this question *now,* we
might discover the key factors and optimal strategies before the system goes fully and irretrievably
out of control. And, third, even with *no* hard
knowledge, we must, as concerned and rational human
beings, at least give it a try. To do otherwise, if
my reading of the ongoing process is correct, is to
passively await the inevitable catastrophe.

The purpose of this paper is, however, more
modest. In it, I hope to sort out some of the factors that appear to be most culpable in making the
global system less and less habitable, and suggest a
few self-correcting arrangements that seem feasible
in the short run, and that might well start us onto
some of those positive, self-amplifying processes
that could move us away from today's dysfunctional
system. Thus, despite the need for radical *transformation,* it is equally important to address those
transitional mechanisms that might give us the time
to start the transformation process and perhaps move
us more rapidly into that critical phase of human
history.

NATION-STATE AND INTERNATIONAL SYSTEM

We begin with the international system as it is
--or, more accurately, as it appears to me--and try
to indicate which of its characteristics makes it
the setting for recurrent war. While examining
these characteristics and their associated processes, we should also be searching out those points
which might offer some leverage for possible system
change.

One of the more important but less obvious
characteristics of modern international politics is
the fact that a single set of individuals finds itself playing the dominant role in both national and
international politics. These are, of course, the
national political elites--those individuals who

comprise what is variously called the government, the regime, the administration, or, less frequently, the court. *Within* the national state there may well be other elites with a fair degree of autonomy who dominate provincial or local politics but who are subordinate to those who comprise the national regime. On the other hand, however, there does not yet exist any legitimate authority *above* the hundred-odd national regimes. Given the extraordinary durability of the doctrine of national sovereignty, most influence in international politics is exerted in a horizontal direction--nation vis-a-vis nation--and almost none in a downward vertical direction. There are, of course, many international organizations and even some supra-national ones, but they remain largely the creatures of their nation members; hence we speak of the global system as "subsystem dominant" (6).

One consequence of this state of affairs is that national elites constitute the major actors in both national and international politics (16). Moreover--and of central concern to us here--the demands of these two systems are often quite incompatible. Behavior which leads to success in one environment may often lead to failure or disaster in the other, and vice-versa. The balance of this paper will be addressed to: (a) the nature of the conflicting incentives, temptations, and constraints which are generated by both sets of systems; (b) the resulting inadequacy of their homeostatic mechanisms; and (c) some possible short-run modifications of a self-correcting nature which might reduce the magnitude of those conflicts which are so inevitably a part of international politics.

What makes a certain level of such conflict almost inevitable? In the global system, given the absence of legitimate supra-national authority, national elites have relied on the ultimate threat of military power as a means of defending "national interests" against possible interference by other nations. This traditional reliance on force as the final arbiter has, in turn, inhibited the growth of an alternative basis for inter-nation harmony: a widely accepted normative code which might permit more adaptive solutions to the inescapable conflicts and clashes of interest. In the absence of both coercive authority and normative consensus, and in the presence of many material and psychic scarcities, the only remaining basis for cooperative behavior is a utilitarian one--a payoff matrix which rewards short-run restraint and accommodative strategies.

And there is the rub. If two nations become involved in a conflict, the general options are two. The most natural, and probably the most frequent, response is to stand firm on the original conflict-inducing position, or perhaps to even increase the original demands. Within most well integrated national societies, this response tends to be applauded, and history suggests that it generally enhances the popularity of the regime. Moreover, this behavioral response tends to reinforce the existing norms of world politics ("this is the way things are done") and hence the probability that other nations will handle subsequent conflicts in the same general manner.[1] But this is a fairly standard and stylized opening round routine, and not particularly pregnant with danger. The critical question is whether the protagonists now succeed in "backing off" sufficiently so that normal diplomatic procedures can be brought into play, or whether one or both parties continue to press their claims in the original and more vigorous fashion.

The other general option is to recognize the opening moves for what they are and to then initiate and reciprocate moves of a more conciliatory nature. But the probabilities are all too high that the competence, courage, or patriotism of one or both sets of elites will then be challenged by the domestic opposition, be it a legitimate political party in a democratic system or a less institutionalized faction in a more autocratic system. Moreover, the efficacy of that challenge from the "outs" will generally be high, due largely to the prior actions of the "ins." That is, political elites cannot man an army and finance a military machine without some sort of psychological mobilization. In persuading an appreciable sector of their society that preparedness is necessary, they inevitably create a climate which must be relatively responsive to jingoistic appeals from the opposition. As a matter of fact, had some minimum psychic and material preparedness *not* existed prior to the conflict, there might well have been no conflict; had the nation been militarily weak or psychologically unprepared, the competitor would probably have had its way *without* any diplomatic conflict.

Having suggested the general linkages between the national and the international systems, creating largely incompatible sets of demands on the national elites, let me now describe some of the feedback processes in greater detail. My purpose here is to indicate more precisely where the self-aggravating

tendencies are greatest, and then go on to suggest
some possible feedback mechanisms whose effects
might tend more in the self-correcting, and less in
the self-aggravating, direction.

SELF-AGGRAVATING FEEDBACK

Given the limitations of space here, the most
feasible procedure is to bypass any thorough description of the structural, cultural, and physical
setting within which foreign policy decisions are
made and executed, and concentrate rather on those
few variables which are critical to the problem
which concerns us here. In my judgment, one of the
reasons for our failure to understand and more fully
control inter-nation conflict is the tendency to
treat such conflicts as discrete and separable
events. By viewing them rather as part of an oft-
recurring feedback process, we might better appreciate that the way in which any single conflict is
handled is both a consequence of prior such experiences and a predictor of the way subsequent ones
will be handled (3). The position taken here is
that intra-national and inter-national events all
impinge on one another in a cyclical and ongoing
process within which the self-aggravating propensities frequently exceed the self-correcting ones by
an unacceptably large amount. As I see it, there
are four points at which the self-aggravating effects of positive feedback are particularly cirtical
during the inter-nation conflict. Let us discuss
them, one at a time, noting how the traditional notions of confrontation between a government and its
citizenry have been replaced by highly symbiotic relationships.

Reconciling foreign and domestic policy needs.
The first point is found precisely at the apex of
the foreign policy hierarchy within the nations
themselves.[2] The political elites, often unwittingly, "paint themselves into a corner" in order to accomplish two short-run objectives when engaged in
diplomatic conflict. One objective is to demonstrate to the *foreign* adversary that they have both
the intent and the capability to stand firm, and the
other is to head off any potential *domestic* attack
based on the inadequacy of that intent and capability. In order to satisfy both these objectives,
however, the elites will oridnarily resort to the
kind of rhetoric which does little more than "raise

the ante" all around. The intended message to the
adversary may be merely one of firm determination,
but since it will be heard at home as well, it cannot be too conciliatory; as a matter of fact, by
making a commitment audible to the domestic audience, the decision makers may hope to make their
foreign policy threats more credible, given the domestic costs, real or apparent, of capitulation.

Assuming for the moment that the early verbal
behavior has demonstrated the appropriate degree of
firmness abroad and at home, what are the likely
consequences? The adversary's regime, of course,
"will not be intimidated," and so responds in public
messages to the several relevant audiences. At this
point in the scenario, if we are fortunate, the interactions shift toward quiet diplomacy, both domestic oppositions turn their attention to other matters, and the publics forget the episode in short
order. Suppose, however, that the prior episodes
had been so handled by the regime, the opposition,
and the media that there was sufficient public hostility toward this particular adversary, and, fur-
thur, that the opposition prefers not to let the issue drop out of sight. Quite clearly, the regime
takes a fairly serious domestic risk if it ignores
the cries for justice, revenge, national honor, and
so forth; but it takes a different (and also far
from negligible) risk of escalating the conflict if
it tries to satisfy the domestic critics.

Escalation. In order to examine the second
point at which positive feedback can get us into
serious trouble, we can focus on another set of factors. Let us assume, reasonably enough, that both
nations in the conflict are moderately well-armed by
contemporary (but nonnuclear) standards, but that
one enjoys a discernbile superiority over the other
in the relevant military categories, and that neither can turn to close allies for diplomatic or military support. The regime of the disadvantaged protagonist, having permitted the conflict to pick up
some momentum, now has the choice of: 1) bluffing;
2) retreating; or, 3) delaying while improving its
military position. The first can lead to a sharpen-
ing of the conflict and a more humiliating retreat
later (or even a stumbling into war), and the second
makes it vulnerable to political attack at home.
Thus, there is always some temptation to try to
close the manpower and weapons gap in order to bargain from a position of parity or even of greater
strength. If this route is taken, the regime will

first need to augment its program of psychological mobilization, without which neither the volunteers and conscripts nor the funds for weapon acquisitions might be forthcoming.

In the process of mobilizing public and sub-elite support for these preparedness activities, however, two new conditions are generally created. First, the adversary is not likely to sit idly by, watching its superiority disappear, and its regime therefore embarks on a similar set of programs. Second, both publics must become more persuaded of the need to resist the menace to their respective nation's security, and as a consequence, offer a more fertile ground for any militant domestic opposition. Given the almost irresistible temptation to exploit this state of affairs, the net effect is to raise hostility levels in both nations and therefore to raise the expectations as to what would constitute a satisfactory settlement, negotiated or otherwise. Since these rising expectations tend to be fairly symmetrical, neither regime is in as good a position to compromise as it was during the first round of the conflict. The probability of further escalation, diplomatic rupture, or war itself is now appreciably greater.

Mass communications. Let me now turn to a third source of danger in the cyclical conflict processes which seem to characterize so much of international politics. To this point, the role of the media has had little attention, yet mass communications would seem to play a particularly central role in helping the self-aggravating process along. Again, the differences between a highly autocratic and a relatively democratic nation are seldom as profound as contemporary Westerners prefer to believe. At almost any point along the autocratic-democratic continuum, the political elites need the media and the media need the political elites, be they regime or opposition. The regime relies on the media to help mobilize the population, to bargain with and ridicule the domestic opposition, and even to communicate with other nations.

While it may be simpler to arrange when the party in power exercises *formal* control over its mdeia, any effective and stable regime has little difficulty "managing the news." First of all, the words and actions of the elite are, by definition, newsworthy, and therefore widely transmitted. Secondly, members of the regime have control over information which can be of great help to the reporter

or commentator to whom it is made available. Thus,
by judicious release or righteous restraint, government officials can all too readily help or hinder
the careers of many media employees. Thirdly, as
regimes become more conscious of the need--and pos-
sibilities--of domestic propaganda, they begin to
recruit media people into their ranks as "public information" officers. Many newsmen are therefore involved in competition for these often attractive
bureaucratic positions, and one way to stay in the
running is to describe the appropriate agency's activities in a generally favorable fashion. While
access to, and control over, the media may not be
quite as simple for the "outs" as for the "ins,"
factions or parties in legal opposition are not
without the sorts of media amplifiers they need to
berate the regime for being devoid of courage, incapable of defending the nation's honor, or "soft ·
on------ism." In some nations, each political party
has its own newspaper, magazine, or radio station,
and in others, the possibility of the opposition
coming to power can make the media somewhat more responsive than might be expected.

I am not, in this section, arraigning the media
of most nations on charges of "selling out," although the charge would be far from groundless.
Rather, despite the existence of a vigorous and independent sector in the media services of many nations, the general impression is that the incentives
work to make these institutions a major factor in
amplifying inter-nation conflicts and contribute
to the positive feedback process.[3]

The societal power elite. The fourth and final
factor to be considered in this analysis is the effect which a nation's participation in an escalating
conflict can have upon the distribution of social,
economic, and political power within the society.
Without accepting those conspiratorial models which
see generals and "munitions makers" actively fomenting rivalry, conflict, and war, one must be extraordinarily naive to expect no systematic biases in
the foreign policy preferences of those who comprise
the military-industrial complex. Even more than
with newsmen, questions of ambiguity will regularly
tend to be resolved in the hard-line direction by
many military officers, corporate executives, labor
leaders, government bureaucrats, civil defense spe-
cialists, and technical consultants, as well as by
the standard phalanx of patriotic organizations.
Given the state of our knowledge about international

politics, most foreign policy problems are indeed matters of opinion, rather than fact, and in matters of opinion the point of view which usually gets the benefit of the doubt (i.e., the conventional wisdom) can be expected to win out most of the time.

The problem here, of course, is that in most nations the major positions of power--as well as the public plaudits--go to those who are in the ideological mainstream; this seems to hold even if the mainstream of the moment is allegedly pragmatic and nonideological, as in the United States of today and (probably) the Soviet Union of tomorrow. Having acquired power, prestige, and credibility by advocating or acquiescing in the modal foreign policy positions, these middle elites are seldom likely to shift toward a position which could be interpreted (or misinterpreted) as giving aid and comfort to the enemy, whoever the enemy of the moment may be.

Furthermore, as the intensity of the inter-nation conflict increases, the higher becomes the value of the professional and extra-curricular services of these middle elites. On top of this, as their individual influence and status increases, the *size* of their sector also increases. When the armed forces expand, officer promotions accelerate, and when more weaponry is being designed and produced, more engineers and technicians are promoted and recruited; even academics in the social and physical sciences find that foreign policy conflicts lead to increased opportunities for money, status, and influence in the modern world. The high energy physicist or the professor of biology has his role to play in the preparedness program, just as the political scientist or anthropologist finds himself consulting on log-rolling tactics in international organizations, military strategy, or counter-insurgency. If for no other purpose than to give intellectual legitimacy to the conventional wisdom, academics arealmost as likely to be co-opted into the foreign policy mainstream as are the more obvious members of the military-industrial complex.

My point here is that it does not take a so-called totalitarian regime to mobilize key sectors of the society. The basic properties of the sovereign national state in the industrial age are such that this mobilization occurs with little effort. No secret police, no dictatorial government, not even any veiled threats are required to generate the joint "conspiracies" of silent acquiescence and noisy affirmation once a nation becomes embroiled in a conflict of any intensity or a preparedness pro-

gram of any magnitude. For the past century or so,
the self-correcting mechanisms have gradually with-
ered, despite the assumptions of economic liberalism
and classical democratic theory. In the absence of
vigorous countervailing forces within the nations or
in the larger global community, the self-correcting
mechanisms of international politics are feeble indeed, with the consequence that all too many of the
inevitable conflicts among nations are free to grow
into costly rivalries and, occasionally, into tragic
wars.
      Is the interaction between and among nations in
global politics as dismal as I have painted it here?
Is the relative potency of our self-correcting mechanisms thus much less than that of the self-aggravating ones? Considering the paucity of scientific,
data-based research on global politics, and the absence of much evidence at either the micro- or
macro-level, it is a bold man indeed who will take
so dim a view and embrace so pessimistic an analysis. The picture may, admittedly, be overdrawn for
the sake of emphasis, and it may even be that as a
science of global politics develops, this character-
ization of the nation-state system will turn out to
have been seriously incomplete or inaccurate. Be
that as it may, responsible scholars must act on the
basis of the little that *is* known, even while working to enlarge that knowledge base, and the interpretation offered here will therefore have to suf-
fice for the moment. The word "act" is used quite
literally, since I intend in the next section to
shift from the diagnostic mode to that of prescription. Having described how these aspects of the
global system look to me, let me summarize a few
modifications that might possibly reduce the probability of any given conflict erupting into war, and
of any given war converting great parts of humanity
into a nuclear rubble. With so much at stake, it is
embarrassing to propose so little, but the approach
offered here may possibly generate some self-amplifying processes of its own.

SELF-CORRECTING FEEDBACK

      Assuming that this formulation is essentially
correct, and having emphasized that a great deal
more rigorous research is called for, I would single
out the communication and norm-setting centers in
the national societies as one of the more high-pri-
ority points of intervention. Until decision makers

become aware of the many ways in which their own behavior exacerbates conflicts, and converts the possibility of win-win outcomes into zero-sum ones, the
chances are they will continue to act in the traditional manner, and often find themselves, unexpec-
tedly, in situations from which extrication is costly or impossible [4] Journalists and commentators,
for example, could pay more attention to the effects
of such moves on the inter-nation conflict itself,
and less to the effects on the regime's popularity
vis-a-vis its domestic opponents (18). The various
private or semi-independent groups that exist to influence foreign policy or the public's attitudes toward it could devote as much of their attention to
the regime's comflict management techniques--and the
opposition's acquiescence in, or exploitation of,
such techniques--as they do to pursuing their own
particular and narrow goals or applauding "our side"
in world politics.

Perhaps more critical, but demanding much more
in the way of short-run self-sacrifice, is the need
for the political "outs" to play a less opportunis-
tic game. Support for a "vigorous defense of the
national interest" may win the opposition a word of
thanks from the regime, and criticism of "a policy
of appeasement" may win it some support from a large
sector of the public, but neither of these tactics
is likely to make the regime's diplomacy any more
successful.

Nor will they have led to any improvement in
the future. This is an utterly critical phenomenon
in all social processes, but it is very rarely acted
upon, or even appreciated, and may deserve more than
this passing allusion. Consider, for a moment, the
relationship between two classes of phenomena in any
social system: beliefs (including norms, values, an
and expectations) and behavior (including verbal,
decisional, and physical). Every public action, especially if taken by a highly visible reference figure, exercises some impact, however minor and however indirect, on the beliefs and attitudes of those
who observe or hear about the act. It may lead to
the strengthening and reinforcement of some attitudes among some people, and to the weakening or
modification of some attitudes among others.

Given this dynamic interdependence, it behooves
us to pay attention to the possible consequences of
every foreign policy action that occurs. Each act
of the opposition--no matter how weak its power, or
how cynical the public--helps shape those attitudes
which will, in turn, shape the behavior of many of

the participants in the foreign policy process. If,
for example, the "ins" and the "outs" are seen to
agree on the rights and wrongs of a foreign policy
conflict, many citizens will conclude that there *is*
no other reasonable position. And if they disagree
to the extent that the regime is accused of appeasement, the regime will either modify its policy in a
more militant direction, or try to *appear* as if the
policy were indeed at least as militant as that advocated by the opposition "outs." Either way, citizen attitudes will be strengthened in a more nationalistic and short-ranged direction.[5] Unfortunately,
many of those so influenced will be reference figures who, themselves, are "opinion influentials."

The importance of these positive feedback mechanisms is relevant not only *during* conflicts and
crises, but before and after. If a conflict is finally resolved in a more or less satisfactory fashion, the contending regimes are likely to emphasize
the diplomatic "victory" they have achieved by their
firmness in the face of the adversary. Once again,
this may enhance their prestige for a few weeks or
months, but the main effect is to increase the popular expectation that all subsequent conflicts will
end in victory-through-firmness. If it ends unsat-
isfactorily for one side, the norm is a refusal to
acquiesce in the "unjust" outcome, and a pledge to
redress the nation's grievances at the earliest opportunity. In either case, the prognosis for peaceful resolution of future conflicts is not favorable.
Likewise, there is a great and naive myth in many
more or less democratic societies that elections
have one function and one alone: to decide which
party or faction shall be in power. Thus, the campaign strategists first try to ascertain the dominant views of the various voting blocs and then proceed to pander to these views. With few exceptions,
then, election campaigns--because they receive fairly wide and sustained publicity--tend to serve as a
powerful reinforcement for existing views on many
domestic and some occasional foreign policy issues.
And, as I have already mentioned with some frequency, these are not views which make it easy for decision makers to pursue peace abroad and honor at
home.

For the information channels to play a useful
part in reducing the dominance of positive over negative feedback mechanisms in inter-national conflict, several groups will have to contribute.
Scholars need to identify which points are most
critical in different classes of conflict and which

behavioral patterns account for most of the self-
aggravating as well as self-correcting tendencies.
Journalists and other media people need to take a
more detached and critical view, accepting the important difference between their professional roles
and those of politicians.[6] Politicians need to appreciate the trade-off between short-run tactical
gains vis-a-vis the domestic opponent and the mid-
dle-run liabilities that accrue when, in negotiating
with foreign elites, they find little room for maneuver.

   At first blush, these look as if they might indeed be steps which individuals and groups in each
nation could take on a unilateral basis. If they
could be taken unilaterally, one might feel somewhat
more optimistic, but the fact is that too much progress along these lines in any single nation could
put that nation at a modest (some would say disastrous) disadvantage vis-a-vis other nations in the
global system (12). After all, each of these steps
implies--almost by definition--some reduction not
only in the level of political and psychological mobilization within the affected nation, but a longer-
range trend toward public resistance to the standard
mobilization appeals. When the attentive public in
a nation becomes more sophisticated, farsighted, and
tolerant of compromise with foreign powers, its regime may be at a disadvantage in diplomatic bargaining. As a matter of fact, a favorite ploy in such
bargaining is to inform the adversary that one's own
public (or legislature, or press, etc.) just would
not accept a particular settlement, and certain con-
cessions must therefore (and regrettably) be requested in order to get an agreement which could be
"sold" at home. If this is indeed an accurate pro-
trayal, the only way to start the trend toward more
realistic diplomacy is for the initiative to be tak-
en by those nations which are clearly in the strongest bargaining position in any such negotiations,
despite the modest risks.

   In addition to the possibility of certain unilateral measures, a number of *negotiated* arrangements should also be mentioned. Given my emphasis
on the role of the media in exacerbating many conflicts, let me begin there. One approach might be
to establish, in line with Quincy Wright's proposal
(19), an international "intelligence" center, whose
mission would be to monitor a representative sample
of the world's radio, film, TV, and newspaper output,
in order to ascertain the levels and growth rates of
self-aggravating (and self-correcting) emissions.

Using computerized content analysis techniques (5, 14,17), such an agency could publish weekly reports, thus providing a type of "early warning" to the governments and publics of the world.

Another approach might be a treaty or agreement, perhaps initiated by a group of nonaligned middle-powers, obliging governments to match each allocation of resources to military preparedness, with an equivalent or larger allocation to a specified nonmilitary activity. Given the upper limit on all nations' resources, the need to increase expenditures in agriculture, housing, education, or research, for each preparedness expenditure might well help to curtail preparedness programs and all that follows in their wake. A variation on this theme might be to base a nation's contribution to the United Nations system on military expenditure levels rather than on gross national product or access to hard currencies.

A third possibility--lying somewhere between the unilateral move and the negotiated arrangement-- is what I have called elsewhere, negotiation by proxy (15). Very simply, the idea is that several nations begin to experiment with the hiring of international law firms to handle certain types of diplomatic negotiations. The assumption is that foreign ministry officials, despite the folklore to the contrary, are indeed susceptible to the domestic political pressures which we discussed earlier, and that international bargaining could be partially de-politicized by assigning the task to skilled "mercenaries." With the intelligent design of procedures and fee schedules, some of the basic incentives for failure in negotiation could be replaced by incentives for success.

CONCLUSION

In this paper, I have tried to describe those relationships and behavioral propensities which account for a great deal of the positive feedback in the international system, and therefore convert many minor disputes into major conflicts. Now some will urge that the mechanisms which I propose in order to strengthen some of the negative feedback tendencies are little more than short-run palliatives, and that the system is basically inadequate in its present design. The charge is probably a fair one, but it is also somewhat beside the point; this is the nature of the system as it now stands, and our immediate concern is to devise those homeostatic mechanisms which will keep the fluctuations in conflict within the safe range.

Moreover, there may well be some "natural" tendencies toward more self-correcting behavior even in the absence of such innovations. For example, war has by and large not been a particularly effective conflict resolving technique in this century, and the nature of the cost-benefit ratio is increasingly appreciated. Certainly, nuclear weapons and missile delivery vehicles can do nothing but increase the ratio. Likewise, the drive for overseas possessions--once a major source of international conflict --has become less and less attractive. Colonialism, at least in its older form, just did not pay. A third element of built-in stability may be the increasing disenchantment with national states and nationalism; many of the world's people are beginning to look for alternative and more efficient forms of human organization (16). If this trend continues, many regimes will find it increasingly difficult to mobilize support for traditional foreign policies.

Despite these favorable possibilities, the need for supplementary control mechanisms nevertheless remains. We must of course explicitly differentiate between mechanisms which are designed to perform a largely homeostatic function, such as those outlined here, and those designed to initiate a self-reinforcing feedback process which might lead to fairly radical system transformation. We have merely alluded to some potential tendencies in this direction, and the need for further investigation is crucial. My major concern, then, has been to point out those properties of the international system which seem most mal-adaptive, and to indicate some possible short-run mechanisms of a more adaptive and self-correcting nature. If certain unilateral and multilateral innovations can be made, we may still be able to keep the dangerous, self-aggravating tendencies within safe limits, and thus retain the opportunity to find and exploit those which might lead us toward a system in which change is possible and violence is beyond the pale.

NOTES

1. Lest there be any misunderstanding, the analysis suggested here does not necessarily apply to *every* conceivable inter-nation conflict. While most such conflicts are, in my judgment, matters of routine

incompatibilities between and among traditionally
defined national interests, some do indeed raise legitimate issues of justice and morality. Unfortunately, we have not yet developed any generally accepted criteria for distinguishing between the two
types of case and even if we could, nationalistic
appeals would often overwhelm them.

2. For the sake of simplicity here, I not only assume that there is a viable opposition in most nations but that the political spectrum is largely
based on a two-faction, quasi-pluralistic division,
with one or the other in power at a given time.
These are, of course, drastic simplifications, but
do not affect the argument which concerns us here.

3. Some informative and suggestive interpretations
of the media's role in foreign policy are Cohen (1),
Kruglak (7), Reston (13), Nimmo (11), and Hale (4).

4. In almost every government agency or corporation, there is a controller (or comptroller) whose
major assignment is to watch budgetary income and
outgo, and to issue warnings when they tend to get
out of balance, or look as if they might do so.
Perhaps every foreign ministry ought to have an an--
alogous officer whose sole responsibility is to
watch for those trends which signal a potential loss
of diplomatic maneuver.

5. There is an extensive literature on bipartisanship in U.S. foreign policy, but it tends to look at
only one part of the problem. Revering the traditional doctrine that "politics must stop at the
water's edge" in the name of patriotism, it seldom
notes the frequency with which bipartisanship produces a conspiracy of silence. Since foreign policy
is rarely an issue in national or local elections,
the electorate is most unlikely to hear any criticism (thoughtful or otherwise) of the regime in this
regard. And when it *is* an issue (usually too late
in the game), the parties usually seek to out-do one
another in simplistic appeals.

6. They could probably get some reinforcement in
this task from the more alert and concerned consumers of national media. One possible mechanism might
be the establishment of some sort of readers' pressure group which could single out certain newspapers
and periodicals from time to time, publicize the
more serious distortions which they perpetuate

and try to organize "subscribers' strikes." If such
errors of fact and interpretation were called to the
attention of publishers and editors by a readership
wich is in a position to impose a temporary boycott,
some progress might be made. And since much of the
propagandistic material in the newspaper and radio
reports must be traced to the wire services, these
transmitters might then begin to demand higher standards from UPI, AP, Reuters, Tass, and the rest.

REFERENCES

1. Cohen, Bernard C. *The Press and Foreign Policy.*
Princeton, N.J.: Princeton University Press,
1963.
2. Deutsch, Karl W. *Nerves of Government.* New
York: Free Press, 1963.
3. Deutsch, Karl W., & Merritt, Richard. Effects
of events upon national and international images.
In Herbert C. Kelman (Ed.), *International Behavior.* New York: Holt, Rinehart & Winston, 1965,
132-187.
4. Hale, O.J. *The Captive Press in the Third Reich.*
Princeton, N.J.: Princeton University Press,
1964.
5. Holsti, Ole R. *Content Analysis for the Social
Sciences and Humanities.* Reading, Mass.:
Addison-Wesley, 1969.
6. Kaplan, Morton A. *System and Process in International Politics.* New York: Wiley, 1957.
7. Kruglak, Theodore E. *The Two Faces of Tass.*
New York: McGraw-Hill, 1963.
8. Maruyama, Magoroh. The second cybernetics: de-
viation-amplifying mutual causal processes.
American Scientist, 1963, *51,* 164-79.
9. Miller, Warren. Voting and foreign policy. In
James N. Rosenau (Ed.), *Domestic Sources of Foreign Policy.* New York: Free Press, 1967, 213-
230.
10. Milsum, John (Ed.), *Positive Feedback.* Oxford:
Pergamon, 1968.
11. Nimmo, Dan. *Newsgathering in Washington.* New
York: Atherton, 1964.
12. Osgood, Charles E. *An Alternative to War or
Surrender.* Urbana, Ill.: University Illinois
Press, 1962.
13. Reston, James. *The Artillery of the Press,* New
York: Harper & Row, 1966.
14. Singer, J. David. Media analysis in inspection
for disarmament. *Journal Arms Control,* 1963, *1*

(3), 248-60.

15. Singer, J. David. Negotiation by proxy. *Journal Conflict Resolution*, 1965, *9*(4), 538-41.

16. Singer, J. David. The global system and its sub-systems. In James Rosenau (Ed.), *Linkage Politics*. New York: Free Press, 1969, 21-43.

17. Stone, Philip *et al*. *The General Inquirer*. Cambridge, Mass.: M.I.T. Press, 1966.

18. Waltz, Kenneth. Electoral punishment and foreign policy crises. In James N. Rosenau (Ed.), *Domestic Sources of Foreign Policy*. New York: Free Press, 1967, 263-293.

19. Wright, Quincy. Project for a world intelligence center. *Journal Conflict Resolution*, 1957, *1*(1), 93-97.

J. DAVID SINGER is Professor of Political Science at the University of Michigan, and a member of its Mental Health Research Institute. After serving in the U.S. Navy during World War II and the Korean War, he took his Ph.D. in International Politics at New York University. Since 1956, he has taught at Vassar College, the Naval War College, and the Universities of Oslo and Geneva, as well as at Michigan. A pioneer in peace research and the scientific study of world politics, he has published 90-odd articles and a number of innovative books in the field; among these are FINANCING INTERNATIONAL ORGANIZATION; DETERRENCE, ARMS CONTROL, AND DISARMAMENT; HUMAN BEHAVIOR AND INTERNATIONAL POLITICS; and QUANTITATIVE INTERNATIONAL POLITICS.

Dr. Singer is the recipient of many honors and grants, including in 1956 serving as a Ford Fellow, in 1957-8 a Ford Foundation grant, in 1959 a Phoenix Memorial Fund grant, from 1963 to 1967 a Carnegie Corporation grant, in 1963-64 appointment as a Fullbright Research Scholar, and from 1967 to 1975 a National Science Foundation grant.

He has served as editor and as a member of the editorial board of many professional journals; at present, he is on the boards of the Journal of Conflict Resolution, Transaction, Journal of Peace Re-Search, Journal of Politics, *and* Political Science Reviewer. *In 1972-73, he was President of the Peace Research Society.*

Dr. Singer has consulted to many agencies including: Institute for Defense Analyses, Bendix Systems Division, Historical Evaluation & Research Organization, U.S. Arms Control and Disarmament Agency, U.S. Naval War College, U.S. Department of

*Defense, U.S. Naval Ordnance Test Station and U.S.
Department of the Navy.*

SOME OTHER PUBLICATIONS BY J. DAVID SINGER

- *Financing International Organization: The United
  Nations Budget Process.* The Hague: Martinus
  Nijhoff, 1961.
- *Deterrence, Arms Control and Disarmament: Toward
  a Synthesis in National Security Policy.* Colum-
  bus: Ohio State University Press, 1962.
- *A General Systems Taxonomy for Political Science.*
  New York: General Learning, 1971.
- *On the Scientific Study of Politics: An Approach
  to Foreign Policy Analysis,* New York: General
  Learning, 1972.
- With Melvin Small. *The Wages of War, 1816-1965:
  A Statistical Handbook.* New York: Wiley, 1972.
- With Susan Jones. *Beyond Conjecture in Interna-
  tional Politics: Abstracts of Data-Based Research.*
  Chicago: Peacock, 1972.
- Editor, with George Kish. *The Geography of Con-
  flict.* Ann Arbor: *Journal Conflict Resolution,*
  1960. (special issue)
- Editor, *Weapons Management in World Politics.* Ann
  Arbor: *Journal Conflict Resolution,* 1963. (spe-
  cial issue).
- Editor, *Human Behavior and International Politics:
  Contributions from the Social-Psychological Sci-
  ences.* Chicago: Rand McNally, 1965.
- Editor, *Quantitative International Politics: In-
  sights and Evidence.* New York: Free Press, 1968.

17. The World Order Models Project: Toward a Planetary Social Change Movement

Ian Baldwin, Jr.

This article describes the first phase of the World Order Models Project (WOMP I) at the Institute for World Order* in New York.   The research directors for the project were as follows:
   SAUL H. MENDLOVITZ, Rutgers University Law School and the Institute for World Order, was overall director of WOMP I.   RAJNI KOTHARI, director of the Centre for the Study of Developing Societies, Delhi, represented an Indian perspective on world order; YOSHIKAZU SAKAMOTO, Faculty of Law, University of Tokyo, a Japanese; ALI A. MAZRUI, formerly Dean, Faculty of Social Sciences, Makerere University, Kampala, now at the Department of Political Science, University of Michigan, sub-Saharan Africa; RICHARD A. FALK, Woodrow Wilson School of Public and International Affairs, Princeton University, the United States; JOHAN GALTUNG, Institut du Development, Geneva, represented a nonterritorial perspective; and GUSTAVO LAGOS, Faculty of Law, University of Chile and HORACIO GODOY, UNDP, Bogota, a Latin American perspective.
   In addition, participants from the Soviet Union, Egypt and an unofficial spokesman for the People's Republic of China took part in many of the discussions and meetings that preceded the publication of the first WOMP I manuscripts.
   The World Order Models Project (WOMP) is a self-conscious part of larger, nonviolent social change processes that, hopefully, will lead toward a planetary social change movement.
   WOMP grew out of an attempt by the Institute

---

*Formerly The World Law Fund.

for World Order to implement a nonviolent but drastic change in the world political system. Six perceptions animate the Fund's approach to this massive
social change task:

(1) The world political system needs to be radically changed if war (and ultimately thermonuclear
war), massive poverty and widespread social injustice are to be eliminated or substantially allevi-
ated.

(2) In any event, drastic system change, positive or negative, is likely to occur soon, that is,
before the end of this century.

(3) Given the suffering and frequently adverse
social results of violence, and given the present,
hideous technological scale of violence, it is the
responsibility of concerned humans to work for nonviolent strategies that could achieve basic changes.

(4) Given the urgency imposed by the time
frame in which serious changes must occur--one to
three decades--and the commitment (which is not,
however, necessarily and invariably an absolute one)
to nonviolent strategies of transformation, serious
efforts must be made to convince elites in and out
of governments that drastic systemic changes should
be implemented as a matter of national, regional and
world policy.

(5) Because political elites are, in effect,
"trapped" by the knowledge and expectations of their
own national constituencies,[1] it is necessary to
generate new approaches to world order within educational environments throughout the world.

(6) Finally, because of the global commitment
to ever higher levels of universal education, a
worldwide curriculum reform movement--which is of
course an inherently nonviolent process--does in
fact have a chance of generating a large planetary
constituency for world order values.

WOMP is the advance guard of a nascent educational movement whose goal is to introduce the study
of the future--organized around the interrelated
questions of *world order*, namely, how do you eliminate the institutional bases of war, poverty and social injustice--into educational settings throughout
the planet. At the outset, the WOMP participants
insisted on the interconnected nature of the global
problems confronting humankind: "It is quite
clear that a world without war is at least as impossible to create in the absence of minimum conditions
of economic well-being, social injustice and political participation as the latter are to achieve in a
war-torn world."[2] World order study and research

investigates these problems as values to be realized
    So saturated with history are the problems of
world order that there is a deep-rooted tendency to
regard them as ineradicable. The elevation of war,
poverty and social injustice (e.g., racial prejudice, religious intolerance) from their preconscious
status as natural phenomena to social problems capable of rational solution is a first step crucial to
their demythologization. To link the task of intellectual understanding of the problems with that of
realization of their countervailing values (war-
peace, poverty-economic welfare, social injustice-
justice) deepens the process that seeks the transformation of global society.
    Comprehension of the problems and clarification
of the values at stake are efforts not sufficient to
give human beings access to a future they desire.
Individuals need to consciously envision the future
each wants. The study of world order (which may be
the cornerstone of any larger effort aimed directly
at the transformation of the world community) requires each student to imagine a world in which the
crucial problems are to a large extent solved--and
the world order values are realized. The involvement of millions of students in deliberate imagining
of concrete, desirable futures might liberate powerful social energies on a worldwide basis.

TOWARD A WORLD CURRICULUM REFORM MOVEMENT

    To launch a world curriculum reform movement,
it was necessary to bring together persons from diverse societies representative of the social complexity of the real world. The legitimacy, and
therefore, ultimately, the effectiveness of such a
movement will depend on the extent to which it has
achieved the creative participation of outstanding
individuals throughout world society.
    Between 1966 and 1969, Saul Mendlovitz, overall
director of WOMP I, recruited outstanding scholars
from Japan, India, West Germany, the Soviet Union,
sub-Saharan Africa, Latin America, the United States
and Norway (representing a nonterritorial perspective). These scholars in turn formed their own
search teams. Each team was responsible for making
a diagnosis of the present world order from its own
national-regional perspective, with specific reference to the values that were to be achieved. The
trends discerned as being unfavorable (and favorable) to the values were then extrapolated to the

decade 1990 in an effort to understand the magnitude
of some of the obstacles (and positive forces) which
lay in the path of the values.

The directors also took as their task the formulation of models which outlined world orders they
believed to be both desirable and achievable by the
decade 1990. Each director agreed that a model of
"world order" is one in which war, poverty and social injustice are minimized, or, alternatively, in
which peace, economic welfare and social justice are
maximized beyond their present levels of realization.
Furthermore, each director was asked to give particular attention to the constitutional dimensions of
his world order model.

Models of world order are not solely preferential descriptions of hypothetical world economic and
political systems in which the fundamental authori-
tative processes of government--at national, regional and world levels--are outlined in some detail.
Each model also had to contain guidelines for its
own creation. Each director had to recommend concrete "transition steps" that could bring the model
into being. In turn, these transitional recommendations had to be grounded in historical social processes which can be seen to operate in a long-term
positive direction. In other words, each director
(or research group) had to work with a theory of social change on which he could build specific action
proposals. Such proposals could take the form of
policy recommendations oriented toward governmental
elites, and/or could be suggestive of culturally
more radical actions likely to appeal to counter
elites. The nature of these transition steps of
course depended on the intensity of the director's
commitment to the specific values to be achieved and
on his own orientation toward what he imagined to be
the "reality" of the world political system.

There was, however, a strong predisposition
among almost all the directors for the achievement
of *drastic* system change by the 1990's. Each was
also oriented toward discovering--through basic research, imagination and action--*nonviolent* strategies of transformation. This latter orientation is
of course inherent in WOMP's commitment to the
achievement of world peace.

As a group, the WOMP participants met well over
hald a dozen times since 1967 in various places
throughout the planet. After some eight to ten
years, most of the directors submitted manuscripts
for worldwide publication and distribution on a regional basis. In addition, each director submitted

an essay, written for the general reader, which has
been published in a single volume of essays, edited
by Saul H. Mendlovitz.* These books help to provide
a core of instructional materials that is now available for use in educational environments throughout
the world. The involvement of increasing numbers of
students, academic and other public figures in the
shaping of other related materials and in the critical evaluation and teaching of this initial set of
materials hopefully will be the first step toward
the creation of a planetary constituency committed
to the realization of world order values.

THE METHODOLOGICAL PERSPECTIVE OF WOMP

TOWARD A PLANETARY-SPECIES ORIENTATION

     WOMP came into being against a background domi-
nated by the persistent failure of world legal, economic and political mechanisms to lessen the incidence and scale of international violence, poverty,
and racial injustice. The core of the problem
rested in the fact that supposedly "world" mechanisms were, of course, inter-nation mechanisms in
which the notion of a *world interest,* articulated on
behalf of the *whole* world community, was never
allowed to emerge in any predominant way. The world
waits, even now, for the articulation of world policy recommendations which, when necessary, can be put
into effect by world, as well as regional, national
and local institutions.
     In confronting the question, where do we begin?
Mendlovitz and the Institute turned to a community

_____

*Saul H. Mendlovitz. *On the Creation of a Just
World Order* (1975).
Other titles published are: Rajni Kothari. *Foot-
steps into the Future* (1974); Richard A. Falk. *A
Study of Future Worlds* (1975); Ali A. Mazrui. *A
World Federation of Cultures* (1977); Gustavo Lagos
and Horacio Godoy. *The Revolution of Being* (1977);
and Johan Galtung. *The True Worlds* (in editorial
development).
All of these books are published in North America
by the Free Press. In addition, some have been
published in Europe by North Holland, in Africa by
the Ohana Publishing Co., and in India by Orient
Longmans. Iwanami Shoten in Tokyo is contracted
to translate the series into Japanese.

of human beings likely to be more free than any other to focus on the objective requirements of the
problems of world order--a community Karl Mannheim
long ago termed the "free intelligentsia." The rise
of a free intelligentsia has provided the world with
a class of human beings who in varying degrees are
able to cross inherited social, economic, political
and cultural boundaries.* As Mannheim put it, "Participation in a common educational heritage progressively tends to suppress differences of birth, status, profession, and wealth, and to unite the individual educated people on the basis of the education
they have received."[3] Mannheim also pointed out
that the social-situational, political-ideological,
fragmented character of all knowledge "implies the
possibility of an integration of many mutually complementary points of view into a comprehensive
whole."[4] Thus WOMP I came into being, not only for
the purpose of investigating the causes of planetary
danger and of making concrete policy recommendations
based on insight into the causes, but also for the
purpose of bringing together a group of scholars and
intellectuals from various nations, cultures, ideologies and races as a first step toward the creation
of a planetary collegium whose members could ultimately share, speak for and act upon a common set of
values and priorities framed within a world interest
perspective.
     Of course, there were many tensions and diffi-
culties built into this complex sociological task.
One of the research directors, citing a major characteristic of WOMP, has described it as an attempt
to deal with world problems in regional perspective,
on the one hand, and regional problems in world perspective, on the other.[5] Each director was asked to
represent what he considered to be the aspirations
and legitimate interests of the region or nation of
which he is a part. At the same time, each director
had to reconcile potential conflicts between the
national-regional interest and whatever he conceived
to be the world interest. In speaking for the group
as a whole Mendlovitz gave some focus to the complexity of the process: "At the very outset we recognized that not only is there a difficulty in the research directors acting as 'true representatives of
(a given) area' but in fact...there is an ambiguity

---

*It should be noted that the Russian participants,
in particular, may not subscribe to the social
theory presented here.

between their acting as representatives of an area
and attempting to perform as world citizens. My own
personal resolution of that problem was to see it as
a crucial methodological issue, and to work with it
as an issue during the process of our joint research
effort."[6]

WORLD ORDER VALUES

     The WOMP participants tried to shape a radical-
ly different perspective on international affairs.
The world order perspective is above all conditioned
by its orientation to an *explicit* set of values.
Yoshikazu Sakamoto stated that the "fundamental
reason why we pay serious attention to the values is
the fact that values are values precisely because
they are not completely realized in the actual
world, and because they will not be realized in the
future unless we make efforts in that direction."[7]
Any problem of a massive, pervasive sort is unlikely
to be solved unless broad sectors of society inter-
nalize a value response to the problem, an internalization that gains enough psychological weight in
enough minds to generate a social movement animated
by the profound desire to solve the problem and
realize the value. (The histories of slavery and
colonialism are perhaps instructive in this respect.) Although no value is absolute, history reflects the significance accorded to certain values
over time.
     At the outset of WOMP I, all the directors
agreed that peace, economic welfare and social justice were core values whose realization throughout
the world was increasingly imperative. Other values
could have been added to this core provided it could
be demonstrated that they were causally related to
the realization of the initial values.
     An essential task of WOMP I was to clarify the
meaning of the values--including the setting of minimal and maximal standards--and to develop indicators for measuring progress or regress of each value
in world, regional, and national settings. Theories
had to be created to show how the values might be
implemented. Built into this process of value clar-
ification and construction of social change theory
were the tensions inherent in the various value combinations. One of the Russian directors reiterated
that values, being hierarchial, were not in themselves the determining social factors, but their
hierarchical arrangement, the differing moral and
political weight assigned to each core value, was

decisive. Their ordering was not "an abstract ethical question, but an entirely practical problem, for
these 'preferred worlds' will be acceptable according to the preference for one or another hierarchy
of values."

Different approaches to the tensions inherent
in any combination of these and related values were
taken by several of the research directors. Since
the process of achieving value consensus had to un-
derlie any attempt to form a nonviolent planetary
social change movement, it is interesting to briefly
review some of the diversity of perception about
values among the WOMP I participants. For instance,
Sakamoto claimed that no value could be introduced
into the core if it were mutually exclusive with one
or more of the core values. The values themselves
must not be incompatible, a situation which could
arise "if one of the values is maximized at the cost
of the other two." Sakamoto went on to point out
"what is essential is the optimization of a set of
values, which is quite different from maximization
of individual values."[8]

In addition to the agreed-upon core, Richard
Falk added the value of "environmental quality" as a
fourth "primary value." Each of these four values
is intimately related, according to Falk, in ways
that vary according to their different possible decisional settings. "Each concrete decisional setting needs to be examined in the light of its expected value consequences and the decision reached
justified by a reasoned explanation of its *net* effects." Thus, a course of policy action that
avoided the use of violence with respect to, say,
the grievances of the blacks in the United States
(economic welfare, social justice) might have to be
abandoned for another policy employing violence, or
some measure or types of violence, in southern
Africa. Falk therefore foresaw great diversity of
policy action flowing from concrete attempts to
realize the four values throughout the planet. According to him, one criterion that might emerge as
universal to the deliberations of policy makers and
social change activists is "a strong presumption
against irreversible damage" that might emerge on a
broad scale as a consequence of any given policy action.

Ali Mazrui suggested the ingenious notion of
"carrier values," at least within the setting of
sub-Sahara Africa. Given the instability and unpre-
dictable nature of political power in Africa, how
could a continued national oppenness to the three

core values be maintained. He asked what the elements were that might make national cultures responsive to the "triple value orientation" of world order, regardless of what regime is in power. "A different set of vaues might have to be added as Trojan
horses to bring in the triple orientation" of welfare, justice and minimization of violence. Mazrui
posited that, at least in the case of sub-Saharan
Africa, three such "carrier values" might help
African societies to be positively oriented to the
world order values: the carriers he posed are "tolerance," "toil," and "teamwork." Mazrui was particularly concerned that tolerance be implanted as a
value in the political socialization process in
Africa. "What Africa needs more than anything else
is *tolerance* in relations between tribes, classes,
races, ideological groups, social class, etc....be-
cause intolerance in African conditions is too brutal. My liberalism is therefore oriented not toward
'individual freedom' initially but toward 'intergroup tolerance' first and foremost."

This world order investigation was thus deliberately prescriptive. It sought social change. "A
social science methodology," according to Johan
Galtung, "that changes from emphasis on 'facts' to
emphasis on 'values' may be more open to human concerns, less fatalistic in its determinism and its
reification of the factual, its elevation of that
which happens to be empirical today into more eternal laws." A social science with an explicit emphasis on specified values is impelled to seek ways in
which those values can be achieved, and thus becomes,
not incidentially, a part of social change processes.
It could become the knowledge template, not on which
the status quo is maintained (as so often has been
the case), but on which an action-oriented movement
could grow and be intellectually nourished.

By themselves values are, nonetheless, inadequate constructs for investigating the future with
the purpose of liberating the present from the bondage to the past.

*WORLD ORDER MODELS: UTOPIAS, RELEVANT UTOPIAS AND
PREFERRED WORLDS*

Investigators concerned about the future have
been warned that failure to work with the imagination to create other and better futures would lead
to endless projections of present trends and a petty
unfolding of technological possibilities which would
in the end leave man crippled."[9] Part of the metho-

dological and social purpose of WOMP I was to provide people with a liberating perspective on world
order problems. The design of utopias (models),
"relevant utopias," and "preferred worlds" was a
central part of the WOMP I undertaking. Here a
utopia was taken to be any description of a social
system qualitatively different from the present.
One function of utopia design was to free the imagination of the investigator; to give him or her the
creative space necessary to break out of patterns of
thinking imposed by inherited, traditional notions
of what constitutes "reality."

The construction of the researcher's model was,
however, usually (though not necessarily) preceded
by other steps. Thus, once the values were established and given some operational meaning, the first
step the researchers usually engaged in was diagnosis of their national or regional and world situations, a diagnosis which was guided by their commitment to maximizing the core values and to minimizing
the corresponding problems. Once a diagnosis was
made, the central tendencies or trends within the
relevant social-political contexts had to be extrapolated to the decade 1990. Given a disparity between the probable world the researcher saw ahead
and the utopia he desired, the researcher had to construct, as concretely as possible, his utopia, that
is, a model or image of the world in which particular attention was paid to "the constitutive order of
the fundamental and general political and social
processes which determine when and how violence will
be used, and the manner in which the values...are
distributed."[10]

Further, to be "relevant" another component had
to be added to the utopia or model: the researcher
had to describe transitional processes and strategies that could bring it into being. These transition steps did not need to be politically feasible;
they had to be sufficiently clear so that probability could be evaluated. The degree to which they
were intellectually credible (within the realm of
possibility) and morally persuasive would determine
the degree to whcih people could be motivated to act
on their behalf. Mendlovitz pointed out that the
process of evaluating the relevance of utopias and
transition steps is deeply complicated by the sociology of knowledge problem: "In formulating and attempting to establish the validity, persuasiveness,
desirability or likelihood of a utopia, we are faced
with the difficulty of overcoming many biases built
into the gathering and selection of facts....The

biases built into the fact-gathering and selection
process can be at least partially overcome if all
formulations of world order models are given a common examination by representatives of as many parts
of world society as possible...What is unfeasible,
unpersuasive, or undesirable to one observer or nation may be feasible, persuasive and desirable to
another...It may, in fact, be likely that the preferred world system which is finally agreed upon,
will consist of components or combinations of various relevant utopias, many of which were thought to
be 'irrelevant' by large numbers of people."[11]

A final step consisted in formulating a "preferred world" by selecting elements from a range of
utopias and relevant utopias and shaping a single
relevant utopia that became in effect the researcher's recommendation for a new world order. Any relevant utopia recommended by a researcher as his model of world order became his "preferred world."

There was some disagreement among the directors
as to the degree of specificity that should be in-
vested in a model or utopia. Falk cautioned against
the "fallacy of premature specificity," advising
that although legal processes could give rise to
normative expectations as well as be the end result
of those expectations, "the mechanics of administrative management are an outgrowth of political consciousness rather than its source." Mazrui took an
even more radical stance with respect to the WOMP I
mandate to provide an explicit constitutional framework for a preferred world. Claiming that the "very
idea of constitutional and judicial solutions was...
itself deeply rooted in American political and legal
experience," he went on to say, "It is a postulate
of the African perspective that the transmission of
ideas and their internalization are more relevant
for world reform than the establishment of formal
institutions for external control."

Just as many value scheme were possible, so too
was a range of model types. The "behavioural" model,
according to Mendlovitz, was detailed, constitution-
ally concrete (along the lines of Clark and Sohn's
World Peace Through World Law); there was little
room for ambiguity about who will make what decisions how. Mendlovitz argued that given the general
erosion of authority in the world, there was an
"openness" in the international system, a political
vacuum in which "it may be most sensible to state
one vision rather definitively. In so doing, we
will have provided a rallying point for the world
peace movement, giving ourselves a measuring rod as

to whether or not we are achieving our goals, and
provide some guidance for a world which sorely
needs it."[12] The danger here is that the organizational forms, which are but political means, tend
to become ends in themselves, at the expense of the
real goals, and that the institutional specificity
of the model may lead the observer to feel there is
a rigidity about it that precludes alternatives and
compromises.

At a time when legal and political flexibility
is an imperative need of the evolving world political order such rigidity could become dysfunctional.
A more open-ended model, on the other hand, would be
based on the perception that there is a constant
self-modifying feedback between the initiatives
made on behalf of a given set of goals and the social and political processes such initiatives set in
motion.   There is an organic social process at work
whose concrete end results are probably always impossible to specify. On the other hand, a model's
lack of clearly specified institutional forms may
render it useless as a political instrument capable
of attracting large numbers of pragmatic people
willing to work for its realization.

VIOLENCE AND THE PROBLEM OF TRANSITION

Probably no intellectual activity in WOMP I--
including the making of a firm diagnosis-prognosis
and a detailed preferential statement of an alternative world system--was more demanding than the formulation of a coherent, persuasive strategy for
drastic world system change. (This is the problem
which, more than any other, continues to enlist the
energies of the WOMP directors.) No model or utopia
could be *relevant* without built-in strategies for
social and political transformation of a potentially
large-scale character; no image of the world could
be preferred that did not confront this essential
task.   The task of creating a relevant utopia was
made even more difficult by the inclusion of the
value "peace." *Violent means cannot readily be recommended for the achievement of the world order values.*

The difficulty of avoiding transition steps
that might employ some measure of violence becomes
more apparent in the context of the future. Whether
the violence is of the direct, physically damaging
sort (e.g., wars) or the indirect, structural sort
(e.g., poverty, racism), its incidence and intensity

seem likely to increase during the remainder of this
century.

Structural violence, no matter how well sanc-
tioned it may be by history, has become increasingly
intolerable for increasing numbers of people. Gustavo Lagos asserted early in WOMP I, that "the
eagerness of marginal persons, nations, and regions
to participate, supported by an egalitarian ideology
of worldwide diffusion, will be the decisive sociological, cultural and political factor" in the
achievement of a preferred world order. Lagos noted
that the egalitarian revolution was an ongoing process with deep historical roots and precedents. The
exposure of masses of human beings, via the media
and transportation systems, to levels of affluence
beyond their reach created a cumulative demand for
access to material values. The exposure of increasing numbers of educated young people to western concepts of justice served to heighten these basic social pressures.

However, at the same time that egalitarian ideologies have generated powerful, historically-rooted
demands for justice and economic well-being, scien-
tific-technological revolutions have made violence
increasingly dysfunctional. In recent centuries,
technology has been a potent subconscious value
whose autonomy has hastened the disruption not only
of social systems but also natural ecosystems--even
at the global level. War itself is no longer solely
a genocidal activity. The so-called "limited" war
in Vietnam was actually a virtually *unlimited* war of
both genocidal and ecocidal proportions, at least
for the people and landscape of Indochina.

Quite apart from the problem of the rising potential for physical violence among the structurally
oppressed vast majority of human beings now alive on
the planet--a problem linked to the achievement of
justice at local, national and higher levels of or-
ganization--is the problem of sacrifice among the
rich nations. For instance, with respect to the
United States, whose privileged position in the
world community is vulnerable (who has more to
lose?), Falk has said, "We expect reluctance, if not
resistance, to merge national destiny in a wider
global destiny involving far larger numbers of people who have been living in a condition of mass misery."

Yet virtually all the WOMP I participants were
committed to searching for nonviolent strategies of
social change. Though there was a general commitment to democratic processes and achieving radical

changes through, in Lagos' phrasing, "consensus, negotiation, persuasion, and a political-cultural mobilization guided fundamentally by the values that
inspire the model of the preferred world," few of
the directors would discount absolutely the necessity of sometimes foresaking nonviolent tactics as a
matter of deliberate policy. Perhaps this position
was most unequivocally articulated by Rajni Kothari,
who said that "resort to coercive instruments by
those seriously affected by social injustices, when
the due constitutional processes prove insensitive
to their plight, must be tolerated (and) ought to be
considered as part of the democratic process."

Quite apart from the problem of violence in
strategies of change, there was the difficulty of
making transitional recommendations that were aimed
not only at transforming national and regional social orders, but also at world society. It soon became clear that transition strategies tailored to a
specific nation or region were infrequently general-
izable to other nations or regions. For example,
one of the German participants insisted that the
labor movement had a much greater revolutionary potential in certain European countries than it did,
for instance, in the United States, nominally a society with much in common with Western Europe.

Despite this difficulty, each WOMP team accepted the goal of *world transformation,* as well as
national and regional transformations. However, a
clear theoretical explanation of the interaction between national, regional and world social and political processes did not emerge among the WOMP I participants. Which level of policy implementation
should have priority, in terms of the pragmatic
achievement of world order goals? For some the "domestic factor" has primacy. Yet none denies the
fact that national policies have an increasingly
perceptible regional and global impact, while world
bodies such as the International Monetary Fund could
implement policies that affect an overwhelming majority of nations.

A range of "prospective actors" are possible
social change agents, from the individual human being to movements and institutions organized to act
at subnational, national, international, regional,
transnational and global levels. Nation states are
but one actor type in a planetary society that includes radical political and cultural movements,
private nongovernmental organizations, multinational
corporations, labor movements, regional economic
groupings, guerrilla organizations, the United

Nations, etc. Any one of these, and others,were or
could become world order actors. It is evident that
as the authority of nation states is eroded, the political space encompassed by the planetary system of
human relations is increasingly accessible to other
kinds of actors.

WOMP - A PROSPECTIVE SOCIAL CHANGE ACTOR?

Perhaps WOMP I will be a fulfillment of Mannheim's description of what social science work
should be. Mannheim cautioned that participation in
the social process one was at the same time observ-
ing did not mean the "facts" involved were falsified
or incorrectly perceived. "Indeed, on the contrary,
participation in the living context of social life
is a presupposition of the understanding of the inner nature of this living context....The disregard
of qualitative elements and the complete restraint
of the will does not constitute objectivity but is
instead the negation of the essential quality of the
(social) object."[13] With respect to WOMP the "object" may be broadly described as the world community. The WOMP I participants were self-conscious
members of that community, actively engaged in a
long-range attempt to help shape it in a preferred
direction. For in creating detailed images or models of the future, the WOMP I participants may have
succeeded in introducing a radically different perspective on world relations into educational environments throughout the planet. If they and others
like them are successful on a worldwide scale,
global social and political changes may ultimately
result.
It is this role and this process Mendlovitz
probably had in mind when, late in the development
of WOMP I, he felt compelled to remark that "we have
probably underestimated the extent to which the presentation of a vivid and compelling image of a future world, capable of dealing with a set of interrelated world problems, is itself part of the transition process" to a preferred world.[14] *The creation of a large and vociferous community of world-
minded educated men and women schooled in visioning
the future will naturally generate pressures for
planetary social change*. A whole earth political
movement, firmly grounded in a knowledge about the
complex nature of world order problems, might then
emerge and give pragmatic shape to a new, world
consciousness.

CONCLUSION

It would be as foolish to underestimate the potential of such a beginning as it would be to overestimate it. Elise Boulding has spoken of the chiliastic enthusiasm that is now beginning to form a basic cultural undercurrent in the world community. This current, "therapeutic and powerful," is not dissimilar from that which generated the millenial thinking a few decades before the year 1,000 A.D. and which helped transform Medieval civilization.[15] In the context of the kind of change connotated by the word millenial, John Platt has discussed the phenomenon of "hierarchial growth," of "sudden changes in structure" in living systems, structural leaps that result in the "sudden formation of larger integrated systems from malfunctioning or conflicting sub-systems."[16] At the underlying level of social thought, of value selection and interpretation, one is reminded of Mannheim's suggestion of the possibility of an integration of many mutually complementary points of view into a comprehensive whole." Such an intellectural integration will probably have to occur, to some critical extent, immediately prior to the formation of fully viable world community political mechanisms. In this connection, Sakamoto has given us the insight that "while the conflict of ideologies is a system of negative interactions from the viewpoint of particular ideologies, it will appear as a set of sub-systems consisting of diverse positive values if it is seen from the viewpoint of man's value system as a whole."[17]

The complexity of planetary life--in its cultural, as well as its specifically economic and political dimensions, and in its ecological dimension--presses upon the minds of human beings. Faced with the demands of such complexity, dogmatism of all political shades is a luxury responsible people tend to shun. Further, as the world becomes an increasingly integrated system of human interactions, the notion of a planetary destiny may lead human beings to acquire a species-wide identity. The formation of such a self concept is probably an indispensible part of the movement to a planetary social system capable of satisfying the basic justice and order needs of humankind.

Against this background it is possible to see the late 1970s and early 1980s as potentially a time of consensus formation. It is precisely this fundamental social and cultural process that must be engaged in if humankind is ever to evolve peacefully out of its six-thousand-year-old statist/chrysalis and into an effective planetary system of justice

and order. It is after such a period of consensus
making that the case for taking big steps can begin
to be made among the peoples of the world.[18]   For
apart from their slowness in achieving the degree of
change needed, small steps for change in the international system lack visibility and as a rule generate little enthusiasm among populaces. *A series of
big steps, such as the creation of a supranational
world police force capable of enforcing racial
equality in southern Africa, for example, or the
creation of an ocean regime empowered to tax devel-
opers of ocean resources for the betterment of the
poor states, or the creation of an environmental
agency empowered to bring enforceable legal action
against criminal ecological offenders, are highly
visible political actions whose effects could be
readily communicated to large numbers of people as
holding forth the promise for rapid and positive
changes in the quality of their lives.* Powerful political energies could be mobilized in favor of big
steps.

Such actions are unlikely to occur, however,
before a good deal more substantive dialogue has
taken place among representatives of the various regions of the planet. In the meantime, the task of
building a consensus among intellectual leaders is
a critical first step. This step WOMP I has helped
initiate.

NOTES

Except when otherwise noted, the WOMP I research directors' remarks are quoted from preliminary sources such as conference transcripts, position papers, and first drafts of the documents, none
of which are generally available or can be construed
to represent a definitive position on their parts.
Therefore, I have made no attempt to footnote most
of the quotations taken from the WOMP participants.

1.   The concept of trapped elites was originally
formulated by Harold Lasswell. See his "Future Systems of Identity" (esp. p. 15) in Black, Cyril &
Falk, Richard, *The Structure of the International
Environment,* Volume IV of The Future of the International Legal Order Series. Princeton: Princeton
University Press, 1972.

2.   Letter from Rajni Kothari to Saul H. Mendlovitz,
dated November 26, 1969 (p. 22 of Memo #21). In

368   IAN BALDWIN, JR.

Saul H. Mendlovitz. "Memos to Research Directors WOMP." Available from the Institute for World Order, 1140 Avenue of the Americas, New York.

3. Mannheim, Karl. *Ideology and Utopia,* translated by Louis Wirth and Edward Shils. New York: Harcourt, Brace & World (a Harvest Book). No date. Originally published in German, 1929, p. 151.

4. *Ibid.*, p. 149.

5. Sakamoto, Yoshikazu. "The Rationale of the World Order Models Project," to be published in the Proceedings of the American Society of International Law. An earlier version of the paper was presented at the UNITAR Conference on "New Perspective in International Cooperation" in September 1971. Available from the Institute for World Order.

6. *Op. cit.*, Memo #18, Letter dated September 17, 1969 to Dean B.S. Murty (p. 2).

7. *Op. cit.*

8. *Ibid.*

9. Boulding, Elise. Futurology and the imaging capacity of the West. Chapter 2 in *Conceptualization of Cultural Futurology,* forthcoming.

10. Mendlovitz, *Op. cit.*, Memo #20, p. 12.

11. *Ibid.*, Memo #21, p. 16.

12. *Ibid.*, Memo #20, p. 11.

13. Mannheim, *Op. cit.*, p. 46.

14. *Op. cit.*, Memo #25, p. 2

15. *Op. cit.*

16. "Hierarchical Growth" in *Bulletin of the Atomic Scientists,* November, 1970.

17. *Op. cit.*

18. See Mendlovitz, Saul H. The case for the big step. In Elizabeth Jay Hollins, *Peace is Possible.* New York: Grossman, 1966, 313-322.

*IAN BALDWIN, JR. writes: I attended Columbia
College as an English and Oriental Studies major
during the late 50s and early 60s. My first encounter with the idea of nonviolence was in reading and
hearing of the New Testament; but it was in the
study of Buddhism at college that the idea took root.*

*I retain a certain amount of fundamental ambiv-
alence toward the ideal of living a life committed
to nonviolence. As a supreme value, such a life retains for me the quality of an aspiration; on the
other hand, it is still difficult for me to be evan-
gelical about such a commitment, especially outside
my own society and race. There is too much intolerable institutionalized violence in the world, violence I do not myself experience directly as a white
Anglo-Saxon male citizen of the United States.*

*In the midst of my senior year at college, I
sold what few worldly goods I had and embarked on a
trip around the world. I returned to New York pen-
niless eight months later having spent some $400,
working my way across oceans and seas in Scandina-
vian freighters. It was on that trip that a planetary-species identity, somehow always latent, became
a conscious part of myself. I returned to finish
college.*

*Revulsion at the atrocities committed by my
country in Vietnam and my acquaintance with several
pessimistic ecologists (through a job I had as editor of biological sciences at Holt, Rinehart and
Winston's college department) led me to search for a
more meaningful vocation than profit-centered publishing could afford. From early 1969 to 1974, I
had the opportunity to work for the Institute for
World Order as editor responsible for helping other
staff and authors publish world order materials. I
was also co-editor of a series of WORLD ORDER BOOKS
published by Grossman/Viking (trade editions) and
W.H. Freeman (college editions).*

*I believe we confront three possible futures.
One involves some form of violent breakdown of world
civilization, either in a single catastrophic stroke
such as a massive nuclear war, or, more likely, in a
series of environmental collapses such as the sudden
and drastic shortage of potable water, fish protein,
petroleum, etc. At its most drastic, such a future
could involve the elimination or genetic transmuta-
tion of the human species. At its least drastic, it
could entail the beginning of a planetary dark ages
in which anarchy and comparatively low levels of
man-man and man-nature violence become the norm.
Many, sometimes including myself, hunger for this
least drastic scenario as a desirable antidote to*

the present course of civilization.

Another, more likely future involves the formation of an oligarchic, repressive world government managed by technocratic elites, whose mandate will be derived from a widely acknowledged necessity to bring order to an endangered system of world relations.

The third, and only desirable future I can presently imagine working for, consists of some form of limited planetary government that is achieved through essentially consensual means. That is, such a government will be created by planetary social processes, and not as a tool of any privileged sector. If such a government is achieved, its mandate will not merely be to bring order into the world system--i.e., the control of large-scale conflict, pollution, population increase, resource depletion-- but to secure as well a far greater measure of justice, most immediately in the form of a more egalitarian distribution of the world's goods and services. In terms of both complexity and sheer human effort, this future will be the most difficult one to achieve.

I am presently on the staff of the Environmental Defense Fund in New York City.

18. The All-Win Approach to Conflict Resolution: Tough-Minded, Humane Power for Social Change

James H. Craig, Ph.D., and Marguerite Craig

> "He drew a circle that shut me out--
> Heretic, rebel, a thing to flout.
> But Love and I had the wit to win:
> We drew a circle that took him in."
> *Edwin Markham*

Power seems intimately involved in the origin, continuation, and resolution of almost every conflict. The initiation of social change seems to involve power, and power inevitably emerges in resistance to social change.

The centrality of power to the concerns of this book encouraged us to reexamine the concept of power and to offer a theoretical framework upon which to erect conflict-resolution and social-change models.

Motivation

Our theory of power is intimately related to our theory of human motivation.[1] We postulate that motivated human behavior emerges whenever a harmonious configuration of four subjective motivational factors arises or is stimulated in a *responder*. The four factors--perception or conceptions--may or may not reflect objective reality.

The four subjective factors comprising a responder's motivational state may be described as follows:

(1)	(4)	(3)	(2)
INSISTENT NEED	IMPLEMENTING ACTION	CONNECTING BRIDGE	APPROPRIATE SATISFIER

The arising of (1) an insistent need, by itself, does not lead to purposive behavior. (It may lead to exploration.) But when people conceive of the existence of (2) an appropriate satisfier, conceive of (3) a bridge to it, and conceive of (4) implementing

371

behavior they are willing and able to carry out, then purposive self-directed behavior follows.

Actually, this model depicts only a portion of a motivational state. People often experience several more or less insistent needs, and may perceive or conceive of one or more possible satisfiers for each need. Additionally, they may have vague or clear conceptions of several possible implementing actions to traverse more or less difficult bridges to achieve some of the satisfiers. The complexity of competing factors complicates the real-life exercise of power, but need not interfere with our understanding of the process.

POWER

In general we define power as the capacity of an *initiator* to intentionally affect a *responder's* behavior so that the initiator is subsequently more satisfied. In terms of our motivational model, the initiator exercises his or her power by affecting the shape and/or the force of one or more of the responder's four motivational factors.

In some instances, such as in a Nazi prison camp, the camp administrator completely controls resources and agents of violence. Consequently he indirectly controls each of the four motivational factors of the prisoners. Basic needs for food, rest, shelter, and avoidance of pain are powerfully insistent in each prisoner/responder. By providing a minimal amount of food, rest, and shelter, and a reasonably clear understanding of how obedience will help the responder minimize suffering, an administrator can motivate most responders to do exactly what is desired of them as long as they are physically able. The rare exceptions, where prisoners defy their guards or plot escape attempts, do not invalidate the model but may instead suggest that the responder has a higher individualistic need that overrides his manipulated needs.[2]

Directive Power

The power exercised by Nazi prison camp administrators is an extreme example of what we will call *directive power*. By directive power we mean any form of power in which the initiator intentionally makes people act against their will, their judgment, or their interests. We will generally describe directive power as coercion and manipulation, and include in those categories the use or the threat of

force, the conditional offer or withdrawal of rewards, and the intentional distortion or withholding
of information.

Many social scientists, philosophers, and lay-
men consider coercion and manipulation as factors
present in all forms of power. Some, such as Lasswell and Kaplan limit power to influence which is
"enforced or expected to be enforced by relatively
severe sanctions" (16, p. 84). Power, so defined,
is a dirty word. Most people are quick to deny
wanting to use power, and often deprecate others for
"seeking power." Humane people especially shrink
from considering the use of power thus identified.

However, the various forms of directive power
do not exhaust the possible ways an *initiator* can
intentionally affect a *responder's* behavior. And
they do not describe much of the tremendous power
exercised by such persons as Buddha and Ghandi.

Synergic Power
The other forms of power fall into a class we
call *synergic power*. Synergic power, like directive
power, is used to affect the behavior of responders
so that the initiator will be better satisfied. It
differs, however, in that its use accords with the
will, the judgment, and the interests of the responders, and it is only effective if the responder
concurs with the initiator. Synergic power is the
power we exercise by sharing information and feelings in nonmanipulative, noncoercive ways, and by
creatively cooperating to discover new solutions to
problems or conflicts. Education and therapy at
their best exemplify synergic power. Pathfinders
and navigators exercise synergic power. The leader
who shares his vision with his followers and receives their enthusiastic support *may be* exercising
synergic power. But the leader who freely shares
his knowledge and vision, encourages free interchange of knowledge and desires with and among his
followers, and helps his followers coordinate their
efforts to carry out jointly-devised programs, is
surely exercising synergic power.

Shifts in Power Styles
Leaders typically shift the nature of the power
they use when they move from establishing an initial
power base to using that power base against outside
forces. Castro, for instance, mainly used synergic
power when he assembled his original band of revolutionaries. He offered his prospective supporters a
credible diagnosis of Cuba's ills, attributing them

to the Batista-U.S. regime. He painted an appealing
picture of a free Cuba, and sketched what seemed to
many Cubans a reasonable way they could work together to achieve the desirable future.

Even though his followers had little to do with
devising their common goal and the plan to achieve
it, Castro appeared to use little manipulation and
no coercion in the first stages of assembling his
initial power base. Later some coercion was introduced to maintain discipline and to discourage de-
fection. However, when Castro led his band against
Batista's regime, he used the most violent forms of
directive power. The shift does not represent a
change in character. It represents the "natural"
difference between the ways prospective friends and
"inevitable" enemies are treated.

The power directed toward allies and potential
allies is usually synergic power, perhaps including
some of the less abrasive forms of directive power:
polite manipulation and gentle bargaining. It may
consist of little more than "showing the way" by
which followers can more easily attain what they already want. It may include helping people see that
they have needs and desires they had not previously
noticed, and/or helping them see that there are ways
to attain what they had previously believed unob-
tainable. Clearly, the manipulation used by adver-
tisers and salespersons closely resembles synergic
power. The obvious similarity should not lead us to
reject synergic power, but should alert us to the
reality that synergic-power *techniques* can be used
to manipulate people. The people toward whom synergic power is directed can safeguard against its manipulative use by insisting on full disclosure of the
initiator's interests and connections, and by participating in goal-setting and program design.

The Four-fold Path
The successful use of synergic power requires
the initiator to help responders assimilate the information needed to undergird a motivational state
that will lead them into cooperative action. Success depends upon the development of (1) a credible
diagnostic analysis of the problem situation, connecting unsatisfied needs with shortcomings in the
current situation, (2) a credible picture of a desirable goal that clearly satisfies insistent needs,
(3) a design of a credible bridge leading to that
goal, and (4) an understanding of what roles which
people can and must play to get the bridge built and
crossed. These four concepts form what we call "the

four-fold path to nonviolent social change." Each concept or strand corresponds to one of the four motivational factors that comprise the responder's motivational state.

When the initiator completely designs the four-fold path, with little feedback and no substantial contributions from responders, the power exercised is a smoothly manipulative form of directive power that has many of the good attributes of synergic power. In a true form of synergic power the initiator would serve as a directive catalyst, involving the responders in uncovering their pressing needs, identifying satisfiers, devising transition bridges, selecting congenial roles, and in insisting that all of them together continually reassess and redesign the path as their progress provides them with fresh vantage points.[3]

When events fail to substantiate features of the four-fold path presented by a leader, a credibility gap tends to open and widen, and the synergic power of the leader tends to fade. Johnson's and Nixon's experiences in Vietnam bear this out. Of course they had been distorting information to manipulate the American people into supporting policies that were primarily beneficial to the military-industrial complex. The credibility gap, hence, did not spell the failure of an exercise of synergic power, but rather the failure of an exercise of manipulative directive power.

Results were quite different for the North Vietnamese administration. Events largely validated their diagnostic analysis of their problems with foreign invaders, whether French, Japanese, or American. The bridge to eventual freedom from foreign interference, despite its cost and the delays, progressed according to design, implemented by a multitude of people who could see what they had to do and who carried out the tasks needed to complete and cross that bridge.

The foregoing discussion suggests that synergic power techniques cannot be used successfully to accomplish *every* end. Only if the people involved desire and value the ends will they be motivated to cooperate. If experience validates the concepts comprising the four-fold path, synergic power techniques are facilitated. But complete validation is not essential. Even the failure of events to confirm the initiator's diagnosis and prognosis may leave his synergic power unshaken *if* he acknowledges the nonconfirmation and openly revises the program, and perhaps even the goals, in light of new information freely shared with responders.

The manipulative leader, particularly if he serves special interests, is much more vulnerable to disconfirming events. As long as his enterprises are successful he may avoid serious challenge. But a serious loss, or a series of lesser failures that are defended by the initiator, or "explained away" lead to crumbling confidence and a change in the motivational state of the responders. To maintain control in such a situation, the initiator is forced to shift from manipulation to coercion, and every semblance of his synergic power disappears, as with Idi Amin. However, if he has approval from enough citizens who agree that coercive forms of directive power are the right thing to use against dissidents, he may be able to remain in control until undone by a coup or by external events.

CONFLICT

Everybody knows what a conflict is, and yet no consensus exists on the exact meaning of the term (9). We have chosen to define conflict in a broad psychological sense that intentionally makes no distinction between conflict and competition.

A *conflict* exists when an individual perceives himself (or his group) frustrated or threatened by the actions or the existence of another individual or group. We do not center our conception of conflict on instances of overt antagonistic behavior. Actually, what is usually thought of as conflict-- the actions taken to relieve frustration or threat-- we consider to be conflict-resolution behavior.

Forms of Conflict Resolution

Conflict resolution may involve aggressive violence, such as the Blitzkreig of Hitler, whose dreams of expansion were temporarily frustrated by the mere existence of the victim states. Or for some weak parties it may be largely limited to appealing for help, as Haile Selassie did to the League of Nations when Ethiopia was attacked by Italy's armed might. But whether labeled conflict behavior or conflict-resolution behavior, we see it as a gross symptom of an underlying conflict. Our concern is to replace the violent forms of conflict resolution with nonviolent forms, or even better, to encourage the early detection of underlying conflicts and provide means for dealing directly with them before they erupt into violent or otherwise inefficient attempts at resolution.

The same kinds of underlying conflict can lead
either to violent or to nonviolent attempts at resolution. Whether an attempt involves violence seems
to be determined less by the nature of the felt
frustrations and threats than by the way the parties
to the conflict view each other. As long as they
view each other as allies, resolution attempts tend
to be nonviolent and noncoercive, although some manipulation is not unusual, and veiled threats may be
included. But against a party viewed as an enemy,
direct violence is much more likely to occur. Conditional threats of violence are common, and quite
open. And manipulation of an enemy is high in
threats and low in conditional promises of rewards.

From Adversary to Ally?

If we want to reduce incidences of violence and
of conditions that breed violence, the simple answer
is to convert our adversaries into allies. That
might sound like a simpleminded solution if there
are, in fact, objective conditions that make some
parties inevitable adversaries.[4] However inevi-
tableness is questionable. World history shows that
some of our most important allies today were our adversaries 30 years ago, and our most threatening adversaries today were allies at that time. If we examine our relations carefully we will see that any
of our allies is also a potential adversary, and any
adversary is also a potential ally. We have common
interests and complementary interests with our worst
adversaries, and conflicts of interests exist between us and our strongest allies. The "inevitable-
ness" of a party's adversary or ally status is dependent upon emphasizing certain aspects of our relationships and disregarding others.

What does a state or an individual seek when it
seeks an ally? It seeks assistance in reducing
frustrations and threats. Could it seek the same
kind of assistance from an adversary? We contend
that it could, and could get more efficient assistance from the adversary which was "causing" the
greatest frustrations and threat, than from an ally.[5]

Parties don't often look to adversaries for assistance because such relations are sensitive, and
difficult to deal with. But Bismarck, the master
strategist did, and so it seems did Kissinger, who
is a student of Bismarck(14). Kissinger notes that
in 1854, during the Crimean War, Bismarck listed
Prussia's options as: (1) an alliance with Russia
against France, (2) an arrangement with Austria,

presumably against Russia, or (3) an understanding
with France against Austria and Russia. The choice
was to be determined strictly on the basis of utility.

Thus, if political "realists" feel no compunction in shifting adversaries to allies from purely
utilitarian considerations, those of us who are motivated by humanitarian considerations shouldn't
feel hesitant about striving for alliances based on
a higher utility: the well-being of all humankind.

An adversary begins to be seen as an ally or
potential ally when he is seen as possibly helping
reduce serious frustrations and threats, or at least
as holding greater potential to reduce than increase
frustrations and threats. Thus, to change an adversary into an ally calls for developing or illuminating positive possibilities, and avoiding behaviors
that appear threatening or frustrating. To plan the
shift from adversary to ally, and to understand specifically what the "pressing needs" and "appropriate
satisfiers" of our motivational model might be, we
need clear conceptions of what frustrations and
threats involve. We've referred to them as if they
were clearly understood and agreed upon, but only in
a very general sense is this true.

The pleasure/pain model of humankind. Some see
people as motivated solely by the avoidance of discomfort and pain and by the seeking of pleasure and
comfort. They see the wide range of behaviors and
accomplishments as simply convoluted ways of seeking
pleasure and avoiding pain. In such a view human
behavior differs from the behavior of a thermostat-
ically controlled furnace only in degree of complexity. People are viewed as tools with two control
levers: reward and punishment. The person who controls overwhelming military or economic power believes that if he can credibly offer enough rewards
or threaten painful enough punishments, he can get
other people to do whatever he wants. Such a belief
underlies the principle of social order through vigorous police action and punitive penal practices.
It also underlies the hope for world peace through
enforceable world law. This view seems to contain a
tacit recommendation for the use of directive power
by those who possess or who can assemble superior
might and resources.

The human-tendencies model of man. A more credible image of man--one that draws heavily on the
contributions of Abraham Maslow (19)--emerges when

we give due weight to humanity's evolutionary roots.
In the course of human evolutionary development rigid instinctual controls have been replaced by conscious control gently guided by instinctual rem-
nants--what we call innate *human tendencies*. Pleasure and pain have lost their motivating force and
now serve as indicators. Conditions that give rise
to pleasure are generally good for life, and those
that arouse pain are generally bad for life. But
those indicators can be overridden, and often are,
as humans consciously and with foresight, respond to
their distinctively human tendencies.

Beyond the universal need for food, shelter,
and a reasonable degree of bodily comfort, humans
seem to have innate tendencies to seek, in one way
or another, (1) self-esteem, (2) self-determination,
a degree of control over what happens to them, (3)
the giving and receiving of companionship and love,
(4) a comprehensible and orderly picture of map of
their society and world, (5) the freedom to express
their feelings, and (6) opportunities to make use of
their innate and acquired capacities in play and
meaningful work.[6] Only when people's higher human
tendencies are seriously frustrated do pleasure and
pain assume a dominant role in shaping their actions
or does violent aggression displace rational coping
behavior. This view of humankind contains a tacit
recommendation for the use of synergic power by
those who hope to bring out the best in their fellow
humans.

Brute force may be used to exterminate people.
It can powerfully shape and distort human behavior.
But it cannot be used to impose peaceful, cooperative living. It cannot provide the soil for the
growth of human potential. It is inefficient because it always generates its own opposition, even
where none had existed previously.

The path from adversary to ally. The foregoing
detour into the nature of humankind strongly suggests how people, acting for themselves or their
state, can facilitate the shift from adversary relationships to alliances. The human-tendencies model
indicates three ways to reduce others' frustrations
and increase their satisfactions *without cost:* (1)
Treating others with consideration and respect responds to their esteem needs. (2) Assuring others
they will participate in all decisions affecting
them responds to their control needs. (3) Being
open and making intentions known responds to their
need for a reliable "map" of their world. And act-

ing in any or all of these three ways contributes to
satisfying the others' friendship needs.

Erecting and maintaining defenses against hostile adversaries may cost more than providing for
some of their material needs, or making it possible
for them to provide for those needs themselves.
This seemingly low-cost method of conflict management has appeal. But it contains hazards. The Lady
Bountiful approach creates a paternalistic relationship, which may ultimately aggravate the conflict.
Only when the self-esteem and control needs of others are also satisfied does assistance in meeting
material needs contribute to an alliance. Dispensing bounty can be a form of directive power. But
for an alliance to prosper, a synergic-power relationship seems essential.

Converting an adversary into an ally does not
automatically resolve any conflict, although it may
reduce some of the threats felt on either side, and
consequently reduce some of the associated tensions.
The effect of reducing tensions may be ambiguous.
On the one hand, it may also reduce the motivation
to resolve the conflict in question, particularly if
the parties are also involved in other more urgent
conflicts. On the other hand, it may make possible
a cooperative search for mutually satisfactory solutions. On balance, particularly when we consider
that allies are less likely to revert to violence
than adversaries, the conversion effort seems well
worthwhile as a first stage in any conflict-resolution process.

CONFLICTS STEMMING FROM THE NATURE OF HUMANKIND

In addition to conflicts stemming from the nature of individual humans, another set of conflicts
stems from features of the social structure which
reflect important aspects of humankind's nature. We
are not interested in providing an analysis of society's power structure. Other authors have done
that much better than we can (15,2,8,18,20). What
we do want to show is that the existence of elites
and the emergence of a ruling elite is inevitable in
any society, given the nature of humankind. And we
want to show, further, that the existence of a ruling elite is an inevitable source of social conflict.

Humankind, as a product of evolution, exhibits
a tremendous range of variation along a multitude of
dimensions. In terms of any characteristic, such as
height or intelligence, most people bunch around the
average. When we move away from the average we find

fewer and fewer individuals as we approach the extreme (i.e., very few basketball giants or mental wizards).

Elites. We hesitate to explicitly categorize people as belonging to elites or to the masses, and yet the term "elite" gives us a conceptual hook for our argument. At the apex of any society we see three elites: a ruling elite, a serving elite, and a passive privileged elite. Most of the people in these elites fall close to the upper ends of whatever dimensions are relevant to exercising power. Together, they make up but a small fraction of society.

These individuals share with the rest of humankind the need to control what happens to them. But because of their exceptional qualities, especially their superior foresight and conceptual powers, they are better fitted than the average to make the most of situations they find themselves in and to get into those situations that hold the most promise. If, in their inevitable conflicts, they exercise great initiative and treat their fellows very objectively as potential resources or obstacles, they have a good chance to make their way into the ruling elite.

The ruling elite. The ruling elite, itself only a small fraction of society's elites, is comprised of those major bankers, industrialists, politicians, and wealth-holders who actively use their wealth and position to maintain the status quo and/ or to reshape society to even better serve their special interests (8). The ruling elite provides society with leadership, but it is a leadership chiefly oriented toward maintaining and expanding its special privileges.[7]

The serving elite. We consider the serving elite as consisting of the upper echelons of professional people: doctors, lawyers, scientists, educators, entertainers, communications media people, writers, and religious leaders. Most of these people do provide services honestly designed to meet needs. However the best and the first of their services generally goes to other members of the elites. And their services are usually delivered in ways that neither threaten nor infringe upon the power of the ruling elite.

The passive privileged elite. Members of this elite neither rule nor serve, but reap the benefits

of their position and do little to disturb the status quo. Many of these people have inherited or
married their wealth. Some are "operators" who are
so busy making deals and scouting society's commercial and financial thickets for the big opportunity
that, despite their money-making activities, they
could be categorized as politically passive in the
larger society. Beyond their automatic support of
conservative politics, their chief impact upon society is through their patterns of consumption.

    Structural conflict. A major conflict, in la-
tent or manifest form, results from the collision
between the needs of each individual for self-determination and the tremendous concentration of direct
and indirect control in the hands of a tiny ruling
elite.

    As long as most citizens are unaware of how
completely an unofficial ruling elite affects the
course of their lives through the implementation of
selected policies and the blocking of others, as
long as they blame fate, or "the government," or
"human nature," or their own incompetence, the basic
conflict can remain latent. But the frustrations
generated will be vented in divisive infighting and
in aggressive actions against any vulnerable target.
    However, when enough people throughout a so-
ciety become aware that they are being used and manipulated for the convenience and/or profit of a
privileged few, then the potential for open conflict
rises to the combustion point. If the people fail
to receive competent leadership, probably from the
ranks of the serving elite, their struggle may merely gain them a coercive ruling elite in exchange for
a manipulative one, as happened to the Greeks a few
years ago under the domination of their colonels.
    We hypothesize that societies weaken and fall
when their elites feed off the efforts of their citizens, and mislead them into actions that are
directly self-destructive.
    We hypothesize that societies prosper when some
important part of their elites fill the role of
leader as servant (11), providing leadership and direction for its citizens so that the actions of many
are coordinated to promote the general welfare.
    The pleasure/pain model of man suggests that,
in principle, conflict could be avoided if satisfiers could be sufficiently increased and/or population sufficiently reduced. Skinner (24) suggests
that comprehensive planning and appropriate schedules of rewards and punishments could so perfectly

coordinate the behavior of all that no conflict need
ever arise. Contrary evidence and our personal preferences lead us to reject both the pleasure/pain
model of man and the notion that conflicts are
avoidable.

The human-tendencies model of man indicates
that conflict is inevitable no matter how plentiful
satisfiers might become. And attempts to centrally
plan and coordinate everyone's behavior would, in
itself, frustrate people's self-determination tendencies and would thus generate conflict. When, for
example, we examine parent-child relationships we
can see the inevitable built-in conflict. The tendencies of a child to be in control, to explore, to
express feelings, and to exercise his developing capacities inevitably frustrate and threaten the tendency of his parents to control and to maintain an
orderly, predictable world. In turn, the expression
of the parental tendencies frustrate the child.

In the larger society the allocation of scarce
resources and desirable positions creates conflict.
And in our culture, particularly, the celebration of
competition and "equal opportunity" among people en-
dowed with very unequal capacities inevitably leaves
many people with unsatisfied material needs and
frustrated needs for self-esteem, or else drives
them into neurotic patterns of rationalization.

THE ALL-WIN APPROACH

The twin goals. It seems clear that much conflict is due to social arrangements that do violence
to many humans. It seems equally clear that a great
deal of conflict is attributable to human nature,
and probably is unavoidable. Hence we have two
goals. One is to devise methods of nonviolent social change in order to modify or eliminate those
social, political, and economic arrangements that
now cause people unnecessary frustration and threat.
The other is to devise nonviolent conflict-resolution methods which are congruent with human nature.

The two goals are inseparable. Attempts at social change will surely arouse or heighten conflict,
and a definitive resolution of any fundamental conflict will probably call for social change. The
best way to approach our twin goals is probably
through resolving an important conflict. Attempting social change where no active conflict exists
probably would be more difficult. As long as conditions are reasonably stable,those who benefit from

the status quo are much more motivated to resist
change than they are to seek a solution for the
problems of others. However, when an active conflict threatens, or especially when it gets hot,
both parties become more open to seeking resolution.

THE ALL-WIN PRINCIPLES

The nine All-Win principles follow from our
conception of human nature. We hypothesize that
conflict-resolution procedures and social change
programs[8] embodying the spirit of these principles
will successfully and nonviolently achieve their
purposes, or at least will provide a solid foundation on which to erect revised programs that will
ultimately achieve success.

The principles are designed to provide conditions that encourage responsible, creative, humane
behavior from great numbers of people, and to avoid
the conditions that foster defensive, hostile behavior. They are designed to convert adversaries into
allies, to resolve conflicts for the benefit of all,
to place the power of the state in the service of
its people, to sensitize people to their interdependence, and to dissipate their feelings of anomie and
impotence.

1.   *Leadership from a serving elite.* Any program calling for significant nonviolent change in
the status quo needs effective leadership by individuals capable of generating synergic power on a
broad popular base.

The problem is serious because the pool of prospective change leaders with the needed capacities
is limited: first, by the natural distribution of
individual differences, which provides few individuals with any given kind of superiority; second, by
the attraction of many to material success in business and free-enterprise professions; third, by the
seduction of many of our brightest young people into
spending their lives solely in scientific pursuits;
and fourth, by the movement of many of our most socially conscious youth into service careers wherein
they limit themselves to alleviating local suffering. The pool of prospective leader/servants is
further limited by the aversion felt by most humane,
socially minded people toward using power, and by
the acceptance of the myth of the expert specialist,
which leaves the use of power to the professional
politician, and more particularly to those who
"buy" his services.

Some political change leaders might be drawn
from the relatively large untapped pool of alert women and members of minorities who have been kept out
of influential positions by prejudice and self-de-
meaning attitudes. They don't need to be coaxed or
dragged, but they do need a relatively clear picture
of just how they might begin to effectively serve
the larger society rather than merely put in their
efforts for some self-serving politician or business
man, or some organization dedicated to a special
interest.
Potential leaders can be drawn from among those
capable, humane people who have never considered exercising power because they have seen all power as
dehumanizing. Many of them will be glad to initiate
synergic power when they understand how it can have
the opposite effect--how it can help both initiator
and responder to live responsible and fully human
lives.

2. *Popular representation.* Whenever a conflict affects more than a few people, not all of
those affected will be able to meet face to face for
its resolution. The use of representatives becomes
a physical necessity. (A suggested model for using
representatives in conflict resolution follows the
listing of principles.) The criteria for selecting
delegates to the face-to-face meeting is a crucial
matter. Three criteria seem very important: (a)
Delegates should resemble the people they represent
so the latter can clearly identify with them. (b)
They should be selected for exceptional characteristics that can make exceptional contributions to the
conflict-resolution process: high intelligence
(however assessed), flexibility, creativity, warmth,
etc. Not all delegates need have all desired characteristics. If each were superior on all counts
they would lose their representative nature. The
selection process aims at assembling people with
complementary characteristics to form a superior
team. The gravity of our conflicts warrants assembling the best teams we can field. (c) Delegates
should not be members of government, the ruling
elite, groups dedicated to special interests, or
"experts." Members of each of these groups cannot
afford to be totally open and frank. To develop the
trust, not only of their counterparts, but of the
people they represent, our representatives need to
avoid all secrecy and be models of openness. Openness is easier to achieve if delegations do not include anyone who must keep secrets or who must en-

gage in self-censorship for fear his words might be
taken to represent an official position of government, organization, or pressure group. Lay representatives can explore novel ideas without the fear
of traditional negotiators that exploration might
weaken bargaining positions. Another important advantage of working with lay people is that they often don't recognize some of the "impossibilities"
that are familiar to experts. With their fresh
viewpoints they may circumvent some of the impossibilities inherent in accustomed ways of treating
conflicts.

When representatives do feel the need for special knowledge of experts, or if they want briefings
from government officials or from special interest
groups, they can consult people possessing the desired information. However, to continue fostering
trust, the consultations should be conducted in open
meetings with representatives from both sides present. Any circumspection and self-censorship on the
part of the consultants should not detract from the
trust developing among the representatives.

3. *All-Win coaching*. To operate effectively,
each team of lay representatives should receive appropriate training and guidance. The key role in
the All-Win process is that of coach. Just as the
performance of an athletic team is dependent upon
its training and coaching, so is the performance of
the All-Win team. Bad habits acquired from participation in, and observation of typical adversary proceedings need to be weakened, and new habits to facilitate cooperative problem solving need to be developed.

Behavioral science professionals experienced in
working with groups[9] can prepare themselves to coach
All-Win teams with a minimal amount of special
training. A coach works exclusively with one team,
training its members and guiding them in their encounters with delegates of other teams.[10] He helps
his team identify the human concerns behind abstract
arguments and fixed positions. He encourages the
surfacing of information crucial to problem solving,
and he guides people through emotional conflicts and
away from the "natural" adversary stances that lead
to deadlock.

The coach and his team are prepared to meet
with the others for as long a time as it takes for
new learnings to occur and for attitudes and values
to shift. The time demand can be put into perspective by contrasting the amount of time required for

All-Win conflict resolution with that used up in our typical ways of dealing with conflict. Compare the time needed by a few coaches and All-Win teams, supported by groups of citizens, to resolve large-scale conflicts, with the time used--millions of hours spent each year by judges, juries, court staff, lawyers, and witnesses--not to solve problems or resolve conflicts, but merely to affix blame and assess penalties.

Ideally, in the All-Win process, all parties to the conflict would select and train teams as suggested in Principles 2 and 3. However, the procedures could still work, though more slowly and roughly, if only one team accepts a coach and training. One well-trained team with a skilled coach should be able to "train" and "coach" their counterparts into reciprocating with All-Win responses.[11]

4. *Grass-roots participation*. As many as possible of the people affected   the conflict in question should be made a part of the conflict-resolution process. In addition to the immediate participants in the conflict, those who support the participants through tax paying, political activity, verbal encouragement, and those who feel threatened should all be made a part of the conflict-resolution process in one way or another. Technological advances in TV and videotape make grass-roots participation technically possible.[12] This principle offers several benefits: (a) New information generated in the All-Win conference by representatives is more credible to people involved in its development. (b) Those who actively participate will be able to learn and "grow" along with their representatives so they will be prepared to give popular support to novel solutions. (c) Participants actively exposed to varied viewpoints will increase their flexibility. And (d), perhaps even more important, the process offers a potent focus around which to do grass-roots organizing. And (e) it develops an informed public opinion which can provide meaningful feedback to the representatives. Such feedback is essential for the design of self-enforcing agreements.

Traditional closed negotiations provide no basis for grass-roots participantion. Representatives who deviate from traditional positions run great risk of being labeled traitor. If they devise truly innovative solutions they are very likely to be repudiated by their rank and file. Representatives taking part in secret negotiations must disregard feedback from an uninformed or misinformed public

which is seen by the negotiators as speaking from
ignorance.

5. *Problem-centered approach*. The initial focus should be on analyzing the conflict in terms of
the frustrations and fears and the unfilled needs
and desires of the individual humans involved in the
conflict (element 1 of the fourfold path). An exchange of demands or proposals (which are, in effect,
unilaterally formulated solutions) has no standing
in the All-Win procedure. Later, bilaterally and
multilaterally formulated solutions will be in order.
The appearance of a conflict provides little
specific information. It clearly signals only that
at least one party is experiencing frustration and/
or threat attributable to another party. Analysis
of the conflict behavior, itself, may also provide
little or no information about the nature of the
conflict. Similarly, analyses in terms of historical roots, perceptions and misperceptions, ideological bases, gross national statistics or average per-
capita figures tend to conceal, not reveal, what
happens to individuals.
There need be little initial effort expended on
clarifying perceptions of adversaries, dispelling
misperceptions, etc. In some cross-cultural workshops, exercises for the exchange of perceptions
have backfired with vague, negative feelings becoming crystallized into specific perceptions that in-
terfered with subsequent attempts at problem solving.
The use of this activity seems dubious. Good, clear,
positive perceptions develop naturally enough when
team members are helped to work together with their
counterparts on common tasks.
Conflict analysis in terms of the costs and benefits to individual humans on both sides seems most
promising. New information is generated as both
sides analyze the costs and benefits to people in
various social positions: industrial stockholder,
soldier, defense worker, retired person, farmer, etc.
The analysis will probably need to be revised as
various solutions are proposed that would affect
different people in different ways.

6. *Search for multiple alternative solutions*.
As conflict resolution moves from defining the problems to devising solutions (element 2), the representatives need to avoid settling upon a single approach (12), and need to consciously work toward
several solutions. *First*, the exploration of new
directions is essential. Obvious approaches have

little chance for success. If the elaboration or
refinement of current approaches could provide a
solution, one probably would have been hit upon and
implemented before now. *Second,* the quality of possible solutions will be upgraded. When we force
ourselves to search for several alternatives, we
stretch our imagination, we keep more people deeply
involved, we exercise the creative human faculties
of more people for a longer time, and we give seren-
dipity a chance to occur. *Third,* the thinking of
our team, and of our grass-roots participants, will
become more flexible. If we have worked out a number of different solutions, we will be able to look
more dispassionately at ideas presented by our adversaries, to pick out acceptable ideas, and to work
in a problem-solving fashion to devise still further
alternatives that may narrow the gaps between us
without compromising the need-satisfactions of any
of the people involved.

    7. *Human satisfactions criteria.* The solu-
tions sought should grow out of the identified needs
of individual human beings. Those needs often will
turn out to have little or no direct relation to national goals or official ideologies. For example,
pursuit of the goals of "freedom" and "self-determination" for South Vietnam meant that members of its
elites were free to continue profiting from the war
as long as they cooperated with U.S. efforts. For
ordinary Vietnamese citizens, however, pursuit of
those goals meant profound suffering and loss.

    Unexamined national goals and ideologies may
serve as an invisible controlling force that can
lead peoples into self-defeating actions. However
goals and ideologies often do reflect people's values and fears. Concealed in their abstractions and
generalities, human needs may be identified. If
people are assisted in recognizing and evaluating
how well or how poorly they can expect their ideologies and traditional goals to serve their human
needs, they become free to retain or revise them as
they choose.

    The application of this principle can lead to
the resolution of apparently intractable conflicts.
For example, interest-group goals or national goals
of adversaries are often mutually exclusive, as in
the case of border disputes or in ideological conflicts. However, when attention shifts to devising
ways to satisfy the various human needs and desires
of the individuals involved, satisfactory solutions
become a possibility.

8. *Revisable agreements*. Each agreement
reached should include a joint commitment to work
for its revision should it later prove unsatisfac-
tory to any party. Thus negotiators' natural inclination to keep all options open is reduced. This
inclination often blocks creative problem-solving.
When delegates don't have to worry about every future contingency, they can concentrate all their efforts on inventing optimal solutions to the defined
problems. Only where proposed agreements might
cause irreparable damage to life or to the environment should future considerations override immediate
human concerns.

This principle might seem to make agreements
pointless. However, it merely recognizes that nothing is ever settled "for once and for all." Only so
long as individuals, groups, and nations find it in
their interest to live up to agreements do they do
so. Much avoidable violence occurs because some
party to a formal or tacit agreement becomes too
dissatisfied with it. This eighth principle makes
the reaching of agreements easier and replaces un-
planned, unilateral violations of agreements with
orderly, cooperative resolutions whenever difficulties arise.

A conflict may continually elude resolution if
each proposed agreement is considered potentially
irrevokable or unacceptably expensive to revise. In
contrast, a conflict is more readily resolved when
there is confidence that a changed situation will
lead to a search for a new solution.

9. *Popular autonomy*. A conflict-resolution
process incorporating the preceding eight principles
is not designed to displace any existing governmental machinery. However, the information it helps
generate and disseminate will affect the international and domestic climate of opinion. It will
bring about changes in people's beliefs and attitudes. It will permit the power of the people to
shift from blind support of possibly defensive and
destructive policies to an active insistence that
constructive policies be pursued. With every argu-
ment--ideological, economic, and political--stripped
down to show how it affects individual human beings,
governments will not be able to justify policies
that serve special interests to the detriment of human welfare. Leaders who honestly want to serve the
people will gain the informed support they need to
be of service.

Effects of All-Win Applications
   Application of the All-Win principles is expected to help (a) explode popular myths about society and humankind, (b) bring the state's power under the informed control of its members, (c) bring
the abilities of society's more capable members into the service of all its people--but not create a
meritocracy that replaces one ruling elite with another, (d) break the status quo wherein society's
benefits trickle down irregularly and uncertainly
only after an elite minority has been served, (e)
erase people's anomie and sense of powerlessness,
(f) foster their sense of interdependence, and (g)
help people develop orderly, meaningful images or
conceptual maps of their society and world so that
they can responsibly use their power to enhance
their own lives and the lives of their fellows, instead of blindly responding like disciplined pawns
to the slogans that reflect their most poignant
feelings of the moment.

ALL-WIN CONFLICT RESOLUTION

   The All-Win method of conflict resolution follows directly from the nine All-Win principles.
The following description shows one way of conducting an All-Win program for either an international
conflict or a conflict over a far-reaching national
policy issue. Scaled-down versions could be adapted
to deal with community conflicts.

   Sponsorship. An existing organization with the
goal of nonviolent conflict resolution, or an organization newly formed for the purpose can sponsor an
All-Win program. The majority of the public need
not be convinced in advance of the value of using an
unproven technique. The support of powerful people
who believe they have vested interests in the status
quo will not be needed. Only a few people of moderate means need be convinced that an All-Win approach
offers a promising bridge to a harmonious, satisfying nation and/or a peaceful, disarmed world.
   At the outset the sponsoring organization will
have to take the initiative, make decisions, arrange
funding, select staff, and assume full responsibility. Later, as the program gets under way, decisions and responsibility can be shared with other
organizations and transnational bodies. The sponsor
and staff, however, retain control of procedural
matters unless and until they are replaced through a

decision reached by an All-Win process.

All-Win format.   The All-Win program operates
on two levels.   (1) At its core an open, widely publicized conference is held between representatives
of groups involved in the focal conflict.   (2) At
the grass-roots level, the people represented are
assembled into a network of groups which "sit-in" on
the core conference by means of closed circuit TV,
or through a circulating library of video tapes.
The group members, aided by group leaders, relate
the conference proceedings to their own lives and
beliefs, and they feed back their personal reactions
and insights to the core-conference delegates
throughout the course of the conference.

Core conference.   The citizen delegates are selected, trained, and coached to be able to openly
explore their own needs, hopes, and fears, and those
of the people they represent.   As a part of the
training of our teams, practice encounters are
staged and those members who lack sufficient flexibility and empathy are either eliminated from the
program or given additional training.   When the
delegate teams are not in agreement as to the needs
of any of the people touched by the conflict, they
are to devise means for getting the needed information.   They might use field trips, surveys, consultants, cross-panel subgroups, etc.   As the delegates
relate identified needs, hopes, and fears to the
supplies of resources, to technologies, and to the
social, political and economic arrangements now in
effect, the roots of the conflict will be uncovered.
The conflict will become disentangled from the abstractions and ideological colorations that so often
conceal underlying human conditions.

Shifting from adversary to ally.   The All-Win
process allows people on both sides--grass-roots
participants as well as core-conference delegates--
to discover that their former enemies are fellow humans with fears and dreams much like their own.   The
ground for creative problem solving is prepared by
that recognition, and by the understanding that today's technology makes possible desired gains for
some without commensurate losses for others.   Delegates, acting as allies, and with help from the
grass-root groups and coaches, can enlist all of
their intelligence and energy in devising a variety
of ways to meet needs, respond to desires, and reduce the frustrations and fears felt on both sides.

The continual emphasis on fitting solutions to the needs of specific humans frees delegates from the search for "straight-jacket" solutions applicable to all. Solutions based on the desirability of "different strokes for different folks" can lead to equal satisfactions for unequal humans.

Implementation of All-Win solutions. Just as there are no "normal channels" through which to initiate the All-Win procedure, there are no "normal channels" for implementing All-Win solutions.[13] Presumably the sponsoring group will assume primary responsibility for implementing solutions devised by the conference. However, throughout the solution-developing phase, the All-Win coach has emphasized that solutions are incomplete until they include practical plans for their implementation (elements 3 and 4). Hence those who strive for implementation will be able to draw on the previous work of delegates and grass-root participants who may well be involved in the implementation. And they will have a ready-made body of informed citizens to support and assist in their efforts.

Contributions to international order. When *typical* negotiations between adversaries produce agreements, they are either dictated by the victors, or they represent compromise--a partial defeat for both sides. The 1919 Versailles Treaty--a dictated agreement--provided much of the fuel that brought the Nazi regime to power. The 1954 Geneva Accords-- compromises that satisfied no one--were supported only until the parties to them believed their interests would be better served by violating them. The failure of the Geneva Accords to win wholehearted general support helped prepare the ground for twenty more years of large scale violence that ceased only after the American people repudiated their government's war policy.
In contrast, any diplomatic agreements reflecting solutions openly reached in All-Win encounters would attract public acceptance. They would receive much more general approval and support--from both sides--than the kind of agreements that emerge (if they ever do) from adversary negotiations.

CONCLUSION

The future of humankind looks very dim unless more people among the serving elite, people who read and write books like this, begin to initiate social change, viewing themselves as leader/servants, and teaching those with less vision to see the problem and to dispossess the self-serving ruling elites.[15]

The All-Win approach assumes that no portion of humankind can confidently expect to prosper for long unless all parts of global society prospers. We have long passed the time when one part can hope to decisively overpower another, or even hold it in check for long. Either we make it possible for all to win, or else all will lose.

We offer the All-Win approach as one possible way for some bright, humane people to begin involving large numbers of their fellows in sharing control over their way of life. All-Win is not offered as the definitive way. We hope that others who want to share more rewarding, more humane lives with their fellows will work to devise many other alternative ways. Any path we devise will be worth following if we remember while we design and traverse it that we may never reach the goals we seek, but that we are certain of every pleasure and pain we experience along the way. Let our passage be joyous.

NOTES

1. This abbreviated version of our motivational theory (5) omits mention of a number of factors, such as emotion and habit, despite their effect on perceptions and cognitive processes. We do not discount their importance, but feel they do not have enough effect on the four postulated motivational factors or the relationships among them to warrant lengthening and complicating the discussion by their inclusion.

2. Victor Frankl (10) reports from his firsthand concentration camp experiences how it seemed that only the prisoner with a personal goal or purpose was able to avoid becoming "completely and unavoidably influenced by his surroundings" (p. 103). "In the final analysis it becomes clear that the sort of person the prisoner became was the result of an inner decision, and not the result of camp influences alone" (p. 105).

3. Waskow (26) emphasizes that "along the way the process of imagination and creation will lead one to change his imagination." He recommends that we design "the future as an open-ended future: a future

which is free to decide on *its* own future..." (p. 37).

4.   The felt need for retribution is a powerful *subjective* obstacle to the conversion of adversary to ally.   Russell (23) in tracing the direct causal relationship between Biblical teaching, adherence to most Christian denominations, and severe authoritarian-punitive attitudes suggests how hard it will be to diminish the desire to punish and to extract retribution from "evil" people--from the enemy.   By recognizing the source in our Judeo-Christian heritage, we may be able to change the attitudes that prevent us from dealing effectively with crime and delinquency as well as with war.

5.   Lewin (17) postulated that any relatively stable conflict situation represents a state of "quasi-stable equilibrium" where each party's position represents a "balance" between restraining forces and driving forces.   If an adversary applies additional "driving forces," such as threats or attacks from the outside, additional "restraining forces as counter-threats or counter-attacks are brought into the field by the defender.   According to this model, if the "defender" can be led to reduce his restraining forces (and he would never do so if under attack), the equilibrium point would move in the desired direction without the application of any external force.   Hence, building an alliance *against* an adversary would lead him to increase his restraining forces, whereas forming an alliance *with* him would lead him to reduce those forces.

6.   Maslow's (19) conception of man has been expanded to encompass White's (28) competence tendency, the "mapping" and ordering tendencies suggested by Kelly (13) and Tolman (25).   We have added a generalized control tendency which seems inevitable in an organism that has substituted, in large measure, cognitive control for preprogrammed instinctual responses.

7.   We do not suggest that the ruling elite comprises an organized entity.   Rather the actions of its members are more or less coordinated by a common ideology, a common view of man, and shared or complementary interests.

8.   The first publicized use of anything like the All-Win approach to real life conflict resolution was used by Blake, Shepard & Mouton (3) for labor-

management conflict. Many of the All-Win principles and techniques stem from that experience. A related approach was used for police-community conflict in Houston (4). Another approach used for police-community problems in Grand Rapids, Michigan was able to avoid direct confrontation on emotion-laden issues until after a climate of mutual trust and skills in joint problem-solving were developed (1). The nearest thing to an All-Win conference was the Fermeda workshop, which brought together in Switzerland unofficial representatives from three African nations involved in a border dispute (6). The Pugwash conferences (7) initiated in 1957 by Cyrus Eaton, and the highly secret Bilderberger conferences (21) initiated in 1954 by Prince Bernhard of the Netherlands resemble the All-Win approach only in their private sponsorship, in their extra-diplomatic nature, and in that delegates are not official government representatives. Neither of these lengthy series of meetings is known to have contributed to resolving any international dispute. The Pugwash series has increased East-West communications and understandings, and probably has contributed from time to time to reduction of tensions. The Bilderberger series, attended by "sophisticated members of the ruling elites and their retainers" (21, p. E9620) may have increased communication and understanding *within* the Atlantic community, but may, consequently have worked at cross purposes to the Pugwash spirit.

9. Qualified professionals are associated with a number of centers, including NTL Institute for Applied Behavioral Science, Washington, D.C.; UCLA Graduate School of Business Administration; Yale University; Veterans Administration Hospital, Houston, Texas; Scientific Methods, Inc., Austin, Texas; and the Center for the Analysis of Conflict, University College, London.

10. Resentment built up at the Fermeda workshop where representatives from three African nations were forced to spend the first half of their week in training before they could get down to the substance of the border dispute that brought them together (6, p. 97). This suggests that preliminary training should be conducted at home, or at least with the teams separated.

11. During the administration of the simulation game "Crisis," the authors and one cooperative

stranger were able to shift the entire course of the
game, involving some 60 participants, from mutually
destructive attack, counter-attacks, and manipulation into a trust-building cooperative enterprise
wherein all benefited. The conductor of the game,
who was initially unaware of our bias, was astonished by the outcome.

12. The MINERVA program, under Amitai Etzioni at the
Center for Policy Research, New York, plans to use
computer-communications hardware for making possible
grass-roots decision making.

13. Rapoport (22) notes: "Because there are no institutions where the theoretical findings of peace
research can interact with practice,...the prospects
for developing an applied 'science of peace' remain
dim" (p. 280). He shows that any program that might
substantially promote the cause of peace will need
to be initiated and supported from outside "the establishment."

14. Warren Weaver, former president of American Association for the Advancement of Science and associated with the Rockefeller and Sloan Foundations, is
only one of an increasing number of respected members of the scientific establishment who sees the
dimension of society's predicament and calls for the
first remedial steps from a serving elite. Weaver
(27) writes, "...Who should be more able than scientists in the attempt to understand in advance the
human, social and environmental consequences?...
Minds that can successfully penetrate the interior
of elementary particles, the reaches of space, the
mechanisms of the cell, the intricacies of the central nervous system, should not be paralyzed by the
complications and difficulties of devising procedures for making science decent, sensitive to the
needs of men, and responsive to the requirements of
a culture; truly rational but also truly humane."
If they take that first remedial step they will find
themselves inextricably involved in reshaping society to be truly worthy of humankind.

REFERENCES

1. Allen, Robert F., Pilnick, Saul, & Silverzweig,
    Stanley. Conflict resolution--team building for
    police and ghetto residents. Report presented
    at the American Psychological Association Con-

vention, San Francisco, September, 1968.

2. Barber, Richard J. *The American Corporation: Its Power, Its Money, Its Politics*. New York: Dutton, 1970.

3. Blake, Robert R., Shepard, Herbert A., & Mouton, Jane S. *Managing Intergroup Conflict in Industry*. Houston: Gulf Publishing Co., 1964.

4. Bell, Robert, Cleveland, Sidney E., Hanson, Philip G., & O'Connell, Walter E. Small group dialogue and discussion: an approach to police-community relationships. *Journal Criminal Law, Criminology & Police Science*, 1969, *60*, 242-246.

5. Craig, James H., & Craig, Marge. *Synergic Power: Beyond Domination and Permissiveness*. Berkeley, ProActive Press, 1974.

6. Doob, Leonard W. The impact of the Fermeda workshop on the conflicts in the Horn of Africa, *International Journal Group Tensions*, 1971, *1*, 91-101.

7. Doty, Paul. The community of science and the search for peace. *Science*, 1971, *173*, 998-1002.

8. Domhoff, G. William. *Who Rules America?* Englewood Cliffs: Prentice-Hall, 1967.

9. Fink, Clinton F. Some conceptual difficulties in the theory of social conflict. *Journal Conflict Resolution*, 1968, *12*, 412-460.

10. Frankl, Viktor E. *Man's Search for Meaning*. (Rev. ed.) New York: Washington Square Press, 1963.

11. Greenleaf, Robert K. *The Servant as Leader*. Cambridge, Mass.: Center for Applied Studies, 1970.

12. Janis, Irving L., & Mann, Leon. *Decision Making*. New York: Free Press, 1977.

13. Kelly, George A. *A Theory of Personality*. New York: Norton, 1963.

14. Kissinger, Henry A. The white revolutionary: reflections on Bismarck. *Daedalus*, 1968, 888-924.

15. Kolko, Gabriel. *Wealth and Power in America*. New York: Praeger, 1962.

16. Lasswell, Harold D., & Kaplan, Abraham. *Power and Society*. New Haven: Yale Univer. Press, 1950.

17. Lewin, Kurt. Group decision and social change. In Guy E. Swanson, T.M. Newcomb, & E.L. Hartley, (Eds.), *Readings in Social Psychology*, (Rev. ed.) New York: Henry Holt, 1952, 459-493.

18. Lundberg, Ferdinand. *The Rich and the Super-Rich*. New York: Lyle Stuart, 1968.

19. Maslow, Abraham H. *Motivation and Personality*. (2nd ed.) New York: Harper & Row, 1970.

20. Mintz, Morton, & Cohen, Jerry S. *America, Inc.: Who Owns and Operates the United States*. New York: Dial Press, 1971.
21. Pasymowski, Eugene, & Gilbert, Carl. Bilderberg: the cold war internationale. *Congressional Record*, September 15, 1971, E9616-E9624.
22. Rapoport, Anatol. Can peace research be applied? *Journal Conflict Resolution*. 1970, *14*, 277-286.
23. Russell, Elbert. *Christianity and Militarism. Peace Research Reviews*. 1971, *4*.
24. Skinner, B.F. *Beyond Freedom and Dignity*. New York: Knopf, 1971.
25. Tolman, Edward. Cognitive maps in rats and men. *Psychological Review*, 1948, *55*, 189-208.
26. Waskow, Arthur I. Looking forward: 1999--who plans your future? *New University Thought*. 1968, *6*(3), 34-55.
27. Weaver, Warren. Science in a troubled culture: a prescription. *AAAS Bulletin*, 1972, *17*(1), 3.
28. White, Robert W. Motivation reconsidered: the concept of competence. *Psychological Review*, 1959, *66*, 297-333.

JIM AND MARGUERITE CRAIG co-direct the Center for the Study of Power which they established in 1968 for research and dissemination of information on conflict resolution and power, and on ways power can be used humanely and responsibly to increase human satisfaction.

Jim received his Ph.D. in psychology from the University of Texas, and was on the faculty there and at California State University at Northridge. The assassination of John Kennedy was Jim's turning point. He suddenly saw that no one is safe in a society that treats many of its children (and adults) as Lee Harvey Oswald had been treated in childhood and early manhood--in ways unwittingly designed to arouse undying anger. As a social psychologist with experience in conducting sensitivity training, he sensed the vague outlines of an alternative society wherein each member would be cherished and helped to achieve a rewarding life in a nonthreatening world. From then on, in all of his activities, he has sought clues for the design and achievement of the caring society--in his college teaching and at a Summerhill-type school; in conducting sensitivity training for failing students, for deaf adults, and for business supervisors; in interviews with ghetto residents after the Watts riots, and with aging San

Franciscans in a self-help program; in his study of drug abuse prevention programs; and in his work with groups that were trying to stop the Vietnam War.

Jim has taught many psychology courses including management psychology, business psychology, human relations, and leadership principles and practices. He consults with groups and organizations seeking to increase the commitment and participation of members, the effectiveness of their meetings, and the scope and effectiveness of their outreach programs.

Marguerite operated a public relations consultation service for health and welfare agencies in Los Angeles for 12 years prior to marrying Jim. She was a founder and driving force in the sister city affiliation between Los Angeles and Salvador, Brazil. She demonstrated to herself the power that one committed person, without formal position, can muster and direct. The lessons learned in this experience were then tested further in her more recent affiliations with the Women's International League for Peace and Freedom, the Committee of Responsibility, the San Anselmo Town Meeting, Unitarian Fellowship of Marin, and local policical campaigns and issues. She co-designs and presents workshops on synergic power with Jim and has co-authored a workbook for women called POWER FROM WITHIN (Berkeley: ProActive Press, 1976). She is also on the staff of the Center for Attitudinal Healing in Tiburon, California, facilitating self-healing workshops for people with glaucoma and other vision disorders.

In 1974, the Craigs co-authored a major volume, SYNERGIC POWER: BEYOND DOMINATION AND PERMISSIVENESS (Berkeley: ProActive Press).

SOME OTHER PUBLICATIONS BY JAMES & MARGUERITE CRAIG

- Craig, Marguerite. Patient--Heal thyself. *Journal Contemporary Psychotherapy*, 1974, 6, 157-164.
- Craig, Marguerite, Johnson, Sheila Merle, & Lautner, Mary Beecher. *Power from Within: A Workbook to Guide Women in Discovering their Power and Expressing it in Creative, Caring Ways.* Berkeley: ProActive Press, 1976.
- Craig, James H., & Craig, Marguerite. *Synergy: Path to Human Liberation.* Berkeley: ProActive Press, 1976. (pamphlet)

Name Index

Subject Index

Activists, 90
Adversary to ally, 377
Aggression, 69,73,122,
137,149,156,175,208;
American, 164-183;
awareness of, 171; con-
cealing, 167; correct-
ing American, 179, re-
lationship to destruc-
tiveness, 208; violent,
376
Agency International De-
velopment, 299,302
Ahmedabad, riots, 258
Algerian War, 229
Alienation, 280,307,308,
310
All-win approach, 371-
400; application, 391,
393; coaching, 386;
conference, 392,396;
format, 392; grass-
roots participation,
387; revisable agree-
ments, 390.
Altruism, 76,90
American Arbitration As-
sociation, 194,199
American Association Ad-
vancement Science
course on peace and
conflict, 229
American Bar Association,
199
American Civil Liberties
Union, 199
American Council Educa-
tion, 190
"American dream," 197
American foreign policy,
171
American Institute Re-
search, 299
American Jewish Commit-
tee, 198
American Legion, 187
American Orthopsychiatric
Association Study Group
Mental Health Aspects
Agression, Violence and
war, 162

Anger, 208
Anti-Semitism, 66
Anti-war demonstrations,
119,141,181; anti-war
movement, 320
Arab oil boycott, 179
Arbitration, 194
Armenians, 103
Arms race, 166
Assassination, John F.
Kennedy, 399
Atomic Bomb, 105,147
Attica Prison, 257
Authoritarianism, 170,395
Awareness, 112; develop-
ment of, 172; terror
of, 177
Baroda, riots, 258
Bataan Death March, 104
Bay of Pigs, 181
Behavior, exploratory,
77; modification, 84;
phylogenetic substrate,
72; programming, 70
Biafra, 133
Big business, 165
Bilderberger Conferences,
396
Bill of Rights (U.S.),
184,187
Blacks, 129,270,358; mili-
tants, 191; Panthers,
131,139,186; power,218
Blitzkreig, 376
Boer War, 166
Bonding, 69,70,76; so-
cial, 74; spiritual, 79
Boycott, 191; Center, 192
Brothels, 28
Brown shirts, 185
Buddhism, 369
Bulletin Peace Proposals,
148
Cain syndrome, 20; ten-
dency, 69
Campus revolts, *see* Kent
State U.
Canadian Peace Research &
Education Association,
17, 18; Peace Research
Institute, 316